I0815812

"Steffaniak makes a clear and compelling case that classical theism's insistence on divine simplicity, immutability, eternity, and impassibility does not point to a cold and distant Deity but rather offers essential support for sustaining the Christian tradition's commitment to God's boundless love and faithfulness. This book is an incredible resource for all those who study, teach, or simply hope to explore the church's long tradition of reflection on the nature and attributes of God."

—BRENDAN CASE, associate director for research, The Human Flourishing Program, Harvard University

"Seeped in the luminaries and confessional statements of the Reformation, especially the Reformed and Baptists, Steffaniak presents a robust case for a Protestant embrace of natural theology and classical theism. Accessible to the lay reader yet still insightful for the expert, this book serves as an excellent call to return to the traditional doctrine of God."

—TIMOTHY J. PAWL, professor of philosophy, University of St. Thomas

"This book has value as both a primer and a plea. It's a primer for engaging very complex material—especially surveying the relevant philosophical debates. And it's a plea for embracing mere classical theism—neither rejecting it as unbiblical nor requiring a more specific version for 'orthodoxy' than history will bear. Without having all the answers, Jordan Steffaniak can help us to frame better questions."

—DANIEL TREIER, Gunther H. Knoedler Professor of Theology, Wheaton College

"Jordan Steffaniak has authored a creative and insightful book on classical theism. He treats both the nature and the history of the doctrine of God. Moreover, significantly, he does so within an ecclesial and ecumenical context—both Catholic and Protestant. He also critically contrasts it with other contemporary notions of God, such as Open Theism and Process Theism. Where he manifests his theological acumen is when he treats the various divine attributes—divine simplicity, immutability, impassibility, and eternity. What I found extremely helpful is that he provides the biblical basis for such philosophical attributes. This is a marvelous book, one that must be read by anyone who values mere classical theism, and even ones who don't."

—THOMAS G. WEINANDY, former member of the Vatican's International Theological Commission

"This book is an insightful, weighty, and well-written study of the Christian doctrine of God, with attention both to the great tradition of faithful believing and also some of the debates carried on by today's theologians. Doxology is always near the surface—a sense of the wonder and awe and contemplation of what St. Paul called 'the deep things of God' (1 Cor 2:10). Recommended highly!"

—TIMOTHY GEORGE, distinguished professor, Beeson Divinity School, Samford University

"In his introduction to classical theism—or what he terms mere classical theism—Steffaniak presents an important book aimed at rehabilitating the doctrine of God, the foundation of the church's theology. He argues that recovering the vision of God found in the great tradition is essential for the church's faith and practice today, especially as it navigates new philosophical and moral challenges. This book is a readable and reliable guide to the attributes of God, certain to encourage and edify any Christian leader seeking to deepen their love for God."

—STEPHEN O. PRESLEY, senior fellow for religion and public life, Center for Religion, Culture & Democracy; associate professor of church history, The Southern Baptist Theological Seminary

CLASSICAL THEISM

CLASSICAL THEISM

A CHRISTIAN INTRODUCTION

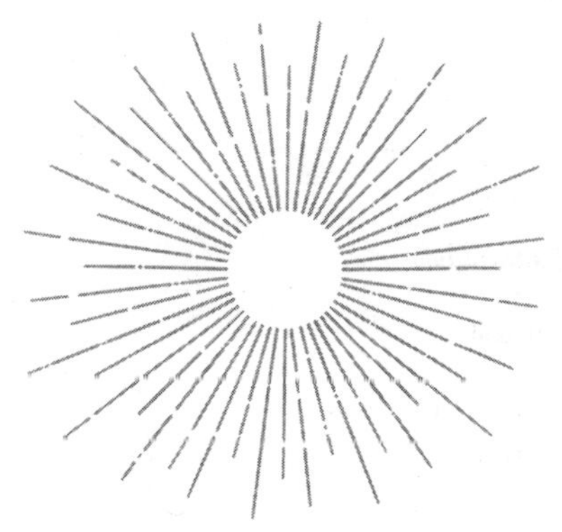

JORDAN L. STEFFANIAK

Classical Theism: A Christian Introduction

Lexham Academic, an imprint of Lexham Press
1313 Bay St, Bellingham, WA 98225
LexhamPress.com

Print ISBN 9781683598688
Digital ISBN 9781683598695

Lexham Editorial: Todd Hains, Robert Hand, Danielle Burlaga, Mandi Newell
Cover Design: Gabriel Eason
Typesetting: Justin Marr

25 26 27 28 29 30 31 / IN / 12 11 10 9 8 7 6 5 4 3 2 1

To my sons
I pray these doctrines grip you

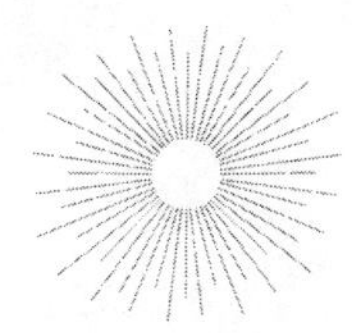

CONTENTS

Contents

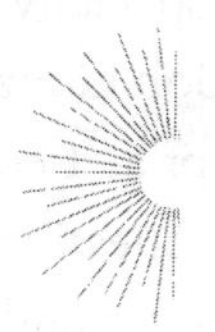

ACKNOWLEDGMENTS

Undertaking the task to write about God is incredibly daunting. It is one thing to muse among friends in informal settings. It is another to put pen to paper. There is a sense of permanence and finality to it. And I am but a man. A sinful man at that. A man that is deeply aware of Exodus 33:20: "You cannot see my face, for man shall not see me and live."

But the Lord has placed an insatiable desire to seek, to see, and to savor the face of God. I believe each one of us has this desire. Our hearts are restless. Our minds are tossed to and fro. The only safe haven is God himself. Therefore, I must first and foremost give thanks to our great God and Savior. It is he whom I pray I've pleased and honored in the pages that follow. Without his meticulous care and providence, I would never have written this book. My interest in the classical doctrine of God began near 2015, toward the end of my graduate studies at the Southern Baptist Theological Seminary, thanks in large part to the associate pastor at my church, Brad Weldy. And it only grew as I pursued a second master's degree at Southeastern Baptist Theological Seminary, where I completed a ThM thesis in defense of the methodology of classical theism under the wise guidance of Greg Welty. Jamie Dew similarly provided keen insight throughout the completion of my thesis and offered numerous helpful questions at my defense.

Many names have aided me in the completion of this book. Each of them has embodied Augustine's own desire: "What I desire for all my works, of course, is not merely a kind reader but also a frank critic."[1] Tim Giovanetto generously copyedited the first two chapters at a very early stage, assisting me with wisdom for becoming a better writer. Garrett Walden and

1. Augustine, *The Trinity*, trans. Edmund Hill (New City, 2015), 3.2.

Tim Stanyon provided extensive comments on the first few chapters. Hunter Hindsman provided stimulating, critical, and spirited feedback on chapter 3 (multiple times as I drafted and redrafted the chapter!). Matt Ntiros provided comments on several chapters, especially chapter 4. His feedback made the chapter significantly better. Bob Gonzalez read and provided tremendous feedback on the manuscript as I completed early drafts of each chapter. His keen eye and helpful questions were invaluable. Tim Pawl read a very early version of chapter 7 and then read the entire draft manuscript upon completion. His wise guidance caused me to rewrite nearly all of chapter 7 in the early stages and made the overall work significantly better. He is not only a model philosopher but a model Christian. I hope one day to be half the thinker and virtuous person he is. Greg Ganssle read chapter 8 and provided insightful commentary. Daniel Pedersen read and provided extremely helpful feedback on chapter 6 in a very short time frame. I owe him. Andrew Hollingsworth has been a tremendous sparring partner through many of these chapters as I've lobbed ideas at him to see his response as someone who is not a classical theist. We even wrote a paper together. He's a tremendous theological "opponent": firm, careful, and charitable. I also owe Joel Chopp and Ryan Modisette acknowledgment as they've acted as sounding boards for many of my curiosities, questions, and confusions. Garrett Walden and Caleb Hawkins have also served me in this way. But I really should thank all of those associated with the London Lyceum. Whether through podcast interviews or our private online Slack group, I've been inspired, challenged, and educated. For that, I am grateful.

My wife, Sarah, and children, Samson, Ezra, and Noah, have each patiently endured the completion of this book. They've sacrificed time with me to see its end and will be rewarded by the Lord, who sees all. But they've also inspired me and given me passion to honor them in my work. I pray I bring respect upon our family through my diligent work. For those I've forgotten to acknowledge, I'm sorry.

In the end, I stand in a long line of Christians. Surely, I will be forgotten. And rightfully so. But I won't be forgotten by my Savior, whom I've sought to know and share herein.

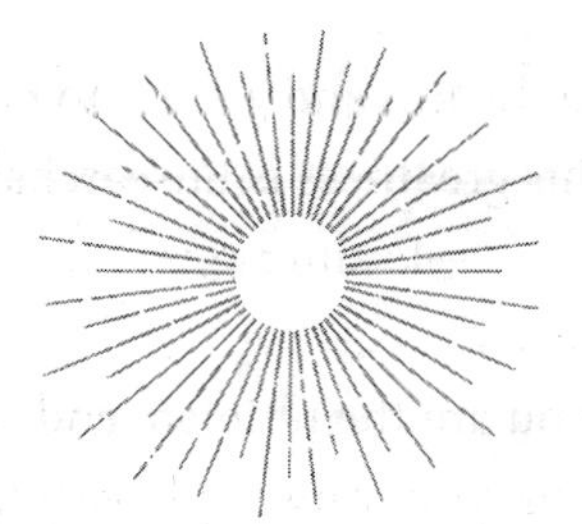

"Great is the LORD, and greatly to be praised,
and his greatness is unsearchable."
—Psalm 145:3

"Lord our God ... you are the ultimate end; you are supreme in perfection; you transcend everything else."
—John Duns Scotus

"Who will enable me to find rest in you? Who will grant me that you come to my heart and intoxicate it, so that I forget my evils and embrace my one and only good, yourself? ... In your mercies, Lord God, tell me what you are to me. 'Say to my soul, I am your salvation' (Ps 34:3). Speak to me so that I may hear. See the ears of my heart are before you, Lord. Open them and 'say to my soul, I am your salvation.' After that utterance I will run and lay hold on you. Do not hide your face from me (cf. Ps 26:9). Lest I die, let me die so that I may see it."
—Augustine

1

INTRODUCING CLASSICAL THEISM

WHAT ARE WE DOING HERE?

It's no secret that so-called "classical theism" has fallen on hard times. While the terminology is new, the general idea is old. Before the nineteenth century, classical theism and its set of claims about a transcendent God above all time, change, and destruction was seen as necessary for any orthodox account of the Trinity, the incarnation, or the atonement.[1] Not so today. But even while it has seen a revival of interest among Protestants over the last decade, classical theism often remains shrouded in mystery, appearing to many as abstract, foreign to the world of the Bible, and potentially harmful for pastoral care. Worse, many of those seeking to retrieve classical theism for our current day have misunderstood it and therefore given it a bad reputation by introducing unhelpful innovations and making unnecessarily narrow dogmatic pronouncements. That's why I wrote this book.

I've written it primarily for graduate students and pastors, especially Protestants. I've done so with classroom pedagogy in mind, whether in a traditional educational setting like a university or seminary or for a teacher

1. Stephen R. Holmes, "The Attributes of God," in *The Oxford Handbook of Systematic Theology*, ed. Kathryn Tanner, John Webster, and Iain Torrance (Oxford University Press, 2007), 56, https://doi.org/10.1093/oxfordhb/9780199245765.003.0004.

in a Sunday school at a local church. I've worked hard to provide formal structured arguments, clear definitions, and organizational consistency that all proves especially useful for such contexts. While my primary audience is not the average layman or laywoman, I hope it is written well enough that those who feel themselves less equipped can benefit because I believe there is no greater study than that of God himself. I've sought to leave enough breadcrumbs along the way that those intimidated by some of the technicalities at times can find their way. So, even if *you*, dear reader, feel daunted at times by some of the necessary technical explanations, I'm convinced the reward is worth the effort.[2]

As a final preliminary note, I must confess that I would have preferred to write this book twenty or thirty years later in my career after having more time to listen intently and learn from the classical tradition in greater depth and breadth. For example, I believe there are untapped mines stocked with treasures untold in the sermons from the classical tradition. Sermons in general are the fuel of the church, the fire of dogma, and the bleeding heart of theology. It is where we encounter the word of God most powerfully. More reckoning with them will only bring greater love, devotion, and clarity. I've barely scratched the surface in my own reading and writing on these sermons to this point in my life. Yet I think we need this book at our current moment. I feel bound to write before I'd like because classical theism needs a fresh explanation for today—especially for Protestants. It needs clarity regarding its place within the so-called "Great Tradition." It needs to be translated into contemporary terminology. It needs to be told as an invigorating story. Classical theism is not merely a cold-hearted analytic syllogism. It has fire within its bones, if only we are willing to experience the tradition afresh. Therefore, I seek to retrieve classical theism in the pages that follow by defining it and defending it.

2. It's rather commonplace today for Christians to bemoan technical theology. However, I am absolutely convinced that technical theology is necessary for the health and joy of the church. Not all theology should be technical, but some must be. What else should we expect, anyway? Should God be easy to understand and lack depth, richness, and mystery? While some (hopefully not most) theology can be *overly* technical and obscure the matter where it should be articulated in a less elitist manner, this isn't always the case. Technical theology remains necessary in its proper context. Just as we should expect medical doctors to read and articulate complicated medical studies for the sake of our health while also giving us examples we can understand, we should expect the theologian and pastor to do the same.

REFORMED CATHOLICITY

The entirety of the book will seek to utilize the catholic creeds and councils, *historical catholic* thinkers, and *Protestant* confessional documents to define and defend classical theism. This means two things. First, when I refer to "classical" theism or the "classical" tradition, I am limiting its scope to *Christian* classical theism and the *Christian* classical tradition. In a very broad sense figures like Plato (428/7–348/7), Avicenna (980–1037), and Aristotle (384–322) are "classical." But when I use the terminology of classical theism or the classical tradition, I am referring to Christianity, unless otherwise noted. Whatever these non-Christian sources think about classical theism is not of primary importance for my project. Thus, if Christianity breaks with them on how we understand God, there is not a pressing need to consider their thoughts or ideas for *this* book. Where their views *are* relevant for certain historical genealogies of doctrines they are engaged for how Christian pastors and theologians interacted with their ideas. But the goal of this project is not to develop non-Christian historical accounts. Second, this general approach among Protestants sometimes goes by the terminology of "Reformed catholicity." This theological program and disposition holds firm to the same necessary dogmas of religion as the church catholic but remains distinctively Protestant in its doctrinal commitments, which are beyond the shared dogmas found in the ecumenical creeds.[3] Therefore, Reformed catholicity is not an attempt to widen the gap between Roman Catholics, Eastern Orthodox, and Protestants more generally. Instead, it is a program that seeks to commune with the church catholic in its shared doctrinal commitments, including the doctrine of God, without ignoring or downplaying its own distinctives. In fact, it finds unique resources from the wealth of its own tradition that are especially suited for furthering the classical tradition.

As a Reformed and Protestant program, the concerns that are ever present for these traditions shape and guide my introduction to some degree. For example, Protestants usually want to see more "exegetical homework" before signing off on a doctrine than other traditions. And so, I do not attempt to ignore or too quickly run past this legitimate desire. But

---

3. William Perkins, *A Reformed Catholic*, ed. Shawn Wright and Andrew S. Ballitch, vol. 7 (Reformation Heritage, 2014), 5.

even with these distinct pressures, when it comes to the doctrine of God, a Reformed catholic will share the same basic doctrinal conclusions as those in other traditions such as Rome or Constantinople but will differ in some of its supporting structure, like the nature of theological authority.[4]

So, when I mention using "historical catholic" thinkers, I just mean Christians who are orthodox in their beliefs. They affirm the same sort of fundamental doctrinal claims like those found in the Apostles' Creed. These thinkers belong to various denominations and traditions, including Roman Catholicism and Eastern Orthodoxy. But it is the use of the standard Protestant confessions of the Reformation era that make the present work distinctively *Reformed* and *Protestant*.[5] Their articulations will sustain, guide, and guard the articulation of God as God, even as they coincide with non-Protestant definitions that are shared by the true church catholic. However, one shouldn't assume that because I write as a Protestant with a goal to focus on Protestant confessional resources that the present volume isn't of use for non-Protestants. Instead, what it should remind non-Protestants is that Protestants too share a deep bond with the church catholic and its central dogmatic commitments as seen in the ecumenical creeds and ecumenical councils. We have a shared heritage that shouldn't be despised. Each of us has unique gifts and treasures from our own heritages that can aid in developing a robust doctrine of God.

I should be clear at this point that there is no substitute for experiencing the Christian tradition in all its glory firsthand. I implore you to read the many primary sources you'll encounter throughout this book. I attempt to expose you to a wide array of theological divines, but most are necessarily muted in their overall contributions in this work, since brief summaries cannot expose you to the breadth or depth of their thinking. And these figures deserve careful reading of their own full

---

4. However, even on topics such as theological authority, Rome had no coherent system that could properly be contrasted with what became Protestantism even as late as the fifteenth century. See Ian Christopher Levy, *Holy Scripture and the Quest for Authority at the End of the Middle Ages* (University of Notre Dame Press, 2012), xiii.

5. While I prioritize the terminology of the Reformed, this should not indicate that the Lutheran tradition is ignored or at odds with my methodology. The Lutheran confessional tradition and several prominent Lutherans do feature throughout this work, though to a lesser degree than more traditionally "Reformed" streams. I use Reformed primarily because of the contemporary terminology of "Reformed catholicity" more than I do to mark out Lutheran dogmatics as distinct.

works in context. So, I recommend chasing these footnotes as they come. Be curious, and read widely. As you read, you'll quickly find out that the story of doctrine is far more complicated than is often suggested. Yet there remains use in having a "30,000-foot view" of the terrain that both consolidates and explains the tradition. This helps to give you an idea of the grand narrative and structure that would be missed if you only saw the ground level alongside a select few figures. Therefore, this book is not a traditional historical theology but an exercise in theological retrieval that is designed to listen and learn from the past while at the same time build upon the work of the past in creative and faithful ways. As such, this is not a true "history" book. I do not provide ideological genealogies within. Instead, I seek to retrieve the ideas and arguments from those that have come before us.

But in retrieving classical theism, I hope you'll discover what I call "*mere* classical theism."[6] It's a classical theism with breadth. It's a hospitable classical theism. It's a classical theism that recognizes the challenges of inventing the terminology of "classical theism" a mere century ago (coined by process theologians no less!) and attempting to fit the majority of the Christian tradition under its banner.[7] It's a classical theism that endeavors to stand on the shoulders of the giants in the Christian faith instead of merely standing in their shadows.[8] In other words, it's an ecumenical or *catholic* classical theism but one that seeks to go beyond mere repetition.

Such a reminder is critical for our current day wherein there has been a miniature revival of classical doctrine about God, especially among Protestants, a revival that I am thrilled to see and hope to fan into flame. But there is an ease of radicalization with paradigm shifts or "aha!" moments with big doctrines. In common colloquial language, this is often dubbed the "cage stage." It's common to hear cage-stage terminology applied to freshly minted Calvinists who, upon discovering the doctrines of grace, have an inability to see anything but Calvinism in the pages of Scripture and act with incredible zeal to mark and avoid anyone that isn't a "pure" Calvinist. I fear that the same can become true of contemporary

6. I must thank my friend Brendan Case for this phrasing.

7. Katherine Sonderegger, *Systematic Theology*, vol. 1 (Fortress, 2015), 164.

8. Thanks to James Eglinton for the expression of standing on shoulders versus standing in the shadows.

classical theists. Suddenly classical theism is found under every rock and in every corner, and heretics lurk behind every shadow. But this posture is unhealthy and can have detrimental effects on the ultimate long-term retrieval of the dogmas so cherished by the zealous.

For example, I recently received an email from a student asking for church recommendations in the area he planned to move. I didn't know the area but had friends who did, and they suggested a particular congregation. The student emailed me later that he reached out to the pastor of the church and was shocked to hear that the pastor had never even heard of classical theism before! Even worse, the student knew one of the elders at this church from a previous church. To his chagrin, he never once heard anything about simplicity, impassibility, and the like from the elder. The student told me this to explain why the church I had recommended was not worth attending or joining. The student had become convinced of the truth of classical theism, and his eyes had been opened to a whole world he'd never known. He felt cheated through the course of his Christian life because of it. While there is joy and passion here that we should praise and encourage, there is also a dangerous youthful zeal. If the congregation has a strong confession of faith, we shouldn't stress over not hearing technical theological terms in regular discourse. The Lord builds up the church by his ordinary means, which often does not include technical theological jargon, though that jargon is precious for the defense and propagation of the faith over generations.

Our priority for recovering classical theism is not to possess more fifty-dollar theological words to impress our friends or to make our pulpits appear more profound. Instead, the recovery of classical theism is about articulating the coherence and foundation of God's everlasting love and covenant faithfulness, which are to take center stage over the intricate details of divine simplicity (necessary as these details are—necessary enough for me to write an entire book about them!). The point is this: Like the foundation of a building, the finer details of the classical attributes of God are usually only seen or discussed by most if they are broken. If I were to say that God is not the same yesterday, today, and forever, the average believer would immediately recognize that something was off in my teaching. They may not have the words to explain exactly what is broken, but they would know something is seriously damaged. So, while the average believer may not be able to pinpoint the error as one of divine immutability (or, in the building analogy, the structural error as one of architectural design hidden away from plain sight), they know the main point better than most of us. God never changes. He is the same yesterday, today, and forever. And it is the content of these beliefs that transforms us.

Therefore, I hope you discover that classical theism is not the exclusive copyright of luminaries like Thomas Aquinas (1224/25–1274). It is okay to reject or revise aspects of Thomas as a classical theist. Nor is it a monolithic program with only one denomination, theological school, or methodological research program. Classical theism is a beautiful tradition full of diversity. There are boundaries to the tradition, and Thomas is surely a bright light, but there remains room for debate within.[9] That's why it is *catholic*. Augustine's (354–430) own lack of dogmatism is instructive. When noting various interpretations of Scripture, he concludes that so long as they are "not otherwise at odds with sound doctrine, we may cheerfully use not merely one interpretation but as many as can be found. For the more ways we open up of avoiding the traps of heretics, the more effectively can they be convinced of their errors."[10] In the spirit of Augustine I say, let's cheerfully confess the beauty of classical theism in all its varied forms.

Alongside Thomas and Augustine, you'll encounter a wide range of resources within the tradition. While there isn't space here to include *everyone* or *everything* (and many remain locked behind needed translation work), I hope the breadth herein displays a classical theism that isn't misshapen by a lack of fellowship with the whole of the Great Tradition. We need all of God's gifted guests throughout the ages to sit at our dinner table and teach us. We need to hear from Christian thinkers across the theological spectrum, from Origen (185–253) to Basil (330–379) to Augustine to Anselm (1033–1109) to Thomas to Scotus (1265/66–1308) to Arminius (1560–1609) to Gill (1697–1771). So, I hope to squeeze more seats at the table of classical theism.

Now, I implore those who feel concerned about this approach—having a sneaking suspicion that "squeezing more seats" is code for twisting cherished doctrines—to hear me out. The goal of my invitation is not

---

9. Thomas Williams, "Introduction to Classical Theism," in *Models of God and Alternative Ultimate Realities*, ed. Jeanine Diller and Asa Kasher (Springer, 2013), 95.

10. Augustine, *The Trinity*, trans. Edmund Hill (New City, 2015), I.4.31.

to attempt a sort of Frankenstein devilry. My goal is to breathe fresh life into our confession of God as all-sufficient and to show that the modern wounds inflicted on this confession are not fatal.[11] I argue that there is a bountiful feast that ought to be shared. Charity demands that hospitality is offered no matter our prior backgrounds or commitments. So, I want to invite you. There's one Lord and one faith (Eph 4:5), and we ought to welcome all who are fellow travelers of the Way.

THE ECCLESIAL NATURE OF CLASSICAL THEISM

I firmly believe that classical theism is unashamedly ecclesial. It's ecclesial because worship is driven by the church's confession of the faith, and the *telos* of classical theism is doxology. It is to confess with Saint Paul, "To the King of the ages, immortal, invisible, the only God, be honor and glory forever and ever. Amen" (1 Tim 1:17). It is to praise alongside David, "Great is the LORD, and greatly to be praised, and his greatness is unsearchable" (Ps 145:3). Throughout Scripture one finds the authors naming and confessing God as acts of prayer and praise.[12] And so, classical theism, as Michael Allen says, "summons the church to confess the incomparable beautiful name of God."[13] It causes us to "remember that his almighty power has been willed toward our flourishing."[14] The very vocation of such theology is worship.[15]

This is why classical theism is not merely abstract or theoretical. In fact, all theology is practical because it is ultimately directed at action—theology informs to excite and impel. And the most fundamental human action is the worship of God.[16] Therefore, classical theism is resolutely practical because it shapes, grounds, and guides our worship. It leads us to stand in awe of God and love him. God delights not in our strength, not in our power, not

11. Tim Pawl, "Review of *God without Parts: Divine Simplicity and the Metaphysics of God's Absoluteness*, by James E. Dolezal," *Faith and Philosophy* 30, no. 4 (2013): 486, https://doi.org/10.5840/faithphil201330445.

12. Janet Martin Soskice, *Naming God: Addressing the Divine in Philosophy, Theology and Scripture* (Cambridge University Press, 2023), 4.

13. Michael Allen, "Divine Attributes," in *Christian Dogmatics: Reformed Theology for the Church Catholic*, ed. Michael Allen and Scott R. Swain (Baker Academic, 2016), 58.

14. Allen, "Divine Attributes," 77.

15. Matthew A. Wilcoxen, *Divine Humility: God's Morally Perfect Being* (Baylor University Press, 2019), 1.

16. Francis Turretin, *Institutes of Elenctic Theology*, ed. James T. Dennison, trans. George Musgrave Giger (P&R, 1994), 1.7.11.

in our wisdom, but in our fear of him and our hope in his steadfast love (Ps 147:11). Our hope and fear of God are both grounded in who he is *as God*. Thus, the church as pillar and buttress of the truth confesses the God who is all-sufficient, all-good, and perfect in every way. Classical theism gives shape and depth to this confession. It allows us to "praise him according to his excellent greatness!" (Ps 150:2). Therefore, classical theism is not only abstractly good for the church. It is a steadfast rock for the grieving widow in her sorrows, who casts her hope on the God who never changes but remains faithful to his creation forevermore. It is a consuming fire for the pastor and the pulpit, fueling the sermonic grandeur of God and kindling the hearts of the congregation. It is a soothing balm for the anxious mother who trusts in the eternally present God who never leaves nor forsakes.

But more than merely revealing the object of worship, classical theism is also designed to safeguard our worship of God. The classical doctrine of God protects the steadfast love of God about which the psalmists so frequently sing. It builds us up to the unity of the faith and knowledge of God so that we are no longer children tossed by every wind of doctrine. Classical theism considers any other foundation to be sinking sand. All the beautiful claims of Scripture—God is loving, faithful, kind, merciful—depend on these doctrines. In doing so, this doctrine is the lifeblood of the liturgical life of the church. As Augustine so long ago advised us, the true function of all knowledge is the preaching of the gospel.[17] And classical theism is the bedrock of this preaching. It is the church's doctrine—or so I hope to argue. It is not the opinion of a few isolated individuals but the communion of saints throughout the ages. And as a "dogma" of the church, classical theism ought to be defended. Therefore, I'll also seek to engage the latest and most potent objections to classical theism.

ORTHODOX YET MODERN

As we seek to explore the rich depth of the tradition on classical theism, we will find that the tradition remains a key resource in articulating contemporary defenses. But you'll also find that there are new and innovative ways to explore the challenges to classical theism that have arisen

17. Augustine, *On Christian Teaching*, trans. R. P. H. Green, Oxford World's Classics (Oxford University Press, 2008), 65.

in our own age. In the shadow of many of the great neo-Calvinists like Abraham Kuyper (1837–1920) and Herman Bavinck (1854–1921), I am likewise committed to the idea that to be truly *catholic* and *classical*, one must be orthodox *and* modern.[18] We must not only be zealous for the old form of orthodoxy but have the courage of orthodoxy that listens to the current questions and develops new answers.[19] Doctrine, then, develops over time, and as it develops we should be eager to preserve it and freshly articulate it. This impulse is not exclusive to neo-Calvinism but is found in patristic thinkers like Vincent of Lérins (d. c. 445) and later Roman Catholic theologians like John Henry Newman (1801–1890). For both the orthodox sense is neither lost nor turned into something new as doctrine develops and takes on new shapes but is preserved while growing. We can and *must* articulate doctrines in new ways without changing the doctrine into new things.[20] Doctrine is not mummified but always growing, *organically*.[21] What distinguishes true growth and acceptable newness rather than aberration and innovation is that when catholic doctrine grows and is enlarged, it does so according to its own nature.[22] It retains the same type, principles, and organization.[23] As Vincent describes:

> For progress requires that the subject be enlarged in itself, alteration, that it be transformed into something else. The intelligence, then, the knowledge, the wisdom, as well of individuals as of all, as well of one man as of the whole Church, ought, in the course of ages and centuries, to increase and make much and vigorous progress; but yet only in its own kind; that is to say, in the same doctrine, in the same sense, and in the same meaning.[24]

---

18. Neo-Calvinism is broadly a tradition that originated in the eighteenth- and nineteenth-century Netherlands that prizes particular virtues such as classic Reformed confessional theology alongside the fruitful engagement of modern resources. See Cory C. Brock, *Orthodox yet Modern: Herman Bavinck's Use of Friedrich Schleiermacher* (Lexham, 2020), 66; Cory C. Brock and N. Gray Sutanto, *Neo-Calvinism: A Theological Introduction* (Lexham, 2023), 3–9.

19. Brock and Sutanto, *Neo-Calvinism*, 48–49.

20. Vincent of Lérins, "The Commonitory," in *Nicene and Post-Nicene Fathers*, ed. Philip Schaff and Henry Wace, trans. C. A. Heurtley, vol. 11 (Eerdmans, 1978), 22.53.

21. Thomas G. Guarino, *Vincent of Lérins and the Development of Christian Doctrine* (Baker Academic, 2013), 18.

22. Guarino, *Vincent of Lérins and the Development of Christian Doctrine*, 16.

23. John Henry Newman, *An Essay on the Development of Christian Doctrine* (Word on Fire, 2017), 141.

24. Vincent of Lérins, "The Commonitory," 23.54.

So, progress is necessary, but so is remaining orthodox. And to distinguish true growth from false is to discern organic growth, like that of a seed to a full-grown tree of the same kind or that of an infant to a mature adult rather than degeneration.

As the disillusionment with modern society continues and Christians seek to resource themselves from within the tradition, there is an ever-present danger of *reverse* chronological snobbery. Just as we can imagine everything new is better, we can imagine there is some past golden age that is in all ways better! But this is not the case. The Spirit of God works in every age, including our own. God's grace and illuminating Spirit did not cease working in our preferred golden age, whether that be the thirteenth century or seventeenth. God continues to teach. Just as orthodox teaching is never confined to one geographical area or one group of believers, neither is it confined to one time period.[25] More will be said about this classical spirit in the chapters that follow. But suffice to say, while this is an introduction to old doctrines, it remains original in some ways, charting out new paths to defend old truths.

As you've seen by now, this is an opinionated introduction! I think classical theism is the true confession of God's goodness and greatness, but I also find some presentations of classical theism more persuasive than others. So, I'll tell you which presentations I think are better than others. But I'll do my best to remain impartial as far as explanation goes. I hope those who are classical theists but disagree with my conclusions will still appreciate the book because it presents their view in the best light, as they would describe it. I also hope non-classical theists will benefit from the book because it doesn't hide from their objections; it's honest about the challenges that face classical theism.

CLASSICAL THEISM AND THE BIBLE

One of those challenges is the elephant in the room. Does classical theism rule over Scripture? Does it place an interpretive straitjacket upon the Bible, twisting and forcing Scripture to say only what is allowable within the classical tradition? Many today think this is the case.[26] And certainly,

25. Guarino, *Vincent of Lérins and the Development of Christian Doctrine*, 5.

26. I could provide several pages of footnotes to prove this, but take these as representative examples: Bruce A. Ware, "An Evangelical Reexamination of the Doctrine of the Immutability of God" (PhD diss., Fuller Theological Seminary, 1984), 387; Bruce A. Ware, *God's Greater Glory: The*

some appear justified when they read recent "classical" proposals that, whether they intend to or not, appear to sideline the relevance of tools such as biblical theology for theological construction.[27] Few have articulated the worry so well as Henri Blocher in an essay investigating the concept of divine eternity:

> Yet, and not without fear and trembling, I dare say that I am not convinced. Is there no other way to conceive of divine perfection? Though the classical tradition extols the incomprehensibility of God—not seldom adorned with Neo-Platonic hyperbole, not seldom verging on agnosticism—I cannot get rid of the suspicion that it dictates to God what his immutable perfection must entail. On the top of the metaphysical Everest of concepts like those of being-itself and *actus purus*, reason may grow dizzy from rarefied oxygen: what is the force of inference? I need more Scriptural explicitness to draw contours of mystery—lest the mysteriousness of God's mystery become an instrument in our hands.[28]

Worries of this sort are understandable. Many likely wonder what value there is in studying the contemporary philosophy of time or medieval scholastic theories of act and potency when these ideas aren't clearly in Scripture. Certainly, most church members, if not most pastors, do not see the value in such abstract and difficult research areas when the Bible tells me all I need to know. And so, these worries, rather than being ignored as ill-informed anxieties, should serve as healthy warnings to the theologian: Beware of vain and empty discussions that promote speculations rather than the stewardship from God that is by faith (1 Tim 1:4). It is the word of God that is "living and active, sharper than any two-edged sword" (Heb 4:12). No philosophical argument has such power. However,

Exalted God of Scripture and the Christian Faith (Crossway, 2004), 138; K. Scott Oliphint, *God with Us: Divine Condescension and the Attributes of God* (Crossway, 2012), 14–15; Jay Wesley Richards, *The Untamed God: A Philosophical Exploration of Divine Perfection, Immutability, and Simplicity* (InterVarsity Press, 2003), 32.

27. See for example: James E. Dolezal, *All That Is in God: Evangelical Theology and the Challenge of Classical Christian Theism* (Reformation Heritage, 2017), xv.

28. Henri Blocher, "Yesterday, Today, Forever: Time, Times, Eternity in Biblical Perspective," *Tyndale Bulletin* 52, no. 2 (2001): 195.

wise warnings as they are, I intend to show this is not the case. Dizzying as such rarefied oxygen might be at times, the Lord gives aid in fresh air and fuels us to soar. For those that faint along the way and grow weary, the Lord will renew their strength and enable them to know and understand the glories that are the divine nature (Isa 40:28–31). It is the very ecclesial nature of the classical tradition that provides fuel for the road ahead through the worship of the local church, the wisdom of the creeds, and the power of the word preached and served in sacrament.

Therefore, I hope that by experiencing the sources firsthand and examining the exegetical foundations, one thing you won't conclude is that the classical tradition and its account of God is either ignorant of Scripture or attempting to jam a square peg into a round hole. In fact, I hope you'll see that the language of the fathers and even of the medievals *is* Scripture. In other words, they speak and think in ways that are so drenched in Scripture that it is sometimes hard to determine when they are intending to quote Scripture, when they are paraphrasing, and when they are speaking for themselves. They also wrote biblical commentaries without any hint of unease or tension between their exegesis of biblical texts and their classical theological beliefs.[29] Just because our own cultural context has taught us that "valuing" Scripture takes a specific form doesn't mean that all eras wrestled with Scripture in the same forms. Of course, you may question whether these theologians properly understood Scripture. But this is the case for everyone in every period! Scripture is sufficient and authoritative, yet we still must interpret it. No one can piously stand up and declare, "My view is simply identical with what the Bible says; no interpretation is needed!" This is what modern theologians call a form of biblicism. It is a naively naked approach to interpretation.[30] Who, then, has the most biblical and satisfying interpretation? This is why church tradition is so valuable, as will be explained in greater detail later. It provides

---

29. Eleonore Stump, *The God of the Bible and the God of the Philosophers* (Marquette University Press, 2016), 37.

30. I have elsewhere written more on the concept of biblicism and its incoherence: Jordan L. Steffaniak, "Everything in Nature Speaks of God: Understanding Sola Scriptura Aright," *Modern Reformation* 31, no. 3 (2022); Jordan L. Steffaniak, "The God of All Creation: A Critique of Evangelical Biblicism and Recovery of Perfect Being Theology," *Journal of Reformed Theology* 14, no. 4 (2020): 358–80, https://doi.org/10.1163/15697312-bja10008.

a wealth of interpretive insights that transcend our own current contexts.[31] But whatever you think about classical theism, I hope to convince you that classical theists deeply care for, revere, and submit to Scripture. They are not merely capitulators to the spirit of their age. Nor is classical theism as a system subject to illicit explanations of a divine mystery that ought to remain locked.

With all this in mind, keep these twin goals at the forefront as we progress: introduction and invitation. The point is both to explore the classical tradition by way of defining it and defending it but also to expand classical theism beyond the narrow mischaracterizations of our current day. I hope to faithfully guide you to the seat reserved for you at the table of classical theism.

WHAT IS CLASSICAL THEISM?

We've been talking about classical theism for a while now, but what exactly is it? If you are familiar with the contemporary Protestant conversation about classical theism, your first thought might be, "It's whatever Thomas Aquinas says." And, truthfully, this isn't a terrible answer. But Thomas wrote an incredible amount of material, and much of it is not related to classical theism. For example, his biblical commentaries and his writings on natural law, virtue, and the like are not directly relevant for classical theism—though they may be indirectly.

Additionally, and more important, Thomas's dominance in contemporary discussion is largely shaped by Pope Leo XIII's initiative in 1879 to reinvigorate Thomism in the Roman Catholic Church followed by Pope Pius X's direction for Catholic professors to teach Thomism in 1914, and the subsequent reception of his thought in the twentieth century. Thomism during this period became "indispensable" for the mission of the church, according to Roman Catholics. Pope Leo XIII's encyclical in 1879 made Thomas the philosopher of choice. He cut off Catholic philosophy, according to Tom Ward, "from the constructive pluralism of the scholastic method." These decisions are understandable when placed in historical context and often mirror many other Christian attempts at

31. Vincent of Lérins, "The Commonitory," 2.5–6.

grappling with the rapid change and development of doctrine throughout the nineteenth and twentieth centuries.[32] For example, Southern Baptists gathered to develop their own definition of faith during this era in the Baptist Faith and Message of 1925, due in large part to external pressures regarding evolution and similar worries. But to understand the impact of this Roman decision with reference to Thomas specifically, imagine if the nineteenth-century Gothic Revival in architecture had revived not the Gothic *style* but one particular Gothic *building*.[33] Later Pope Pius X declared Thomism the philosophical foundation of the church's theology.[34]

The result from these decisions was that philosophy and theology supposedly progressed until Thomas Aquinas and then regressed afterward. Therefore, any disagreement with Thomas, even in the slightest respect, is not progress but regression.[35] As Trent Pomplun helpfully narrates:

> Catholic writers largely dismissed eclecticism in favor of an ill-defined Thomism. Even so, the Catholic genealogies of the late nineteenth-century took their inspiration almost wholly from the secular and liberal Protestant historians that preceded them; if they attacked Descartes, Locke and Kant—with Duns Scotus or Scotists occasionally caught in the crossfire—they happily borrowed the elevation of Thomas and the vilification of Scotus from the very modern philosophers they opposed.[36]

But in Thomas's own day, he was one of many important "classical" thinkers.[37] His views represent one member in the family of views that is properly captured by the term *classical theism*. I don't mean to

---

32. Douglas A. Sweeney, *The Substance of Our Faith: Foundations for the History of Christian Doctrine* (Baker Academic, 2023), 124–38.

33. Thomas M. Ward, *Ordered by Love: An Introduction to John Duns Scotus* (Angelico, 2022), 5–9.

34. Ward, *Ordered by Love: An Introduction to John Duns Scotus*, 33.

35. Trent Pomplun, "John Duns Scotus in the History of Medieval Philosophy from the Sixteenth Century to Étienne Gilson (†1978)," *Bulletin de Philosophie Médiévale* 58 (2016): 426.

36. Pomplun, "John Duns Scotus in the History of Medieval Philosophy from the Sixteenth Century to Étienne Gilson (†1978)," 422.

37. Richard Cross, *The Medieval Christian Philosophers: An Introduction* (I. B. Tauris, 2014), 105; Richard Cross, "An Accidental Reformation?," *The Hanover Review* 3, no. 1 (2024): 5–6; Romanus Cessario, *A Short History of Thomism* (Catholic University of America Press, 2005), 24–28. Such historiography is critical to understanding why "Thomism" has become so popular among many Protestants and evangelicals over the last several decades. There are important sources that are being relied upon that follow the Catholic requirement of Thomism, such as the work of Étienne Gilson.

say that Thomas isn't relevant for classical theism. He is! And you'll encounter him many times over in this book. I've found Thomas to be a treasured friend over the years as I've sparred with his thoughts on all matters of doctrine. He's been an invaluable partner in thinking wisely about God and about his world. But classical theism is not Thomism. And it's important to recognize this from the outset. If we begin by assuming the identity of classical theism with Thomism, the Great Tradition of the Christian church will be misshapen and misunderstood. Any approach to the "Great Tradition" that sees Thomism as the only home of orthodoxy is illusionary. It is an attempt to "whitewash all traditions from one pot."[38] Even if we wanted it to be true, a unitary Great Tradition to this extent is what Richard Cross has called a "figment of the modern imagination."[39]

Knowing this, I do have reservations about some of the evangelical Thomistic retrieval which has taken off recently. I am concerned because it has unhelpfully identified classical theism with Thomism. And yet I'm not critical because those efforts are making Thomas more accessible or making him more relevant. That's good! Thomas is a much greater resource than any number of recent evangelical thinkers. By my lights, spending time with Thomas is far more profitable than most any thinker after the eighteenth century. It is not coincidence that his thought has generated one of the most compelling traditions of all time. However, ironically, I caution against some of the recent evangelical material because that material is not sufficiently conversant with *Thomas*. We don't need less of Thomas. We need more. More on his biblical exegesis. More on his moral theology. More on his understanding of atonement, sacrifice, and sacraments. More on his pneumatology. More on his eschatology. More on his sermons and personal life. Only then can we rightly access his legacy and decide how best to appropriate his work for contemporary use.

See figure 1.1 for one way to think about it. (Note my emphasis on *one* way to think about it—these charts are not meant to be exact representations but illustrative and directionally accurate.) Thomism *about*

---

38. Martin Chemnitz, *Examination of the Council of Trent*, vol. 1 (Concordia, 1978), 220.

39. Cross, "An Accidental Reformation?," 10–11.

the doctrine of God is a subset of classical theism. If we expand our thinking beyond the doctrine of God to a more general "classical consensus," this chart would look slightly different. Therefore, while it is true that Thomism is a form of classical theism, the two are not identical. If Thomism were identical to classical theism, then "classical" thinkers who were Thomas's own contemporaries like Bonaventure (1221–1274) and Henry of Ghent (1217–1293), or later Reformed giants like John Calvin (1509–1564), or even earlier figures like Augustine wouldn't be classified as classical theists! If classical theism is reduced to Thomism, the terminology loses its meaning, since classical theism is supposed to be a term that can pick out a large and diverse group of thinkers. Thomism is a narrow, though influential, segment of this tradition. And not all that Thomism confesses is required for classical theism. One can reject aspects of Thomism and yet remain a classical theist.

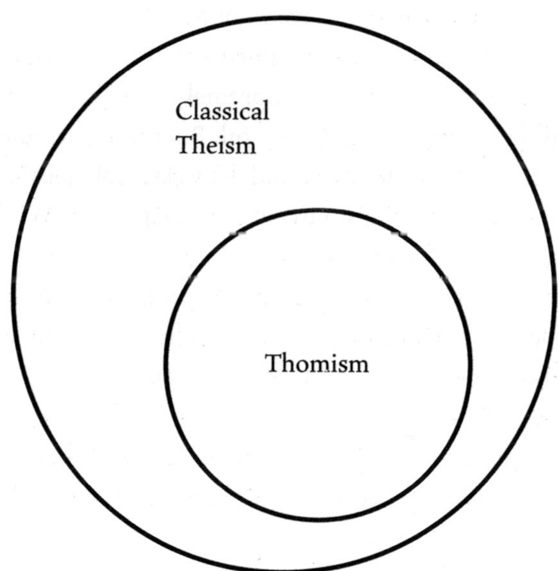

Figure 1.1

But other times, when someone speaks of classical theism, they are simply thinking about Trinitarian doctrine. They may think of the Latin model of the Trinity compared to modern "social" Trinitarian models (which is an admittedly ambiguous term).[40] But while there are "classical" doctrines of the Trinity, when the term *classical theism* is used today, it usually refers to the divine attributes. Therefore, I intend to largely avoid Trinitarian discussions, though they can't be altogether avoided since Trinitarianism remains the core of true Christian dogmatics. No truly Christian account of God can avoid presupposing the Triune God of Scripture. But the depth and nuance required to properly explicate a classical model of the Trinity is far too difficult to complete alongside a comprehensive introduction to the classical view of the divine attributes. If it takes book-length treatments to simply work through various periods of church history on the doctrine of the Trinity with care, it is certainly unwise for me to attempt to deal with *both* the Trinity and the divine attributes in one introductory volume.[41]

However, even the divine attributes aren't properly what is meant when speaking of classical theism. For example, divine attributes such as love, goodness, omnipresence, omniscience, and omnipotence are not what most theologians primarily have in mind when they refer to classical theism. Certainly, classical theism affirms all these attributes; it seeks to exalt and defend the God who is supremely loving, omnibenevolent, everywhere, all-knowing, and all-powerful. But these attributes are also defended by those who seek to revise and deny classical theism. Therefore, it is best to define classical theism by what is *unique* to it. While it's true that all classical theists think God is omniscient, so do process theists in their own way. But it is not merely unique aspects but *necessary* aspects that ought to define it. Thus, I think Ryan Mullins is exactly right when he defines classical theism as a model of God that believes God is *simple, immutable, impassible*, and *eternal*.[42]

These negative "attributes" are unique to classical theism, whereas others (e.g., love, omnipotence, etc.) are shared by rival models of God.

---

40. For an extensive (and excellent!) treatment of the possible various senses of "social" Trinitarianism, see Thomas H. McCall, *Analytic Christology and the Theological Interpretation of the New Testament*, Oxford Studies in Analytic Theology (Oxford University Press, 2021), 137–76.

41. For an example that covers an especially rich period of Trinitarian thought, see Russell L. Friedman, *Medieval Trinitarian Thought from Aquinas to Ockham* (Cambridge University Press, 2013).

42. I should note that I've chosen the language of *eternal* over *timelessness*. My logic will be further explored in future chapters. R. T. Mullins, "Classical Theism," in *T&T Clark Handbook of Analytic Theology*, ed. James Arcadi and James T. Turner (T&T Clark, 2021), 85.

Therefore, when I refer to classical theism throughout this book, I am referring to a model of God that confesses God as simple, immutable, impassible, and eternal. These attributes are properly *negative* in scope—denying imperfections of God—rather than positive in content. They are not positive properties in the traditional way we think about the world. Saying God is immutable isn't the same as saying my house is white. It is a form of "apophatic" theology in which theological terms are intended to "regulate" our speech by denying certain things more than proclaiming what is positively true.[43] It is very important to keep this in mind as we proceed, since there is a constant temptation to reify these classical attributes (e.g., immutability, etc.), which typically leads classical theism into trouble. These terms, in themselves, could be interpreted in ways that are decidedly *not* classical, which is why each will have an entire chapter. So, while attributes like omniscience, omnipresence, and omnipotence aren't my focus, they still play a role in what follows. And it is true that classical theism shapes how we understand these other attributes. They are not siloed off. Classical theism has wide-ranging effects, which we will see as we go on.

I'll use my artistic skills once more to give you an idea of where classical theism fits in comparison to several other models in their approach to the divine attributes. In figure 1.2, you'll see that there is some overlap between these different models. I will explain in more detail in the next chapter. But for now, it's helpful to know that different groups, whether neo-classical theists, Thomists, or classical theists, *all* want to affirm statements such as "God is good" or "God is love." So, there is space where these all overlap. A classical theist and process theist both agree that God is love in some sense. But the way this is understood by each theological model can vary greatly between them. Though, there is more overlap between some models than others. Note

43. Apophatic theology has a long and illustrious history in the Christian tradition. Fundamentally, it is an approach to knowing God that is negative. Instead of positively attributing things to God, it denies things of him. God is *not* like this. He is *not* like that. And through knowing what God is not like we know, in a shadowy sense, what he must be like. There is a range of applications of apophatic theology throughout the tradition as well, some totalizing it to the point that we can almost know nothing about God while others using it as an interpretive tool at various points. I'll have more to say about this general posture in chapter 3 on methodological sensibilities.

that these figures are *illustrative* and not based on exact scientific figures that would give proper proportions and overlap for each model.

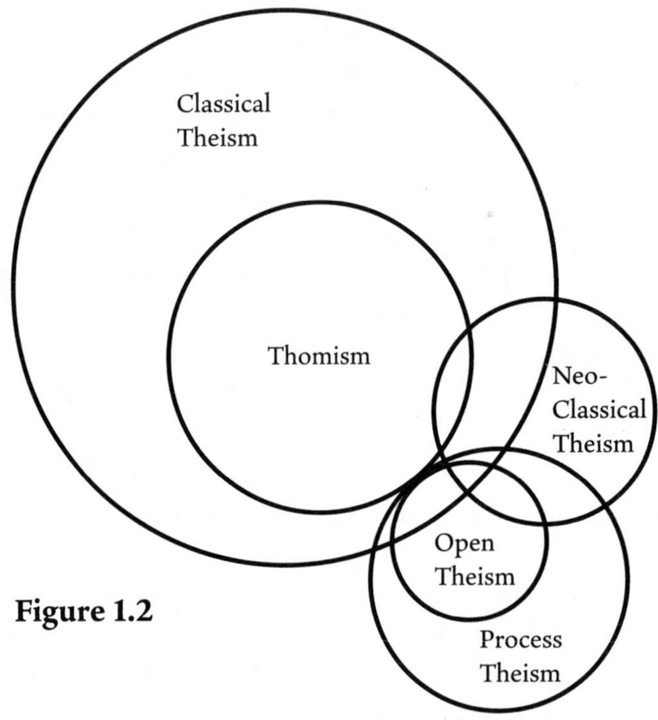

Figure 1.2

WHAT IS RETRIEVAL?[44]

Next, I want to give a crash course in the theology of retrieval, since it's an underlying presupposition throughout this book. In its essence, theological retrieval is a disposition and project that values the past for the benefit of the present. In some sense, we are all practicing theological retrieval as we engage with Scripture and the Christian tradition. Some of us are more critical, while others are more constructive or reparative of well-worn paths.[45] But the best of theological retrieval is a project of careful historical research that reappropriates the insights

44. Much of this section comes from my essay on Herman Bavinck: Jordan L. Steffaniak, "Retrieving Reformed Philosophy of Mind: Herman Bavinck's Eclectic Harmonism as Gateway to Neo-Aristotelianism," *Evangelical Quarterly* 94 (2023): 3–5, https://doi.org/10.1163/27725472-09401006.

45. Simeon Zahl, "Tradition and Its 'Use': The Ethics of Theological Retrieval," *Scottish Journal of Theology* 71, no. 3 (2018): 308, https://doi.org/10.1017/S0036930618000340.

gleaned for a modern context.[46] It is first a receptive posture that sees the task of theology as fundamentally given rather than generative. The content of theology is not a singular moment of grace. The entire context of theology is marked by grace—waiting and receiving from the Lord, the giver of every good thing.[47] As the Baptist John C. Ryland (1723–1792) explains, theology is "marked by its religious responsibility to God as an act of worshipful gratitude ... what follows for theology is not further divinely inspired teaching but rather hearing, receptivity, and confession of that which has been given 'once for all' (Jude 3)."[48] Thus, it gives priority to the self-description of the Christian community throughout the ages but is conscious of its own social location, seeking to advance theology for *today*.

A posture of retrieval doesn't entail an approach to theology that would force Christianity to be subservient to any era of theology, whether modern, premodern, or otherwise.[49] The past, rather than being dead and gone, speaks to us today and provides both a conceptual grammar for healthy theology and imaginative resources for further theological work.[50] The past is seen as our inheritance we as faithful sons and daughters must receive and make something of.[51] It is not merely a series of footnotes or proof-texts but rather provides actual source material for today with living relevance.[52] This requires that any proper retrieval of the past do more than "mine" (or Google!) for quotes that agree with the conclusion. It is more than an archaeological activity. It requires the patience to read thinkers of the past in their full context, understanding their overall argument, along with competing thinkers that differ in sometimes significant ways. It then requires the imagination and courage to invest our inheritance in today.

---

46. Brock, *Orthodox yet Modern*, 54.

47. Michael Allen, *The Fear of the Lord: Essays on Theological Method* (T&T Clark, 2022), 180.

48. Tyler Wittman, *God and Creation in the Theology of Thomas Aquinas and Karl Barth* (Cambridge University Press, 2019), 9.

49. David F. Ford, "Introduction," in *The Modern Theologians: An Introduction to Christian Theology since 1918*, ed. David F. Ford and Rachel Muers, 3rd ed, The Great Theologians (Blackwell, 2005), 2–3.

50. David Bentley Hart, *The Experience of God: Being, Consciousness, Bliss* (Yale University Press, 2013), 13.

51. Charles T. Mathewes, *Evil and the Augustinian Tradition* (Cambridge University Press, 2001), 69.

52. Brian E. Daley, *God Visible: Patristic Christology Reconsidered* (Oxford University Press, 2018), 3.

Therefore, theologies of retrieval listen and learn from the Christian tradition while at the same time building upon that tradition in creative and faithful ways. The past functions as both a resource to receive and a resource to inspire. As such, there is no one monolithic path to retrieval,[53] though there is a shared heritage, posture, and community of authoritative texts and friends.[54] The past is a *community* that leads us to think well, as Bavinck has explained:

> The dogmatic theologian no less than the ordinary believer is obliged to confess the communion of the saints. How wide and long, how high and deep the love of Christ is. A love that surpasses all knowledge can only be grasped with all the saints in communion. It is first of all in and by means of their fellowship that a theologian learns to understand the dogmas of the church that articulate the Christian faith. Above everything else, the communion of the saints provides empowering strength and superb comfort.[55]

Such a listening to the community of ages past is not merely good advice from dead theologians. It is also given christological and Trinitarian warrant in holy Scripture. Hebrews 13:7–8 commends us to remember our leaders, to consider their way of life, and to imitate their faith. Sitting at the feet of departed saints, then, is a spiritual exercise in humility and wisdom. It awakens us to the blindness of our presuppositions when we hear of strange words from different lands and times. It shocks us to the lack of attention we've given to various scriptural teachings. It eliminates our propensity to be rugged lone wolves that attempt to know and

53. Khaled Anatolios, *Retrieving Nicaea: The Development and Meaning of Trinitarian Doctrine* (Baker Academic, 2018), 281.

54. The precise nature of this authority is often debated among differing segments of Christianity. Roman Catholics and Protestants will have differing answers to questions such as who these authorities are and how absolute or relativized their authority is. While I do engage these sorts of questions to a minimal extent in this book, I do not seek to offer a comprehensive account. I minimally assume that authority in some sense is necessary for any Christian doctrine, especially our doctrine of God, which is what I take to be the basic claim of retrieval theology. The past matters for the present and exerts some form of influence on our present understanding. On the question of authority in general, see Avery Dulles, who reminds us that rejecting authority is not a mark of adulthood but a sign of adolescence: Avery Dulles, *The Resilient Church: The Necessity and Limits of Adaptation* (Doubleday, 1977), 94–96.

55. Herman Bavinck, "Herman Bavinck, 'Foreword to the First Edition (Volume 1) of the *Gereformeerde Dogmatiek*,'" trans. John Bolt, *Calvin Theological Journal* 45 (2010): 9.

understand God as isolated individuals. God has given us heroes in the faith that have gone before us who then invite us to participate in the living tradition of the church. But such a practice is not a call to mimicking or repeating them exactly but to considering with wisdom how we ought to live similarly for our own setting.[56]

Therefore, the end goal in hearing from the Christian tradition is *not* revolution, restoration, or even repristination. The end goal *is* a serious and creative use of the past for the present.[57] Unfortunately, there is always a temptation to revolt, restore, and repristinate the past, but we must be resolute in our commitment to the living faith through which the Spirit continues to guide us into all truth (John 16:13).

As such, the Christian task of retrieval understands tradition as a living reality, refusing to exalt the past (or future) as fundamentally different than our own existence. The past bears no more promise than our own age. And yet the Lord has worked in each age, and we ought to critically appropriate each age as such. The Almighty has brought the Christian tradition from darkness to light but has yet to glorify it.[58] Herman Bavinck explains the task far better than I: "To cherish the ancient simply because it is ancient is neither Reformed nor Christian. A work of dogmatic theology should not simply describe what was true and valid but what abides as true and valid. It is rooted in the past but labors for the future."[59]

In contrast to theologies of retrieval are theologies of repristination. Theologies of repristination cherish the ancient simply because it is ancient. They calcify doctrinal discoveries of ages past in stone. They make these ancient discoveries immovable as if there were a golden age of doctrinal development that is final.[60] In our case, they often canonize and lionize certain figures like Thomas Aquinas.[61] This approach is one

---

56. Allen, *The Fear of the Lord*, 198–99.

57. See Gavin Ortlund, *Theological Retrieval for Evangelicals: Why We Need Our Past to Have a Future* (Crossway, 2019), 17–18, 25, 45, 71.

58. Allen, *The Fear of the Lord*, 181–82.

59. Bavinck, "Herman Bavinck, 'Foreword to the First Edition (Volume 1) of the *Gereformeerde Dogmatiek*,'" 10.

60. Ortlund, *Theological Retrieval for Evangelicals*, 74.

61. See, for example: Matthew Barrett, *The Reformation as Renewal: Retrieving the One, Holy, Catholic, and Apostolic Church* (Zondervan, 2023), 114–204.

of imitation. It seeks to be *like* the model. But theologies of retrieval seek to emulate the model and thus *surpass* them.[62]

Retrieval seeks to surpass on at least three grounds. First, those involved in the work of retrieval seek to work like their models instead of merely copying the results of their models' work. Second, they display greater sensitivity to context by seeking to think like their exemplars would in our current context. Third, retrieval allows novel expressions of form. Theologians engaged in retrieval allow themselves to shape their mode of presentation and style in their own excellent ways.[63] Such an approach is like a habit of mind that is fundamentally contemplative, considering how one might expand and innovate but always as an apprentice to a wise set of masters.[64] Therefore, retrieval is a form of *participation* in the whole of the Christian tradition. When we seek to inhabit the world of our exemplars and explore their ancient wisdom for today, we find them beautiful and inspiring.[65] As Henri Blocher has well argued: "We treasure tradition not by servile adherence to it, but by, as it were, sitting on the shoulders of fathers and elder brothers who were giants indeed, and thus do we hope to be granted the grace of seeing even further and even more clearly."[66]

Robin Le Poidevin offers a lucid comparative illustration between these approaches. He contrasts what he calls "period" metaphysics with "contemporary" metaphysics, which I am loosely connecting to theologies of repristination and retrieval. In so doing he compares them to the debate over instrumental music from given periods. Some argue that music from any given period, whether the eighteenth century or the 1980s, should be played only on period instruments. There is a certain aesthetic experience that must be replicated by using all the exact same instruments and the like. But if this is true then it is impossible for us to listen to the music properly since our hearing of the music will be tainted

62. Jennifer A. Herdt, *Putting on Virtue: The Legacy of the Splendid Vices* (University of Chicago Press, 2012), 116–19.

63. Herdt, *Putting on Virtue*, 116–17.

64. Justus H. Hunter, "Postmodernity and Univocity," Syndicate, accessed April 20, 2023, https://syndicate.network/symposia/theology/postmodernity-and-univocity/.

65. Herdt, *Putting on Virtue*, 119.

66. Henri Blocher, *Original Sin: Illuminating the Riddle* (InterVarsity Press, 2004), 13.

by the memory of other instruments in our own period. Analogously, if we are to truly inhabit classical theism, then we must inhabit whatever the chosen golden century's presuppositions, epistemology, and metaphysics are—fourth or fourteenth centuries. Otherwise, we risk misunderstanding and departing from the original ideas and aims.[67] But of course, such slavish devotion is impossible. We do not live in the fourth or the fourteenth century. We live today. And we shouldn't despise God's providence in placing us to theologize today.

Thus, it is wise to avoid theologies of repristination. They are neither fruitful nor healthy. They are biased and prevent us from enjoying the entirety of the Lord's bountiful harvest. This is why I am committed to an approach of confessing orthodoxy while living in the present. Instead of rejecting our current day out of hand, as if God's common grace ceased in the eighteenth century (or whichever century you might find especially nasty and the root cause of our problems), I find even greater vigor in theologizing for the church as a theologian of *today*. Indeed, I find encouragement from some of our greatest modern theologians like John Webster, who laments similarly:

> However necessary "anti-modern" protest may be on certain occasions, however much it may empower the re-engagement of neglected constructive tasks, it should not betray theology into the illusion that all that is required for successful dogmatics in the present is the identification and repudiation of an error in the past. Such a stance can indicate the same illusion of superiority as that sometimes claimed by critical reason. Moreover, it can fail to grasp that the problem is not modern theology but simply theology. All talk of God is hazardous. Modern constraints bring particular challenges which can be partially defeated by attending to a broader and wiser history, but there is no pure Christian past whose retrieval can ensure theological fidelity.[68]

67. Robin Le Poidevin, *And Was Made Man: Mind, Metaphysics, and Incarnation* (Oxford University Press, 2023), 12–13.

68. John Webster, "Theologies of Retrieval," in *The Oxford Handbook of Systematic Theology*, ed. Kathryn Tanner, John Webster, and Iain Torrance (Oxford University Press, 2007), 596, https://doi.org/10.1093/oxfordhb/9780199245765.003.0033.

Therefore, a properly "theological theology" of retrieval requires more than restating the past. It requires a "going forward." Every age must receive, retrieve, and rearticulate doctrine afresh. And while the mystery of God and his gospel has been clarified, it is never fully comprehensible. It is not merely a problem to be solved. So, we should always be open to further development and clarification. As Thomas Weinandy has quipped, "The depth of mystery can still be plunged further."[69] And this is just what the Christian tradition has offered us in all its variegated glory.

CLASSICAL MOTIVATIONS

Finally, I'd like to give several reasons why classical theism is important. What are the motivations that have compelled so many to confess a similar understanding of God as simple, immutable, impassible, and eternal? I think there are at least four good reasons to both confess and inhabit this tradition.

First, the *telos* of classical theism is doxology. As noted earlier, it is to confess with Saint Paul, "To the King of the ages, immortal, invisible, the only God, be honor and glory forever and ever. Amen" (1 Tim 1:17). This is why classical theism is at its core an ecclesial doctrine. It breathes wind into the sails of the church's worship. It fuels and gives speech to our prayers. Classical theism is no mere dry and arid academic study of religion. It is earnest doxology to the all-sufficient Yahweh. Our happiness depends on it.[70] This, by and large, is why so many have been drawn to classical theism. It is serious about worshiping God. It is serious about ascribing every conceivable perfection to him. It is serious about divine transcendence—maintaining God's rightful place outside the created order. God is not another thing in the universe but something different altogether.

Now, this isn't to say that non-classical thinkers aren't serious about worshiping God! I know too many good and godly men and women who love God with every fiber of their being and yet find classical theism troubling. We should treat all those who share the confession of the Nicene and Apostles' Creeds as brothers and sisters in the one faith—even if we think they fail to properly understand the meaning or entailments of those

69. Thomas G. Weinandy, *Does God Suffer?* (University of Notre Dame Press, 2000), 36.

70. John C. Ryland, *Contemplations on the Beauties of Creation and on All the Principal Truths and Blessings of the Glorious Gospel; with the Sins and Graces of Professing Christians* (Thomas Dicey, 1779), 2:327.

confessions. Instead, I am saying there is a certain disposition found in many classical thinkers that prioritizes reverence and awe in conceiving of God.

Second, classical theism is a *biblical* doctrine. While there is an ever-present danger, especially in our contemporary period, to think that to accept classical theism is to depart from Scripture, making philosophy king and twisting the Bible into a pretzel to fit one's own prized philosophical system, this ought not be. When you cut classical theism, it ought to bleed Bible. There is a deep and wide exegetical tradition that gives life to classical theism. Unfortunately, this hasn't been made clear in recent times. For example, Craig Carter has claimed that "classical theism refers to what can be known about God by reason working on general revelation."[71] While it's true that classical theism does make use of reason and general revelation, as *Christian* classical theism it does not exist apart from the font of Scripture. Apart from Scripture, the classical Christian understanding of these attributes is severely misshapen. Classical theism for today ought to return to the heritage of the church that not only made philosophical claims with reference to Plato, Aristotle, or even Jewish and Muslim sources, but was fundamentally anchored in Scripture and reverent worship.[72]

Third, classical theism has a vast and wide historical pedigree (and consensus!). While most Protestants today do not take historicity as a major authority, it's far more authoritative and meaningful than our own individual interpretations. God promised his Spirit to guide his church into all truth. Therefore, it is wise to inhabit the traditional thinking about who God is, lest we inadvertently distrust God's own effectiveness to achieve his promises.

Fourth, classical theism has philosophical firepower. It has developed over the centuries to include highly sophisticated and refined arguments in its defense. Philosophy is not everything for the Christian. But formidable argumentation from many of the Christian tradition's greatest thinkers is a reason to confess and inhabit the tradition of classical theism.

---

71. I should note that Carter does provide a significant amount of exegesis in his own work, dedicating nearly half his book to biblical commentary on Isaiah. However, this claim is indicative of a misshapen explanation of classical theism. Craig A. Carter, *Contemplating God with the Great Tradition: Recovering Trinitarian Classical Theism* (Baker Academic, 2021), 25.

72. Soskice, *Naming God*, 3.

WHAT'S NEXT?

Now for a more formal road map for what's next. The first section, in which this chapter is included, is the "prolegomena" to classical theism. Before we move to discuss the unique attributes of classical theism, it's necessary to define more closely various rival models of God (including classical theism itself) to better orient ourselves. The focus of chapter 2 is devoted to this conceptual heavy lifting. Chapter 3 provides much of the groundwork for how classical theists think about Scripture and doctrine. The chapter explores various interpretive sensibilities that many within the classical tradition have employed to think well about God. Apart from this hermeneutical foundation much of the logic of classical theism will appear confusing or foreign. Chapter 4 gives an overview of some of the metaphysical concepts necessary to understanding classical theism. This chapter also provides a general overview of the consensus and minority report on various metaphysical commitments. The section concludes with chapter 5, which provides the theological foundations for classical theism. These are God's aseity and goodness.

The next section begins the introduction to Christian classical theism proper. Chapters 6 through 9 examine, explain, and defend the four unique attributes of classical theism: divine simplicity, immutability, impassibility, and eternity. Each of these chapters concludes with the ecclesial importance of these dogmatic and sometimes difficult doctrines. Therefore, this book isn't merely for budding scholars of the doctrine of God or senior scholars interested in understanding this doctrinal locus better—it's for the church. Pastors ought to see this as a resource for their own preaching and teaching ministries. They should find it to be a resource for their own discipleship ministries with their elders and deacons as well. While some of the terrain can be difficult at times, I promise it's rewarding. As Baptist luminary John Brine (1703–1765) argues, "Learn to distinguish well, or you never will be able to preach well."[73] The careful thinking and careful distinctions that you find in the classical tradition only serve our confession of God. So, classical theism is a dogma for the church!

---

73. Quoted in Robert Hall, *God's Approbation, the Study of Faithful Ministers* (J. W. Piercy, 1771), 15.

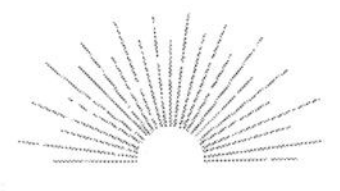

2

CLASSICAL THEISM AND MODELS OF GOD

One of the first rules for biblical interpretation is that context is king. The same rule applies when thinking about classical theism. If we want to know what it is, it helps to know its context. When we know what other views say about God, we will have a better grasp of classical theism itself. In contemporary terminology, these differing views are called "models." Just as there are different models of trucks, where you may have a Ford F-150, a GMC Sierra, or a Ram, you have different models of God. The main models I explain in this chapter alongside classical theism are neo-classical theism, open theism, and process theism. I also explain certain subsets of these models, such as Thomism, but I take the aforementioned as the primary headings. Each primary model refers to a "family" of views on the divine attributes, but each are Christian in the sense that they believe (or at least *can* believe) God is triune, God the Son was incarnate and atoned for sins, and the like. Many would likely be unhappy to call process theism *Christian* in any traditional sense, but for the sake of building a robust context to understand classical theism, I include it. While categorizing models based on family resemblances can be somewhat fuzzy around the edges, it remains useful to designate a consensus among certain thinkers. Once I've given a general description of these models, I discuss more fully the notion of *mere* classical theism and the flexibility and limits of the classical tradition.

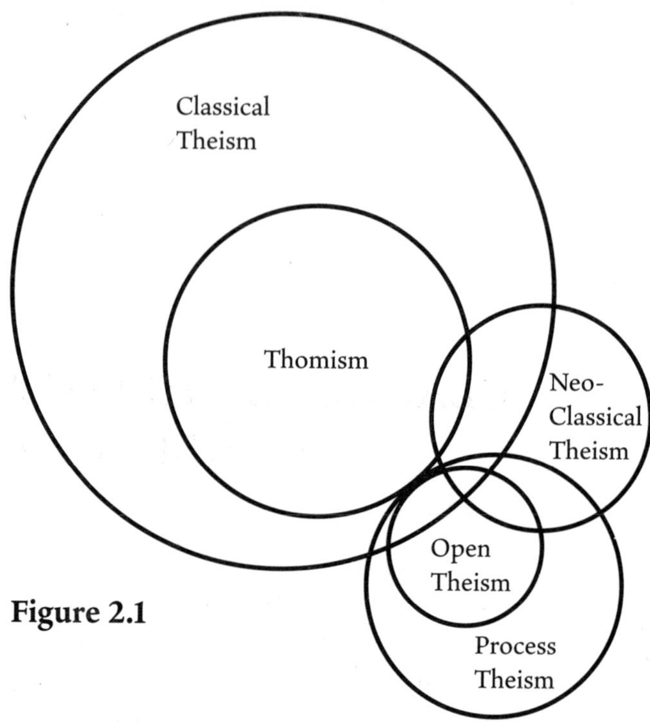

Figure 2.1

MODELS OF GOD

As I summarize these various models of God, I should make three preliminary remarks. First, these are not intended to provide explanations for *why* each model understands God in the way that it does. The point is to summarize the basic claims that each model makes. Therefore, my goal in this chapter is not primarily to offer evaluative judgments or expansive explanations for them. Non-classical models will be evaluated and judged thereafter as fits the occasion. Second, "models of God," as I'm using the phrase, is intended to pick out a view of God's attributes and not necessarily the nature of the Trinity, incarnation, or anything else. Third, I eschew the now-popular terminology of "relational theism" or "theistic mutualism" throughout. While it has become en vogue to classify everything that isn't classical theism as relational theism or theistic mutualism, I find such categorizations rather unhelpful and confusing.[1] Whatever the

1. See, for example, Craig Carter, *Contemplating God with the Great Tradition: Recovering Trinitarian Classical Theism* (Baker Academic, 2021), 16; James E. Dolezal, *All That Is in God* (Reformation Heritage, 2017), 1; David Bentley Hart, *The Experience of God* (Yale University Press, 2013), 127–28.

case may be, the mutualists or relationalists are the theological "bad guys." And they are indeed very bad. However, this terminology is typically only used as a theological pejorative. Such is obvious when few (if any) so-called mutualists or relationalists willingly adopt the label.[2] It's helpful to keep figure 2.1 in mind as we proceed. While it doesn't include all of the models and subsets (lest it become more akin to a twenty-first century prophecy chart), it should be directionally useful for what lies ahead.

CLASSICAL THEISM

Classical theism, given its storied tradition, has many robust definitions throughout the ages. They are worth re-reading and slowly unpacking. Consider the below two examples as entryways into understanding it. First, John of Damascus (675/76–749) says:

> So then, we both know and confess that God is without beginning, without end, eternal and everlasting, uncreated, immutable, unchangeable, simple, non-composite, incorporeal, invisible, impalpable, uncircumscribed, limitless, ungraspable, incognizable, unfathomable, good, just, almighty, the creator of all created things, sovereign over all, overseeing all, exercising foresight over all, having supreme power over all, and judge of all.[3]

Similarly, Augustine explains:

> Thus we should understand God, if we can and as far as we can, to be good without quality, great without quantity, creative without need or necessity, presiding without position, holding all things together without possession, wholly everywhere without place, everlasting without time, without any change in himself making changeable things, and undergoing nothing.[4]

These descriptions are quite similar. Both stack up terminology about what God is. God is without need, beginning, or end. He is perfect, omniscient,

2. William Wood, *Analytic Theology and the Academic Study of Religion*, Oxford Studies in Analytic Theology (Oxford University Press, 2021), 159.

3. John of Damascus, *On the Orthodox Faith*, trans. Norman Russell (St Vladimir's Seminary Press, 2022), 61.

4. Augustine, *The Trinity*, trans. Edmund Hill (New City, 2015), V.prol.2.

omnipotent, omnipresent, and omnibenevolent. Such a description of classical theism as a model is a fair starting point. But other models also want to say that God is perfect, omniscient, omnipotent, omnipresent, and omnibenevolent. Therefore, to understand classical theism, we need to know what makes it unique. Traditionally, what has set classical theism apart is that it also claims that God is *simple, immutable, impassible,* and *eternal.* It is these four attributes that comprise the uniqueness of classical theism and mark it off as a distinct model of God. If you are unsure of what any of these attributes mean, stay tuned, as each requires the necessary space to unpack properly.

Classical theism was the primary model of God for most of Christian history. Isolating classical theism from orthodox Christian doctrines of the incarnation, atonement, and the like into a generic theism would allow for Platonic, Neoplatonic, and Aristotelian philosophy and for many Jewish and Muslim thinkers to be categorized as "classical theists" as well.[5] But since I am defining classical theism within a Christian context that requires other classical doctrines like those found in the Apostles' Creed, pagan Platonists or Muslims are not categorized as classical theists. They may hold some classical doctrines, but they reject others.

Despite widespread agreement among classical theists, there is room to question and provide alternative explanations for a simple, immutable, impassible, and eternal God. By this I mean that there is no uniform explanation for what divine simplicity or what divine impassibility *must exhaustively* mean within the classical tradition. While there are guardrails and views that are decidedly nonclassical, there are various strands and textures throughout the tradition. Given that the latter half of this book is dedicated to extrapolating these four key attributes, I won't spend further time examining them here.

Some may wonder afresh why Thomism isn't just identical to classical theism at this point. As I mentioned in the introduction, there are doctrines that standard Thomism requires that are not required by classical theism. Thomism is a theological school that is dedicated to the principles, conclusions, and rationality of the thought of Thomas

5. Thomas Williams, "Introduction to Classical Theism," in *Models of God and Alternative Ultimate Realities*, ed. Jeanine Diller and Asa Kasher (Springer, 2013), 95.

Aquinas.[6] Based on this definition of Thomism, alternative intellectual traditions and movements such as Augustinianism, Scotism, and the various Protestant traditions, according to Romanus Cessario, "entirely eschew Thomism."[7] Thomists are dedicated to a "pristine adherence" to Thomas Aquinas's own principles.[8] But classical theism is a shared confession of God as *simple, immutable, impassible,* and *eternal* and not a confession of all doctrines as Thomas Aquinas, Bonaventure, Augustine, or anyone else understood them. Classical theism is not a confession of a particular version of virtue theory, the metaphysics of the sacraments, or metaphysics of human persons. While they may overlap in some respects, and sometimes be connected in deep ways, these are distinct doctrinal *loci*. And as Robert Pasnau reminds us, "It is good to keep in mind that Thomism—contrary to what is often supposed—was always a minority view during the scholastic era."[9]

But even if we restrict Thomism to the doctrine of God alone, there remain differences. For example, the formal distinction from John Duns Scotus (which I will explain in further detail in later chapters) is often thought to be inconsistent with the thinking of Thomas Aquinas. Yet both are committed to upholding the basic claims that derive from divine simplicity.[10] If their articulations of simplicity do amount to real differences, then we should not limit classical theism to Thomism (or Scotism) alone. Similarly, the approach to divine simplicity from those like Basil the Great and Gregory of Nyssa (335–395) has often been thought to be inconsistent with the Thomistic identity thesis, or as James Dolezal has sharply suggested, "entirely repugnant to the later version of simplicity" and "entirely nonsensical."[11] If Basil and Nyssa are

6. Romanus Cessario, *A Short History of Thomism* (Catholic University of America Press, 2005), 1, 11–28.

7. Cessario, *A Short History of Thomism*, 16. It should be noted that Cessario also mentions a more modern "eclectic" form of Thomism that allows for a piecemeal approach to Thomas's thought alongside commitments to traditions like those within Protestantism. Cessario ultimately rejects this categorization as useful. I agree and seek to use the more traditional "wide" definition of Thomism throughout. If one objects to my categorization and prefers the eclectic form of Thomism, I wouldn't mind. But I think such usage of the term obscures more than it clarifies.

8. Cessario, *A Short History of Thomism*, 19.

9. Robert Pasnau, *Metaphysical Themes: 1274–1671* (Clarendon, 2011), 588.

10. Gisbertus Voetius, "God's Single, Absolutely Simple Essence," trans. R. M. Hurd, *The Confessional Presbyterian* 15 (2019): 21.

11. James E. Dolezal, "Review of Basil of Caesarea, Gregory of Nyssa, and the Transformation of Divine Simplicity," *Westminster Theological Journal* 73 (2011): 387.

classical thinkers and yet they disagree with Thomas about aspects of simplicity, then we should not collapse the identity of classical theism to either the Cappadocians or the Thomists. Therefore, no classical school, whether Thomism or otherwise, should be thought of as *identical* to classical theism.

Classical theism is also unbound by the technical scholastic distinctions and their meanings as found in Thomism—*actuality, potentiality, matter, form, substantial form*, and the like. This doesn't mean these terms are irrelevant or should be cast aside. They can be, and often are, of great service to classical theism. Their vocabulary and "grammar" are ubiquitous. But the doctrinal formulations of these terms as found in orthodox Thomism are not all necessary conditions for classical theism. For example, it is not necessary to follow the Thomist maxim that all physical bodies have only one substantial form. Pluralism about substantial forms is not inconsistent with classical theism. But even more, Thomism can be quite variegated itself![12] So, even if Thomism were flexible enough to be used interchangeably with classical theism, if one is really dedicated to getting into the weeds of Thomism, one will find further bewildering complexity. But this is true of any school of thought within the classical tradition. The point is this: Classical theism is a family of views that by its very nature is broad enough to include various theological "schools." Classical theists should feel free to inhabit Thomism, Scotism, or other variegated traditions without immediate worry that they are no longer inhabiting the classical Christian tradition.

NEO-CLASSICAL THEISM

Neo-classical theism is a model or family of views about God wherein God is independent and self-sufficient (this is the doctrine of aseity, being *a se*, from nothing but himself), omniscient, omnipotent, omnipresent, and omnibenevolent. He is perfect and possesses every possible perfection. On these general descriptions, classical theism and neo-classical theism overlap in large measure, and process theism would be at odds. Yet in this model, God is *not* simple, immutable, impassible, and/or eternal like he is for classical theism. God remains omniscient, omnipotent, omnipresent, and so on, while also suffering, going "back and forth" with

12. Cessario, *A Short History of Thomism*, 14–15.

his creation, grieving, and the like. God remains unchangeable in his essential nature and existence but engages in genuine "give-and-take" relationships where he is vulnerable and changeable.[13] But there are various ways to be a neo-classical theist, and the boundaries can be somewhat vague because of this.[14] One could reject all four of the so-called classical attributes, or one could reject or modify only one or two of them. Thus, a clear description of the family of views is rather difficult to provide except by way of various examples.

As a beginning example, consider someone who claims that instead of God being simple, he is unified. This is a weaker claim than divine simplicity, though it is similarly affirmed by classical theists. Therefore, someone who rejects divine simplicity but affirms divine unity could say that God is complex in the sense that he has distinct attributes, though they are coextensive and necessary. And instead of modifying any of the other attributes, someone with this view only modifies simplicity. Properly speaking, such a view is best understood as neo-classical theism, even though it overlaps with classical theism in nearly every other way. The reason it is neo-classical theism in this instance is because it rejects a necessary tenant of classical theism. But most often, a neo-classical theist will either modify or reject all four hallmarks of classical theism.

As another example, many neo-classical theists reject a strong account of divine immutability. Instead, God is immutable in his essential properties but can change in his nonessential properties. He can change from not Creator of the world to Creator. He can change from not Redeemer to Redeemer. He can change from hating sinners to loving them. He can change from not hearing our prayers to hearing them. Likewise, instead of God being eternal in the sense of experiencing no temporal succession, God is eternal in the sense of having infinite duration. Therefore, God has no beginning and no end. He will exist forever. But he experiences a succession of moments.[15] Finally, instead of God being impassible in the

13. John C. Peckham, *Divine Attributes: Knowing the Covenantal God of Scripture* (Baker Academic, 2021), 1–23.

14. Kevin Timpe, "Introduction to Neo-Classical Theism," in *Models of God and Alternative Ultimate Realities*, ed. Jeanine Diller and Asa Kasher (Springer, 2013), 202.

15. R. T. Mullins, "The Difficulty with Demarcating Panentheism," *Sophia* 55, no. 3 (2016): 331, https://doi.org/10.1007/s11841-015-0497-6; Richard Swinburne, *The Coherence of Theism*, 2nd ed. (Oxford University Press, 2016), 228–44.

sense of being unaffected by outside action, he can be affected by others and experiences emotions besides infinite beatitude. However, he is never controlled by external stimuli that would impact his emotional state and always willingly receives them. He intimately relates to creation and feels all that's "feelable."[16]

OPEN THEISM

Open theism, while less popular now, was all the rage in decades past. It is like neo-classical theism (and even classical theism in some respects!), typically affirming God as a necessary being who possesses the maximal set of perfections *essentially*.[17] Some open theists even suggest their model is a "relatively conservative *modification* or *correction* of the classical tradition."[18] So, open theists are in some agreement (or at least are *attempting* some agreement) with classical theism and neo-classical theism, yet their account of God's perfections in relation to God's knowledge and the future are quite distinct. For open theism, God lacks exhaustive foreknowledge. The future, in many respects, is both casually and epistemically open. It is yet to be determined. Not even God has control over it. While there remain patterns and regularities in the progress of history, it remains uncertain where the future will lead. God, like creation, experiences time and progress, as the future doesn't yet exist.[19] So, while the possibilities aren't endless for God, they are certainly *open*. God cannot predestine, predetermine, or even *know* the future.[20] The future simply doesn't exist yet. The reasons given for such claims are partly philosophical and partly biblical. Suffice it to say, there is a strong intuition in open theism that only such a model can call God truly personal and interactive.[21]

---

16. Thomas Jay Oord, *Open and Relational Theology: An Introduction to Life-Changing Ideas* (SacraSage, 2021), 58.

17. John Sanders, "An Introduction to Open Theism," *Reformed Review* 60, no. 2 (2007): 35.

18. Alan R. Rhoda, "Generic Open Theism and Some Varieties Thereof," *Religious Studies* 44, no. 2 (2008): 226, https://doi.org/10.1017/S0034412508009438. Emphasis original.

19. Oord, *Open and Relational Theology*, 28; Alan Rhoda, "The Philosophical Case for Open Theism," *Philosophia* 35, no. 3–4 (2007): 302, https://doi.org/10.1007/s11406-007-9078-4; Rhoda, "Generic Open Theism and Some Varieties Thereof," 227.

20. Oord, *Open and Relational Theology*, 33; Clark H. Pinnock, "Open Theism: An Answer to My Critics," *Dialog: A Journal of Theology* 44, no. 3 (2005): 238, https://doi.org/10.1111/j.0012-2033.2005.00263.x.

21. Pinnock, "Open Theism," 237.

But limiting God's knowledge in such ways impacts other divine attributes besides omniscience. In open theism, God is also temporal, or eternal, like he is for many neo-classical theists. His knowledge changes over time as he learns new things and as the future comes to pass. He is also passible, since God's knowledge depends on the choices that free creatures make.[22] Furthermore, he is mutable, since his knowledge, will, and actions are always changing. But open theism remains distinct from neo-classical theism, given the latter's account of omniscience as including exhaustive foreknowledge.

PROCESS THEISM

Process theism is often identified with thinkers like Alfred North Whitehead (1861–1947) and Charles Hartshorne (1897–2000), who were the intellectual giants of its modern promulgation. Three main ideas can distinguish process theism. First, one of God's *essential* attributes is being involved in and affected by temporal processes. In other words, God is necessarily related to his creation. While neo-classical theism and open theism may affirm that God is involved in these ways, he's not *necessarily* involved.[23] He could choose to do otherwise. Therefore, instead of a radical distinction between God and creation, process theism (usually in the form of pantheism) collapses the distinction and says God and creation are either identical or necessarily related. Process panentheism is something in between the identity found in pantheism and the necessary relation in generic process theism. For process pantheism the universe is in God, but somehow God is more than the universe.[24] What exactly this means is mysterious, at least to me.

Second, process theism is usually intent on denying the omnipotence of God. He is *not* all-powerful. The reason is that an omnipotent God would be either coercive or entirely responsible for evil.[25] Process theism

---

22. Rhoda, "Generic Open Theism and Some Varieties Thereof," 228.

23. Donald Viney, "Process Theism," in *The Stanford Encyclopedia of Philosophy*, ed. Edward N. Zalta (Metaphysics Research Lab, Stanford University, 2022), https://plato.stanford.edu/archives/sum2022/entries/process-theism/.

24. Mullins, "The Difficulty with Demarcating Panentheism," 326; William Mander, "Pantheism," in *The Stanford Encyclopedia of Philosophy*, ed. Edward N. Zalta (Metaphysics Research Lab, Stanford University, 2022), https://plato.stanford.edu/archives/spr2022/entries/pantheism/.

25. Thomas Jay Oord, *The Death of Omnipotence and Birth of Amipotence* (SacraSage, 2023), 4–7.2023

seeks to reject such entailments by suggesting that God is limited in power. Instead, he is persuasive.[26]

Generally, this culminates in a third distinction: a rejection of the traditional doctrine of creation out of nothing. In process theism, God has quite literally always and necessarily been relating to creation.[27] The reason for this is not because God "needs" creation but because the entire structure of reality is social. While God does not require any particular universe to exist, he does require *a* universe, given the necessity of love, giving, and receiving.[28]

MERE CLASSICAL THEISM: THE FLEXIBILITY AND LIMITS OF THE CLASSICAL TRADITION

Given these classifications, when I put forward the notion of classical theism, I refer to a family of views about God that affirms that God is simple, immutable, impassible, and eternal. What these terms mean exactly can be debated, which is why it is "classical" and not something else, such as Thomism or Scotism, which would be narrower in its approach to the attributes. But there is a commitment among classical thinkers to champion these predicates. The God of the Bible, according to classical theism, is simple, immutable, impassible, and eternal. Now, to initially demonstrate what a classical approach is and why it is justified, I will briefly examine Scripture, catholic creedal beliefs, and the Protestant confessional tradition. It will quickly be seen that such predicates as simplicity, immutability, impassibility, and eternity are necessary for the classical tradition, and yet there remains conceptual space for some level of disagreement.

THE GOOD DEPOSIT

Whatever else comes to mind about classical theism, when we think of Christian classical theism we ought to think of a strong reverence for holy Scripture. Classical theism is an attempt throughout the ages of the church to guard the good deposit—to follow the pattern of sound words heard first

26. Barry L. Whitney, "Process Theism: Does a Persuasive God Coerce?," *The Southern Journal of Philosophy* 17, no. 1 (1979): 133.

27. Oord, *Open and Relational Theology*, 63–64; Mullins, "The Difficulty with Demarcating Panentheism," 326.

28. Mullins, "The Difficulty with Demarcating Panentheism," 326.

from saint Paul (2 Tim 1:13–14). While not all defenses and explanations of classical theism dwell in the Scriptures as they ought, this doesn't invalidate those which do remember that all the treasures of wisdom and knowledge are hidden in Christ, who is revealed to us in Scripture (Col 2:3).[29]

For example, Augustine argues that the first and foundational rule for understanding God is "to know these books; not necessarily to understand them but to read them so as to commit them to memory or at least make them not totally unfamiliar."[30] It is Scripture that plays the fundamental role in shaping the theologian's thoughts and speech about God. Again, Augustine says, "The most expert investigator of the divine scriptures will be the person who, first, has read them all and has a good knowledge—a reading knowledge, at least, if not yet a complete understanding—of those pronounced canonical."[31] Augustine assumes a strong proficiency and knowledge of the whole counsel of God for any theologian worth his or her salt. And it isn't difficult to see that Augustine practices what he preaches. While some may disagree with his exegetical and theological conclusions, it's obvious that Augustine was a deeply *biblical* theologian. He found Scripture to be the foundation of his theology.

Even those who are often thought of as pure philosophers stuck in ivory towers, like Thomas Aquinas, are committed to the primacy of

---

29. For an example of a classical theist who self-consciously downplays certain forms of exegetical reflection regarding God (at least in print; certainly, charity demands that unclarity, lack of context, or my own limits may be the actual culprit), see Dolezal, *All That Is in God*, xv. He says, "But it seems to me that biblical theology, with its unique focus on historical development and progress, is not best suited for study of theology proper. The reason for this is because God is not a historical individual, and neither does His intrinsic activity undergo development or change." But of course, such an argument can be adapted to critique his own approach quite easily: "But it seems to me that contemplative theology, with its unique focus on intellectual concepts and their logical relations, is not best suited for study of theology proper. The reason for this is because God is not an intellectual concept, and neither is he a logical relation between intellectual concepts." I am indebted to Greg Welty for this perceptive insight. However, this critique isn't to suggest that Dolezal seeks to downplay *Scripture* itself. But downplaying the constitutive role of exegetical practices like biblical theology is concerning. With that said, it is possible Dolezal is thinking more broadly of the theological academy and how in decades past it was very popular to dismiss traditional philosophical insights so that one could provide a metaphysical system based on the narrative of Scripture itself. And so, his reference to "biblical theology" may refer to this naive practice of assimilating a long series of flat-footed readings that is then taken to carry weight because it strings a bunch of texts together. If this is Dolezal's target, my criticism is less substantial and more pedagogical. We should avoid denigrating a valuable theological method simply because others lack the ability to do two things at once. At minimum, we should labor to be clear in what exactly we are criticizing.

30. Augustine, *On Christian Teaching*, trans. R. P. H. Green (Oxford University Press, 2009), II.30.

31. Augustine, *On Christian Teaching* II.24.

holy Scripture. John Wippel says that "if one wishes to become a philosopher in the Thomistic sense ... one should first become a theologian and philosophize from within one's theology."[32] Such a methodology is a classic version of John Webster's "theological theology." And this isn't just Wippel's imagination. Thomas is quite clear himself. He writes, "For whatever is found in other sciences that is inconsistent with the truth of this science is to be condemned as utterly false."[33] "This science" from Scripture stands above all resources for knowing God. The Christian faith is "based on the revelation made to the Apostles and Prophets who wrote the canonical books rather than on any revelation that might have been given to other doctors."[34]

Now, claims to biblical authority do not entail classical theism by themselves. There must be exegesis and theological reflection to prove such doctrines are congruent with Scripture, since there is no one biblical text that says, "God is simple, immutable, impassible, and eternal, just like Thomas Aquinas said." If there were, our situation would be much easier! But Scripture isn't designed to work that way. It's a text of wisdom that calls us to contemplation. So, Scripture by itself, without contemplation, *is* underdetermined. Scripture has "an open texture" that intends and "licenses us to fill in."[35]

This doesn't mean Scripture is a wax nose that can be shaped to mean whatever we please. It doesn't mean we place less value on the Bible. It doesn't mean that we would be better off examining trees and spiders to know God than we would contemplating holy Scripture. But it does mean we have to do the hard work of exegesis and contemplation by the power of the Holy Spirit. It means we cannot move from the claim that "God is light" (1 John 1:5) to a robust doctrine of divine simplicity without a well-formed interpretive process in which the Holy Spirit guides us into all truth. For the Spirit is "the sole foundation of truth" and "the key that

32. John F. Wippel, *Metaphysical Themes in Thomas Aquinas II*, rev. ed. (Catholic University of America Press, 2007), 21.

33. Thomas Aquinas, *The Treatise on the Divine Nature: Summa Theologiae I, 1–13*, trans. Brian J. Shanley (Hackett, 2006), I.1.6 ad 2.

34. Leo Donald Davis, *The First Seven Ecumenical Councils (325–787): Their History and Theology* (Liturgical Press, 1990), 2.

35. Brian Leftow, *God and Necessity* (Oxford University Press, 2015), 10.

unlocks for us the treasures of the kingdom of heaven."[36] Therefore, divine illumination from the Spirit of God is necessary to set the "created intellect in motion, arousing the exercise of the powers which God bestows and of whose movement he is the first principle."[37] However, there are certain bedrock Scriptural assertions that ought to guide any and all models of God. Though the Bible does not provide the sort of specificity expressed in the creedal and confessional tradition, it will place significant limits on our theorizing. These will be explained throughout the remainder of the book.

THE CATHOLIC CREEDAL TRADITION

Believe it or not, the Christian church has a cherished treasure in its ecumenical creedal formulas and the ecumenical councils' acts and definitions. Many Protestants are sadly unaware of this rich shared heritage. And even those who know the creedal formulas are often unfamiliar with the full creedal proclamations. Indeed, there are thousands of pages from the early church councils, and most of them haven't even been translated into English![38] But these creeds and their synodal proclamations are of great value for understanding classical theism for at least two reasons. First, because they are ecclesiastical documents to which the universal church is supposed to assent. Therefore, they provide a baseline for determining the nature of classical theism. Second, because they reckon deeply with *Christology*. While it may appear odd to invoke the necessity of Christology for theology proper, Christ makes all things new, including our understanding of God himself.[39] As the author of Hebrews reminds us, Christ "is the radiance of the glory of God and the exact imprint of his nature" (Heb 1:3). Basil similarly explains that the way to the "knowledge

---

36. John Calvin, *Institutes of the Christian Religion*, ed. John T. McNeill, trans. Ford Lewis Battles (Westminster John Knox, 2006), 2.2.15; 3.1.4.

37. John Webster, *The Domain of the Word: Scripture and Theological Reason* (Bloomsbury, 2012), 57.

38. Donald Fairbairn, "Interpreting Conciliar Christology: An Overview in the Service of Analytic Theology," *Journal of Analytic Theology* 10 (2022): 363, https://doi.org/10.12978/jat.2022-10.050013031403.

39. In making all things "new," that doesn't mean all things are different in a substantial sense, as if God were something else prior to his coming. Instead, it means that he illumines the truth that was always true but was hidden and partially understood.

of God is from the one Spirit, through the one Son, to the one Father."[40] Therefore, our reckoning with the nature of God is given a radical revelation in Jesus himself. Christology is given an utterly unique and illuminating role in understanding who God is.[41]

Consider first the Council of Nicaea (325). All orthodox Christians affirm this creedal formula that was agreed upon so many centuries ago. It is axiomatic for the Christian faith. The formula itself seems rather innocuous for determining which model of God is properly "creedal." But few have taken the time to examine beyond the formula itself. For example, hidden within the anathemas of the creed is a claim about divine immutability. It says: "But those who say ... that he is mutable or alterable—the Catholic and Apostolic Church anathematizes."[42] This is an anathema directed at those who would suggest the Son is mutable, and hence that God is mutable too. Therefore, according to the council of Nicaea, to deny immutability in a broad sense is to deny the Nicene Creed.

But even the creed itself has classical underpinnings. Nicaea confesses that God is "creator of heaven and earth and all that is seen and unseen." The creed indicates there is absolutely *nothing* that God did not create.[43] Therefore, models of God like process theism, which suggest God necessarily exists with creation, violate a fundamental claim of the Nicene Creed. It is also possible to argue that any model of God that posits eternally existing abstract objects (e.g., numbers, Platonic universals, etc.) alongside God are in violation of the creed. This is a harder claim to justify than the former but is a common intuition. However, the creed does not provide robust accounts of the meaning and role of the divine attributes, like divine simplicity. One can certainly examine what the thinkers behind the creed understood them to mean, but they are not elevated to creedal status, which is no small matter for the Christian committed to sharing in the one faith of our Lord.

---

40. Basil, *On the Holy Spirit*, trans. Stephen M. Hildebrand (St. Vladimir's Seminary Press, 2011), 18, 47.

41. Thomas Joseph White, *The Incarnate Lord: A Thomistic Study in Christology* (Catholic University of America Press, 2017), 5.

42. Davis, *The First Seven Ecumenical Councils (325–787)*, 60.

43. William Lane Craig, *God over All: Divine Aseity and the Challenge of Platonism* (Oxford University Press, 2016), 16, 40.

Beyond the creedal formulas themselves, numerous documents also received the council's approval as orthodox interpretations of the creeds. For example, Cyril of Alexandria's (376–444) *Second Letter to Nestorius* received synodal approval at both the Council of Ephesus (431) and Chalcedon (451) and is considered a "*de facto* definition of the faith."[44] Within this letter, Cyril flatly states that God is impassible because he is incorporeal.[45] In his *Third Letter to Nestorius,* which received synodal affirmation at the Second Council of Constantinople (553), Cyril argues that "the one who abides eternally, according to the scriptures, is entirely unchanging and immutable."[46] Likewise, Chalcedon affirmed Pope Leo's (400–461) *Tome* as orthodox as read against the backdrop of Cyril.[47] Leo later provided a more mature reflection, his *Second Tome,* in which he asserts that the divine essence is immutable, impassible, and eternal.[48]

While these proclamations are not primarily theological accounts of the attributes of God, it remains clear that confessing God as simple, immutable, impassible, and eternal is necessary for creedal orthodoxy.[49] There is a deep intuition of a true "orthodox sense" by which the creeds must be interpreted. It is not merely a grammatical exercise to verbally confess certain words ignorant of their overall meaning and logic. There is a rule of faith of sorts, wherein individual doctrines fit a larger pattern.[50] Therefore, correctly understanding conciliar statements requires a key, which is the right interpretive tool.[51]

---

44. Richard Price and Michael Gaddis, trans., *The Acts of the Council of Chalcedon*, vol. 1 (Liverpool University Press, 2007), 24.

45. Cyril of Alexandria, "Second Letter to Nestorius," in *The Cambridge Edition of Early Christian Writings*, ed. Mark DelCogliano, trans. Matthew R. Crawford (Cambridge University Press, 2022), 568, https://doi.org/10.1017/9781107449640.041.

46. Cyril of Alexandria, "Third Letter to Nestorius," in *The Cambridge Edition of Early Christian Writings*, ed. Mark DelCogliano, trans. Matthew R. Crawford (Cambridge University Press, 2022), 628, https://doi.org/10.1017/9781107449640.046.

47. Fairbairn, "Interpreting Conciliar Christology," 376–77; Price and Gaddis, *The Council of Chalcedon*, 1:67.

48. Leo of Rome, "The Second Tome (Letter to Emperor Leo)," in *The Cambridge Edition of Early Christian Writings*, ed. and trans. Mark DelCogliano (Cambridge University Press, 2022), 120–21, https://doi.org/10.1017/9781009057103.005.

49. Tim Pawl, *In Defense of Conciliar Christology: A Philosophical Essay* (Oxford University Press, 2016), 181–90.

50. Cyril of Alexandria, "Third Letter to Nestorius," 626.

51. Richard Cross, "On the Interpretation of Church Councils," *TheoLogica: An International Journal for Philosophy of Religion and Philosophical Theology* 4, no. 2 (2020): 203, https://doi.org/10.14428/thl.v4i2.60613.

THE PROTESTANT CONFESSIONAL TRADITION

One of the beauties of the Protestant tradition is its herculean effort at drafting a number of confessions of faith. All these confessions are exceptional achievements in their own rights. They are documents forged out of the church for the life of the church. They are designed to summarize the consensus positions that would function as dogmatic keys. While these confessions are far more robust than the early creedal formulas, and sometimes polemical to set themselves apart from other Protestant denominations, they are crucial to understand for those seeking to know and understand classical theism. The reason for this is threefold. First, these documents are ecclesial in nature. And as I've claimed, classical theism is an ecclesial doctrine. It is the bedrock of the church's life and worship. Therefore, the *telos* of these confessions and the dogma of classical theism are intertwined. Second, these documents are consensus statements, designed to formalize the agreed-upon beliefs of large groups. Therefore, they are signposts for what the Protestant church has understood about God. They are not merely the beliefs of individuals but of communities.[52] Third, as you'll find, whether Lutheran, Reformed, or otherwise, Protestants historically confessed a unified belief in a classical God.

The Thirty-Nine Articles: Anglicanism on God

Anglicanism historically receives the Thirty-Nine Articles (1571). Within Article I, the church confesses God's nature: "There is but one living and true God, without body, parts, or passions." While this statement is not as robust as others we will consider, note that the phrasing later repeated in other Protestant confessions, "without body, parts, or passions," is found here. Of all attributes that could be explicated, this confessional phrase is of such great importance that it must be located alongside the existence and unity of God. The phrase is shorthand for God's spirituality, simplicity, and impassibility, and by extension his immutability and eternity. While there is obvious room for debate about what entailments arise from saying God is without body, parts, or passions, the language here is set. A truly faithful Anglican *must* confess God as without body, parts, or passions.

52. Bruce D. Marshall, *Trinity and Truth* (Cambridge University Press, 2002), 19.

The Augsburg Confession: Lutheranism on God

The Lutheran Augsburg Confession (1530) in Article 1 seeks to inhabit the ancient tradition of Nicaea as "true and to be believed without any doubting" and focuses especially on God as triune but also speaks to the divine attributes, claiming: "There is one Divine Essence which is called and which is God: eternal, without body, without parts, of infinite power, wisdom, and goodness, the Maker and Preserver of all things, visible and invisible." Again, we see the language of God being without body and parts, though without "passions" is lacking from the statement. We also see additional language that is relevant, like God's eternity, which Lutheran theologian Johann Gerhard (1582–1637) has explained along the traditional Boethian definition as the simultaneous possession of an everlasting life. Therefore, by "eternal" it is meant that God's life is interminable, indivisible, and independent in duration. Therefore, there is absolutely no succession.[53]

The Belgic Confession and Synopsis of Purer Theology: The Continental Reformed on God

The Belgic Confession, written in 1561 by Guido de Brès (1522–1567), is the formal confession of the Dutch Reformed in the Netherlands and many other Reformed churches. It forms part of the Three Forms of Unity and has seen wide use since its creation. It begins in Article 1 by stating: "We all believe in our hearts and confess with our mouths that there is a single and simple spiritual being, whom we call God—eternal, incomprehensible, invisible, unchangeable, infinite, almighty; completely wise, just, and good, and the overflowing source of all good."

Herein we find God being confessed as *simple* and spiritual, eternal, and unchangeable, among other traditional divine attributes. These attributes receive significant explanation among the many Reformed confessional theologians who subscribe to the confession.

Later, in the *Synopsis of Purer Theology* (1625), God is described in section 6.17 as "a spiritual essence, entirely simple and infinite, that is eternal and immeasurable, and immutable." The traditional "classical" attributes are listed here and confessed save impassibility, which is likely assumed.

53. Johann Gerhard, *On the Nature of God and on the Most Holy Mystery of the Trinity*, ed. Benjamin T. G. Mayes, trans. Richard J. Dinda (Concordia, 2007), 139.

The Second London Confession of Faith: The Reformed, Congregational, and Baptistic on God

The Second London Confession of Faith (1677/1689) is a slight revision and modification of the Westminster Confession of Faith (1646) and the Savoy Declaration (1658). I include it over these two because it is slightly more precise in this section. It states in Article 2.1:

> The Lord our God is but one only living and true God; whose subsistence is in and of Himself, infinite in being and perfection; whose essence cannot be comprehended by any but Himself; a most pure spirit, invisible, without body, parts, or passions, who only hath immortality, dwelling in the light which no man can approach unto; who is immutable, immense, eternal, incomprehensible, almighty, every way infinite, most holy, most wise, most free, most absolute; working all things according to the counsel of His own immutable and most righteous will, for His own glory; most loving, gracious, merciful, long-suffering, abundant in goodness and truth, forgiving iniquity, transgression, and sin; the rewarder of them that diligently seek Him, and withal most just and terrible in His judgments, hating all sin, and who will by no means clear the guilty.

As can be seen, the Second London Confession is quite robust in its articulation of God. The traditional formula of "without body, parts, or passions" once again appears amid the other traditional divine attributes. However, this confession also includes an explicit appeal to God as immutable in essence *and* will. It should also be noted how the confession juxtaposes these classical doctrines with those that revisionists have sought to pit against classical theism: God's love, mercy, long-suffering, forgiveness, and atonement. These Protestants had no problem affirming that God is wholly immutable and impassible and yet also deeply involved in working out the counsel of his *immutable* will in history—loving his creation, showing mercy, forgiving, and avenging justice.

The Orthodox Creed: General Baptists on God

It is not only Reformed Protestants who confess God as simple, immutable, impassible, and eternal. The General Baptists—those who deny definite atonement, among other classically held Reformed doctrines—also confess similarly the nature of God. In An Orthodox Creed (1678), Article I, it states: “We verily believe, that there is but one, only Living and true God; whose Subsistence is in and of Himself; whose Essence cannot be comprehended by any but Himself; a most Pure, Spiritual, or Invisible Substance: who hath an Absolute, Independent, Unchangeable, and Infinite Being; without Matter or Form, Body, Parts, or Passions.” As can be seen, their confession is like others, including the Second London Confession, claiming once again the classic phrase that God is without body, parts, or passions. But their confession becomes even more explicit in Article II when it claims:

> Every particle of being in Heaven and Earth, leads us to the Infinite Being of beings, (namely God) who is Simplicity, (viz.) one meer and perfect Act, without all Composition, and an Immense Sea of Perfections; who is the only Eternal Being, everlasting without Time, whose Immense Presence, is always every where present; having Immutability without any alteration in Being, or Will, (In a word) God is Infinite, of universal, unlimited, and Incomprehensible Perfection, most Holy, Wise, Just, and Good; whose Wisdom is his Justice, whose Justice is his Holiness, and whose Wisdom, Justice, and Holiness, is Himself. Most Merciful, Gracious, Faithful and True, a full Fountain of Love, and who is that Perfect, Sovereign, Divine Will, the Alpha of Supreme Being.

Here is a hearty treatment of classical theism—far narrower than many other widely confessed documents. God is simple as one perfect act, without composition, eternal without time, immutable without any alteration in being or will, and identical to his perfections.

THE FLEXIBILITY OF CLASSICAL THEISM

Given these brief summaries, one ought to quickly see that there is a strong Christian and Protestant consensus that the God of classical theism is the God of the Bible. He is simple, immutable, impassible, and eternal. Each of these attributes will be developed and explored throughout the tradition in greater detail in their respective chapters. But a natural question arises at this point: How flexible is classical theism? What exactly can I modify, and how much can I modify without abandoning classical theism? Do we need to allow non-Christian resources to exercise a level of judgment over the meaning of concepts? Is it appropriate to read a historical document and say, "I understand this differently"? Is this an example of "reader-response" theory of interpreting texts, allowing them to mean whatever we want apart from their historical context?[54] What sort of authority, if any, does the past have for us today in understanding what classical theism is? These questions will need to be more fully worked out as we proceed, but I offer a provisional framework for an answer now.

I suggest that the grammatical framework of the creeds and confessions is a *necessary* condition for classical theism, though it is not *sufficient*. By grammatical framework I am referring to the language used in general. If the creeds or confessions say God is "without passions," we should adopt that as axiomatic for classical theism. Anyone who would flatly reject one of the standard divine attributes (omnipresence, omnipotence, omniscience) or the standard classical attributes (simplicity, immutability, impassibility, eternity) is straightforwardly rejecting classical theism. However, if one seeks to modify one of the classical attributes, like simplicity, while maintaining the terminology, the grammatical formulas alone are insufficient to determine what counts as classical theism. After all, the fathers thought it was a crime to innovate beyond the Nicene faith.[55] The fathers at Chalcedon were clear: "accursed who innovates."[56] Cyril of Alexandria is representative when he explains that there is a tacit refusal to go beyond Nicaea *even in the slightest respect*.[57] Athanasius (296/98–373) at the Council of Alexandria (362) issued a letter that quite clearly outlaws those who "pretend to cite the faith confessed at Nicaea" but "do nothing more than in words deny the Arian heresy while they retain it in thought."[58] For Athanasius and company, it is not sufficient for language alone to guard the faith once delivered to the saints—the meaning underlying it must be affirmed too. While the creeds were intentionally

54. James Renihan argues that we cannot make any such modifications. Whatever the authors thought in their own context is necessary. See: James Renihan, *To the Judicious and Impartial Reader: A Contextual-Historical Exposition of the Second London Baptist Confession of Faith* (Founders, 2022), 7.

55. Price and Gaddis, *The Council of Chalcedon*, 1:22.

56. Price and Gaddis, *The Council of Chalcedon*, 1:170.

57. Cyril of Alexandria, quoted in Price and Gaddis, *The Council of Chalcedon*, 1:182.

58. James Stevenson and W. H. C. Frend, eds., *Creeds, Councils, and Controversies: Documents Illustrating the History of the Church, AD 337–461*, 3rd ed. (Baker Academic, 2012), 80.

minimalistic to gain widespread support, the early church still saw it as necessary for supplementary documents to be used as guides to faithful interpretation of the creeds.[59]

Therefore, I suggest that what is required additionally in these scenarios is a strong *consensus* view. If there are significant variations within the tradition of Christian thought on how to understand the divine attributes, then there ought to be flexibility in how the tradition is understood. But if there *is* a consensus, it is wrong to classify deviations as "classical theism." But what a "consensus" entails is ambiguous (and likely appears like a lot of work to determine!). Does it refer to a specific group consensus? All Christians? All theologians? All bishops present at Chalcedon? Do Arians or Nestorians get to count? What about Unitarians? What about Muslims? Is this setting us up for a No-True-Scotsman fallacy where avoiding doctrinal requirements is as simple as saying a council or confession erred and isn't *really* "consensus"? For example, I could argue that the consensus of the Christian tradition on the divine attributes is a strict theory of divine simplicity wherein there are no distinctions whatsoever. You could then point to several examples that admit of various distinctions. But my reply could be that they aren't *true* members of the Christian tradition because they deny the strict theory of divine simplicity! It is an easy appeal to purity. So, what then is the threshold to meet a "consensus"? Must it require every member of a particular group without exception to be counted as a consensus?

I suggest that we should adapt the general framework of Vincent for defining a consensus. Scripture is the ultimate authority for all matters, but there are multiple derivative interpretive authorities. First, ecumenical councils and the ecumenical creeds declare the faith once for all delivered to the saints with the greatest level of authority beneath Scripture. These are gatherings and summaries of the whole church that have received support across time and culture and so are well tested. Where we do not have a council or creed, Vincent encourages us to look to the numerous important theological masters who remain within the church as guides where there is a consensus among them.[60] I think this

59. See Mark DelCogliano, "The Emergence of the Pro-Nicene Alliance," in *The Cambridge Companion to the Council of Nicaea*, ed. Young Richard Kim (Cambridge University Press, 2021).

60. Vincent of Lérins, "The Commonitory," in *Nicene and Post-Nicene Fathers* (Eerdmans, 1978), 3.8; 27.70; 29.76–78.

initial hierarchy is on the right track but can be helpfully buttressed by the confessional tradition of the church that is developed well after Vincent. Confessions can serve as a second clarifying consensus below ecumenical councils and creeds.

I especially focus on the Protestant confessions that expand on, without revising, the earlier creedal tradition and their ecumenically approved documents. These are all artifacts that were approved by a majority of Christian pastors and theologians and authorized with ecclesiastical force. They are the proper standards of appeal and "impart a definite character and historical continuity."[61] This isn't to deny the role every Christian plays. Like John Henry Newman argued, the normal everyday Christian was the "ecclesiastical strength" of Athanasius and Hilary (310–367).[62] They remain so today. But there is a specific representative value that comes with especially qualified persons that join together to affirm a confession of faith. These especially qualified persons, depending on the tradition, are typically the office of pastor (or elder/bishop/overseer) alongside teachers in the church that provide a specific role in defining and defending the faith once delivered to the saints.

In a way, this is an appropriation of Cardinal Joseph Ratzinger's (1927–2022) argument that catholicity is measured not "just by numbers, but by the importance of the see."[63] Likewise, Avery Dulles argues that we do not measure the sense of the faithful "by counting noses but by weighing opinions."[64] Therefore, I suggest we can appropriate these insights by locating the consensus in the strength and usage of the conciliar, creedal, and confessional documents. These documents "weigh" far more than any one individual or small tribal group. Therefore, I take it that the items within the creedal formulas have a privileged status whereas "what is held in common" by the various confessional documents should be understood as an additional support for determining the "consensus." Where an item is not carefully described in one of

---

61. E. A. Litton, *Introduction to Dogmatic Theology* (Elliot Stock, 1882), 4.

62. John Henry Newman, *On Consulting the Faithful in Matters of Doctrine*, ed. John Coulson (Rowman & Littlefield, 2006), 76.

63. Joseph Ratzinger, *God's Word: Scripture–Tradition–Office*, ed. Peter Hünermann and Thomas Söding, trans. Henry Taylor (Ignatius, 2020), 33.

64. Dulles, *The Resilient Church*, 100.

these documents a strict consensus view that has normative value for the life of the church is likely too difficult to enforce on others, whether for classical theism or any other doctrine or dogma.

By focusing on "what is held in common," my consensus methodology is concerned with discrete historical periods but intends to weigh the entirety of the historical tradition and its unfolding more heavily. In this way, it values the discrete judgments of the creeds, councils, confessions, and theological masters in their own immediate context, but also focuses on the developing theological concepts that become more refined.[65] Therefore, the creeds, councils, confessions, and theological masters can all be seen as sorts of "waypoints" in a full and continuous Christian tradition that must be read as a whole to be understood properly.[66]

So, the ecumenical creeds and the consensus position of the Protestant confessions could be understood as guardians. They are like the Argonath statues in the Lord of the Rings that were designed to impose awe and fear upon Gondor's enemies, standing nearly 800 feet tall, etched in the stone of the cliffs. The creeds and confessions function similarly. They warn the would-be revisionary about the dangers of destruction of its people, way of life, and borders.

But the question remains about how literally we must interpret the creeds and confessions. Sarah Coakley's seminal essay from twenty years ago offers four models of understanding the meaning and function of the creeds, which is instructive for determining the limits of classical theism: (1) literal regulation, (2) linguistic regulation, (3) apophatic regulation, and (4) metaphorical regulation.[67]

The strictest option, literal regulation, includes *everything* that could be included as necessary for creedal affirmation. It includes all the ontological baggage. Whatever the framers of the creeds believed at the time ought to be believed—whether divine simplicity or geocentricism. It often

---

65. Adam R. Renberg, "Is Eusebius of Caesarea a 'Nicene'? A Contribution to the Notion of Conciliar Theology," *International Journal of Systematic Theology* 25, no. 2 (2023): 293, https://doi.org/10.1111/ijst.12583.

66. Renberg, "Is Eusebius of Caesarea a 'Nicene'?, 310.

67. Sarah Coakley, "What Does Chalcedon Solve and What Does It Not? Some Reflections on the Status and Meaning of the Chalcedonian 'Definition,' " in *The Incarnation: An Interdisciplinary Symposium on the Incarnation of the Son of God*, ed. Stephen T. Davis, Daniel Kendall, and Gerald O'Collins (Oxford University Press, 2002), 144.

requires us to also believe later theological and logical concepts that articulate the judgments within the creedal affirmation.[68]

The second option, linguistic regulation, is a grammatical framework approach. It requires those who seek to confess the creeds to utilize its terminology in all formulations but allows ambiguity as to the metaphysical underworking. So, the terms are linguistically distinguished but not given definable content. Instead, it offers a paradigm or pattern of predication.[69] Those who seek to affirm the creeds (or confessions) must confess in the same pattern as they do and cannot deviate. There is good reason to believe the framers of Chalcedon themselves would have adhered to a linguistic-regulatory version of creedalism, since the bishops were wary of adding anything to Nicaea. The goal was to reaffirm and provide a "regulatory grid" for interpretation.[70]

The third option, apophatic regulation, is Coakley's preferred model, as she thinks it is impossible to separate the linguistic from the ontological in the way that the second option attempts to do.[71] Language refers to reality.[72] Therefore, the apophatic model argues that the creedal formulas are *more* than mere grammatical rules. They also function as riddles that simultaneously show us novel interpretations precisely through telling us what is not the case.[73] Therefore, the apophatic regulation model, like the linguistic regulation model, suggests the creeds do not offer a full systematic account with a complete and precise metaphysic. Their function is to (1) rule out various aberrant interpretations, (2) provide a rule of language, and for the apophatic model also to (3) give a "riddle" of negatives by which some positive new content in the form of deepening and clarifying may be understood.[74]

---

68. See Renberg, "Is Eusebius of Caesarea a 'Nicene'?" He examines the case of Eusebius of Caesarea and shows that he is truly orthodox and Nicene in the purely historical sense and yet as doctrinal formulation became clearer and more precise it is important to not categorize him as Nicene. So, in one sense, he is. But in another sense, he isn't. But this requires a decision for how one intends to understand historical figures and to evaluate them: either historically or theologically. The binary isn't perfect here, but it's helpful heuristically to see the distinction between the two methodologies.

69. Coakley, "What Does Chalcedon Solve and What Does It Not?," 146.

70. Coakley, "What Does Chalcedon Solve and What Does It Not?," 145.

71. Coakley, "What Does Chalcedon Solve and What Does It Not?," 149.

72. Coakley, "What Does Chalcedon Solve and What Does It Not?," 150.

73. Coakley, "What Does Chalcedon Solve and What Does It Not?," 156.

74. Coakley, "What Does Chalcedon Solve and What Does It Not?," 161.

The final option, metaphorical regulation, is the most flexible, being what Coakley has termed a "post-Kantian" rendition wherein any sort of interpretation of the creeds is given conceptual space, since *all* language of God is radically improper. The creeds then become "harmlessly ornamental *and* simultaneously 'radically improper.' "[75] Even more, the formula can make quite literally no sense—it has no conceptual content whatsoever.[76]

My approach requires, at minimum, a linguistic regulation model, though, along with Coakley, I hold there must be some ontological content behind the language that is required. This is why I offer a second necessary condition of strong consensus—though this is *not* intended to be like the literal regulation model that requires belief in *everything* the framers believed. There is some conceptual space for disagreement since the conciliar creeds themselves demonstrate an attitude and style that is willing to tolerate a significant number of differences "in the service of an irenic ecumenism."[77] However, there remains a strong consensus that innovation from the touchstone of Nicene orthodoxy is an unacceptable invention.[78] The later creeds, then, function as negative boundary markers, defining the limits of Nicene orthodoxy.[79]

But what does such an approach look like in practice? I would distinguish between several ways of rejecting or modifying classical theism. First, there are beliefs that are directly incompatible with classical beliefs. This is rather black and white. If one says that God is not simple, they are denying classical theism and no longer can be meaningfully classified as such. Second, there are beliefs that may lead to undermining classical beliefs. Maybe someone constructs a model of divine simplicity that ultimately removes the rationale for it and hollows out any meaningful content. Third, there are beliefs that are incompatible with implications (or good and necessary consequences) of classical beliefs. These are even more difficult to spot and require rigorous argumentation, syllogisms, and persuasion to prove. Maybe someone constructs a model of dependence relations that appears to invite a denial of divine simplicity or divine

---

75. Coakley, "What Does Chalcedon Solve and What Does It Not?," 151.
76. Coakley, "What Does Chalcedon Solve and What Does It Not?," 153.
77. Cross, "On the Interpretation of Church Councils," 208.
78. Price and Gaddis, *The Council of Chalcedon*, 1:8–9.
79. Price and Gaddis, *The Council of Chalcedon*, 1:58.

aseity. But if this is the case, it would need to be a model that does not have a consensus, *and* it would need to be proven to undermine classical beliefs. And finally, there are beliefs that may undermine implications of classical beliefs.[80]

CONCLUSION

Attempting to explain the nature of God is the greatest of all challenges that humans face. It is also the most important. Therefore, it is with fear and trembling that I've sought to offer some of the main Christian models of God thus far. These should serve as a useful backdrop for understanding what makes classical theism *classical* theism. But even more, I've sought to entice you with the creedal and confessional tradition. There is much to know and learn from those who have gone before us. Thus, it is wise to allow the consensus documents of the creeds and confessions guide our articulation of God. We will see that as we continue, but before we move to the specific doctrinal claims of classical theism, we ought to attend to the hermeneutics of classical theism.

80. My thanks to my friend Joel Chopp for developing this sort of framework.

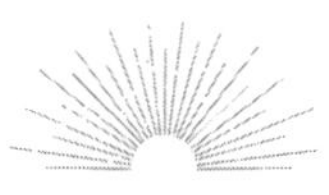

3

THE METHODOLOGICAL SENSIBILITIES OF CLASSICAL THEISM

What follows serves as the engine for the theological imagination of classical theism. It is not just the material content of classical theism that is important, but the *way of reasoning* is crucial as well.[1] Apart from understanding these theological strategies for understanding Scripture and theology, much of the edifice of classical theism may appear strange. While I use the terminology of "method" throughout, what I canvas is not properly a method in the sense of having a strict set of formulas that ensure the proper result. Rather, it is more akin to a sensibility that is rooted in the ontology, authority, and unity of Scripture. The Christian tradition, rather than having a strict hermeneutical theory that all employ, uses a variety of interpretative strategies based on one's theological convictions about Scripture and the Triune God.[2] These strategies serve as key ingredients for reasoning toward and defending classical theism. Those that reject the various classical tools I describe here often end up rejecting the dogmatic results of classical theism.

However, it is true that, as with all aspects of the classical tradition, there is variance, diversity, growth, and development. The difference

1. Cyril of Alexandria, "Second Letter to Nestorius," in *The Cambridge Edition of Early Christian Writings*, ed. Mark DelCogliano, trans. Matthew R. Crawford (Cambridge University Press, 2022), 567.

2. J. Todd Billings, *The Word of God for the People of God: An Entryway to the Theological Interpretation of Scripture* (Eerdmans, 2010), 163.

between unity and uniformity or similarity and identity should be remembered and appreciated.[3] Therefore, none of these "sensibilities" are strictly necessary as I articulate them for every classical thinker. Further, I do not recount these sensibilities strictly as historical elements but as a retrieval theologian searching for the various tools of the past to aid in the present. So, in what follows, I seek to capture some of the common features of classical reasoning throughout the ages, some of which are more central than others. I introduce six separate *loci* for classical approaches to theological construction as it relates to the doctrine of God. Each of these aspects will be apparent throughout this work—particularly when developing arguments in favor of the classical attributes of God.

Unfortunately, not all the methodological sensibilities from the classical tradition are surveyed here. Such a treatment would require a full book in itself.[4] Rather, my goal is to explicate *some* of the main consensus of the tradition that contribute significantly to the doctrine of God. The main point I hope to convey is that there are some shared practices in the Christian tradition, but there remains freedom within the overall epistemological process. And while these six methodologies are not set in stone as timeless types—some in the tradition are skeptical of some of these practices—they are more than historically located and contingent movements. They span a great breadth of the Christian tradition. It's to these six loci that I now turn.

DOGMATIC THEOLOGY

The terminology of "dogmatic" theology is relatively new. We don't see Saint Basil offering a *dogmatic* account of the Spirit or Boethius (480–524) giving a *dogmatic* account of God and time. So, it may seem surprising to incorporate the term within a description of *classical* methodologies. Why force new wine into old wineskins? Because the wine of dogmatic theology is quite old.[5] While the language is new, the employment of its way of

3. Brandon D. Smith, *Taught by God: Ancient Hermeneutics for the Modern Church* (B&H, 2024), 5.

4. For two recent examples surveying exegetical reasoning, see R. B. Jamieson and Tyler Wittman, *Biblical Reasoning: Christological and Trinitarian Rules for Exegesis* (Baker Academic, 2022); Keith D. Stanglin, *The Letter and Spirit of Biblical Interpretation: From the Early Church to Modern Practice* (Baker Academic, 2018).

5. It is also partly because my project is not exclusively historical in nature, where employing later terms may be confusing on historiographical grounds. It is instead a constructive retrieval of wisdom from the past articulated for the present.

reasoning stretches throughout the tradition. So, using the terminology gives a shared language to many of the key theological intuitions, goals, and intellectual contexts that are common throughout the classical tradition.

Dogmatic theology is chiefly an ecclesial theology.[6] It lives and breathes the life of the church, which nurtures, guides, and guards sound doctrine. There is no cold detachment from the worship of the church or the authority of the community. Dogmatic theology, instead, is the activity of ordering our thoughts and directing the attention of the church to the realities of the God of the gospel.[7] Rather than doctrines being developed and understood in disconnected fashion, dogmatics works from an organizing principle.[8] And it is the work of the entire church catholic throughout the ages—not merely that of the individual or even of a particular church.[9] Therefore, dogmatic theology is an ecclesial theology that is primarily interested in the ways the faith has been articulated and received throughout the ages in the creeds and confessions of the church.[10] As an ecclesial theology it inhabits the classrooms of the church across generations, believing that Christ speaks through his Spirit and dwells richly in us through ecclesial teaching, admonishing, and singing (Col 3:16–17).[11] It intentionally allows the church's liturgical practices and eschatological aims to shape and drive theological development. It is neither outside nor above the church but partakes of its life.[12] It is this overall intentional ecclesial posture that marks the Christian tradition. Dogmatic theology defends the faith recognized and confessed by the church with its end goal as doxology.[13] In this same vein, the classical tradition has sought to

---

6. Ratzinger, *God's Word* (Ignatius, 2020), 61.

7. John Webster, *Holiness* (Eerdmans, 2003), 8.

8. Herman Bavinck, *Reformed Dogmatics*, ed. John Bolt, trans. John Vriend (Baker Academic, 2003), 1:125.

9. Bavinck, *Reformed Dogmatics*, 1:116.

10. Oliver D. Crisp, *Analyzing Doctrine: Toward a Systematic Theology* (Baylor University Press, 2019), 4.

11. Michael Allen and Scott R. Swain, "Introduction," in *Christian Dogmatics: Reformed Theology for the Church Catholic*, ed. Michael Allen and Scott R. Swain (Baker Academic, 2016), 4.

12. E. A. Litton, *Introduction to Dogmatic Theology* (Elliot Stock, 1882), 3.

13. I intentionally use the generic sense of "church" to mean the universal church catholic. This is not to ignore the action of particular church bodies. I simply choose this for the sake of elegance to avoid belaboring the various ecclesial distinctives. Whatever they may be, there is a shared universal practice I intend to call attention to. See: Bavinck, *Reformed Dogmatics*, 1:46.

maintain that the *telos* of classical theism is doxology. So, like classical theism, there is an eminently practical aspect to the nature of dogmatics that leads to the end goal of worship. Therefore, dogmatic theology is the ecclesial reception of, participating in, and defense of the Christian faith.[14]

As receptive, dogmatic theology listens intently to holy Scripture and the received tradition of the church, especially as it relates to the doctrine of God that classical theism seeks to explain. But reception is more than mere listening. It assumes that some doctrines have a degree of authority that requires ecclesial recognition. It reminds us to be slow to speak against the consensus doctrinal positions because there is both wisdom and divinely ordered authority before us. In other words, by recognition, it is meant that dogmatic theology is elaborated, guarded, and confessed by the church.[15] The church, whether Roman Catholic, Lutheran, Presbyterian, Baptist, or otherwise, has determined that some theological conclusions are true and necessary for unity in the faith and thus should be affirmed by all members.[16] The most important of these are so-called dogmas, which are those doctrines that are fundamental to the Christian faith and not just constitutive of a segment of the Christian tradition.[17] Just as Paul confesses, there is one body and one Spirit; there is one Lord, one faith, one baptism, one God and Father of all, who is over all and through all and in all (Eph 4:4–6). Likewise, the received doctrine of God maintains a level of dogmatic authority and should be privileged above alternative models of God. This doesn't make it infallible, but it does warn us of the perils of innovation and revision.

For Protestants, the authority found in dogmatic theology is recognized—*not created*—through the ecumenical reasoning of the church catholic and the rule of faith. The power of the church is not sovereign and legislative but ministerial and declarative.[18] John Gill (1697–1771)

---

14. Crisp, *Analyzing Doctrine*, 57.

15. Steven J. Duby, *Divine Simplicity: A Dogmatic Account* (T&T Clark, 2016), 55; Basil, *On the Holy Spirit*, trans. Stephen M. Hildebrand (St. Vladimir's Seminary Press, 2011), 27, 66.

16. The precise nature of how authority is realized in local churches differs among various Christian traditions. I do not intend to defend any one model herein since the acceptance of the ecumenical creeds as faithful and authoritative summaries of orthodox doctrine is widely shared. The underlying mechanics are not the main point here. Bavinck, *Reformed Dogmatics*, 1:28–31.

17. Avery Dulles, *The Resilient Church* (Doubleday, 1977), 45.

18. Bavinck, *Reformed Dogmatics*, 1:32.

illustrates the nature of this reception and resultant authority by explaining that the Apostles' Creed was received, embraced, and professed by the church *because of* its congruence with Scripture and ought to be recognized as the "rule of faith" with a similar authority. Our interpretations of Scripture ought to comply with its own dogmatic shape.[19] This is why Protestant dogmatics remains likewise fixed upon holy Scripture as the norm and limit of all theological reflection upon which ecclesiastical reception is built.[20] The sacred page itself is the primary resource for theological reflection, shaping and inspiring dogmatic priorities. The true dogmatic theologian is not only attentive to the church catholic but also chiefly to Scripture in all its depth, listening to its repetitions, connections, and emphases, allowing our theology to be continually reshaped by Scripture's own set of values.[21] Dogmatic theology, then, requires an artful dance between the material content of Scripture and the ecclesial reflection of the church.

All of this is in stark contrast to many Protestants over the last century. For example, Jürgen Moltmann complains that dogmatics "freezes living Christian tradition solid."[22] His concern seems to be that dogmatics is merely the practice of defending what Robert Jenson calls "irreversible communal" dogmas.[23] In one sense, this is right. Dogmatics is narrower than doctrine or theology construed broadly. It is more focused on, or limited by, the decisions of authorities that are meant to rule faith and practice.[24] But dogmatics needn't be understood or developed in a stringent fashion that would literally freeze us solid—nor must it be seen as an entirely modern enterprise. Instead, dogmatics can be seen as "creative and constructive," interacting with the wide range of theological source material in biblical theology, the history of theology,

---

19. John Gill, *What Is Theology?*, ed. Christopher Ellis Osterbrock (H&E, 2022), 56–57.

20. The traditional "order of knowing" for Protestant dogmatics is seen in most works in the Reformed tradition, beginning with exegesis before moving to other authorities and modes of discourse. Michael Allen, *The Fear of the Lord* (T&T Clark, 2022), 143.

21. Michael Allen, *The Knowledge of God: Essays on God, Christ and Church* (T&T Clark, 2022), 53.

22. Jürgen Moltmann, *The Crucified God* (SCM, 2015), 17.

23. Robert W. Jenson, *Systematic Theology*, vol. 1 (Oxford University Press, 1997), 22.

24. Douglas A. Sweeney, *The Substance of Our Faith* (Baker Academic, 2023), 99.

and contemporary philosophy.[25] It is this sort of approach that marks the classical tradition.

THE TASK OF DOGMATICS

Given the nature of dogmatics, the church's dogmatic *task,* according to Herman Bavinck, is "to preserve, explain, understand, and defend the truth of God entrusted to her."[26] The dogmatic theologian, therefore, begins by accepting in faith what has been revealed and confessed by the church and reasons, reflects, and understands *from* such a starting point.[27] Assuming in faith that dogmatic theology is true from the start is not an attempt to avoid defending the rationality of doctrine. Instead, it is about making use of the truths that the church has confessed as central to the gospel. For example, Markus Bockmuehl has offered a perceptive illustration:

> Road engineers know that when you are trying to build a new road from A to B, quite often the best route is more or less to follow the course of the old road from A to B. Thus one can make all the necessary road safety improvements while gaining from one's predecessors collective understanding of the local terrain.[28]

This approach is distinctively receptive in posture, being dependent upon divine testimony in Scripture and divine guidance through ecclesial casting of divine testimony. As Saint Paul advised Timothy, theology is an enterprise of stewardship from God by faith rather than speculation (1 Tim 1:4). Therefore, while the dogmatic task is primarily negative, it also remains positive. It negatively seeks to preserve and defend received teaching, and it positively seeks to explain, understand, and ultimately worship.

---

25. Cornelis van der Kooi and Gijsbert van den Brink, *Christian Dogmatics: An Introduction,* trans. Reinder Bruinsma and James D. Bratt (Eerdmans, 2017), 16.

26. Bavinck, *Reformed Dogmatics,* 1:31.

27. Michael Gorman, *Aquinas on the Metaphysics of the Hypostatic Union* (Cambridge University Press, 2017), 8.

28. Markus Bockmuehl, "A Commentator's Approach To the 'Effective History' of Philippians," *Journal for the Study of the New Testament* 18, no. 60 (1996): 58, https://doi.org/10.1177/0142064X9601806003.

Whereas others pursue different models of God, the classical tradition has understood classical theism as a dogma of the faith.[29] Given the ecumenical consensus on doctrines such as simplicity, immutability, impassibility, and eternity, the classical tradition theologizes under the presupposition that these are true. There is a great weight to departing from the traditional understanding of God. This does not mean that it is impossible to pursue new constructive theology that explains these dogmatic positions in fresh ways. While the apostolic deposit itself cannot grow (i.e., new and original truths will not be discovered), the church's understanding can and must grow.[30] Therefore, there *must* be new and fresh ways to understand the same ancient dogmatic truths but not new dogmatic truths. And so constructive theology has room to flourish, even within dogmatic theology. This again is simply what thinkers in the past like Vincent, John Henry Newman, and the neo-Calvinists argued for.

THE CONTEXT OF DOGMATICS

The *context* of dogmatic theology for the classical tradition is the church. As briefly described above, since the God-ordained *telos* of theology finds its completion in the worship of the church and ultimately in the beatific vision, the context of the church plays an essential role in healthy theology. There are two main ecclesiological aspects that shape the context of dogmatics: the *liturgical life* of the church and the *eschatological end* of the church. Theology developed outside this context or for purposes apart from this end will be deficient. As such, the classical tradition is primarily an ecclesiastical enterprise. As Bavinck argues, "Dogmatics is possible only for one who lives in the fellowship of faith with one Christian church or another."[31]

The liturgical life of the church is manifold. By this I mean that in the church, the Spirit guides its social and intellectual culture and shapes her by certain texts, traditions, attitudes, practices, and aspirations. It is through these sets of shared texts, traditions, attitudes, and aspirations that classical

29. This is not to equate the church universal with the classical tradition. There are members of the church catholic that revise the received doctrine of God and thus reject classical theism.

30. Michael Allen and Scott R. Swain, *Reformed Catholicity: The Promise of Retrieval for Theology and Biblical Interpretation* (Baker Academic, 2015), 43.

31. Bavinck, *Reformed Dogmatics*, 1:85.

theism flourishes. This enables and directs proper contemplation of the divine.[32] The liturgical practices of the church shape human persons and their thoughts about God in ways that are impossible to obtain apart from word, sacrament, and the community of the saints. God speaks especially through revelation, Spirit, conciliar activity, and liturgical tradition.[33] Therefore, public worship is necessary for the health and proper orientation of the theologian.[34]

For example, confessing the Nicene Creed or Apostles' Creed with the saints each Lord's Day, sitting under the authority of the word proclaimed, sharing in the Lord's Table, and singing spiritual songs all create habits of mind. They shape how one thinks, focus one on particular topics, and encourage asking specific questions. They also reorient the theologian to the priorities of holy writ itself.[35] Singing, confessing, hearing, praying, and fellowshiping all serve a critical purpose for healthy theology.[36]

These liturgical practices are thus *preconditions* for good theology. Without prayer, contemplation, and worship, there are not only insights that will be unlikely to be had but *impossible* apart from attention to the social location wherein the manifold wisdom of God is made known (Eph 3:10).[37] These churchly considerations found in dogmatic theology are those we find replete throughout the classical tradition. This doesn't mean that *all* aspects of classical theism or true theology more generally are impossible to obtain in the strongest possible sense for those outside the proper social location. It is certainly possible that even a non-Christian can understand some things about God, like his eternal power and divine nature. However, apart from the context of the church many truths about God will be hidden, ignored, or misunderstood. It is contrary to modern sensibilities that we need an ordinary community of people to discern the fullness of God, but this is both how holy Scripture and the Christian tradition describe our journey to God.

32. Allen and Swain, *Reformed Catholicity*, 19.

33. Ratzinger, *God's Word*, 87.

34. Steven J. Duby, *God in Himself: Scripture, Metaphysics, and the Task of Christian Theology* (IVP Academic, 2019), 57.

35. Duby, *God in Himself*, 57; Billings, *The Word of God for the People of God* (Eerdmans, 2010), 41.

36. For a fuller treatment of prayer in the Christian intellectual life see Peter W. Martens, *Origen and Scripture: The Contours of the Exegetical Life* (Oxford University Press, 2014), 187.

37. Sarah Coakley, *God, Sexuality and the Self: An Essay "On the Trinity"* (Cambridge University Press, 2013), 16.

The school of Christ remains the church forevermore, and his lessons are sometimes found in the joyful toddlers and faithful widows of the church.

The eschatological end of the church must also always be kept in view. The end of the church is worship of the Triune God. Theology constructed without this aim in view will lack wisdom and the fullness of truth. While it may contain truths, it will not possess all that ought to be confessed of God. For example, while a biologist may be right to say that humans are made of certain fundamental particles, if they do not understand the whole or purpose of humans, they will fail to properly explain them. We are more than our elemental particles, lest aspects like our moral nature be completely ignored.

But the eschatological goal of the church also includes the glorification of the saints. Because of this the classical tradition is replete with claims regarding the moral character of the theologian. No one can understand God apart from purification.[38] One must fear him and seek holiness to know him.[39] These claims, though, should not be shocking to the Christian theologian since they are simply what Scripture itself teaches. The pure in heart will see God (Matt 5:8). The fear of the Lord is the beginning of knowledge (Prov 1:7).

NATURAL AND SUPERNATURAL THEOLOGY[40]

Given the nature of dogmatic theology and classical theism's own dogmatic posture, it is useful to further explicate the process of ecclesiastical *recognition*. Many of history's greatest classical thinkers employ natural theology to arrive at the God of classical theism. Divine simplicity, immutability, impassibility, and eternity are developed and defended with recourse to natural theology. But those leery of dogmatic theology, particularly dogmatic classical theism, are suspicious of classical theism precisely due to this perceived overreliance on natural theology. They worry that the classical tradition inflates natural theology to an authoritative position

---

38. Augustine, *On Christian Teaching*, trans. R. P. H. Green (Oxford University Press, 2008), 12.

39. Augustine, *On Christian Teaching* 33–34.

40. Much of this section comes from material I previously published in these two sources. Given the significant conceptual overlap, I do not cite each instance. Steffaniak, "Everything in Nature Speaks of God: Understanding Sola Scriptura Aright"; Steffaniak, "Natural Theology and the Uneasy Conscience of Modern 'Calvinism,' " The London Lyceum, July 10, 2022, https://www.thelondonlyceum.com/natural-theology-and-the-uneasy-conscience-of-modern-calvinism/.

over Scripture.[41] The Bible then becomes a mere puppet for whatever it is that one's own dogmatic tradition has deemed true theology. The rough edges of Scripture, which are God-ordained, are artificially smoothed out to resolve tensions that should remain. As one New Testament scholar has remarked, these sorts of systematic theologians look more like systemagicians than systematicians.[42] Plato and Aristotle may argue for classical attributes like immutability, but they aren't Christians, so their ideas shouldn't be given the weight they often are given by classical thinkers. But these worries, while legitimate, misunderstand natural theology.

DEFINING NATURAL AND SUPERNATURAL THEOLOGY

Understanding natural theology requires us to understand four general terms: *natural revelation, natural theology, supernatural revelation,* and *supernatural theology*. Revelation, whether natural or supernatural, is the objective work of God, whereas theology, whether natural or supernatural, is the rational engagement with God's objective revelation. The basic idea here is that God reveals himself to us through two means. One is natural and found in creation; the other is supernatural and found in Scripture. They are equally revelation from God but differ in origin and scope of material content. Natural theology, then, according to Franciscus Junius (1545–1602), "is that which proceeds from principles that are known in relation to itself by the light of the human understanding, in proportion to the method of human reason."[43] Natural theology is a sort of theology that is "through" the natural order, compared to supernatural theology, which is "from beyond" the natural order.[44] Supernatural theology, in contrast, has a superior quality, extent, and depth.[45]

---

41. Bruce Ware, "An Evangelical Reexamination of the Doctrine of the Immutability of God," PhD diss., Fuller Theological Seminary, 1984, 63–65.

42. See Constantine Campbell's remarks here: *The Theological Interpretation of Scripture Roundtable*, YouTube (The London Lyceum, 2023), https://www.youtube.com/watch?v=LWOC-LB2x-U&t=1614s.

43. Franciscus Junius, *A Treatise on True Theology*, trans. David C. Noe (Reformation Heritage, 2014), 143.

44. Jordan Steffaniak, "The God of All Creation," *Journal of Reformed Theology* 14, no. 4 (2020): 360; Bavinck, *Reformed Dogmatics*, 1:307.

45. Matthias Joseph Scheeben, *Handbook of Catholic Dogmatics*, trans. Michael J. Miller (Emmaus Academic, 2019), 2:42.

For example, when someone observes the natural beauty of the world and infers that there is a creator God, this is natural theology because it is based on the material content of natural revelation. However, if someone-someone learned of God as Triune, this would be a form of supernatural theology since the material content of God as Triune is only discoverable through Scripture. But suppose someone discerned God as creator from supernatural revelation and *then* saw the beauty of the world and realized, "Yes, creation does point to God as creator!" Does the fact that someone arrived at this conclusion because of supernatural revelation mean that they must rely upon supernatural revelation to know that there is a God? No. We can know that there is a God even without supernatural revelation. (This is the whole point of Psalm 19 and, especially, Romans 1:18–32.) This is why the pagans are rightly judged by God: because without supernatural revelation they know there is a God and suppress this knowledge.[46] Therefore, these natural facts are properly the domain of "natural theology."

Consider one more example for the sake of clarity. Never could we attain to the divine mysteries of Christ as redeemer from nature alone because the human mind apart from supernatural guidance lacks the material content in creation itself to discern God as redeemer. The grace of supernatural revelation is necessary because it provides additional information that our natural rational capacities could not otherwise obtain. Apart from God procuring the additional knowledge of Christ as redeemer to us, the human intellect operating within its own speculative horizon could not come to knowledge of it.[47] While we can reason *some* about God, morality, virtue, and the like apart from supernatural revelation, we will lack the extent of that knowledge.[48] Since we have a nature tainted by sin, our natural reason is negatively affected such that any genuine insight is hard fought, only gained after a long time, and mixed with error in many places.[49]

---

46. Thanks to David Haines for helping me to clarify this section. In previous publications I had disagreed minimally with his articulation of natural theology, but after conversation with him, I've realized I misunderstood.

47. Thomas Joseph White, *The Incarnate Lord* (Catholic University of America Press, 2017), 73–74.

48. John Brine, *A Vindication of Some Truths of Natural and Revealed Religion* (London, 1846), 36–42.

49. Thomas Aquinas, *The Treatise on the Divine Nature: Summa Theologiae I, 1–13* (Hackett, 2006), I.1.1c; Junius, *A Treatise on True Theology*, 150.

The revelation found in nature is readily accessible to all. The "light of nature" remains in humanity after the fall by virtue of which humanity can know things about God, natural things like protons and electrons, general moral principles, the necessity of virtue, and the like.[50] The work of theology is "inferred" and contemplated from one of these material sources, either natural or supernatural.[51] Stephen Charnock (1628–1680) provides a standard account of these distinctions:

> There is a natural as well as a revealed knowledge, and the book of the creatures is as legible in declaring the being of a God, as well as the Scriptures are in declaring the nature of a God; there are outward objects in the world, and common principles in the conscience from which it may be inferred. For (1) God, in regard of his existence, is the discovery not only of faith but of reason. God hath revealed not only his being, but some sparks of his eternal power and Godhead in his works as well as his word. … Faith supposes natural knowledge, as grace supposes nature.[52]

Charnock further clarifies that these two modes of revelation and theology are not in conflict. They are not, as Bavinck suggests, "two independent powers engaging in a life-and-death struggle with each other."[53] Instead, as Francis Turretin (1623–1687) says, supernatural theology, rather than destroying natural theology, "perfects it" and makes it clearer.[54] Jesuit Francisco Suárez (1548–1617) summarizes rather well:

> Although divine and supernatural theology depends on the divine light and on principles revealed by God, nevertheless, since it is perfected by human reasoning and rational discourse, it is also assisted by truths known by the light of nature, and it employs

---

50. See the Synod of Dort Article 4 for some of this language.

51. Willem Arie den Boer and Riemer A. Faber, eds., *Synopsis of a Purer Theology* (Davenant, 2023), 3.

52. Stephen Charnock, *The Existence and Attributes of God*, ed. Mark Jones (Crossway, 2022), 46.

53. Bavinck, *Reformed Dogmatics*, 1:616. As a note of clarity, I am agreeing with Bavinck's assertion here.

54. Francis Turretin, *Institutes of Elenctic Theology*, ed. James T. Dennison, trans. George Musgrave Giger (P&R, 1994), 1.9.5.

> these as servants and instruments in order to perfect its reasonings and illuminate divine truths.[55]

Supernatural theology, then, is aided by natural theology as they work together.

There is a further lack of certainty in natural theology compared to supernatural. Supernatural theology directs us with a "firm hand," whereas natural theology "easily lets itself be captivated by fantasy and its own limitations."[56] In a way, natural theology sees in a glass dimly, though sparks do glow. For example, most in the Christian tradition have thought that the existence of God is discoverable by the light of nature.[57] Only the fool says in his heart there is no God. Then, in Scripture, we are given a hand, inflaming our hearts and instructing our minds in ways beyond nature.[58]

Unfortunately, natural theology in the contemporary Protestant milieu is often misunderstood. Part of this is due to the differing definitions one can find in monographs and popular-level works. When definitions range from natural theology as *pure philosophy* about God's nature to the modest project of providing support for religious beliefs based on non-religious premises, it is no wonder confusion occurs.[59] But there is also the problem of the morass of the internet and polemics that can often blind us to nuance and careful precision. But, sometimes, it might truly be fair to wonder if many are just syste*magicians*, pulling theological rabbits out of mysterious hats since so many fail to show their work. Therefore, it is wise to also note what natural theology *isn't*.

1. Natural theology *isn't identical* to the arguments for the existence of God (e.g., the cosmological argument, the teleological argument, etc.).[60]

---

55. Francisco Suárez, *Metaphysical Disputation I: On the Nature of First Philosophy or Metaphysics*, trans. Shane Duarte (The Catholic University of America Press, 2021), 11.

56. Scheeben, *Handbook of Catholic Dogmatics*, 2:41.

57. Brine, *A Vindication of Some Truths of Natural and Revealed Religion*, 36–37.

58. Leo, *Sermons*, trans. Jane Patricia Freeland and Agnes Josephine Conway (The Catholic University of America Press, 1995), 121.

59. For the former example, see Johnson. For the latter, see Alston. Jeffrey D. Johnson, *The Failure of Natural Theology: A Critical Appraisal of the Philosophical Theology of Thomas Aquinas* (Free Grace, 2021), 10–11; William Alston, *Perceiving God: The Epistemology of Religious Experience* (Cornell University Press, 1995), 289.

60. David Bradshaw, "Introduction," in *Natural Theology in the Eastern Orthodox Tradition*, ed. David Bradshaw and Richard Swinburne (IOTA, 2021), 1; contra Alvin Plantinga, "Reason and Belief in God," in *Faith and Rationality: Reason and Belief in God*, ed. Alvin Plantinga and Nicholas Wolterstorff (University of Notre Dame Press, 1983), 63.

2. Natural theology *isn't* a means of understanding God in *contradiction* to supernatural theology (Scripture).
3. Natural theology *isn't* required to *begin apart from* Scripture.
4. Natural theology *isn't* a *foundation* from which supernatural theology is built.
5. Natural theology *isn't* a project of natural *salvation* apart from Scripture.

I could list other faulty (or at least incomplete) features of natural theology, but I think these get the idea across. Some of them may be surprising to you, but that's part of the point. I hope that you realize the boogeyman under the bed really isn't all that scary. Natural theology is not intended to be an isolated means of salvific knowledge that rules over Scripture. It's not some hyper-speculative enterprise designed to insulate oneself from God's supernatural revelation in Scripture. It isn't designed to take its life and being apart from God's word, which is the only true generator of reality.

SUPERNATURE ON NATURE

It is not merely the catholic tradition that testifies to the validity and use of natural theology. Scripture itself validates natural revelation as a source of knowledge and theological construction. Psalm 19 and Romans 1 unequivocally confess the validity of natural theology. Psalm 19:1 exclaims that "the heavens declare the glory of God," and Romans 1:20 states that God's "invisible attributes, namely, his eternal power and divine nature, have been clearly perceived, ever since the creation of the world, in the things that have been made." Therefore, as Steven Duby suggests, "In light of Romans 1, it is not just reason but faith itself ... that compels us to affirm the reality of a natural knowledge of God."[61] It is not as if natural knowledge of God is obtained by following a pathway that Scripture rejects. Scripture speaks of humanity knowing God *in* creation itself (e.g., Rom 1:20). We can know God as Creator, as Basil suggests, "through what he

61. Duby, *God in Himself*, 68.

has made."[62] Calvin echoes these sentiments, saying, "This skillful ordering of the universe is for us a sort of mirror in which we can contemplate God, who is otherwise invisible."[63] Baptist divine John Gill similarly has no issue claiming that Romans 1:20 speaks of the perfections of God since it is not about his Triune nature.[64] Calvin also assumes saint Paul means that the whole of the divine nature—excluding his Triune being—can be ascertained from creation. However, while the unregenerate can come to knowledge of God's nature from creation, only the Christian, with the eyes of faith, can know the invisible reality toward which creation points, namely the Triune God.[65]

Natural theology, for the Christian, is merely an expansion of commands such as 2 Timothy 2:7 to "think over" what God has spoken. Knowledge of God not only includes contemplation over supernatural revelation but natural revelation as well. Our contemplation of the divine from these twin sources is what Matthew Levering calls a "difficult metaphysical *ascesis*—the limp of Jacob, the awe of Moses."[66] It is a difficult and joyous wrestling with God's revelation in supernature *and* in nature by means of the light of nature through the divinely given gift of reason. The intellect is impelled to explicate the faith.[67]

---

62. Basil, *Against Eunomius*, trans. Mark DelCogliano and Andrew Radde-Gallwitz (The Catholic University of America Press, 2011), 1.14.

63. John Calvin, *Institutes of the Christian Religion*, ed. John T. McNeill, trans. Ford Lewis Battles (Westminster John Knox, 2006), I.5.1. Calvin has a generally negative view of natural theology, saying that despite its "very great clarity, such is our stupidity that we grow increasingly dull toward so manifest testimonies." Therefore, natural theology is a somewhat vexed topic for Calvin. Regardless, avoiding the exegetical dispute, I take Calvin's positive understanding of natural theology at face value—God reveals himself in nature. Natural theology is unprofitable for the nonbeliever because it only renders him unexcused. But for the Christian, it can be of great profit.

64. See also John C. Ryland, *Contemplations on the Beauties of Creation and on All the Principal Truths and Blessings of the Glorious Gospel; with the Sins and Graces of Professing Christians* (Thomas Dicey, 1779), 2:235.

65. John Calvin, *Commentaries on the Epistle of Paul the Apostle to the Romans*, trans. John Owen (Christian Classics Ethereal Library, n.d.), 49.

66. Matthew Levering, *Scripture and Metaphysics: Aquinas and the Renewal of Trinitarian Theology*, Challenges in Contemporary Theology (Blackwell, 2004), 3.

67. Oliver D. Crisp, "Theology in Search of a Handmaiden: Reason and Philosophy," in *Theology and Philosophy: Faith and Reason*, ed. Oliver D. Crisp et al. (T&T Clark, 2012), 1.

THE TWO MODES OF NATURAL THEOLOGY

While natural theology is limited, there is a further distinction that deserves clarification. It is important to distinguish natural theology as being done in two modes. The first mode is for *everyone* regardless of salvific status. This universal mode includes both immediate non-inferential knowledge, which is commonly known in Protestant circles as the *sensus divinitatis*—the immediate impression of the divine—and inferential argument-based knowledge. The non-Christian sees the same sunrise and sunset as the Christian and has the same intellectual capacities as the Christian as they too are created in the image of God. But non-Christians are darkened in their understanding and hardened in their hearts (Eph 4:18).

The second mode of natural theology is a positive Christian task. Natural theology for the Christian does not supersede supernatural theology but serves it as a handmaiden. As Baptist Dan Taylor (1738–1816) reminds us, "The light of nature will in some degree assist us in thinking and reasoning."[68] However, for the Christian, natural theology is not intended to exist apart from the context of faith but obtains its life from it. It is a faith that seeks understanding.[69] Faith is continually fortified by reason rather than replaced by it.[70] Take Anselm as the paragon example here. While he attempts to argue in his *Monologion* from reason alone, apart from Scripture, he never reasons in contradiction to Scripture or in ignorance of it. Holy Scripture taught him, informed him, and controlled him. Yet he still sought to contemplate the divine through natural means.

CHRISTIAN NATURAL THEOLOGY

Given these explanations, I define natural theology this way, calling it "Christian" to distinguish it as a subset of natural theology beyond what the unregenerate are capable of:

> *Christian natural theology:* The task of utilizing the material content of natural revelation via our renewed reason in service of

68. Dan Taylor, *Fundamentals of Religion in Faith and Practice* (Leeds, 1775), 1.
69. Alister E. McGrath, *A Scientific Theology* (Eerdmans, 2003), 1:266.
70. Martens, *Origen and Scripture*, 103.

> theological construction under the authority of Scripture, the guidance of the Holy Spirit, and the context of the church.[71]

There are several parts to this definition that deserve further clarification. First, natural theology is primarily a discipline of reasoning from natural revelation. While it does reason under the authority of Scripture for the Christian, where Scripture always chastens its ideas, natural theology seeks to develop ideas from resources beyond Scripture. It may begin with a scriptural idea (say, God created us male and female), then it will consider examples in creation (say, chromosomes, gametes, hormones, etc.), and finally, it will develop theological concepts about human sex and gender.

Second, Christian natural theology does not reason using resources in nature in a way that is ignorant of Scripture. If a theological judgment contradicts holy Scripture, then that judgment is jettisoned. The work of Chrisitan natural theology impels the Christian to continually return to the deep well of Scripture seeking strength, refreshment, and surprise. The Christian remembers that the content, logic, and order of Scripture has wisdom we shouldn't ignore. There is a keen desire to read "with the grain of Scripture" and not against it.[72] So, when it comes to the nature of God, it recognizes the pattern of revelation in Genesis begins with the transcendent Creator of the universe *before* revealing his

---

71. Some may wonder if the unregenerate are really incapable of this. For example: "Why couldn't God give someone the ability to do this work without regenerating the person? He gave Aristotle amazing abilities without regeneration, and he didn't even have access to special revelation. Or think of apostates who leave the faith but still have the skills required to do the work of the faithful. They still have the same proficiencies, the same reasoning skills, the same knowledge of scripture and tradition, and so on." While true, the unregenerate cannot be properly ordered toward true theology with its ultimate doxological end apart from faith. This does not elevate all true theology above the unregenerate person's capabilities. God creates human nature as sufficient for these tasks. A non-Christian can read the same Bible as a Christian and see that it describes Jesus as God and that salvation comes through faith. A non-Christian can likewise rationally deliberate the origins of the universe and conclude that only a creator God can explain it. But the non-Christian cannot come to understand these truths in the same mode with the same resultant state of love and worship. Without love and worship, it is hard to understand the non-Christian as possessing the same form of knowledge as the Christian. Thanks to Tim Pawl and Hunter Hindsman for pressing me on this point. While they may still be unsatisfied with my articulation, I must confess my debt!

72. Cody Floate, "Hosea, Figuration, and Impassibility: A Passioned Prophet and the Yahweh Without Passions," *Journal of Classical Theology* 1 (2022): 108.

covenantal condescension.[73] But it also remains attentive to the Lord's gifts, wherever they may be found.

Calvin likens supernatural revelation to that of spectacles for the old or bleary-eyed. Without the spectacles, we could thrust any array of beautiful works before their eyes, but they would be unable to take up and read. But with the aid of spectacles, they suddenly can see and know what is before them. In the same way, without the aid of Scripture's spectacles, we lack the true ability to form a coherent and accurate understanding of God—though this neither denies the objective character of natural theology nor the ability to see and understand it with the aid of supernatural revelation.[74] This doesn't mean that Scripture is necessary to understand natural revelation. Rather, it means that Scripture clarifies and makes sense of it.[75] Nature is not destroyed or neglected because of supernatural theology; rather, it is clarified and magnified.

Third, natural theology as a Christian task is done through renewed reason. Christ delivers us from the lies of the demons that led reason astray and imparts to us the heavenly wisdom that could not be discerned by nature alone in supernatural revelation (e.g., the Trinity, incarnation, reconciliation to God through faith). And the Spirit restores our hearts and renews our minds so that we can reason according to the same natural processes regarding the same content to a higher degree of effectiveness and consistency. It is this renewed mind, by the guidance of the Spirit of God, that considers all of God's world as a gift from him to teach us about him. As Basil explains, the Spirit is an "intellectual light for every rational power's discovery of truth."[76]

Therefore, Christian natural theology is not one that anyone can attain to—whether redeemed or not. It is a distinctively Christian natural

73. Allen, "Divine Attributes," 75–76.

74. Calvin, *Institutes of the Christian Religion*, 1.6.1.

75. Contra Bavinck, *Reformed Dogmatics*, 1:304. Bavinck suggests that the Reformed radically change the older understanding of natural theology to the point that Scripture is *necessary* for understanding even natural revelation. Thus, natural theology is strictly impossible as a pagan. But such a view is inconsistent with how the tradition, by and large, has understood natural theology. While there is a superiority of the natural theology of Christians illumined by the Spirit of God, this does not negate all common knowledge. I am thankful to my friend Ryan Modisette for pointing out this inconsistency in Bavinck. See Duby, *God in Himself*, 112–13.

76. Basil, *On the Holy Spirit*, 9, 22.

theology that utilizes *renewed* reason. The Christian is in a continual process of explicating the faith once for all delivered to the saints and building up and constructing a robust and coherent system of theology to the worship of the Triune God. It is true that natural theology in general is possible in many respects. Plato and Aristotle certainly were able to discern a great deal about the structure of reality, morality, and even aspects of God. As the apostle Paul says, "What can be known about God is plain to them" (Rom 1:19a). They, in principle, have access to the same content that everyone else has, redeemed or not.[77] For instance, natural duties are revealed by the light of nature and include obedience to the moral law, the necessity of worship, prayer to the one true God, and so on. A natural person can know the pertinent content and has power to obey these duties. If a natural person encounters supernatural revelation, they may rationally understand some of it too, but they have neither the grace nor power to obey it. Only the faithful receive the grace and power to understand and obey.

Natural theology, then, for the non-Christian is like dumping a 5,000-piece jigsaw puzzle on the table without letting them see the complete picture on the box. They can recognize some patterns and find pieces that match and complete important sections of the puzzle, but a Christian is enabled through the power of the Holy Spirit to view the complete image on the front of the box and then return to the pieces to work on the puzzle.[78] Irenaeus (130–202) illustrates this by asking us to think of the writing of Homer. While someone could pull various lines from his writing and assert that he meant one thing apart from context, those familiar with the whole of Homer would quickly spot the errors because they knew the overall story. Similarly, those acquainted with the whole of Scripture and renewed by the Spirit see how each aspect is fitted together to portray the likeness of the king rather than the fox.[79]

77. Of course, they didn't have access to the special revelation found in Scripture (or if they really did somehow have access to Moses as some have surmised, they didn't have all of special revelation). But in principle, had they been given it, they would have the same access to the same content as anyone else.

78. Thanks to Garrett Walden for this illustration.

79. Irenaeus, *Against Heresies*, ed. Alexander Roberts and James Donaldson (Ex Fontibus, 2010), I.IX.4.

Fourth, natural theology is a project done within and for the life of the church. It is not a vain and idle attempt to build a sort of theological Babel reaching up to God by our own strength and ingenuity. Rather it remains a dependent discipline, relying on the Spirit and the community of saints to think well about God. It never attempts to be a lord of our faith but a helper of our joy.[80]

ECLECTIC OPPORTUNISM[81]

Classical theism, historically speaking, has inhabited a certain intellectual spirit that I call "eclectic opportunism."[82] By eclectic opportunism, I mean two things. First, the classical tradition is *eclectic* in its usage of sources. It is not beholden to any one philosophical school—be it Platonic, Aristotelian, Stoic, Humean, or Berkeleyan. It is willing to incorporate a vast array of resources that together build a beautiful symphony in support of its doctrinal claims. While there are definite fault lines along which the tradition and subsegments of the tradition have fallen—far more deeply Platonic than Skeptic, for instance—there is no one main "school." Some utilize Neoplatonic elements, like Augustine. Others appropriate Aristotelian philosophy, like Thomas, or others use Berkeleyan philosophy, like Jonathan Edwards (1703–1758). But each of these thinkers, *despite their varying philosophical toolkits*, are within the classical tradition. While they each have different instruments and each hit different notes at times (some of which emphatically disagree), they harmonize to perform a symphony that is consistent with regards to the articles of the faith and classical theism—though some are more creative than others. The fundamental reason for this is that it is *Christianity* that is the primary theological "school" that each classical thinker inhabits and defends. Other philosophical schools are merely appendages to the true central commitment. It is Christianity

80. John Owen, *The Holy Spirit—The Helper*, ed. Andrew S. Ballitch, vol. 7, The Complete Works of John Owen (Crossway, 2023), 221.

81. This section is largely identical, with some additions and adjustments, to a section in my forthcoming essay: Jordan L. Steffaniak, "Plundering the Moderns: A Classical Defense of the Eclecticism of the Christian Tradition," *Pro Ecclesia*.

82. For a similar usage of the terminology as applied to Reformed theologians, see Simon J. G. Burton, *Ramism and the Reformation of Method: The Franciscan Legacy in Early Modernity*, Oxford Studies in Historical Theology (Oxford University Press, 2024), 34.

that is the "universal philosophy" and not Platonism, Aristotelianism, or anything else.[83]

Constructing a dogmatic theology in an eclectic opportunistic spirit is less common today than in ages past—at least in Protestant communities. Whatever the reason for this, whether due to our hyper-specialized academies, wherein we lack collaboration with a wide array of disciplines, or otherwise, it wasn't always this way. For example, Tom Ward has described the nature of the medieval scholastic:

> To have the dialectical right to state an opinion, a Scholastic master needed to acknowledge all that was true and wise in the many voices which preceded and surrounded him, carefully distinguishing different shades of meaning and doing his best to resolve disputes between authoritative sources.[84]

For the scholastics, it was *required* to be conversant in an incredibly wide array of philosophical ideas. Such a program lent itself to wider and more critical appropriation of insights from other schools.

Second, by *opportunism*, I mean that the classical tradition's construction of theology is what Scott Shalkowski has called a "context-relative matter."[85] In other words, there is a reason certain thinkers gravitate to certain philosophical schools or certain philosophical insights and utilize them. While it is true that most fundamentally they utilize them because they think they communicate *truth*, there is a further social dimension. These schools present an opportunity to advance and defend classical theology that either didn't exist in times past, has been forgotten and overlooked, or has been unfairly criticized.

Therefore, eclectic opportunism, as it relates to the classical tradition, is in one sense a "dogmatic minimalism" in which the metaphysical commitments that undergird classical theism seek to say as little as doctrinally

---

83. Frances M. Young, *Scripture, the Genesis of Doctrine* (Eerdmans, 2023), 110; Willemien Otten, "Christian Platonism: Some Comments on Its Past and the Need for Its Future," *The London Lyceum Ledger* (blog), August 3, 2022, https://thelondonlyceum.com/christian-platonism-some-comments-on-its-past-and-the-need-for-its-future/.

84. Thomas Ward, *Ordered by Love: An Introduction to John Duns Scotus* (Angelico, 2022), 6.

85. Scott A. Shalkowski, "Theoretical Virtues and Theological Construction," *International Journal for Philosophy of Religion* 41 (1997): 78.

possible while making clear that certain ways of thinking are off limits.[86] They take the ecumenical creeds and their own traditions' confessional statements as guardrails from which to theologize. Aspects that are not codified in publicly available creeds or confessions are subject to debate. Of course, depending on one's prior commitments, such talk of minimalism may appear rather robust! But I take it that traditional accounts of God, Christ, and the like are for Christians expected.

The sort of eclectic opportunism described here is well summarized by Brendan Case:

> I take it that the practice of constructive theology requires a potentially reckless disregard for the sub-disciplinary boundaries that cordon off the various theological sub-disciplines from one another and from the other university disciplines. This is because the theologian is bound to think and speak and write under the discipline of the LORD's unified self-revelation in the Old and New Testaments as they have been received in the broad catholic theological tradition.[87]

Eclectic opportunism, then, displays a sort of "reckless disregard" for being put within the straitjacket of extrabiblical frameworks—allowing both Scripture and tradition to shape, critique, and even direct us to newer models that serve us better. For example, while the authors of the Chalcedonian definition may very well have assumed all matters of theological and metaphysical content, not all of it is authoritative. While the authors may well have assumed that men are ontologically superior to women, such a belief is not necessary to affirm the substance of the definition. Similarly, while the authors may have been Platonic dualists about human persons, or held some other convoluted view, these beliefs are not restrictive for the classical thinker. While they should be taken seriously, they can equally be seriously rejected in favor of other models.

But even more, eclectic opportunism is *deliberately* eclectic in its philosophical commitments. It functions in this way because it seeks to be

86. Oliver D. Crisp, *The Word Enfleshed: Exploring the Person and Work of Christ* (Baker Academic, 2016), 80.

87. Brendan Case, *The Accountable Animal: Justice, Justification, and Judgment* (Bloomsbury Academic, 2021), 11.

reserved in its theological claims that could be beholden to any one philosophical program. Such an approach avoids placing classical theism at the mercy of transient fashion.[88] Given the eclectic opportunist's rejection of any specific tribe as totalizing of the entire tradition (certainly, one *should* inhabit their own tradition as they seek to resource the greater tradition), this approach allows one to take history far more seriously than in a project of repristination, wherein one can be all too tempted to valorize one's heroes. Yet the eclectic opportunist isn't a totally unstructured scavenger through the theological junkyard. Resourcing ourselves is only useful insofar as the resources lead us to thinking about God in a faithful way.[89]

It's useful to provide a few examples of this approach within the classical tradition itself. First, let's look to two paragon examples of classical theism in Augustine and Thomas. Augustine is rather famous for his claim to "plunder the Egyptians."[90] The logic behind his claim is that we should always be ready to plunder the very best of our neighbor's philosophy and take it captive to Christ. We are given "mines of providence" that we did not create but dug and received treasures.[91] As he argues, "A person who is a good and a true Christian should realize that truth belongs to his Lord, wherever it is found, gathering and acknowledging it even in pagan literature."[92] What Augustine models here is a relative eclectic opportunism—modifying other philosophical schools where necessary and rejecting where they are incompatible with the classical Christian faith. All truth is God's truth. Of course, Augustine isn't the first to deploy this example or to use its logic. Justin Martyr similarly argues that "whatever things were rightly said among all people are the property of us Christians."[93] The plundering logic is replete throughout the classical tradition.

Second, Thomas is famous for reworking the most cutting edge and persuasive areas of philosophy and Christianizing them. He was motivated to take Aristotle captive to Christ because he was an eclectic opportunist who saw intellectual resources available to him. Roman Catholic

88. Bruce D. Marshall, *Trinity and Truth* (Cambridge University Press, 2002), 13.

89. Allen, *The Fear of the Lord*, 141.

90. Augustine, *On Christian Teaching* 65.

91. Augustine, *On Christian Teaching* 65.

92. Augustine, *On Christian Teaching* 47.

93. Justin Martyr, *The First and Second Apologies*, trans. Leslie W. Barnard (Paulist Press, 1997), 84.

theologian Michael Gorman is surely fair in his analysis that "Aquinas is, for the most part, rather opportunistic and occasional in his use of comparisons or similitudes in theology."[94] Again, this doesn't mean Thomas or Augustine are *reckless* in their philosophical commitments. It doesn't mean they are scavenging as homeless theologians. However, it does mean they aren't content with assuming the validity of schemes not clearly given in Scripture and are willing to buttress classical theology with new developments as they come.

Third, the post-Reformation historian *par excellence* Richard Muller explains how theologians of the past sought to drink from both the tradition and the contemporary progress in metaphysics. He says, "The relative philosophical cohesion of any one of the many theological systems of the later Middle Ages, sixteenth, and seventeenth centuries was not achieved by an exclusive allegiance to a particular thinker in the classical tradition."[95] Elsewhere again, "The object of the scholastic theologian or philosopher was, typically, not so much to be 'Aristotelian' as to be the formulator and mediator of a Christian philosophical model that both used and refused various elements of the classical tradition."[96] Now, listen to Muller at length describe the logic of the Reformed permutation of the classical tradition:

> The philosophy (or philosophies) of the late sixteenth and seventeenth century Reformed ought to be understood as a concerted effort to draw on the tradition of classical and western thought for the sake of constructing a philosophical perspective suitable both to the altered theological and churchly context and to the academic needs of the rising Protestant colleges, academies, and universities of the post-Reformation era. What is more, in the course of these debates, the Reformed orthodox did not merely look backward into the Christian philosophy of the scholastic past, they stood in dialogue with the philosophy of their own time and often can be

94. Gorman, *Aquinas on the Metaphysics of the Hypostatic Union*, 44.

95. Richard A. Muller, "Reformation, Orthodoxy, 'Christian Aristotelianism,' and the Eclecticism of Early Modern Philosophy," *Nederlands Archief Voor Kerkgeschiedenis* 81, no. 3 (2001): 321.

96. Muller, "Reformation, Orthodoxy, 'Christian Aristotelianism,' and the Eclecticism of Early Modern Philosophy," 314.

> seen to parallel (perhaps even sometimes anticipate!) the work of thinkers like Malebranche and Leibniz. To call such theology and philosophy "Aristotelian" rather misses both its content and its context. Thus, the "Aristotelianism" of the Christian tradition in its movement through the Renaissance and Reformation into the era of orthodoxy appears, not as a philosophical program rooted in the historical Aristotle but rather as a highly variegated tradition grounded in long-standing discussions of the hylomorphic understanding of substance and its corollary, a conceptualist theory of knowledge that grounds knowledge of a thing in the thing and/or in the ability of the knower to abstract forms from things.[97]

This is the essence of the classical tradition: both eclectic and opportunistic. Unafraid to revise. Unafraid to appropriate. Yet resolute in its core commitments and willing to appropriate whatever will assist in defending them. It is for this reason that prominent classical theologians like Alister McGrath have argued that "the natural sciences today offer to Christian theology today precisely the role that Platonism offered our patristic, and Aristotelianism our medieval forebears."[98]

Lest you remain unconvinced and think I am selling our classical birthright for a mess of stew, hear from Richard Muller once more:

> The Reformed theology of the orthodox era reflects primarily the later medieval and Renaissance modifications of Christian philosophy (again, Thomist, Scotist, and nominalist) and only secondarily a classic Aristotelianism. It is certainly more useful to characterize many of the Reformed orthodox as holding a form of modified (sometimes highly modified) Thomism often with Scotistic or nominalistic accents, sometimes with strong affinities for the philosophies of the day, whether that of Suarez or of Descartes, than to speak of them as simply Aristotelian.[99]

---

97. Muller, "Reformation, Orthodoxy, 'Christian Aristotelianism,' and the Eclecticism of Early Modern Philosophy," 322.

98. McGrath, *A Scientific Theology*, 1:7.

99. Muller, "Reformation, Orthodoxy, 'Christian Aristotelianism,' and the Eclecticism of Early Modern Philosophy," 323.

These classical theologians did not fear deviating from consensus figures like Thomas or Augustine (just like their medieval predecessors!). They did not fear appropriating Scotus, forms of nominalism, Suárez, or even sometimes Descartes (1596–1650). They embodied an eclectic opportunistic spirit, which allows for freedom to appropriate from the very best philosophy, and there is no fear of one day realizing such metaphysics is unhelpful, misguided, or fundamentally at odds with the basic core doctrinal commitments of classical theism. That is because classical theism is not meant to codify literally everything. It is meant to codify certain claims about God, like his being eternal, immutable, simple, and impassible. And whatever metaphysics can assist in defending and explaining these doctrinal positions is to be appropriated.

Finally, consider the modern theologian Herman Bavinck. For Bavinck, modern insights and appropriations are not diametrically opposed.[100] Cory Brock has argued at length, through examining Bavinck's usage of Friedrich Schleiermacher, that Bavinck is "orthodox yet modern." While Bavinck is resolutely committed to his orthodox and confessional tradition, modern theology is given space to advance dogmatic theology, so long as it refrains from contradicting the tradition.[101] He blends, as Brock and Sutanto put it, "principled orthodoxy and irenic learning."[102] Bavinck can blend these two worlds because there is no pristine era of theology. Repristination of any specific era of theology is a fool's errand. The goal of the dogmatic and the classical thinker is reappropriation, and thus, modern insights and modifications are *necessary*.[103] As Brock puts it, "Dogmatics looks back but pays attention above all to today."[104] This vision of dogmatics fits well with Bavinck's own claims regarding retrieval:

100. Cory C. Brock, *Orthodox yet Modern: Herman Bavinck's Use of Friedrich Schleiermacher* (Lexham, 2020), 5.

101. Brock, *Orthodox yet Modern*, 19, 267.

102. Cory Brock and Nathaniel Gray Sutanto, "Herman Bavinck's Reformed Eclecticism: On Catholicity, Consciousness and Theological Epistemology," *Scottish Journal of Theology* 70, no. 3 (2017): 311, https://doi.org/10.1017/S003693061700031X.

103. Brock, *Orthodox yet Modern*, 54; Brock and Sutanto, "Herman Bavinck's Reformed Eclecticism," 312.

104. Brock, *Orthodox yet Modern*, 270.

> With Calvin, Luther, and Zwingli we differentiate that which is essential and truly reformed, from that of the spirit of the age. We do not return to them after the fact, to repristinate them and their work as much as to respect their value in general ... but through their teaching, better than even they, to hold fast to and speak out a reformation principle ... not to return to them but to go forward from them is our motto.[105]

Herein Bavinck is clear that the goal of theology is *not* repristination—not a return—but a going forward. Thus, Bavinck's own methodology encourages such eclectic opportunism.

But it is not only Bavinck's posture toward modern resources that is amiable to the eclectic opportunist. It is his own theological and philosophical eclecticism. Bavinck is not beholden to a single philosophical tradition. Consider his claim against the need for a specific tradition of philosophy for the Christian faith:

> Theology is not in need of a specific philosophy. It is not per se hostile to any philosophical system and does not, a priori and without criticism, give priority to the philosophy of Plato or of Kant, or vice versa. But it brings along its own criteria, tests all philosophy by them, and takes over what it deems true and useful. What it needs is philosophy in general.[106]

Bavinck's own philosophical vision is exactly as I would sketch the broad classical tradition: resolutely committed to orthodox doctrine but eager to pillage from any and all resources to buttress such doctrine. There is no law that one must be a Platonist, a Kantian, or anything else. While some philosophical programs or insights are better than others, and some are essential, not all require allegiance.

The classical tradition in this way is like a great feast. Think about whatever your favorite one is. Mine is Thanksgiving. All great Thanksgiving feasts require a main dish, and if you ask me the only appropriate one is turkey, though ham is suitable. Whatever your

---

105. Quoted in Brock, *Orthodox yet Modern*, 132.

106. Bavinck, *Reformed Dogmatics*, 1:609.

persuasion, there is an essential aspect to the main dish for the feast. While there is some flexibility, it is limited in scope. I cannot simply substitute a side dish or marinade for the main dish. What would your family think if I brought a cucumber and served it as the main dish? Certainly, cucumbers are delicious, but they cannot feed a family gathering. The nourishment we need requires a hearty dish at the center. Or what if I brought a racoon carcass I found on the side of the road while driving to the gathering? Not only would this be disgusting, but it would be toxic. In this way, some philosophical programs are out of bounds, some are useful only in certain contexts, while others are flexible and amendable. To continue with the feast analogy, some delicious foods have bad aftereffects. While they are delightful in the moment and appear to complement the meal, they end up giving heart burn or lethargy. And so, the classical tradition is like a great feast with room to appropriate within a set of options.

DIVINE NAMING

Another common practice throughout the tradition, which becomes nearly ubiquitous by the time of Zwingli (1484–1531) through the Reformation, is to begin with the divine names as the revelatory epicenter of the divine nature.[107] These names are divine revelations that offer insights into who and what God is in utterly unique and profound ways.[108] They possess a significance that spans the biblical canon and goes well beyond the mere grammatical arrangements themselves.[109] As Herman Bavinck says, "All that we can learn about God from his revelation is designated his Name in Scripture."[110] His names function as signs that reveal honor, worth, individuality, and the like. Again, Bavinck guides, noting that "there is an intimate link between God and his name. According to Scripture, this link too is not accidental or arbitrary but

107. Richard A. Muller, *Post-Reformation Reformed Dogmatics: The Rise and Development of Reformed Orthodoxy, ca. 1520 to ca. 1725*, 2nd ed. (Baker Academic, 2003), 3:246.

108. Petrus van Mastricht, *Theoretical-Practical Theology*, ed. Joel R. Beeke, trans. Todd M. Rester (Reformation Heritage, 2018), 1.2.4.III; Thomas Aquinas, *Summa Contra Gentiles: Book One; God*, trans. Anton Charles Pegis, vol. 1 (University of Notre Dame Press, 1975), 22.10.

109. Tyler Wittman, *God and Creation in the Theology of Thomas Aquinas and Karl Barth* (Cambridge University Press, 2019), 278.

110. Bavinck, *Reformed Dogmatics*, 2:97.

forged by God himself. We do not name God; he names himself."[111] The divine names function as a *biblical* and fatherly doorway into necessarily difficult discussions on the nature of God.[112]

For example, it is often understood that Yahweh/Jehovah denotes his essence as *a se*, immutable, and eternal.[113] Above all it communicates his *enduring* existence.[114] As John of Damascus says, "He gathers together and contains all being in himself like an infinite and unbounded sea."[115] While other names are what John Calvin calls "epithets," Jehovah is his "essential" name indicating that "nothing is more peculiar to God than eternity ... because He has existence from Himself, and sustains all things by His secret inspiration."[116] But Exodus 3:14 remains the *locus classicus* for the practice of knowing God through his names. Moses is confronted by God, who provides the ever-mysterious description, "I am who I am." Despite its mystery and its philosophical reception through the tradition, it is quite clearly foundational to our understanding of God to know *this* name. And it is a name that tells us of God's love, kindness, and nearness. It is his gift to his people in their time of need.[117]

However, contemporary Old Testament scholars often shy away from philosophical glosses on this divine revelatory encounter. The fact that most classical and medieval thinkers didn't know Hebrew, and the Greek and Latin translations of the Old Testament translated this text as "the one who is" or "the being-one," give all the more reason for pause.[118] Most commentators and biblical theologians note that the context of Exodus 3:14, together with other passages that feature the divine name (Exod 6:2–8; 33:19; 34:6–7), suggest the idea of faithfulness or covenant keeper as that which the name would have communicated to Moses and the Israelites.

---

111. Bavinck, *Reformed Dogmatics*, 2:98.

112. Muller, *Post-Reformation Reformed Dogmatics*, 3:248.

113. Mastricht, *Theoretical-Practical Theology*, 1.2.4.VIII; Wilhelmus à Brakel, *The Christian's Reasonable Service*, ed. Joel R. Beeke, trans. Bartel Elshout (Reformation Heritage, 1992), 1:84.

114. Francis J. Hall, *The Being and Attributes of God* (Longmans, Green, 1909), 228.

115. John of Damascus, *On the Orthodox Faith*, trans. Normal Russell (St. Vladimir's Seminary Press, 2022), 84.

116. John Calvin, *Commentaries on the Four Last Books of Moses Arranged in the Form of a Harmony*, trans. Charles William Bingham (Baker Book House, 1981), 127.

117. Janet Soskice, *Naming God* (Cambridge University Press, 2023), 13.

118. Andrew Davison, *Participation in God: A Study in Christian Doctrine and Metaphysics* (Cambridge University Press, 2019), 24–25.

But it is standard in the tradition to understand it as conveying a strong doctrine of aseity. God is, will be, and was *being* itself—he is from and of himself, in need of no one. He remains the eternally unchanging faithful one.[119] For example, Calvin understands this divine name to mean that God has "perpetual duration of time" and self-existence.[120] If one finds such interpretative approaches unsatisfying, it remains available to the theologian to take the concept of God's covenant faithfulness and raise the question, "What sort of God must God be in order to have and exercise the kind of covenant faithfulness in view?" From that question, one can then argue that divine aseity, immutability, and eternality are necessary preconditions of divine covenant faithfulness.[121]

DIVINE ACCOMMODATION[122]

Divine accommodation is the warp and woof of classical biblical interpretation. The basic idea behind accommodation is that God and creatures are different—radically so. Because of this difference, there is an inability to understand *directly* and *literally* what God is. He transcends created categories, so we have nothing with which we can truly compare him.[123] Therefore, God must use "accommodative" language to help us understand what he is like. God is *like* a rock, *like* a tree, and *like* a lion. These examples give us some ability to make theological judgments, limited as they are. So, as Saint Augustine says, "The divine scriptures then are in the habit of making something like children's toys out of things that occur in creation."[124] In other words, God uses creation to reveal himself in "a manner suited to human senses," because it is the only category possible for created beings to know.[125]

Such an interpretive practice may be surprising to our modern ears. It might seem this would destabilize our ability to know anything about God.

---

119. Bavinck, *Reformed Dogmatics*, 2:143.

120. Calvin, *Commentaries on the Four Last Books of Moses Arranged in the Form of a Harmony*, 73.

121. Thanks to Bob Gonzalez for this insight.

122. Portions of this section are from my essay: Jordan L. Steffaniak, "On the Inferiority of 'Revisionary Metaphysics': A Review Essay", *The Hanover Review* 3, no. 2 (2025): 67-81.

123. Basil, *Against Eunomius* 1.14.

124. Augustine, *The Trinity*, trans. Edmund Hill (New City, 2015), I.1.2.

125. Augustine, *The Trinity* II.3.7, 12.

But consider for a moment several examples. Is God literally *seated* on the cherubim, as Psalm 80:1 claims?[126] Surely it is quite intuitive to allow for metaphors like this to communicate something besides literal truth, lest we be content to assume that God also has literal eyes, legs, and arms. We must be willing to allow some level of divine accommodation. So, while some predications are proper, like love, others are improper and metaphorical, like circumscribed location. By distinguishing between a proper and improper sense I am following a standard classical approach that sees some terms being entirely metaphorical (this doesn't mean untrue), whereas others are more naturally literally predicative of God.[127]

Take two common examples to prove the validity of the distinction. First, think about the prophecies found in Revelation. I take these to be primarily metaphorical. This doesn't mean they lack meaning; rather, what is being explained is simply using images that don't map *literally* to reality. There won't be a dragon or a seven-headed scorpion at the end of time. Ignoring the exegetical complexities, I think we can agree that the basic idea isn't totally far-fetched. So, when talking about God, who is far greater than a dragon or seven-headed scorpions, why wouldn't we expect language to be metaphorical in many senses? Why assume every depiction of God is completely literal?

Let's take a second example. Imagine I was born into an indigenous tribe in Africa with no contact to the outside world. Then several decades later, some loud and obnoxious American finds my tribe and attempts to explain electricity to me. How do you think he would do that? Would he be able to speak of the scientific nature of electricity and how the power grid works to me? No, I don't think so. He'd need to use metaphors to explain what it is "like." He would use concepts I was familiar with and attempt to explain it in the best way he could.

None of this means accommodation is *literally* "baby talk," as Peter Leithart worries. It doesn't mean that the grownups in the room should put away these childish games for the "grown-up language about God,"

---

126. Augustine, *The Trinity* V.2.8, 9.

127. The nature of theological language is more complicated than I have neatly summarized here. I am assuming for the sake of argument my summary of the material for the sake of space. There are monographs and numerous journal articles dedicated to the topic one can consult for fuller accounts.

which "turns out to be metaphysical language."[128] Leithart suggests that any doctrine of accommodation is "theologically insupportable."[129] He argues accommodation entails a *second* condescension from God: creation and *then* accommodation. To employ these "ticks and tricks" that posit a second condescension is to suggest "creation is not *entirely* good."[130] But none of this is true. Leithart misunderstands the nature of accommodation, which attempts to provide hermeneutical tools for understanding and interpreting the varied modes of divine communication. It does not mean we need something more than Scripture. It just means that we should be patient as we read the biblical text and allow the various signposts found throughout Scripture that warn us of the danger of reading metaphorical language as literal to have their pride of place. And why worry about a second condescension beyond creation, as if that were necessarily bad? Certainly, the incarnation is a condescension after creation, and I'd put money on that being good.

Now, it is important to hear directly from the classical tradition on the logic of divine accommodation, given its importance. I mainly focus on the dynamic Johannine duo of Chrysostom and Calvin since they are relevantly representative.

First, hear from the "golden-tongued" John Chrysostom (347–407). He says, "But the distance between the essence of God and the essence of man is so great that no words can express it, nor is the mind capable of measuring it."[131] His idea is that God is radically different from his creation, which entails that he transcends all creational concepts. He is beyond our intelligence and comprehension.[132]

Yet despite being beyond our comprehension, God does offer revelation of himself in comprehensible terms. Chrysostom explains this as condescension:

> What is this condescension? God condescends whenever he is not seen as he is, but in the way one incapable of beholding him is able to

128. Peter J. Leithart, *Creator: A Theological Interpretation of Genesis 1* (IVP Academic, 2023), 16.

129. Leithart, *Creator*, 17–20.

130. Leithart, *Creator*, 21–22.

131. John Chrysostom, *On the Incomprehensible Nature of God*, trans. Paul W. Harkins (Catholic University of America Press, 1984), II.37.

132. Chrysostom, *On the Incomprehensible Nature of God* III.5.

> look upon him. In this way God reveals himself by accommodating what he reveals to the weakness of vision of those who behold him.[133]

God stoops low to his creation and makes himself known within created realities that lack exact representation. The only exact imprint of God is the Son (Heb 1:3). So, while God reveals himself, the knowledge God brings is not exhaustive knowledge of himself.[134]

Second, listen to John Calvin, theologian *par excellence* of accommodation. Accommodation is one of, if not *the*, chief facets to Calvin's theology of revelation.[135] For Calvin, like Chrysostom, God must accommodate himself to human terms in human ways due to the gap between the Creator and the creature.[136] Now, accommodation doesn't depreciate the reality that God gives self-revelation to his creatures that corresponds to reality, even if "tempered to our feeble comprehension."[137] It merely locates the knowledge of creatures in a different category—true yet incomplete.

But there is a third John that testifies. As John of Damascus argues:

> Many of the things about God that are perceived obscurely by the mind cannot be expressed with precision. On the contrary, we are obliged to speak about what transcends us in terms of our own experience, as when we attribute to God sleep, anger, indifference, hands and feet, and so on.[138]

Since God is divine, exalted, and immaterial, we can only speak of God with images, types, and symbols that we are familiar with.[139] The

---

133. Chrysostom, *On the Incomprehensible Nature of God* III.15.

134. Chrysostom, *On the Incomprehensible Nature of God* V.38.

135. Michael Horton, "Knowing God: Calvin's Understanding of Revelation," in *John Calvin and Evangelical Theology: Legacy and Prospect*, ed. Sung Wook Chung (Westminster John Knox, 2009), 1; Michael H. Kibbe, "Present and Accommodated For: Calvin's God on Mount Sinai," *Journal of Theological Interpretation* 7, no. 1 (2013): 116; Jordan L. Steffaniak, "Bound by the Word of God: John Calvin's Religious Epistemology," *Puritan Reformed Journal* 10, no. 2 (2018): 135–36; Calvin, *Institutes of the Christian Religion*, 1.10.2; 2.11.13; 2.16.2; 3.2.14.

136. Paul Helm, *John Calvin's Ideas* (Oxford University Press, 2004), 200; Calvin, *Institutes of the Christian Religion*, 1.10.2; 3.2.14.

137. Calvin, *Institutes of the Christian Religion*, 2.16.3; Robert L. Reymond, "Calvin's Doctrine of Holy Scripture," in *A Theological Guide to Calvin's Institutes*, ed. David W. Hall and Peter A. Lillback (P&R, 2008), 57.

138. John of Damascus, *On the Orthodox Faith* 60.

139. John of Damascus, *On the Orthodox Faith* 85.

implication of this is that much of Scripture is given to us improperly. There are metaphors that seek to describe who and what God is by similitude rather than by identity. This is why it is not problematic to take various scriptural claims as metaphorical rather than literal. It is the typical practice of God to describe himself in ways that we can understand. So, while Scripture may say that God changed his mind, this isn't something that is supposed to be literally mapped directly back onto God's being. We must be careful readers. We cannot read Scripture with an overly simplistic approach and assume we understand it at first pass. We must contemplate in dependence on the Spirit.[140]

THE THEOLOGICAL WAYS

Finally, it is time to explain the theological ways. These are the way of eminence (*via eminentiae*), negation (*via negationes*), and causality (*via causalitatis*). These are commonly termed the *via triplex*. Through them we know about God by three *ways*: eminence, negation, and causality.[141] The *via eminentiae* is mostly analogous to what is called "perfect being theology" in contemporary theology.[142] This practice takes every discernable good, strips it of any imperfection, and predicates it of God to the highest possible degree by its proper proportion. The *via negationes* denies every discernable limitation of God.[143] It highlights divine transcendence. God transcends every possible created reality or category, even the category of being itself! Therefore, there is nothing that can adequately define what God is.[144]

It is important to note two things about these two approaches. First, these two are intertwined. The ways of excellence and denial engage in a

---

140. There is additional debate that connects to this discussion around "univocity" and "analogy" that often centers on those like Thomas and Scotus. I do not think it is necessary to engage this debate for the purposes of my book. I tend to think Scotus and Thomas are saying substantially the same thing but using different terms. If it turns out that they aren't, I would side with Scotus. But this debate is not the same as accommodation, though it can overlap at times. See Thomas M. Ward, "Duns Scotus, Classical Theist: A Vindication," *The Hanover Review* 3, no. 1 (2024): 19–22.

141. Gisbertus Voetius, "God's Single, Absolutely Simple Essence," *The Confessional Presbyterian* 15 (2019): 38.

142. Some will quibble with this, especially many Thomists. But in general, large strokes, I argue it is true.

143. Stephen R. Holmes, "The Attributes of God," in *The Oxford Handbook of Systematic Theology*, ed. Kathryn Tanner, John Webster, and Iain Torrance (Oxford University Press, 2007), 56.

144. John of Damascus, *On the Orthodox Faith* 66.

sort of reciprocal analogical process.[145] Second, the "classical" divine attributes are primarily *negative* in scope, though they are generated by divine perfections. Finally, the *via causalitatis* follows the effects of God's works to him as the cause, and attributes divine perfections to him through this causal chain. In what follows, I primarily focus on explicating the interplay between the way of eminence and the way of negation, which I take to function under the contemporary terminology of perfect being theology.

UNDERSTANDING PERFECT BEING THEOLOGY[146]

While the terminology of "perfect being theology" may be unfamiliar to some of the classical tradition or may be potentially anachronistic, the basics of the approach are ancient and pervasive.[147] Therefore, we ought to retrain our minds when it comes to perfect being theology. It is not primarily the domain of analytic philosophers of religion but of the classical tradition. Anselm is the archetype with his claim that God is that "than whom nothing greater can be thought." Such a claim summarizes the key contention of perfect being theology and the way of eminence—God is the greatest possible/conceivable being, exhibiting maximal perfection.[148] More than exhibiting this maximal perfection at one point in time, God has perfection necessarily, eternally, absolutely, and limitlessly.[149] But perfect being theology is not merely positive. It is also negative. The perfect being theologian doesn't think we can understand perfection in all its detail, and so while it is designed to emphasize the incomparable perfection of God, it emphasizes the *incomparability*. Because there is nothing we can compare God to, our ideas about him fail, but not out of poverty. They fail out of the abundance of his being.[150]

---

145. Aquinas, *The Treatise on the Divine Nature* I.13.1c.

146. Much from this section and the following (6.1–6.2) are informed by my previous essay: Steffaniak, "The God of All Creation."

147. Holmes, "The Attributes of God," 56.

148. Anselm, *Monologion*, ed. Brian Davies and G. R. Evans, Oxford World's Classics (Oxford University Press, 1998), 5. Note that there can be a significant distinction parsed out between *possible* and *conceivable* being. While this is a worthy exercise, I do not find it necessary for the overall point I am intending to make.

149. William P. Alston, *Divine Nature and Human Language: Essays in Philosophical Theology*, Cornell Paperbacks (Cornell University Press, 1989), 124; Katherin A. Rogers, *Perfect Being Theology* (Edinburgh University Press, 2000), 13.

150. Davison, *Participation in God*, 2.

The standard approach you'll find in the classical tradition is to begin by considering a formal topic of any sort—any possible perfection in creatures, say, wisdom. Then you remove all imperfections. As Scotus says, "When we apply this analysis to God, we must remove the imperfections."[151] At this point, you are capable of ascribing the original notion of wisdom in the ultimate degree of perfection to God. Wisdom is then ascribed in the most elevated and loving manner to God.[152] This is what Stephen Charnock does with knowledge. He says, "As to what knowledge is, if we know what knowledge is in man, we may apprehend what it is in God, removing all imperfection from it and ascribing to him the most eminent way of understanding."[153] But it is more than just abstract reasoning that leads us down this path. The traditional method is to use this approach as a hermeneutical lens. As the Baptist pastor John C. Ryland quips, "Let every scripture be agreeable to all the divine perfections."[154]

So, perfect being theology of this sort is a contemplative exercise of natural theology that understands God to possess/be the sum total of all conceivable perfections and to be infinitely removed from all defects and limitations. Whatever it is better to have, God has. Whatever it is better to not have, God lacks. So, *F* is a divine attribute *if and only if F* is a perfective excellence.[155] Such a belief also arises from Scripture's own description of God. God is "perfect love" (1 John 4:18), God's "work is perfect" (Deut 32:4), his law is "perfect" (Ps 19:7), his gifts are "perfect" (Jas 1:17), his "way is perfect" (2 Sam 22:31), and he is "perfect in knowledge" (Job 37:16). No one is greater than him (Heb 6:13–14; Pss 77:13; 95:3; 96:4; 145:3; Exod 18:11). Jeremiah 10:6 says, "There is none like you, O Lord; you are great, and your name is great in might." Psalm 145:3 says, "Great is the Lord, and greatly to be praised, and his greatness is unsearchable."

---

151. John Duns Scotus, *Selected Writings on Ethics*, trans. Thomas Williams (Oxford University Press, 2017), 73.

152. John Duns Scotus, *Philosophical Writings: A Selection*, trans. Allan B. Wolter (Hackett, 1987), 25; Bonaventure, *Breviloquium*, trans. Dominic Monti (Franciscan Institute, 2005), 30; Thomas Aquinas, *Summa Contra Gentiles: Book One; God*, trans. Anton Charles Pegis (University of Notre Dame Press, 1975), 1.1.30.2.

153. Charnock, *The Existence and Attributes of God*, 618.

154. Ryland, *Contemplations on the Beauties of Creation and on All the Principal Truths and Blessings of the Glorious Gospel; with the Sins and Graces of Professing Christians*, 2:229.

155. Aquinas, *Summa Contra Gentiles: Book One; God* 1.28.

Thus, perfect being theology is reverent faith seeking understanding—not an idealized and isolated philosophical intuition seeking a god in its own image.[156]

THE CLASSICAL TRADITION AND PERFECT BEING THEOLOGY

As noted from the outset, perfect being theology is ubiquitous in the classical tradition. From the patristics to the Reformed orthodox, there is universal support.[157] Yujin Nagasawa is so bold to say that it is "arguably the most widely accepted form of traditional monotheism."[158] Several examples ought to make this plain. The fathers deploy perfect being theology as a general way to govern their thought about God. Predications of God *must* be understood in a way "fitting to God" (*theoprepos*) or "worthy of God" (*deo dignam*).[159] These are not mere remarks about describing a "pretty fancy" God but the ultimate perfect being. Therefore, these conceptual tools are proto–perfect being theology, functioning to ensure all thoughts about God are consistent with his maximal greatness. Fathers such as Didymus, Basil, Gregory of Nyssa, Origen, Athanasius, and Cyril of Alexandria all use this language. For example, Basil argues that we must have rules of interpretation that safeguard "worthy concepts about God."[160] Gregory of Nazianzus similarly wonders how a non-perfect being could even be worthy of worship when he exclaims, "The grossness of it, to say that deity has no properties superior to ours! How could it be worth worship were it bounded?"[161] Augustine likewise thinks that we can "never think about him as he deserves" because "no words of ours are capable of expressing him."[162] These are ways of practicing perfect being theology that are firmly rooted in the classical Christian tradition.

---

156. Contra Ware, "An Evangelical Reexamination of the Doctrine of the Immutability of God," 238.

157. Muller, *Post-Reformation Reformed Dogmatics*, 320–24.

158. Yujin Nagasawa, *Maximal God: A New Defence of Perfect Being Theism* (Oxford University Press, 2017), 7.

159. Mark Sheridan, *Language for God in Patristic Tradition: Wrestling with Biblical Anthropomorphism* (IVP Academic, 2015), 19, 116.

160. Basil, *Against Eunomius* 1.14.

161. Gregory of Nazianzus, *On God and Christ: The Five Theological Orations and Two Letters to Cledonius*, trans. Frederick Williams and Lionel R. Wickham (St. Vladimir's Seminary Press, 2002), 28.7.

162. Augustine, *The Trinity* V.1.1.

But perfect being theology is not only present in the more ancient philosophically inclined era. It is also among leading Reformed thinkers. Consider Petrus van Mastricht (1630–1706), who argues in his *Theoretical-Practical Theology* against the Socinians on the basis that they teach "various things that are incompatible with the infinite perfection and sufficiency of God." Since they remove everything that is agreed to "connote perfection, and which ought to be possessed by the one who is perfect in the highest degree, and without which he cannot be perfect in that way," they error.[163] His reasoning is straightforward. The Socinian error is not ascribing all the perfections to God. This approach is the heart of perfect being theology: Whatever is perfect, God has, and whatever isn't, he lacks. Mastricht's accusation is that his opponents don't attribute everything that is perfect to God and that some things they do attribute to him conflict with his overall perfection. But it is not only Mastricht who employs such a practice. Herman Bavinck does too.

God is the sum of all perfections for Bavinck. Whatever perfections we discover in the world ought to be attributed to God preeminently.[164] John Owen (1616–1683) strikes a similar note, claiming that

> God is absolutely perfect; whatever is of perfection is to be ascribed to him; otherwise he could neither be absolutely self-sufficient, all-sufficient, nor eternally blessed in himself. He is absolutely perfect, inasmuch as no perfection is wanting to him, and comparatively above all that we can conceive or apprehend of perfection.[165]

He goes on to argue for a particular understanding of omnipresence based on this very principle. Omnipresence is a perfection because to lack omnipresence is to be limited in some way—to be less than perfect. This is perfect being theology. These are not Reformed lightweights. They are some of the most sophisticated and robust thinkers in the Reformed tradition.

---

163. Mastricht, *Theoretical-Practical Theology*, 2:1.2.21.

164. Bavinck, *Reformed Dogmatics*, 2:250.

165. John Owen, *Vindiciae Evangelicae; or, The Mystery of the Gospel Vindicated and Socinianism Examined*, ed. William H. Goold, vol. 12, The Works of John Owen (Banner of Truth Trust, 1966), 95.

CONCLUSION

In conclusion, I have shown six areas within the classical tradition that make up some of the methodological sensibilities of the classical tradition. They function as broad ways of reasoning that assist in developing doctrinal claims. They are not like mathematical formulas where we can simply plug in the inputs and always get the guaranteed outputs. Instead, they are an entire way of thinking—a theological culture that teaches us to reason well. While I haven't examined every exegetical practice that gives rise to classical theism, I suggest that these six practices are regular ingredients for thinking well about God. As we turn to the classical attributes themselves, we will find these practices on display either behind the scenes as schematic frameworks or explicitly invoked as tools for making theological judgments. Much of the debate over the classical attributes ends up ignoring the foundational role that these interpretive methodologies play. The reason many come to vastly different conclusions is because they reject these methodological sensibilities.

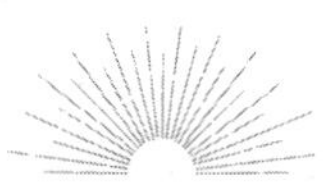

4

CLASSICAL METAPHYSICS

Metaphysics is a word that is often tossed around by theologians without much understanding. This shouldn't be surprising since most theologians (really, most *anyone*) receive no formal training in metaphysics. What is learned about metaphysics is primarily through secondhand acquaintance. And yet it is common to argue that if we believe in important Christian doctrines like the Trinity and incarnation, we will be committed to some form of classical metaphysics.[1] But if metaphysics is necessary—especially *classical* metaphysics—some introductory material will serve us well in thinking about God.

The resources provided in what follows will be deployed throughout the remainder of the book as we seek to understand classical theism. Instead of getting bogged down in some of the more technical material in each chapter, we can lay out the tools here and put them to work later. So, there is a pedagogical advantage to summarizing the general metaphysical topics that are most important for classical theism in one detailed chapter rather than continually introducing ad hoc discussions throughout the work. Describing each topic in detail here allows for a consistent and unhurried unpacking of each concept. But this won't cover all metaphysics. Many traditionally important aspects of metaphysics will be left untouched or significantly underdeveloped. While they play a role in the classical attributes, it is limited for my explanation and so I encourage you to read standard metaphysics introductions to learn more about topics

1. Thomas Joseph White, *The Incarnate Lord* (Catholic University of America Press, 2017), 66.

like causation, persistence, and many of the specific theories that I do not outline in detail here.[2] Instead, I focus on a selective portion that is more germane to the classical attributes we will examine.

As a note before we embark on this journey, I encourage you, if all this material is relatively new to you, to stay the course. While metaphysics can appear overly technical and obtuse at times, it has been jointly understood as the closest science to theology. It is difficult but majestic. Similar to the beauty of standing atop a mountain peak that is paired with the arduous journey to the top, metaphysics is like an intellectual peak that requires intellectual exercise beyond your average daily rhythm. But the truth is, no one complains when technical medical data is required to be understood or when technical mathematical formulas are required for computer engineering. And why would we expect it to be any less difficult when thinking about God? But with great difficulty comes great reward. Once we reach the peak of a mountain that has beaten us down along the trail, we feel a sense of great accomplishment. But unlike a lonely mountain trek, studying metaphysics, and all Christian theology, is a communal enterprise that requires others committed to the same goal to encourage, protect, and spar with. So, stay the course. The payoff is well worth it.

METAPHYSICS AND CHRISTIANITY

Spend any time around a toddler, and you'll quickly be reminded of how natural it is for us to wonder *why*. Why does the sun heat the world? Why do weeds grow in our garden? Why do our bodies need water? Why are some old men bald? And, well, you get the point. Similarly, metaphysics is the grown-up version of asking "Why?" but with a special title for the study. It is relentless in its focus on the most fundamental and general aspects of reality and why they are the way they are.[3] But metaphysics is

2. For general introductions at a beginner to intermediate level, I suggest starting with these (I should note that Inman's volume is unique in that it explains metaphysics with an explicit commitment to Christianity, which will prove especially valuable for those working in ecclesial contexts): Robert C. Koons and Timothy H. Pickavance, *Metaphysics: The Fundamentals* (Wiley Blackwell, 2015); Michael J. Loux and Thomas M. Crisp, *Metaphysics: A Contemporary Introduction*, 4th ed. (Routledge, 2017); Nikk Effingham, *Introduction to Ontology* (Polity Press, 2013); Anna Marmodoro and Erasmus Mayr, *Metaphysics: An Introduction to Contemporary Debates and Their History* (Oxford University Press, 2019); Peter Van Inwagen, *Metaphysics*, 4th ed. (Westview, 2015); Ross D. Inman, *What Is Reality? An Introduction to Metaphysics* (IVP Academic, 2024).

3. Marmodoro and Mayr, *Metaphysics*, 2.

concerned not just with the most fundamental and general explanations of why things are the way they are in reality. It also concerns "what" there is in the most general and fundamental sense. In this sense, it's concerned with the fundamental structure of reality as well.

But is metaphysics really that important for Christian doctrine? Utter the word "metaphysics" to many theologians and laymen alike over the last century, and you'd likely be looked on with disdain. It's not merely absent from the Bible and totally impractical, it's akin to death. It's dry, dead, and toxic. Karl Barth (1886–1968) warned of its fatal speculation while T. F. Torrance (1913–2007) and Colin Gunton similarly saw a large divide between lifeless metaphysics and the joy-filled God of Scripture.[4] But, spoiler alert, I argue that Barth and company are wrong. Metaphysics isn't dry, dead, or toxic. While it can be hard as a specialized academic discipline, we are all junior metaphysicians in some sense, making common-sense judgments about why things are the way they are and what there is.

BUT METAPHYSICS ISN'T IN MY BIBLE!

First, for those unfamiliar with metaphysics, such a discussion may appear as esoteric jargon from the ivory tower. Terms like *supervenience*, *reductionism*, *ostrich nominalism*, and *bloated ontologies* aren't part of our regular vocabularies. Even if some claim it necessary to believe in a certain metaphysic, there's a sneaking suspicion that the Bible is just fine without it. There's no proof text that tells us, "Thou shalt study metaphysics," or, "Beware of false metaphysics lest your doctrine perish." However, metaphysics matters, even if we don't have a Bible verse that I can hang over my office door reminding guests of its importance. While the Bible isn't a metaphysical textbook, it does assume metaphysics and even provides robust metaphysical implications. For example, even in the very beginning of Genesis we see Moses narrating the creation story of natural kinds—the phrase "according to their kinds" is repeated over and over. For example: "God created the great sea creatures and every living creature that moves, with which the waters swarm, *according to their kinds*, and every winged bird *according to its kind*" (Gen 2:21, emphasis mine). This is metaphysics. It's what metaphysicians like to call "carving the world at its joints."

4. Steven J. Duby, *God in Himself* (IVP Academic, 2019), 3–5.

While Moses doesn't give us a philosophy disputation akin to Aristotle, metaphysics is at work by describing and categorizing reality.

And we mustn't think that we are free to leave metaphysics in the background since it can become quite complicated at times. While most of the biblical authors probably would look at you funny if you mentioned ostrich nominalism (who wouldn't!?), they would all vigorously defend a certain way of understanding the world and its importance. For example, the apostle Paul was not a metaphysician, but he understood basic metaphysical principles and assumed their validity. His esoteric argument in 1 Corinthians 11 aside, he speaks of "nature" teaching us in 1 Corinthians 11:14. Whatever he means in that verse, it's clear he thinks something "carves the world at its joints." There is something intrinsic to nature that explains why certain things are the way that they are. There is a sort of "blueprint" that gives directions for how things exist and what their proper function is. Paul wouldn't allow us to simply reject his argument by saying, "Well, that's just metaphysics. I don't need any of that stuff. I just need my Bible."

But some might remain anxious, confidently claiming: "We must stay close to the text of Holy Scripture! I don't see the Bible speaking of nominalism, essentialism, natures, or anything else! Metaphysics is just blind speculation beyond Scripture." Certainly, this is a pious intuition. We should be partial to using the language of Scripture itself. But the anxiety is misplaced. First, the Bible isn't afraid to use some of these metaphysical terms. It does so without embarrassment. Talk of "kinds" and "nature" is relatively common. If the previous examples weren't enough, consider Paul in Romans 1:20, where he speaks of God's "attributes" and "nature," or Peter in 2 Peter 1:4, who also mentions "nature."

But even if we couldn't find all these philosophical words, it's not the words themselves that matter as much as the ideas they communicate. For example, there are nonbiblical words used in the ecumenical creeds to safeguard orthodox thinking about God. They aren't all *biblical* words in the sense that they can be found explicitly in the Bible, but they describe *biblical* ideas. Just like how we can't find the word *Trinity* in the Bible despite its biblical meaning, these words won't always be literally in our Bibles. That's okay. We need extrabiblical words to communicate what is in the Bible. This shouldn't scare us. The fathers of the early church certainly thought words like *homoousios* safeguarded and extrapolated biblical ideas. It was the biblical terminology of Christ as word, wisdom, and image that fundamentally motivated their dogmatic claims.[5] This is why when we come to the discussion of the classical attributes, we shouldn't fear their metaphysical tenor.

BUT METAPHYSICS ISN'T FOR THE CHURCH!

Another common objection to "metaphysics" talk is that it is utterly impractical. Maybe the words or the concepts are in the Bible, but we really don't *need* metaphysics. The church can do just fine without it. I don't speak of metaphysics when I share my faith or when I sing a song on Sunday. But, I suggest, when Christians reject the need for metaphysics, they are doing so while assuming the importance of metaphysics. As the saying goes, they are cutting off the branch they are standing on. While having an awareness of metaphysics and all its technical aspects isn't necessary for Christian faith, it both undergirds it and is necessary for advancing in knowledge of God. For example, while the highly technical workings of the medical profession may appear unnecessarily technical to the untrained eye, it is critical for the advance of medicine. And it is lifesaving. Similarly, while metaphysics may require attentive discipline and a highly refined vocabulary, it pays a lifetime of dividends. The wisdom won through deep thinking is part of the rhythm of sanctification.[6] The very center of our eternal life in the new heavens and new earth is *seeing* God, which entails knowing him in all his beauty and richness, exploring and reveling in the breadth and length and height and depth of his love that surpasses knowledge (Rev 22:4–5; Eph 3:18).

This is why Francisco Suárez argued that metaphysics especially serves sacred theology: because "it most nearly approaches cognition of divine things, and also because it explains and confirms those natural principles which embrace all things, and in a certain way support and sustain every doctrine." He continues, explaining how "those higher mysteries can scarcely be dealt with in a worthy fashion (or not even

---

5. Khaled Anatolios, *Retrieving Nicaea* (Baker Academic, 2018), 283; Jordan L. Steffaniak, "3 Terms about the Trinity You Should Know & How We Got Them," Word by Word, April 2023, https://www.logos.com/grow/hall-three-trinitarian-words/.

6. Michael Allen, *The Fear of the Lord* (T&T Clark, 2022), 136–37.

scarcely)" without metaphysics.[7] So, Suárez defends the necessity of metaphysics in two ways. First, it is the closest subject of study to sacred theology. In it we draw nearer to God than any subject besides sacred theology itself. Second, and most important, it explains and confirms natural principles that support and sustain doctrine. Without metaphysics doctrine is scarcely possible!

But maybe the worry is more about sophisticated metaphysics. The people of God have gotten along just fine with "basic" metaphysics without any need for the technical distinctions we find developed later in theology, such as the scholastics. And there are plenty of useful theologians throughout the history of the church that have underdeveloped metaphysics. While it is true that we don't need a sophisticated metaphysic of every jot and tittle to be a faithful Christian or to be a useful theologian, it remains a special divine aid to knowing and understanding God and our world. And the reality is, most theologians in the history of the church *have* developed sophisticated metaphysical structures to defend sound Christian doctrine and to elevate our worship of the Triune God.

METAPHYSICS IN HISTORICAL PERSPECTIVE

Now, given the common insistence on classical metaphysics by those committed to classical catholic doctrine, it is wise to understand what is meant by "classical" in a historical sense prior to examining the actual content of the metaphysics. If we assume that classical theism must be joined at the hip to classical metaphysics, we will limit classical theism if we limit classical metaphysics. In the same way, by understanding classical metaphysics, we will be inspired to better understand the various explanations, judgments, and distinctions made regarding classical theism.

Traditionally, classical terminology refers to a wide range of subjects, but when discussing metaphysics, it usually refers to the consensus views prior to the Enlightenment. Now, classical metaphysics doesn't disappear during this period, but it does undergo reexamination, revision, and often rejection. To best understand what these consensus views are, it's necessary to clear some ground and explain what it isn't first.

---

7. Francisco Suárez, *Metaphysical Disputations I*, trans. Shane Duarte (Catholic University of America Press, 2021), 11.

WHAT CLASSICAL METAPHYSICS ISN'T

In decades past *classical* could often be equated with lifeless orthodoxy. Thankfully this narrative has largely been put to death. But now, in some popular Western theological literature, a sort of new "decline" narrative is painted, following the same trajectory as those who waxed of dead orthodoxy: whatever is modern is not classical and vice versa. The only difference is that these new authors want us to return to the past instead of forgetting it. Now the old classical ideas we need to recover are sometimes equated with an anti-modern Christianized Platonism.[8] Such simplistic accounts of classical metaphysics abound.[9] But the current trend to create a simple binary between modern and classical, as well as the universal valorizing of Platonism, does not properly define classical metaphysics for several reasons. While no one should suggest the modern era is one of pure growth, neither should they posit a narrative of pure decline.[10]

First, it is important to distinguish between "modern" and "classical" in the historical sense (as referring to thought in a period of time) and in the ideological sense (as referring to a set of commitments associated with a period but which can be present in any historical period).[11] A conflation of these two senses can lead to simple binaries between classical (or premodern, scholastic, etc.) and modern that lean on poor accounts of history and the development of ideas. For example, one might attempt to examine the historical record to understand what is meant by classical metaphysics in an ideological sense. Read whatever the great premodern fathers or medieval scholastics thought, and dub that as "classical." But a purely historical approach to understanding classical metaphysics is insufficient because historians of philosophy rarely date "modern" with the advent of the Enlightenment. It can refer to pretty much *any* period

8. See, for example, Craig A. Carter, *Contemplating God with the Great Tradition* (Baker Academic, 2021); Matthew Barrett, *The Reformation as Renewal* (Zondervan, 2023), 226.

9. For two similar examples, though different in quite important respects, see John Milbank, *Theology and Social Theory: Beyond Secular Reason*, 2nd ed. (Blackwell, 2006); Barrett, *The Reformation as Renewal*. Milbank and Barrett both deal in relatively simple binaries, using watchwords like nominalism, voluntarism, and univocity. Whoever is the theological villain is bound to be infected with one of these "viruses," if not all three! However, Barrett is far more aware than Milbank of the variegated nature of theology. Unfortunately, he continues to paint with a broad brush throughout. See my forthcoming essay "Plundering the Moderns" for a more detailed engagement on this topic.

10. Simon J. G. Burton, *Ramism and the Reformation of Method* (Oxford University Press, 2024), 4–6.

11. Thanks to my friend Matt Ntiros for clarifying this distinction and its use for this section.

after the twelfth century, depending on the thinker.[12] As Roger Ariew has argued, "There is very little content to the concept of modernity except as a term of contrast with antiquity and the Middle Ages, and what is signified as 'modern' changes, depending upon the specific contrast one wishes to make."[13] Even if we wanted to pick an arbitrary date, we are doing so anachronistically. For example, the medieval themselves used the terms "modern," and they did it with the simple meaning of "current," without importing any ideology into the term.[14]

So, it is not as simple as suggesting we all travel back in time to a more pristine era of theology to find the classical metaphysics we need for classical theism where we can finally be free from the toxic sludge of modernity. We can't set our DeLorean to 400 BC, 400 AD, 1274 AD, or any other period to find the declaration of classical metaphysics. The rise of modern philosophy and the waning of medieval philosophy is a complex narrative of events that cannot be explained entirely by a set of new doctrines.[15] Therefore, just saying classical metaphysics is premodern metaphysics might narrow our scope some, but it fails to properly specify. Even if it did focus on one era, the premodern era also had numerous philosophical schools. And even today we are seeing a renaissance of Aristotelianism, making it even more curious to equate modern with the rejection of the classical. In other words, we shouldn't say that nothing outside of the classical period in the historical sense can be called classical in the ideological sense (hence anything from the modern period is anti-classical and wrong).

Second, the idea that classical metaphysics can be equated with any one school, such as "Christian Platonism," fails because Platonism doesn't have a stable and unified set of metaphysical beliefs. When the historical record is examined, one realizes that the commitments required of Platonism, whether of Plato himself or of those devoted as followers, are entirely too thick to define what is classical. While there is a significant

12. Robert Pasnau, *Metaphysical Themes: 1274–1671* (Clarendon, 2011), 1–2.

13. Roger Ariew, "Modernity," in *The Cambridge History of Medieval Philosophy*, ed. Robert Pasnau (Cambridge University Press, 2009), 114, https://doi.org/10.1017/CHOL9780521762168.

14. Trent Pomplun, "John Duns Scotus in the History of Medieval Philosophy from the Sixteenth Century to Étienne Gilson (†1978)," *Bulletin de Philosophie Médiévale* 58 (2016): 356–57.

15. Ariew, "Modernity," 118, 126.

amount of overlap between Platonism and Christianity, any attempt to describe Christianity as fundamentally Platonist is doomed to fail. Platonism simply isn't ubiquitous in the classical era *and* is often strongly rejected—many times on distinctively theological grounds.[16] For example, Athanasius is the great hero of the patristic era, and it's his insistence on standard Christian doctrines like creation out of nothing that revises to a great degree the Platonic tradition.[17] The Platonism of the patristic era is simply much too eclectic in its own philosophical commitments to be of much use as a stable term. It is a syncretistic synthesis. It happily departs from traditional Platonic understandings for its own purposes.[18] This isn't to say that there aren't clearly universal beliefs like the reality of the immaterial. However, it is to suggest that we cannot obtain a usefully worked-out definition of classical from this approach.

Instead, Christianity by premodern standards was seen as a rival philosophical school of its own. It wasn't parasitic on any Greek school but was generative and foundational in itself. Origen is indicative when he contrasts the wisdom of Plato and the philosophers, true as it may be, with the wisdom of the apostles. Plato and the philosophers have "nothing beyond human nature about them," whereas Christian philosophy was "given by God and convinced men by spirit and power."[19] This doesn't mean Christianity didn't borrow resources from other schools, but it did self-identify as its own philosophical school.

Third, anyone familiar with classical thinkers, ranging from the patristic to at least the medieval era, knows that while they may share a similar style and vocabulary, this can conceal enormous differences in beliefs.[20] It is not simply a matter of stacking quotes to determine which metaphysical system is truly "classical." For example, one cannot assume that because

16. Jordan L. Steffaniak, "Which Plato? Whose Platonism? Summarizing the Christian Platonism Symposium," The London Lyceum, September 2, 2022, https://www.thelondonlyceum.com/which-plato-whose-platonism-summarizing-the-christian-platonism-symposium/; Andrew Louth, *The Origins of the Christian Mystical Tradition from Plato to Denys* (Clarendon, 1981), xiv.

17. Louth, *The Origins of the Christian Mystical Tradition from Plato to Denys*, 78.

18. Salvatore Romano Clemente Lilla, *Clement of Alexandria: A Study in Christian Platonism and Gnosticism* (Oxford University Press, 1971), 54–55; Charles Bigg, *The Christian Platonists of Alexandria* (AMS, 1970), 5.

19. Origen, *Origen: Contra Celsum*, trans. Henry Chadwick (Cambridge University Press, 1980), III.68, https://doi.org/10.1017/CBO9780511555213.

20. Pasnau, *Metaphysical Themes*, 2.

Gregory of Nyssa is quoted more in a particular author or set of authors, even favorably, that Nyssa's "metaphysics" are supported by the author. It's far more complicated than that. What is required is a deep understanding of the primary sources and the various metaphysical systems throughout the ages. Instead, I fear that many theologians, when reading from ages past, lack careful historical acumen. They stack the deck in their favor. If their favorite historical author is quoted or cited in a neutral or favorable way, that is evidence whoever they are reading is consistent with them.

For example, in decades past much scholarship argued that Calvin was anti-scholastic because he oftentimes pejoratively speaks of the "scholastics." This, supposedly, must mean that Calvin rejected the medieval scholastic era of theology (like their metaphysics). Calvin, instead, was a biblical theologian in contrast to the abstract medieval. But on closer inspection, such a thin read of Calvin is far too simple. These readers of Calvin assumed that he was referring truly to the *entire* medieval period when he said "scholastic" pejoratively. But in Calvin's native tongue, his French edition, he uses different terminology for them and clearly differentiates between a sort of school theology that is preoccupied with vain subtleties and the general scholastic method. So, Calvin isn't anti-scholastic but anti-school theology in a truly negative sense, meaning theology that is obsessed with theological quibbles and totally divorced from the life of the church. The confusion was due to translation and lack of attentiveness to his entire corpus.[21]

But the temptation here is to overcorrect. Because of the obvious paradigm shift, scholars then begin to see not only is Calvin not fundamentally critical of scholasticism, but he must be a scholastic himself since he utilizes scholastic and Aristotelian categories. The idea is that since Calvin uses these categories, this makes him scholastic (or insert your favorite medieval here—Thomas, Bonaventure, whomever). But this doesn't follow. There must be a far deeper understanding of how sources are used and how ideas are used. Calvin is more akin to the humanist tradition than he is the scholastic. But truly, Calvin isn't anti-scholastic, he's just an eclectic Reformer, helping himself to categories as he sees fit. We sometimes can

21. Richard A. Muller, *After Calvin: Studies in the Development of a Theological Tradition* (Oxford University Press, 2003), 29–30.

be too quick to force thinkers of ages past into our favorite paradigms. But rarely is history this neat or tidy—in part because each of us is finite and holds inconsistencies and ignorance.

It should be added to this third point that it's not uncommon for an author to attribute views to thinkers that the thinkers themselves don't actually hold. It can be done for several reasons. Sometimes there is a common, though false, attribution to someone that is merely assumed. Sometimes there is no opportunity to read the original primary source. Other times it's just difficult to understand what a thinker means. Duns Scotus is notorious for having false views attributed to him as "Scotist." He is accused of voluntarism, univocity about God's being, and all manner of villainous theology.[22] But these accusations are typically inaccurate and based on hearsay or a lack of patient and attentive reading of the primary sources that allows them to speak on their own terms. So, even when reading apparent "consensus" opinions, we must always remember that no one is an infallible interpreter. The reality is that the history of theology and philosophy is often a troubled game of telephone, where mistakes are passed down the line without awareness of the primary sources.

Fourth, some have assumed a simple binary between modern and classical is sufficient to explain "classical" metaphysics because of a thin understanding of its connection to the terms *via moderna* and *via antiqua*. The idea seems to be that these conceptual terms map back onto this old debate in a one-to-one fashion. Therefore, whoever is classified with the *via moderna* is "bad," unorthodox, and non-classical, and whoever is of the *via antiqua* is good, orthodox, and classical. But there are several problems here that must be developed lest our understanding of classical theism be misshapen by incorrectly rejecting the voices of many members of the classical tradition from the start.

It is anachronistic to equate these labels. The terms *via moderna* and *via antiqua* had little significance beyond temporal designations (modern meaning "contemporary," etc.). This is the standard way the medievals themselves used the terms, without any ideology implied.[23] This did

22. See for example: Barrett, *The Reformation as Renewal*, 9–11, 15, 205, 228–50.

23. Pomplun, "John Duns Scotus in the History of Medieval Philosophy from the Sixteenth Century to Étienne Gilson (†1978)," 356–57.

change in the fifteenth century when they took on polemical tribal badges.[24] Only at this point does the *via moderna* became identified with the "nominalist way."[25] Therefore, anachronistically inserting these terms onto earlier figures without careful historiographical retelling is irresponsible.

These terms are also far narrower than supposed. They reflect a very specific older debate about the true doctrine of Aristotle and not the wide-ranging metaphysic that is supposed to be captured by the term *classical.* With the growth of the German Empire, the *via moderna* became the theological and philosophical villain of the day. These nasty nominalists attributed definitions to terms and not things and thus denied, principally, the "correct" interpretation of Aristotle that was found in the *via antiqua* of Thomas, Scotus, and Albert the Great.[26] Therefore, the main battleground centered on the method used to interpret Aristotle, the resultant interpretation, and the authorities one relied on. If you relied on newer sources and denied the older ways of understanding Aristotle, then you were of the *via moderna.* If one hopes to equate premodern with *via antiqua* one will find a term that is too narrow to define what is classical. Nominalism in the fifteenth century just isn't a thesis about whether order exists in the universe, whether moral norms exist, and the like. It is limited in scope.

The narrowness mentioned here leads to another problem. In 1474 the French King Louis XI banished the so-called nominalists and rendered the "proper" authorities to be those like Averroes, Albert the Great, Thomas, Bonaventure, and Scotus.[27] If the simple binary is supposed to render those like Scotus as villain and Thomas as the great hero, then the history tells a different story. While it's true that Thomas is a hero, others like Scotus, rather than being villains, are part of the cast of theological

---

24. Heiko A. Oberman, "Via Antiqua and Via Moderna: Late Medieval Prolegomena to Early Reformation Thought," *Journal of the History of Ideas* 48, no. 1 (1987): 24.

25. Claude Panaccio, *Mental Language: From Plato to William of Ockham*, trans. Joshua P. Hochschild and Meredith K. Ziebart (Fordham University Press, 2017), 179.

26. Maarten J. F. M. Hoenen, "Via Antiqua and Via Moderna in the Fifteenth Century: Doctrinal, Institutional, and Church Political Factors in the Wegestreit," in *The Medieval Heritage in Early Modern Metaphysics and Moral Theory, 1400–1700*, ed. Lauge O. Nielsen and Russell L. Friedman (Kluwer Academic, 2003), 12–13; Pekka Kärkkäinen, "Nominalism and the Via Moderna" (Oxford University Press, 2017), https://doi.org/10.1093/acref/9780190461843.013.266.

27. Theodor Dieter, "Luther as Late Medieval Theologian: His Positive and Negative Use of Nominalism and Realism," in *The Oxford Handbook of Martin Luther's Theology*, ed. Robert Kolb (Oxford University Press, 2014), 32, https://doi.org/10.1093/oxfordhb/9780199604708.013.002.

masters and heroes in the *via antiqua.* We cannot assume that whatever Scotus thinks is modern or non-classical whereas whatever Thomas says is premodern and classical. For example, to claim that Scotus is a nominalist, denies participation, or affirms a univocity of being is simply to either misread Scotus or rely on faulty secondary sources.[28] But Bonaventure, too, differs markedly from authorities like Thomas on any number of doctrines and is yet the *via antiqua.* While it is tempting to draw neat boundaries around our favorite and least favorite theologians, history is messy. And hence the boundaries of "classical" theism are likewise messy.

WHAT CLASSICAL METAPHYSICS IS

What then is "classical" metaphysics? Is there any unifying set of beliefs? Admittedly "classical" is a wax nose. Yet there are some ideas that are common to the classical era, however one dates it, that should give us a sense for what might be true of classical metaphysics in an ideological sense. Prior to the Enlightenment there was a wide consensus commitment to a substance-based ontology.[29] Substance, in this sense, refers to things that bear properties, underly change, persist through time, and have a nature and principle of unity.[30] These are things like people, lions, tigers, bears, etc., and not heaps of sand. After later centuries, especially beginning in the seventeenth and eighteenth, a proliferation of different ontologies that either reject or ignore substance becomes commonplace. They begin to propose various other accounts of substance: world-sized, microscopic, scattered, or none at all. Robert Pasnau cheekily admits, "For those who delight in train wrecks, such chaos can serve only to enliven the subject."[31] Even today, the prevailing opinion among scientists, biologists, and some philosophers is fundamentally Humean in character. Substances as those things that stand under and possess accidents but that are distinct from them are fictions. We may talk of substances (in this thick sense), natures, and essences, but they don't really exist. All that exists is the particles themselves arranged in different ways.

---

28. Thomas M. Ward, *Ordered by Love: An Introduction to John Duns Scotus* (Angelico, 2022), 33–38.

29. Pasnau, *Metaphysical Themes*, 6–7.

30. Marmodoro and Mayr, *Metaphysics*, 25.

31. Pasnau, *Metaphysical Themes*, 633.

Teleology, if it exists, is not grounded in natures. To deny such beliefs would require, as biologist Dan McShea argues, "a metaphysic that is unacceptable in modern science."[32]

For classical thinkers, however, substances exist and are the most fundamental realities. This approach to metaphysics has seen a great revival over the last decade and often goes by the terminology of neo-Aristotelianism today.[33] But Aristotle was not the only classical figure in the premodern world. While I prefer neo-Aristotelianism as a metaphysical scheme myself, it's unfair to fit the tradition within its narrower bounds. For example, Platonic philosophy also prioritizes substances and natures. Therefore, it is better to speak of the classical tradition as a substance-based metaphysical scheme, clunky as the terminology may be.

But we should be more specific than merely mentioning substances as being important to classical metaphysics. Robert Pasnau in his magisterial work on metaphysics during the medieval era expands on four themes that are shared because of the commitment to substance-based metaphysics:

- We have knowledge of substances and the kinds into which they fall.
- Our ordinary kind-distinctions carve things up according to their true essences.
- Ordinary substances (dogs, trees, stones) are real entities.
- Substances naturally and ordinarily come and go, in and out of existence.[34]

These commitments likely look like common sense to most. Trees exist. They are real entities. They have a kind into which they fall. Therefore, a tree obviously isn't in the same "kind" as a beaver. It's right to carve the world up with the distinction between a tree and a table. Their natures

---

32. Daniel W. McShea, "Evolutionary Trends and Goal Directedness," *Synthese* 201, no. 5 (2023): 178, https://doi.org/10.1007/s11229-023-04164-9.

33. For a contemporary defense of substance-based metaphysics, see Ross D. Inman, *Substance and the Fundamentality of the Familiar: A Neo-Aristotelian Mereology* (Routledge, 2018).

34. Pasnau, *Metaphysical Themes*, 633.

determine what kind of thing they are and what their purpose is.[35] When a tree is cut down and made into a table, it is no longer a tree and goes out of existence. But while these may be common sense, they are often rejected in contemporary thought. And rejecting these fundamental assumptions is one of the reasons classical theism is often rejected by contemporary thinkers since it generally assumes these standard accounts of reality.

It should be noted that such classical metaphysical beliefs are supposed to be held by most everyone, whether Platonic, Aristotelian, Stoic, or otherwise. Christianity fits here as well, with its own metaphysical tradition. While Christianity critiques and rejects areas of Platonism, Aristotelianism, Stoicism, and the like, it also depends on and shares certain elements like natural kinds and substances.[36] In this way, the older polemical terms of the *via moderna* and *via antiqua* might be of some use, with the *via antiqua* being more committed to a substance-based metaphysic, and willing to admit of nominalism in certain areas, so long as it doesn't deny ordinary kind distinctions.

I should note that Lloyd Gerson has recently offered a somewhat similar attempt at categorizing the commonalities, or fault lines, throughout the classical era. He argues there are five main areas of agreement, what he calls "Ur-Platonism." These are shared commitments of anti-materialism, anti-mechanism, anti-nominalism, anti-relativism, and anti-skepticism. Gerson elsewhere summarizes these five tenets "as fundamental antinaturalism, that is, the philosophical position according to which naturalistic or bottom-up explanations for all problematic phenomena are in principle insufficient."[37] I think the general idea from Gerson is right and consistent with how others like Pasnau explain the medieval era. However, the terminology of Platonism is confusing because Platonism usually refers to Platonic doctrines—some of which would be modified and rejected by Aristotle. More important, beside my concerns about the terminology, his explanation of the unifying themes is more negative in scope, less clearly focusing on the

---

35. William M. R. Simpson, "From Quantum Physics to Classical Metaphysics," in *Neo-Aristotelian Metaphysics and the Theology of Nature*, ed. William M. R. Simpson, Robert C. Koons, and James Orr (Routledge, 2021), 21.

36. Johannes Zachhuber, *The Rise of Christian Theology and the End of Ancient Metaphysics: Patristic Philosophy from the Cappadocian Fathers to John of Damascus* (Oxford University Press, 2022), 2.

37. Lloyd P. Gerson, *From Plato to Platonism* (Cornell University Press, 2017), 16.

agreement on substance. While his five tenets are generally true, they lack the robust explanatory power that comes with the explicit focus on substance-based metaphysics. Therefore, I suggest we focus on classical metaphysics as a substance-based metaphysic. The ordinary, medium-sized objects we encounter in everyday life, like trees, people, and animals, are real entities with natures that determine their proper functioning. Substances are those natural objects that have an intrinsic principle by which they operate.[38] And it is a classical metaphysic, based on these beliefs, that is necessary for thinking responsibly about God. Apart from a substance-based metaphysic, a host of classical doctrines, including especially those found in classical theism, are left without a firm foundation.

CATEGORIES: SUBSTANCE AND ACCIDENT

One of Aristotle's most important works is the *Categories*. Whether one agrees with his thought or not (which might include later Aristotle himself!), this work plays a massive role in theological and philosophical development since it was one of his only works available from ancient times throughout the Middle Ages before the rediscovery of his metaphysics and other works.[39] Aristotle's basic framework throughout this short work is that there are two sorts of things: substances and accidents. Substances are those things that are subjects for everything else—in his own words, it "is that which is neither said of a subject nor in a subject."[40] Accidents are the characteristics said of or in a subject, like quantity (being five feet tall), qualification (being blue, being wise), where (in my house, at the baseball stadium), and when (yesterday, tomorrow), and the like. None of these can be said without substances. They depend on them for their existence.[41] He offers ten total so-called categories.

The important point here isn't what Aristotle means or how his view possibly changes from the *Categories* to the *Metaphysics*.[42] What we need

38. Edward Feser, *Scholastic Metaphysics: A Contemporary Introduction*, Editiones Scholasticae 39 (Heusenstamm: Scholasticae, 2014), 164–65.

39. Diogenes Allen and Eric O. Springsted, *Philosophy for Understanding Theology*, 2nd ed. (Westminster John Knox, 2007), 65.

40. Aristotle, *Categories and De Interpretatione*, trans. John L. Ackrill (Clarendon, 1994), 2a11, 2b29.

41. Aristotle, *Categories and De Interpretatione* 2a4.

42. For example, Aristotle notoriously makes substance talk more confusing when he introduces at least four possible ways to use the term. See Aristotle, *Metaphysics: Zeta, Eta, Theta, Iota; Books*

to understand is that Aristotle sets the agenda for our basic metaphysical framework and vocabulary. There are substances and accidents. Theologians, by and large, work with this same framework as they think about the structure of reality and God's relation to it. But take note that as frameworks, these lack significant metaphysical commitment. They are basic categories that can be deployed in various ways. As with all areas of philosophy and theology, there are several ways to skin the cat. There is no such thing as *the* theory of substance, accident, or any related term like *form* and *prime matter*. They are pliable catchwords that take on substantive meaning when developed further.[43] This is especially important for when we start to examine the classical attributes, wherein many classical thinkers go to great lengths to deny accidents of God. What exactly are these accidents?

Accidents inhere in or depend on substances (or, at least, accident-instances depend on substances for some Platonists). This is a fairly standard way of defining accidents. But the devil is in the details. Traditionally accidents are understood in a "deflationary" sense, as "modes" of a substance. That's a technical way of saying that there isn't any existing thing over and above the substance that explains the accident. That is how thinkers like Thomas understand them.[44] But some, like Duns Scotus, as a deeply committed realist, argue that accidents are real, over and above the substance.[45] Such metaphysical commitments impact theology in differing ways. But there are further distinctions that are made regarding accidents that can color one's theological commitments, like contingent accidents and proper accidents. Proper accidents are those that "flow" from a thing's nature. They are natural to a particular nature, though their exercise can be frustrated. Think of things like humor or free will. In most ordinary circumstances we can exhibit these as human persons, but they aren't necessarily exhibited in every

---

VII–X, trans. Montgomery Furth (Hackett, 1985), 28b33.

43. Pasnau, *Metaphysical Themes*, 179.

44. See: Jeffrey E. Brower, "Aquinas on the Problem of Universals," *Philosophy and Phenomenological Research* 92, no. 3 (2016): 715–35, https://doi.org/10.1111/phpr.12176; Jeffrey E. Brower, *Aquinas's Ontology of the Material World: Change, Hylomorphism, and Material Objects* (Oxford University Press, 2014), 22; Cross, "An Accidental Reformation?," 8.

45. Pasnau, *Metaphysical Themes*, 181–83.

scenario. What makes proper accidents special is that they depend on our nature in a unique way. Contrast this to contingent accidents, like the color of our skin being light or dark or the color of our car being blue or green. These do not depend on our nature as such.[46]

Substances, on the other hand, are those objects that exist *per se*. They have a unity that mere aggregates lack. A heap of sand, shaped into a sandcastle by my five-year-old at the beach, isn't a substance because it doesn't have the right sort of unity. Therefore, it's an aggregate. Its existence is composed of parts that have their own natures and exist independently of the whole. The grains of sand all retain their identity while being composed as a sandcastle. However, each part, in a substance, depends on the substances for its nature and existence.[47] Hearts do not exist on their own apart from animal bodies. Therefore, for substances, wholes exist over and above their parts.[48]

So, substances are numerically one and can receive "contraries" as they persist over time.[49] They can be pink-skinned one day and then red-skinned the day after a sunburn and yet be the same object. They aren't metaphysically *grounded* in other particulars. They are the ultimate subjects of properties and survive through change.[50] Of course, the kind of changes a substance can undergo without ceasing to be are fixed by its form or essence/nature. It should be clear that this independence for substances isn't a radical absolute independence that only God has, lest there only be one substance.[51] Those objects that are substances are living things and natural inanimate objects (molecules, trees, mountains, planets, etc.).[52] God, however, is typically not thought to be a substance since he is not the subject of accidents for most thinkers prior to the Enlightenment.[53] Therefore, God is properly *being* but improperly *substance*.[54]

46. Feser, *Scholastic Metaphysics*, 192.
47. Simpson, "From Quantum Physics to Classical Metaphysics," 26.
48. Inman, *Substance and the Fundamentality of the Familiar: A Neo-Aristotelian Mereology*, 83, 94.
49. Aristotle, *Categories and De Interpretatione* 4a10.
50. Koons and Pickavance, *Metaphysics*, 104.
51. Pasnau, *Metaphysical Themes*, 104.
52. Koons and Pickavance, *Metaphysics*, 104.
53. Pasnau, *Metaphysical Themes*, 108.
54. Augustine, *The Trinity*, trans. Edmund Hill (New City, 2015), VII.3.9.5, 10.

These distinctions between a substance and an accident are especially relevant for divine simplicity and immutability. Of course, they are relevant for impassibility and eternity as well. But they play a special role in making sense of the simple, unchanging God. Without this background it can be difficult to follow some of the arguments for each doctrine.

UNIVERSALS AND PARTICULARS

Whereas the discussion of substance and accident seeks to understand *what* sort of things there are, universals and particulars are meant to explain *how* things are the way they are. There are all sorts of particular things in the world: trees, persons, and baseballs. But there is a *way* each of these things exists. The tree is 70 feet tall. The person is comedic. The baseball is juiced. Properties are the ontological items (also called features, characteristics, or attributes) that each of these objects exemplifies.[55] The tallness, comedy, and juice are all properties that characterize the particular tree, person, and baseball. So, the way the person is, his being funny, is the property. Then there's the word we use to describe that quality—*comedic*—and the statement we use to express it—"Bob is comedic." When considering properties, we are thinking of *how the world is*, not merely *how we talk about the world*. Not every way we talk about the world necessitates a distinct property to be had by a thing. "Bob is comedic" might well require Bob to have a certain disposition to be humorous. But "Bob is a mammal" need not require a distinct property, mammality, to be true.[56]

For those committed to some form of a realist metaphysical framework, properties exist independent of beliefs, linguistic practices, conceptual schemes, and so on.[57] We do not invent or project these properties onto things but recognize and receive them.[58] In some sense these properties can wholly and completely be exhibited in several spatially discontinuous

55. Koons and Pickavance, *Metaphysics*, 76.

56. Bob's being a mammal might be made true by his being a human, not by something in addition to his being human. My thanks to Tim Pawl for this clarification.

57. Alexander Miller, "Realism," in *The Stanford Encyclopedia of Philosophy*, ed. Edward N. Zalta, Winter 2021 (Metaphysics Research Lab, Stanford University, 2021), https://plato.stanford.edu/archives/win2021/entries/realism/. This is realism about a specific subject: properties. It is not realism about ethics, existence, God, causation, mathematics, or science. While a metaphysical "realism" may include or entail realism about these other things, it's not always cut and dried.

58. Andrew Davison, *Participation in God* (Cambridge University Press, 2019), 1.

particulars at the same time—hence, their universal scope.[59] On this account I can be human and Jack can be human at the same time, though we are different objects. The "humanness" is universally exemplified by us both. It isn't a mere similarity. There is something that explains the resemblance beyond particulars alone—there is a unity of sorts. Likewise, I can be red, and Clifford the big red dog can be red at the same time, though we are different objects. The redness is universally exemplified by us both. But just what these properties are and how they are had is a matter of significant debate. What does it mean to say I am a *human* and Jack is *human*? Is there an actual, existing universal form of humanity existing somewhere that explains how we can both be human in some relevant sense, or is there nothing beside us as particulars, Jordan and Jack, that explains it? Or is there a more complicated story that might be told to account for resemblance without universals? Nominalists will say there is nothing beside the particulars. They deny unity for concepts and kinds altogether. There is *nothing* that can unify redness between Clifford and me or humanness in Jordan and Jack beside relations of resemblance.[60] There are only particulars. Moderate realists will typically deny universals as well. Thomas, for example, thought things are the same kind by virtue of possessing distinct (hence, particular and not universal) but resembling natures.[61] My humanness and Fred's humanness are not identical, although, they are exact *duplicates* with the particularity coming from external facts. Like tropes, they differ solely in virtue of being related to distinct bare particulars.[62] Here lies the debate over universals and particulars.

Those committed to a more Platonic view of the world are likely to think there is a real existing universal in the world that particular objects somehow instantiate when they share the property of "redness" or "human." When I am red and Clifford is red, we both somehow share in the universal property of redness. The universal is either multiply located wherever we both are simultaneously or not located anywhere at all. Those committed to a more Aristotelian view of the world are likely

---

59. Loux and Crisp, *Metaphysics*, 19.

60. Ward, *Ordered by Love: An Introduction to John Duns Scotus*, 63.

61. Brower, "Aquinas on the Problem of Universals," 723.

62. Brower, "Aquinas on the Problem of Universals," 729.

to think "universal" properties exist in the particulars themselves and not some externally existing, free-floating universal. So, Aristotelians agree that there are universals, or at least there are things that have resemblance characteristics that amount to what we would often call universals, but locate them in particulars rather than in a Platonic realm. Such a dichotomy is oversimplifying the matter but should help to explain the debate from a pedagogical perspective. In the history of theology and philosophy these various ways of thinking about universals are refined and given special theological character, such as moving Plato's forms to the divine mind.

But regardless of which view one finds as more likely, there is a further important distinction of properties we should know: *intrinsic* and *extrinsic*. Intrinsic properties are those an object has independently from everything else, whereas extrinsic are those dependent on things external to itself.[63] In other words, an intrinsic property is a property that is true in virtue of the way we are, and an extrinsic property is true in virtue of the way we interact with the world. So, extrinsic properties would be those like being an uncle, being in debt, being ten miles from London, and so on. Intrinsic properties are those like internal structure, charge, or shape.[64] One could be a more realistic Platonist about universals or even an anti-realist and still find this distinction valuable.

Relatedly, and important for this discussion, there is also a distinction between an intrinsic and an extrinsic *predicate*. An intrinsic predicate is a predicate a thing satisfies—a predicate truly applicable of the thing—in virtue of intrinsic features it has and not necessarily intrinsic *properties* it has. Your soul is not itself a property, but "you are ensouled" is an intrinsic predication about you. An extrinsic predicate, by contrast, is a predicate you satisfy *not* purely in virtue of intrinsic features you have. "Uncle" is an extrinsic predicate; you satisfy that predicate if you are a male whose sibling (or whose spouse's sibling) has a child. Notice that "uncle" requires some intrinsic features on your part—it requires that the person be male. But it also requires something extrinsic, and so the predicate counts as an extrinsic predicate. This distinction between intrinsic and extrinsic

63. Ross P. Cameron, "Intrinsic and Extrinsic Properties," in *The Routledge Companion to Metaphysics*, ed. Robin Le Poidevin et al. (Routledge, 2009), 265.

64. David Lewis, "Extrinsic Properties," *Philosophical Studies* 44, no. 2 (1983): 197.

properties and predicates will play an important role in understanding the nature of change and divine immutability in chapter 7.[65]

MEREOLOGY: PARTS AND WHOLES

Mereology is the study of parts and wholes. Most intuitively grasp this. I am a whole made up of parts. I have parts such as arms, legs, and lungs, yet I am a single whole. But mereology can be about anything—parts of weeks, numbers, structural universals, and so on. For example, a star is composed of the parts hydrogen and helium; a house has a roof, wall, and foundation that are all parts; parts of wood compose my desk; computer parts compose my laptop; and embarrassingly, Sour Patch Kids compose me (at least as I write this sentence tonight). These are all material examples, but parts and wholes can relate to immaterial objects as well. When thinking about the nature of parts and wholes, there are several questions that arise naturally. Much is made of Peter van Inwagen's "special composition question": When is it true that the *x*'s compose *y*?[66] Important as the composition question is, it is not entirely relevant for our discussion of the divine attributes. However, what is crucially important, especially for divine simplicity, is *what is a part*?

"Part" for metaphysicians amounts to any item that composes a whole or any item that is a product of being divided from a whole.[67] In this sense, part is used loosely from our common colloquial sense. Parts are not just physical aspects of wholes. There are logical parts, metaphysical parts (e.g., prime matter, accidental forms, and substantial forms), temporal parts, spatial parts, and so on.[68] So, if something has any of these parts, they are considered metaphysically "complex." Most contemporary metaphysicians also distinguish between proper and improper parts. Proper parts are the parts mentioned so far—physical parts, temporal parts, and so on. Improper parts are the things themselves.[69]

65. My thanks to Tim Pawl for this helpful clarification.

66. Peter van Inwagen, *Material Beings* (Cornell University Press, 1995), 30.

67. Andrew Arlig, "Medieval Mereology," ed. Edward N. Zalta and Uri Nodelman, *The Stanford Encyclopedia of Philosophy* (Fall 2023), https://plato.stanford.edu/archives/fall2023/entries/mereology-medieval/.

68. Pasnau, *Metaphysical Themes*, 607.

69. Effingham, *Introduction to Ontology*, 152.

DISTINCTIONS AND RELATIONS

There is a further metaphysical category that deserves attention, especially for theological work on the doctrine of God and the nature of divine simplicity: the categories of distinction and relation. These terms are deployed throughout the theological literature. Nearly everyone in the medieval and early modern scholastic era dedicated significant focus to the topic of relations.[70] And they deploy these terms assuming readers have the prior training and education to properly understand what they mean and the various ways they can be understood. For example, Francis Turretin says, "The relative attributes do not argue composition, but distinction. The formal nature of relations is not to be in, but to be to."[71] Here, a theologian is deploying an account of relations, and is explaining it, but only in a brief sentence. Most contemporary theologians and pastors do not have the background training to understand how Turretin will go on to use the term. Therefore, it is of great importance to carefully explain this concept.

THE METAPHYSICS OF DISTINCTIONS

The nature of distinctions is vital for understanding many of the complicated debates about the doctrine of God. If you read widely, you will find a wide array of views on God's attributes, the Trinity, and his relation to the world all invoking certain sorts of distinctions. Therefore, a taxonomy of these distinctions is beneficial for those seeking to understand the theological rationale of the classical tradition. But it should be made clear that distinctions *on their own* have "nothing to do with the question whether a real relation or only a mental relation accompanies a real distinction." Relations will, therefore, be considered separately. Distinctions, by themselves, are "concerned solely with the foundation on which such relationship may be based."[72] While some thinkers posit more degrees of

---

70. Sydney Penner, "Suárez on the Reduction of Categorical Relations," *Philosophers' Imprint* 13, no. 2 (2013): 1.

71. Francis Turretin, *Institutes of Elenctic Theology*, ed. James T. Dennison, trans. George Musgrave Giger (P&R, 1994), 3.7.15.

72. Francisco Suárez, *On the Various Kinds of Distinctions*, trans. Cyril Vollert (Marquette University Press, 2007), 17.

distinctions whereas others have fewer, it is standard to minimally accept a "real" distinction and a "mental," "logical," or "rational" distinction.

But the reader should be warned that while I attempt to provide a standard explanation of each distinction, there is far from uniform usage. What Thomists, Scotists, nominalists, and other medieval groups mean when they use some of these terms—*virtual, modal, formal, virtual,* and so on—is by no means isomorphic. And the picture is further complicated by the reception and employment of the Protestant Scholastics. Difficulties aside, it is hard to convey the importance of understanding these terms and concepts for classical theism (and alternative models of God), especially those that seek to be conversant with the older theological literature and not just developed in a complete vacuum. These distinctions will play a crucial role in distinguishing various senses of divine simplicity.

Real distinctions are the most natural distinctions to be made. These are typically between one thing and another thing. But for some, like Scotus, there is more nuance to be had. Either way, real distinctions reflect differences in extramental reality.[73] In other words, they carve nature at its joints. I am really distinct from the computer that I use to type this sentence. The distinction is independent from any process of mental abstraction. This distinction would remain if all minds ceased existing. Yes, this is far-fetched, since God can't stop existing. But we can reason from counterpossibles to make the point. A real distinction between this rock and that rabbit remains when all the minds go away.[74] But the distinction between, say, "human" and "rational animal" no longer remains, since that's a distinction mentally drawn. So, you are really distinct from this book as you read it. The apple is distinct from the tree despite hanging on it. These can be known when the concepts are separable in nature.[75] It's quite obvious that while I type on my computer, I'm not composed of it and thus can easily be separated.

Mental distinctions are those that require the reflection and activity of the intellect. There are generally two kinds of mental distinctions. There are purely logical distinctions, which have no foundation in reality. They

73. Suárez, *On the Various Kinds of Distinctions*, 16; Feser, *Scholastic Metaphysics*, 72; Pasnau, *Metaphysical Themes*, 241.

74. Thanks to Tim Pawl for helping me to clarify this properly.

75. Suárez, *On the Various Kinds of Distinctions*, 40; Penner, "Suárez on the Reduction of Categorical Relations," 10.

are purely mental and are often called in the scholastic literature a distinction of *reasoning reason* because they arise "exclusively from the reflection and activity of the intellect."[76] For example, the distinction between a human being and rational animal is purely mental because there is no distinction in reality between them. The *only* difference resides in our concepts.[77]

Beyond the real and mental distinction is much debate as to what kinds of distinctions might be between these two poles of separability and inseparability.[78] It is fairly common, especially among Thomist-inclined thinkers, to describe a further distinction called "virtual," which is a type of mental distinction that has a foundation in reality.[79] In this sense, it has an aspect that is extramental.[80] Therefore, it is not merely our intellectual concepts that create this distinction. There is a *single real* "truthmaker," prior to the work of the intellect, that explains the various differing concepts. These are often called *reasoned reason* in the scholastic literature. The intellect recognizes but doesn't constitute these distinctions. For example, consider the distinction between rationality and animality. These concepts have real foundations since they can exist separately. There are animals that lack rationality, and there are beings such as angels that have rationality yet lack animality. Similarly, the body and soul of a person are virtually or eminently distinguished from the nature of the thing.[81] Therefore, the distinction we conceive of with our intellect, which is the only way we come to understand the distinction, has a ground or foundation in reality, but it is an absolutely single ground.[82] Garrett Walden has formalized a definition of the virtual distinction that proves useful:

> A virtual distinction is a kind of mental distinction wherein two concepts identify the same *res*, but where that *res* relates to those two concepts distinctly, such as concepts X and Y identify the same

76. Suárez, *On the Various Kinds of Distinctions*, 18.

77. Pasnau, *Metaphysical Themes*, 147.

78. Richard Cross, *Christology and Metaphysics in the Seventeenth Century* (Oxford University Press, 2022), 65.

79. The virtual distinction is also called the eminent distinction at points. These terms are supposed to be interchangeable.

80. Feser, *Scholastic Metaphysics*, 72–73.

81. Martinus Becanus, "Summa Theologiae Scolasticae," trans. Michael Lynch (Lyon, 1620), I.1.9, https://michaellynch.substack.com/p/martin-becanus-on-divine-simplicity.

82. Suárez, *On the Various Kinds of Distinctions*, 18; Feser, *Scholastic Metaphysics*, 73.

> *res* Z, but X identifies Z with respect to A, and Y identifies Z with respect to B, and A and B are not identical.[83]

For those with Scotist inclinations, there is also the hotly contested formal distinction. The formal distinction means that prior to any act of the intellect on our part there is an extramental ground or foundation for a distinction *in* the thing itself. As Scotus himself explains, the formal distinction "precedes every act of created and uncreated intellect."[84] Unlike the virtual distinction, then, the potential for the mind to conceptually make this distinction *really* belongs to the object.[85] For example, rationality and animality, or body and soul, are *not* identical in individual humans on the formal distinction, though they are inseparable from them. There is, therefore, on the formal distinction *two* distinct truthmakers for rationality and animality and not just *one*, as on the virtual distinction.[86] Yet, like the virtual distinction, there is no real distinction that would amount to a different *thing* or *separability*.[87] However, many are critical of the formal distinction for various reasons. Those like Feser think the formal distinction either collapses into a real or mental distinction.[88] Suárez, similarly, is representative when he bemoans that "Scotus does not explain with sufficient clarity whether this distinction, which he himself calls formal, is actual in the real order or merely fundamental or virtual. Sometimes he refers to it as virtual, and so there are various interpretations among his followers."[89]

---

83. Garrett M. Walden, "Revisiting John Gill's Doctrine of Eternal Justification," *International Journal of Systematic Theology* 26, no. 2 (2023): 176–96, https://doi.org/10.1111/ijst.12668.

84. John Duns Scotus, "Ordinatio," trans. Peter L. P. Simpson (n.d.), I, d. 2, pars 2, q4, n. 389, https://www.aristotelophile.com/Books/Translations/Ordinatio%20I.pdf.

85. Mary B. Ingham and Mechthild Dreyer, *The Philosophical Vision of John Duns Scotus: An Introduction* (Catholic University of America Press, 2004), 35.

86. Cross, *Christology and Metaphysics in the Seventeenth Century*, 66–67.

87. Scotus, "Ordinatio," I, d. 2, pars 2, q4, n. 400; Thomas H. McCall, "Trinity Doctrine, Plain and Simple," in *Advancing Trinitarian Theology: Explorations in Constructive Dogmatics*, ed. Oliver Crisp and Fred Sanders (Zondervan, 2014), 52.

88. Feser, *Scholastic Metaphysics*, 76.

89. Suárez, *On the Various Kinds of Distinctions*, 24.

THE METAPHYSICS OF RELATIONS

The concept of relations is critical for classical theology because of the oft-repeated charge that on classical theism God has no "real relation" to creation. Therefore, metaphysical background on the meaning of relations is useful. However, relations are notoriously difficult and complicated. Any attempt to summarize the entire metaphysical landscape of relations for non-philosophers is a fool's errand. So, I intend to only focus on the general concept of relation and then on what constitutes a "real" relation.

Most basically a relation is the ontological ground for a relational truth between two things (what you'll see called by their Latin term, *relata*) For example, consider the relation of creation that holds between God as creator of Michael Jordan. If only one of them existed there would be no relation between them. But since both exist, and God is creator, there is a relation between the two: the "created" relation. Or consider the love relation between Abelard and Heloise or the unjust punishment relation between Major League Baseball and the cheating Astros. Each of these is a relation that grounds a *truth*. Distinctions are a species of relation. That is say, not all relations are distinctions, but all distinctions are relations. Thus, if *x* is distinct from *y*, then *x* stands in a certain relation to *y*—namely, that of being distinct from (or non-identical to) *y*.

Relations belong in the category of accidents. Accidents, for scholastic thinkers, further break down into real accidents and conceptual accidents. Real accidents are genuine, irreducible, and exist in their own right—even if they inhere in a substance. Therefore, separability from the substance is neither necessary nor sufficient for a real accident.[90] Real accidents are a distinct kind of thing (*res*) that are irreducible and exist just like substances, whereas conceptual accidents can be modes (a real item in the world but not a thing), a kind of structure (a feature of reality but not a thing over and above the thing itself), a purely conceptual or linguistic thing, or wholly eliminable.[91] It was during the fourteenth century that real accidents became the dogma of the day.[92]

90. Pasnau, *Metaphysical Themes*, 191.

91. Pasnau, *Metaphysical Themes*, 238.

92. Pasnau, *Metaphysical Themes*, 222, 252.

With the general concept of relation in view, I can better describe the classical notion of a "real" relation. This terminology is not only found in the medieval and Reformed era but throughout contemporary literature as well. But, despite being a term of art, most moderns simply don't have a careful understanding of it. If I asked most people what is meant when I say God does not have a real relation to creation, the reaction would likely be one of bewilderment because they would assume real relation meant something like "love, care, or relationship." But in the theological and philosophical tradition there is a *very specific* sense in which something is a "real relation."[93] For much of the classical tradition, a relation is real only if it satisfies the following conditions: "The relation R of *a* to *b* is *real* for *a* if and only if: 1) *a* is related by R to *b* 2) *a* and *b* are really distinct extra-mental things, 3) there is a real extra-mental foundation in *a* for R."[94]

The third condition is the important distinction to be made. It means that there is an *intrinsic* extra-mental foundation in *a* that grounds the relation's obtaining between *a* and *b*. Without such careful distinctions in hand when reading older theological and philosophical literature, one will be handcuffed in understanding what is going on behind the scenes in some of the arguments they make.

THE METAPHYSICS OF TIME

In Augustine's *Confessions* he spends book 11 exploring the difficult nature of time and eternity. When countering an objection to those who ask, "What was God doing before he made heaven and earth?" he recounts the cheeky reply: "He was busy preparing hells for people who inquire into profundities." Augustine finds such a response unhelpful given the depth of the question itself.[95] Nonetheless, many of us can resonate with such humor. We rarely think about the nature of time

93. It is due to this rather technical usage of the phrase that I often suggest avoiding the terminology of "no real relations" altogether. It serves to confuse and obfuscate more than clarify. The concept can be communicated without the specific terminology. In this I follow Thomist Michael Gorman. See Michael Gorman, *A Contemporary Introduction to Thomistic Metaphysics* (Catholic University of America Press, 2024), 204.

94. Mark Gerald Henninger, *Relations: Medieval Theories, 1250–1325* (Oxford University Press, 1989), 7.

95. Augustine, *Confessions*, trans. Henry Chadwick (Oxford University Press, 2008), XI.xii (14).

in our lives, but when we begin to consider it, we realize how difficult it is to understand and conceptualize. It's easy enough to describe the past, present, and future, but when we start asking more precise metaphysical questions, things can become quite fuzzy. And since God's relationship to time is of great importance for the classical tradition, it is necessary to give thought to what time *is* to understand how God relates or doesn't relate to it.

TWO THEORIES OF TIME

There are generally two broad accounts of the ontology of time in philosophy. The accounts split over whether the "flow" of time is a real feature of the world. So, when we think about how Nero watched the Roman world burn, we think of that as the *past*. When we think about reading this sentence, it is the *present*, though soon past. In each case, most of us assume naturally that time has passed as we've read on, or some time has passed since Nero fiddled along. If you've enjoyed reading this book so far, you might even think "time flies," which suggests time has moved since you began reading. But as is often the case in philosophy, the world might not be as clear-cut as we thought.

Those who think the passage of time is real and independent of our own conscious experience of it hold to a *dynamic* view of time. Since time does flow, not all events equally exist, for an event not located in the present may not exist. Dynamic theories of time have a variety of models to explain the passage of time, and all view the present as metaphysically special in some sense. It is not necessary to recount them all, but three common views should give a fair sense of the options. First, there is the intuitive *presentist* view, where only the present exists. The future and past do not exist. The past once did and the future eventually will, but only the present is "real." All events both come into existence (from the future) and go out of existence (into the past). Second is the *moving spotlight theory*, which claims that the present moves across the series of events, illuminating them like a moving spotlight. In some sense the events that are highlighted by the spotlight are "more real" than the events that have been highlighted in the past or will eventually be illuminated in the future. Third is the *growing block theory*, which says the present and past exist, but the future does not. This is because the present continuously adds new existence to a past that continues to exist even after the present has moved on. Reality, then, is like a block that grows over time.

On the other hand, those that think the passage of time isn't real go by various names, most commonly eternalism, where the "now" of the present has no special privileged place. Instead, like space, where my being in Australia or North America isn't ontologically privileged in any sense, times coexist too. When I say I'm "here" in space, it doesn't mean to say other spaces aren't equally "real." Likewise, when I say "now" in time, it doesn't mean other times aren't equally real. So, in this sense, while dinosaurs don't exist *now*, they do exist per se.[96] The claim for the eternalist is *not* that all times exist at once simultaneously but that they exist together like two different locations in space despite succession.[97]

There are other categories within the discipline of time, debating whether time is an ordered series of events (called relationism) or whether time exists independently of what happens in it (called absolutism), but for now, the general divide between dynamic and eternalist theories of the ontology of time suffices.[98] So, the eternalist will say that "all times and events timelessly coexist, and all are equally real; temporal passage is unreal."[99] The dynamic theorist says that "temporal passage is real, and time is not an ensemble of coexisting times and events."[100]

TWO THEORIES OF TENSE

However, there is a further relevant distinction in the metaphysics of time that should be addressed. There are two families of temporal terms and concepts. These are two ways of thinking about the series of events that constitute the "timeline" of time. In contemporary metaphysics they are called the A and B theories.

If we assume time is real (not necessarily that the *flow* of time is real, just time itself), the differences between the two conceptual theories

96. Nikk Effingham, "The Wave Theory of Time: A Comparison to Competing Tensed Theories," *Journal of the American Philosophical Association* 9, no. 1 (2023): 172–73, https://doi.org/10.1017/apa.2021.49.

97. Barry Dainton, *Time and Space* (McGill-Queen's University Press, 2001), 8.

98. Robin Le Poidevin, *Travels in Four Dimensions: The Enigmas of Space and Time* (Oxford University Press, 2003), 27.

99. Dainton, *Time and Space*, 11.

100. Dainton, *Time and Space*, 12.

are easier to understand. When we compare two events in terms of past, present, or future, using *tense,* we are using the A-theory of time. On the A-theory events come into existence and go out of existence. For example, at one time, the apostle Paul existed. That time has now passed, and he is long dead. However, there will be a future time when he is resurrected and lives again. But these times do not equally exist. So, the A-series views the timeline as dynamic and tensed, and not all events are equally real at all times.

On the other hand, when we compare two events as earlier, simultaneous, or later without reference to tense (past, present, or future), we are using the B-theory of time. On the B-theory, time is an eternally fixed framework where all times have the same ontological status (nothing is privileged to say "now"). It is another dimension alongside the three spatial dimensions.[101] Reality, then, is fundamentally tenseless. The "series" of time, then, is static and tenseless, and all events are equally real at all times. So, time is analogous to space, ontologically speaking. All times, just like all spaces, exist. Now, both theories *can* make use of these terms, but they uncover the main divide over whether there is an objective fact of the matter about which events are past, present, and future. For the B-theory, there is no such objective fact, whereas on the A-theory there is. The B-Theory assumes all tensed features of reality fundamentally reduce to tenseless facts.[102]

Let me explain with a few examples. The A-theory of time is probably natural for most people. On this account, when we want to talk about the fact that it is raining on a certain day, we might say, "It is raining *now*," or "It *was* raining yesterday." When we speak like this, we are explaining time with reference to the past, present, and future. On a dynamic ontology of time called "presentism," this means giving the present a "privileged" status. The present is the only time that really exists. The past no longer exists, and the future doesn't yet exist. Such an account is rather plausible because it's hard on first pass to think about how we could explain the fact that it is raining now without reference to tensed language like *now*.

101. Koons and Pickavance, *Metaphysics*, 182; Loux and Crisp, *Metaphysics*, 205.

102. Thanks to my friend Matt Ntiros for helping me think through this section.

But on the B-theory, this is the wrong way to think about time. Instead, it is possible to reformulate all of these tensed facts in neutral terms.[103] So, I can know that it is raining on Monday, May 30, 2023 (instead of *now*). Further, Babe Ruth, the apostle Peter, and Socrates all really exist. They aren't individuals who used to exist but no longer do. Many today are committed to the B-theory because of its congruence with special relativity. Essentially, Einstein's theory of relativity suggests there is *no* absolute simultaneity, and thus there is no absolute present that could be ontologically privileged.

CONCLUSION

Metaphysics is important for anyone seeking to confess the God of classical theism. The discipline covers a host of important topics that impact how we can make sense of who God is and how he relates to the world. What I've attempted to show here is a broad sense of what metaphysics is and some of the various options available on any given subdiscipline that is especially relevant to the nature of God. I've attempted to prove that a classical theist needs classical metaphysics in the sense that they must affirm substances and kinds, but there are several ways we can make sense of other metaphysical topics like time, universals, and ontology more generally. Some of the terrain is difficult in part due to the subject matter itself but also due in part to the centuries-long traditions of reflection on these topics. Most of us modern readers of older works on classical theism, ranging from Thomas to Turretin, lack the necessary conceptual tools to make sense of their arguments. This is designed to properly equip us with at least an elementary grasp of the subject matter. It will likely prove useful to return to this chapter at various points throughout the rest of the book to regain a sense of some of the more technical concepts that might be unfamiliar to you.

103. Paul Helm, *Eternal God: A Study of God without Time*, 2nd ed. (Oxford University Press, 2010), 73–94.

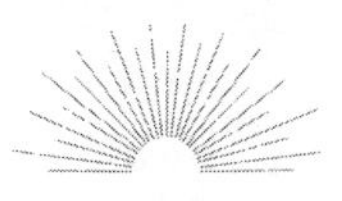

5

CONFESSING GOD AS GOD: THE THEOLOGICAL FOUNDATION OF CLASSICAL THEISM

Christians ought to, as Tyler Wittman says, "confess God *as God*." That might sound strange at first reading, a tautology of sorts adding no real meaning. But the basic idea is vital. Consider the words of saint Paul, who laments that "although they knew God, they did not honor him as God" (Rom 1:21a). Though they "knew" God, they didn't honor him *as God*. Paul makes a distinction on which life depends. The Christian must not only know God but honor him *as God*. Confessing God *as God* requires both the right predications (God is perfect, wonderful, beautiful, faithful, etc.) and the right posture toward such knowledge. To confess God as God is to confess the *truth* about God (Rom 1:25a: "because they exchanged the truth about God for a lie") and to *acknowledge him as such* (Rom 1:28a: "and since they did not see fit to acknowledge God").[1] It is to speak of God in ways that are fitting and worthy of him and to do so with a Christian posture of reverence and worship. All models of God ought to share this concern.

SEEKING THE FUNDAMENTAL

While this entire book is designed to be an exercise in confessing God as God, especially as it relates to the "classical" attributes, it is also necessary to expand our horizons so that we may inhabit the proper context from which

1. Tyler Wittman, *God and Creation in the Theology of Thomas Aquinas and Karl Barth* (Cambridge University Press, 2019), 5.

to explore these attributes. I have defined classical theism as a family of views that seeks to confess God as simple, immutable, eternal, and impassible. And yet there is a danger in focusing mainly on these "negative" attributes at the expense of others. These attributes *are* a necessary part of confessing God as God. They are the perfections of God's sheer freedom from limitation. They are about his transcendence beyond created realities. Yet they are *not* the theological foundation for who God is, and an overemphasis on them will misshape our doctrine of God. If we discover the riches of divine simplicity or divine immutability apart from more fundamental claims about who and what God is, we will not only impoverish ourselves but endanger ourselves. Such negative attributes do little to tell us *what* or even *who* God *is*. Rather, they protect us from faulty conceptions of God. These negative attributes derive from more fundamental positive perfections. So, if we are to confess God as *God*, we must begin with these more fundamental truths that we find in his own self-descriptions. These will lead us by the hand to the truth that he lacks complexity, lacks change, lacks temporality, and lacks passions.

Now, not all positive perfections are equally fundamental. And when I speak of "fundamental," I intend to convey the idea of being logically prior. I am *not* using *fundamental* in the contemporary philosophical sense of metaphysical grounding that would make God have various metaphysical explanation relations between his attributes. Instead, I mean to say that some perfections are theologically and epistemically loaded. They have the force and power of a freight train. While they may not be given equal airtime throughout Scripture, they have greater weight and significance than others because they are eminently biblical and necessitate other perfections. Therefore, they serve as "epistemic priorities" that help to make sense of the rest of Scripture and our understanding of God.[2]

For example, it is natural for a Christian to assume God's oneness as a necessary precondition for all true theology. Any belief that would divide God into three separate beings ought to be rejected from the start. Deuteronomy 6:4 is a lynchpin text and influences all understanding of who God is—he is *one*.[3] As Jesus said, "I and the Father are one" (John 10:30).

2. Bruce Marshall, *Trinity and Truth* (Cambridge University Press, 2002), 157.

3. It should be noted that there are at least five different ways to translate Deuteronomy 6:4, ranging from God being one to God being unique. However, the various translations are not mutually exclusive. Moses could easily have had several meanings in mind, none of which would contradict

He didn't merely say the Father "is one," but the Son and the Father "are" one.[4] Or consider how God's goodness serves as the ground for his love, mercy, and kindness. It entails them. So, while John 4:24 tells us God is spirit; Matthew 19:17 tells us God is good; and Exodus 34:6 tells us God is merciful and gracious, slow to anger, and abounding in steadfast love and faithfulness, not all of these are as theologically loaded. Each play various epistemic roles for us.

It's important that I tread carefully here and nuance these claims to avoid misunderstanding. All of God's perfections are necessary, and they all depend logically on one another. God's justice is not independent from his goodness. Nor can God be good without his justice. However, from our created viewpoint, some perfections play a more fundamental theological role in explicating the other divine perfections. This is not to sideline any attribute or to suggest some are "more important." It is merely to note that some perfections play a significant role for the theologian and church person as they seek to know God in all his fullness. For example, consider how Jonathan Edwards explains what he sees as the three fundamental attributes:

> The whole of God's internal good or glory, is in these three things, viz. his infinite knowledge; his infinite virtue or holiness, and his infinite joy and happiness. Indeed there are a great many attributes in God, according to our way of conceiving or talking of them: but all may be reduced to these; or to the degree, circumstances and relations of these.[5]

As Edwards notes, there are "a great many attributes in God, according to our way of conceiving or talking of them." Even so, we are right to theologically arrange them for the purpose of knowing and worshiping God as God. This approach is often simply assumed. Some attributes entail others and are

the significance of God's oneness. Furthermore, the Christian tradition has certainly interpreted the text as one of divine unity. Therefore, it remains biblically faithful to utilize such a text as a theological presupposition of sorts. See Daniel L. Block, "How Many Is God? An Investigation into the Meaning of Deuteronomy 6:4–5," *Journal of the Evangelical Theological Society* 47, no. 2 (2004): 196.

4. Augustine, *The Trinity*, trans. Edmund Hill (New City, 2015), V.2.10.

5. Jonathan Edwards, "Dissertation I: Concerning the End for Which God Created the World," in *Ethical Writings in Works of Jonathan Edwards Online*, ed. Paul Ramsey, vol. 8 (Yale University Press, 2008), 528.

thus fundamental in a sense. Again, as an example, Mastricht explains that God's spirituality and aseity explain simplicity and immutability.[6]

The necessity of theological work to properly confess God as God is also why we must keep the entire canon of Scripture in view lest we be tempted to overemphasize or misunderstand certain descriptions of God. It is not a matter of "stacking" verses together, counting the descriptions that appear most frequently, to confess God as God. Certainly, it is true that God is a multitude of perfections. But how God is characterized in Scripture is largely dependent upon the narrative purpose of the biblical text. Therefore, much of the Bible's descriptions are occasional in nature and not purely systematic or logical. But the task of the theologian is to synthesize what the Scriptures teach and how the tradition has received them and understood them, and to logically arrange them in such a way as to make sense of who God is. This shouldn't cause fear or anxiety for the faithful Protestant committed to the supremacy of Scripture *alone*. The Bible is written in such a way as to invite us into a divine wrestling match, akin to Jacob and the angel of the Lord. We wrestle with Scripture until we are blessed by God with intimate understanding. It is not a textbook with an answer key in the back. It is a book full of wonder and divine mystery calling us to deeper contemplation of the God who is.

For the classical theologian (or classical pastor or simply classical Christian!), given the scope of Scripture and the tradition's reception of Scripture, I argue that the most fundamental attributes of God are his aseity and goodness. Aseity explains the classical attributes, and goodness properly contextualizes them. By "explain" I mean that attributes like aseity metaphysically "ground" other attributes like simplicity. In other words, if one is willing to accept that God is *a se* they should then accept the classical attributes since there is a relation of necessity between them. While other descriptions of God, even those systematized by the theologian, are important—like his perfection and infinity—these are modes of existence that characterize all of the attributes rather than being individual attributes themselves. As the Second London Confession of Faith leads with in its description of God, he is "infinite in being and perfection" (2.1).

6. Petrus van Mastricht, *Theoretical-Practical Theology*, ed. Joel R. Beeke, trans. Todd M. Rester (Reformation Heritage, 2018), 2:129.

This is why I often prefer to speak of attributes like aseity and simplicity as perfections or infinite perfections. *Infinite* and *perfection* speak to the character of all God's attributes.

Aseity is traditionally used as a fundamental attribute throughout the tradition.[7] For example, Mastricht claims, "All the attributes of God are grounded on this aseity, independence, and primacy."[8] But goodness is variously described. Sometimes it is understood as a subset of other attributes like holiness, wherein goodness is merely the *action* of the divine essence.[9] Yet, I suggest that it is dangerous business to only mention divine aseity as fundamental. I resolutely believe that ignoring God's goodness as fundamental will improperly contextualize the classical attributes. Part of the rationale for the classical doctrines is to protect and wonder at God's goodness. He is so good that he is *immutably* good. Nothing could change his goodness. His faithfulness endures forever.

Therefore, I suggest that considering the "classical" attributes apart from these two fundamental attributes is perilous. It is so because an overemphasis on the classical attributes to the exclusion of aseity and goodness is liable to lead us to an unhealthy imbalance and temptation to prioritize them more than they ought. Second, it is perilous because without divine aseity and divine goodness, God can be seen as cold rather than hot with the never-ending strength to care for his creation. Apart from God's aseity and goodness he can appear too propositional rather than infinitely and unbreakably loving. Aseity and goodness together aren't far from some of C. S. Lewis's descriptions of Aslan in *The Lion, the Witch and the Wardrobe*:

> "They say Aslan is on the move—perhaps has already landed." And now a very curious thing happened. None of the children knew who Aslan was any more than you do; but the moment the Beaver had spoken these words everyone felt quite different.[10] ... Once again that strange feeling—like the first signs of spring, like good

---

7. Ross D. Inman, *What Is Reality? An Introduction to Metaphysics* (IVP Academic, 2024), 59–65.

8. Mastricht doesn't mean to suggest there are three separate attributes but that independence and primacy are part of what aseity means. Mastricht, *Theoretical-Practical Theology*, 2:84.

9. William G. T. Shedd, *Dogmatic Theology*, 3rd ed. (P&R, 2003), 304.

10. C. S. Lewis, *The Lion, the Witch and the Wardrobe* (HarperCollins, 2005), 141.

> news—had come over them. … "Is he—quite safe? I shall feel rather nervous about meeting a lion." … "Safe?" said Mr. Beaver. "Who said anything about safe? Course he isn't safe. But he's good. He's the King, I tell you." "I'm longing to see him," said Peter, "even if I do feel frightened when it comes to the point."[11]

There is a mixture of proper fear, awe, and trust in divine aseity and goodness where the beginning of knowledge meets. As *a se* and good, God is never unstable in his capacity or desire for faithfulness to his promises. Third, it is perilous because the classical attributes cannot stand on their own. It is divine aseity and divine goodness that ground them and provide their coherence and explanatory power. To remove or ignore aseity or goodness is to destabilize the classical attributes.

In what follows I give a general dogmatic description of both aseity and goodness alongside extended exegesis of holy Scripture. Classical theism is supposed to bleed Bible when you cut it. So, it's important to make good on such promises. If aseity is rooted in Scripture and explains the classical attributes like I've suggested, then any of its "good and necessary consequences," like the classical attributes, will equally be rooted in Scripture, even if not materially. However, supernatural revelation does not exhaust the infinite well of God's being, though it does serve as the proper starting point—especially for these two perfections I cast as "fundamental" for logically subsequent perfections.

DIVINE ASEITY

Minimally, confessing God as God is to confess God as *a se* (*a se* is simply the Latin for "from" or "by itself").[12] This is the grand doctrine of God's aseity. God as *a se* is not unique to classical theism. It is also emphasized and gladly confessed by neo-classical theists and by some open theists.[13] For example, noted neo-classical theist William Lane Craig devoted an entire book to using the doctrine of aseity as a theological tool for

11. Lewis, *The Lion, the Witch and the Wardrobe*, 146.

12. Wittman, *God and Creation in the Theology of Thomas Aquinas and Karl Barth*, 13.

13. This is contra the claim of Carter, who states that "modern relational theism" denies aseity. He makes this claim with no source material. Craig A. Carter, *Contemplating God with the Great Tradition* (Baker Academic, 2021), 19.

critiquing Platonism.[14] The classical theist should not fear sharing dogmatic foundations with other models of God. Such a recognition does nothing to reduce God's glory. Instead, it offers opportunity to share common ground that serves to build friendships that create space to convince one another of the appropriate way to confess God as God.

APPROACHING A DOGMATIC DEFINITION

God's aseity is his fullness of life from himself and no one else. As Genesis 1:1 says, "In the beginning, God created the heavens and the earth."[15] Nothing existed alongside God prior to creation. It was God and God alone. No one created God. He exists necessarily through himself. And God is overflowing with unbounded life. These are the general aspects of aseity. Yet, while intuitive and ubiquitous among Christians, aseity has various glosses among theologians. Chief among them is the negative property of being independent and, I argue, the positive property of having fullness in oneself.[16] In other words, God is not dependent on anything to be who he is or do what he does, and he has all that he has in and of himself.[17] An initial definition then could be stated as follows:

> *Divine aseity:* God is *a se if and only if* God is (1) completely independent of *everything besides himself* and (2) completely full through himself.

However, there are questions to be had regarding what "independence" requires and what it means to be "full." It is important to remember there is no true analogue for being totally independent and having fullness in oneself.[18] Of course, it isn't totally equivocal, as we do have some comparisons from which to draw a sense of meaning.

It is useful to begin by looking to the Second London Confession of Faith in section 2.2, which expands on divine aseity to great degree:

---

14. William Lane Craig, *God Over All* (Oxford University Press, 2016).

15. Thanks to my friend Hunter Hindsman for drawing my attention to the theological implications of this text.

16. John Webster, *God Without Measure: Working Papers in Christian Theology* (T&T Clark, 2016), 20.

17. Steven J. Duby, *Jesus and the God of Classical Theism: Biblical Christology in Light of the Doctrine of God* (Baker Academic, 2022), 23.

18. Webster, *God Without Measure*, 14.

> God, having all life, glory, goodness, blessedness, in and of Himself, is alone in and unto Himself all-sufficient, not standing in need of any creature which He hath made, nor deriving any glory from them, but only manifesting His own glory in, by, unto, and upon them; He is the alone fountain of all being, of whom, through whom, and to whom are all things, and He hath most sovereign dominion over all creatures, to do by them, for them, or upon them, whatsoever Himself pleases.

The confession calls God "all-sufficient," an apt designation for aseity. So, based on the confession, aseity means by "independence" that nothing stands above God—he is wholly underived—and by "fullness" that there is nothing that gives him life, glory, goodness, or blessedness that he doesn't already possess. He is the fountain of all being, which harkens to the preaching of Paul in Acts 17:24–25: "The God who made the world and everything in it, being Lord of heaven and earth, does not live in temples made by man, nor is he served by human hands, as though he needed anything, since he himself gives to all mankind life and breath and everything." God is the one who gives. He needs nothing. It is he alone who is the foundation and fountain for all life and breath—*everything*. Everything not identical to God is dependent on God.

It remains useful to hear from the tradition on aseity as well. Not everyone dedicates a unique "section" to aseity in their systems, but it is at least assumed by Christian theologians. Indeed, some contemporary thinkers even argue that aseity is primarily concerned with the negative aspect of independence rather than the positive aspect of fullness.[19] Consider several examples to start.

Anselm grounds divine self-sufficiency in God's creation out of nothing. What exists through something has a different explanation for its existence than does God who exists through himself as uncreated.[20] Jonathan Edwards explains how "God is infinitely, eternally, unchangeably, and independently glorious and happy: that he stands in no need of, cannot

19. Michael Allen, *The Knowledge of God* (T&T Clark, 2022), 8.

20. Anselm, *Monologion*, ed. Brian Davies and G. R. Evans (Oxford University Press, 1998), 6–8.

be profited by, or receive anything from the creature; or be truly hurt, or be the subject of any sufferings or *impair* of his glory and felicity from any other being."[21] Similarly, Herman Bavinck explains that aseity means that "all that God is, he is of himself. By virtue of himself he is goodness, holiness, wisdom, life, light, truth, and so on."[22]

Elsewhere in the tradition we find more explanations for what independence means. It requires that God be free from *every* cause. This includes all four of the traditional Aristotelian causes (causes is used loosely here, for us contemporary readers; we likely only think of the "efficient" cause as a true "cause"): efficient, material, formal, and final.[23] There is nothing that actively causes God to be who he is, there is no "stuff" from which God could be made or caused, there is no type or design from which God conforms to, and there is no end or purpose for which God must conform to external to himself.[24] Herman Bavinck similarly explains that aseity means that God must be independent in everything: existence, perfections, decrees, and works.[25]

These dependency relations could likewise be categorized as historical and contemporaneous. God must have neither. So, God has no historical dependency. Whereas I owe my existence to my parents, God has no such parents to depend on. Whereas I am a human because my parents are human, and I am this person because I have this individual body and soul, there is no such ancestry in God. Likewise, God has no contemporaneous dependency. Whereas I depend on oxygen for my existence,

---

21. Edwards, "Dissertation I," 420.

22. Herman Bavinck, *Reformed Dogmatics*, ed. John Bolt, trans. John Vriend (Baker Academic, 2003), 2:151.

23. For those not familiar with the Aristotelian causal framework, the material cause is what something is made out of, the formal cause is the essence of a thing, or whatever explains its "whatness," the efficient cause is what we typically think of causation as today, and the final cause is the end for which the action was done. The classic Aristotelian example is a statue. Take any statue you like, say one of George Washington. The material cause is the marble it is made of, the form of George Washington is its formal cause, its efficient cause is Fred, who sculpted it, and its final cause is its reminder of America's founder to the general public.

24. Mastricht, *Theoretical-Practical Theology*, 2:86.

25. Bavinck, *Reformed Dogmatics*, 2:152.

God needs nothing to exist. He does so necessarily. There is nothing that God needs or that could make him vulnerable.[26]

What should not be taken from this is that God is aloof or cold. It does not follow that because God is totally self-sufficient that he is totally self-interested in the sense of being an egotistical maniac that cares for only himself. Rather, as Steven Duby has described, "it implies that God acts from a rich benevolence and liberality in the economy, without ever looking upon the creature as an instrument of his own self-realization."[27] It means that God can never abuse. While he has infinite power and strength, he never has the need or desire to use others as instruments for his own self-gratification at their expense. He is infinitely full.

BIBLICAL EXEGESIS

The doctrine of aseity is not merely a teaching stolen by Christians from Greek philosophy. It is much more. Nor is it a useful fiction crafted by theologians in need of a theological crutch to prop up their favorite dogmas. Rather, it is drawn from the Scriptures, principally from the Hebrew Scriptures themselves before any trace of the tired Hellenization thesis can be found.

The God Who Is: Yahweh and Aseity

While there are many biblical texts that describe God's aseity, his own self-disclosure as *Yahweh*—the God who is—in Exodus 3:14 casts a wide shadow across the entirety of the Scriptures and theological reflection upon them. As John of Damascus comments, "He gathers together and contains all being in himself like an infinite and unbounded sea."[28] From the beginning, God is *a se*. Moses experiences God describing himself first-hand as *a se*. Nothing compares to God in his independence and fullness. No one can properly categorize him underneath a general class of concepts that others fit within. John 5:26 echoes the sentiment of

---

26. William E. Mann, "Divine Sovereignty and Aseity," in *The Oxford Handbook of Philosophy of Religion*, ed. William J. Wainwright (Oxford University Press, 2009), 48, https://doi.org/10.1093/oxfordhb/9780195331356.003.0003.

27. Steven J. Duby, *Jesus and the God of Classical Theism* (Baker Academic, 2022), 26.

28. John of Damascus, *On the Orthodox Faith*, trans. Norman Russell (St. Vladimir's Seminary Press, 2022), 84.

Exodus 3:14—God has "life in himself." Similarly, Revelation 1:8 extols God as the Alpha and Omega, the one "who is and who was and who is to come, the Almighty." These biblical descriptions are traditionally deployed as foundations for the doctrine of aseity.

The Holy One of Israel: Isaiah and Aseity

There are also entire biblical books that are permeated with the theme of aseity. For example, consider the book of Isaiah. The most common title for God throughout Isaiah is "the Holy One of Israel," which is ascribed with a surprising amount of evenness (1:4; 5:16, 19, 24; 10:17, 20; 12:6; 17:7; 29:19, 23; 30:11, 12, 15; 31:1; 37:23; 40:25; 41:14, 16, 20; 43:3, 14, 15; 45:11; 47:4; 48:17; 49:7a, 7b; 54:5; 55:5; 57:17; 60:9, 14). Essentially, this title is used to describe God in his *otherness*.[29] It is a mark of his transcendence, meaning that God transcends all created categories. Such a description is central to the concept of aseity. The fact that God is totally self-sufficient means that no category can adequately capture him. Isaiah uses this term for God more than three times as many times as the entire rest of the Old Testament uses it.[30] The title is used so often throughout that it could very well be the very center of Isaiah's entire theology: God is *a se*.

The Fullness Is Mine: Psalm 50 and Aseity

One of the richest biblical texts for aseity is Psalm 50. In many ways Acts 17 draws upon the treasures of Psalm 50. The psalm is non-traditional compared to many other psalms, however. It is a judgment psalm designed to disorient the reader with the grandeur of God.[31] It is designed to portray a prophetic covenant lawsuit with God being both the judge and plaintiff against the Israelites, who are the guilty defendants. The Israelites are under God's judgment for their idolatry, distorting God's true being for an image conjured up by other neighboring false gods. This distortion is important to confront because it causes a misrepresentation of God

---

29. John Goldingay, *Isaiah*, New International Biblical Commentary (Hendrickson, 2001), 15.

30. J. A. Motyer, *The Prophecy of Isaiah: An Introduction & Commentary* (InterVarsity Press, 1993), 18.

31. Willem A. VanGemeren, "Psalms," in *The Expositor's Bible Commentary: Psalms, Proverbs, Ecclesiastes, Song of Songs* (Zondervan, 1991), 372; Robert Alter, *The Book of Psalms: A Translation with Commentary* (W. W. Norton, 2009), 176; Walter Brueggemann, *The Message of the Psalms: A Theological Commentary* (Augsburg, 1984), 89.

himself and his ability to relate with his people.[32] Such a picture reminds us of the importance of our doctrine of God. It is not mere taste or preference from which we may describe God. When we misunderstand his nature, we are guilty of idolatry. We are called to confess God *as God*.

The psalm begins with an introduction of the judge himself (vv. 1–6), which includes a threefold naming of God using El, Elohim, and Yahweh. This is followed by a section indicting Israel for misunderstandings regarding sacrifice (vv. 7–15). The Israelites have missed that God is in fact spiritual and not human like them. The third section (vv. 16–21) charges the Israelites as hardened hypocrites for their actions against God's covenant, missing that God is righteous and just. The final section (vv. 22–23) ends with the implications of the trial, pronouncing the judgment and proclaiming a promise.

The opening section is dominated by the verbal idea of "speaking" ("speaks" in v. 1, "does not keep silent" in v. 3, "calls" in v. 4), which is contrasted with God being silent in verse 21.[33] God's calling and speech denote his power. The God who speaks matter into existence controls the world by his mere word. But God also "shines" and "comes." These denote the character of God. God's shining indicates his intrinsic beauty and purity, and the warmth we obtain from him. We've all experienced the power of the sun, especially those of us with fair skin—the sun quite literally heats our skin and reminds us of its power. God's coming denotes his sacrificial love. He is a God who comes to the lowly and rebellious. But it also denotes his authority and echoes the coming of Genesis 3. These are relevant as they buttress the nature of aseity as the God of all power, purity, and warmth. Aseity is not designed to be a cold and lifeless doctrine. It is put to real pastoral work in the Scriptures.

The rapid pace of verbs and imagery are designed to create anticipation as the psalm progresses.[34] God triple summons the world, heavens and earth, and Israel. But the earth and heavens have been assembled to witness the trial, not to answer it. And what greater witness than these?

---

32. Johanna W. H. Bos, "Oh, When the Saints: A Consideration of the Meaning of Psalm 50," *Journal for the Study of the Old Testament* 7, no. 24 (1982): 73, https://doi.org/10.1177/030908928200702404.

33. Bos, "Oh, When the Saints," 67.

34. Bos, "Oh, When the Saints," 70.

The usual role in the psalms is now reversed, with the people of Israel hearing and God speaking.[35]

> "Hear, O my people, and I will speak;
> O Israel, I will testify against you.
> I am God, your God.
> Not for your sacrifices do I rebuke you;
> your burnt offerings are continually before me.
> I will not accept a bull from your house
> or goats from your folds.
> For every beast of the forest is mine,
> the cattle on a thousand hills.
> I know all the birds of the hills,
> and all that moves in the field is mine.
>
> "If I were hungry, I would not tell you,
> for the world and its fullness are mine.
> Do I eat the flesh of bulls
> or drink the blood of goats?
> Offer to God a sacrifice of thanksgiving,
> and perform your vows to the Most High,
> and call upon me in the day of trouble;
> I will deliver you, and you shall glorify me." (Ps 50:7–15)

The pointed and stinging rebukes from God are startling. He begins by asserting what he is not rebuking them for: their offering of sacrifices. But while they perform these, he isn't interested in such sacrifices. There is a deeper significance behind the liturgical act that is sought. For example, not for praise songs, giving of money, hearing of sermons, fellowshiping with the church, taking of the sacraments, mission trips, sponsoring of Compassion children, reading of books, taking of seminary classes, sharing of testimonies, or volunteering in the sound booth or children's ministry does he rebuke them.

To show this, God gives a threefold repetition of his ownership, showing how unnecessary sacrifices are on his part. Every beast is his. The cattle are his. The birds are his. The world and its *fullness* are his. There

---

35. Robert Davidson, *The Vitality of Worship: A Commentary on the Book of Psalms* (Eerdmans, 1998), 164.

is nothing that escapes his grasp. And even so, he doesn't need what he owns! He isn't the sort of being that can experience hunger or thirst.

He makes it clear that he is not the one in need of sacrifices; indeed, he never needed them, but the people desperately need them.[36] The language here is satirical at heart, poking fun at the assumed weak and hungry "god" of the Israelites who so desperately needed each and every sacrifice.[37] At bottom the true God of Israel is mocking the "god" who lacks aseity. For God, as *a se*, would never need *anything*. The Israelites had come to assume that God was like the pagan gods of their neighbors who needed sacrifices to survive. But an all-sufficient God is totally different. He transcends our created categories and is completely independent. He doesn't need food, sacrifices, or anything else. He is fullness itself.

As such, God shatters the imposed false idol of himself that the Israelites had unknowingly constructed. The point of the sacrificial system was not to fulfill the needs of a pathetic god but to create thanksgiving within the fallen people. It was through the covenant, through the sacrificial system, that it was made possible to thank God and be in relationship with him.[38] God was always sufficient within himself.[39] The Israelites had taken after the neighboring nations by allowing themselves to think that their sacrifices met the needs of their God like that of the other pagan gods.[40] This was a grave insult to the all-sufficient Creator, and therefore he rebukes his people for their faulty idolization.[41] Divine aseity here is being deployed as the basis for the rebuke. So, through multiple lines in this first discourse, God asserts his sovereignty, independence, and complete otherness.[42] In other words, he is *a se*. He is fully independent of any need or desire that anyone may conjure up of him. And such a doctrine is a divine oasis of goodness for those desperate for good news. The true Christian God is never in need of anything and shares out of

36. Peter C. Craigie, *Psalms 1–50* (Word, 1983), 365.

37. Craigie, *Psalms 1–50*, 366.

38. Craigie, *Psalms 1–50*, 366.

39. John Calvin, *Commentary on the Book of Psalms*, trans. James Anderson (Baker Book House, 1979), 268.

40. Calvin, *Commentary on the Book of Psalms*, 268.

41. Geoffrey Grogan, *Psalms* (Eerdmans, 2008), 341.

42. Brueggemann, *The Message of the Psalms*, 90.

his abundance. His all-sufficiency means he is an ocean full of tenderness and care. He is overflowing with love and forgiveness toward those who believe.

DIVINE GOODNESS

Divine goodness is likely one of the more intuitive and universal divine attributes. All theists will confess that God is good. Christians may fail to trust that God is good when faced with suffering and evil, but their response is one of doubt and not outright rejection. Only atheists would positively entertain the idea that God *isn't* good. We are confronted from the very beginning of the Bible that God is good and does good. Indeed, he does *very good*. As Moses narrates, "And God saw everything that he had made, and behold, it was very good" (Gen 1:31). While there is much that could be said about goodness as a perfection in general, in what follows I focus primarily on how it should shape our thought about the classical attributes. The reason for this is because besides aseity, goodness ought to be at the forefront of our minds whenever we think of God as simple, immutable, impassible, or eternal. He is these things, or he lacks these properties, while being the most *good*. And while goodness is important for all matters of theology, I argue it is also crucial for knowing the classical divine attributes. After all, as many theologians have argued, goodness *is* the divine nature itself.[43] For example, certainly we must remember divine goodness when considering God's omnipotence lest we imagine he be a wicked tyrant of infinite strength. We must labor to prevent a divorce of divine goodness from any aspect of the divine life.[44]

APPROACHING A DOGMATIC DEFINITION

While it's clear that God *is* good, it's not altogether clear what goodness is *per se*. It's sort of like asking someone what time is. It's easy to say we understand it until we are asked to give a careful definition. If I said, "The thief is a good burglar," the predicate "good" is being used differently than most would want in relation to God since he has no need to steal nor

43. Katherine Sonderegger, *Systematic Theology* (Fortress, 2015), 1:xiii.

44. Paul L. Gavrilyuk, "God's Impassible Suffering in the Flesh: The Promise of Paradoxical Christology," in *Divine Impassibility and the Mystery of Human Suffering*, ed. James F. Keating and Thomas Joseph White (Eerdmans, 2009), 137.

does he have any desire or propensity to do so! In this sense, goodness wouldn't be so good.

So, it is reasonable to begin with the idea that goodness means, at least, that there is no defect or blemish in something.[45] It is a lack of "badness." But most Christians have thought that evil is an ontologically privative notion, whereas goodness has real existence, real being. So, it must be more than a lack. While it is right to "strip away" any negative connotations when we think of goodness and God, it is more than a negative attribute. As Aristotle suggested many centuries ago, the good is what everyone *seeks*.[46] There is something positive about goodness beyond a mere lack.

Given the positive nature of goodness, some Christians identify goodness with perfection in general, such as Bavinck, Thomas, and Mastricht.[47] Similarly, Gill explains goodness as the "*summum bonum*"—the sum and substance of all felicity.[48] Goodness then could be like Aristotle's chief end of happiness.[49] Goodness in this sense is the "bounty" of God.[50] So then, any kind of excellence is good. Beauty is good. Economic value is good. Skillfulness is good.[51] And so on. But these definitions, while useful, still lack descriptive clarity on what *makes* goodness *good* beyond shared intuition.

Whatever goodness is, we know that it is who God is and what God does. As Psalm 119:68 reminds us, "You are good and do good." The psalmist's distinction here reminds us of what moral philosophers call the intrinsic good and instrumental good. An instrumental good is something that is good *for* something, whereas an intrinsic good is a good *in itself*.[52] For example, money is good because of what it does. It buys me a coffee and quenches my need for caffeine. It pays my mortgage payment and provides the shelter I need. So, God is intrinsically good in himself but also instrumentally good as he works in creation.

---

45. Thomas V. Morris, *Our Idea of God: An Introduction to Philosophical Theology* (InterVarsity Press, 1991), 48.

46. Aristotle, *Nicomachean Ethics*, trans. Terence Irwin, 2nd ed. (Hackett, 1999), 1094a.

47. Bavinck, *Reformed Dogmatics*, 2:211; Mastricht, *Theoretical-Practical Theology*, 2:331; Thomas Aquinas, *The Treatise on the Divine Nature*, trans. Brian J. Shanley (Hackett, 2006), I.5.1c.

48. John Gill, *A Body of Doctrinal Divinity* (George Keith, 1769), 163.

49. Aristotle, *Nicomachean Ethics* 1095a15.

50. Stephen Charnock, *The Existence and Attributes of God*, ed. Mark Jones (Crossway, 2022), 1199.

51. John M. Frame, *The Doctrine of God* (P&R, 2002), 402–3.

52. Russ Shafer-Landau, *The Fundamentals of Ethics*, 5th ed. (Oxford University Press, 2020), 23.

Katherin Rogers has utilized similar terminology in a distinctively theological way by distinguishing between what she calls the metaphysical good and moral good.[53] Metaphysical goodness is an ontological sort of goodness, a fullness of being (e.g., aseity). For this type of good, God is good because he is complete and without flaw with respect to being.[54] Such an account assumes that existence is a good and that existent things are good insofar as they possess the perfection appropriate to their natures.[55] For example, it is good for a dolphin to have the ability and skill to swim well, whereas such an ability is not a good for the ant that has a nature not designed to live underwater. So, when we think of a good dolphin or a good ant, the goodness we refer to will be appropriately different since goodness is determined in part by ontology.

Moral goodness, on the other hand, is the propensity to do the right thing. It is practical in nature. The propensity to act in a good way can be understood twofold: goodness of duty and goodness of benevolence. The goodness of duty is a good that is obligatory in a situation, whereas benevolence is not required and thus is a superadded good. So, benevolence is going beyond duty by doing good that is not only unrequired but unmerited, undeserved, unobligated, and non-necessitated.[56] For example, it is a duty to help my neighbor evacuate his home if it is on fire, but it is not a duty for me to mow his lawn or install a fence on his property without a prior debt. More so, if my neighbor had intentionally destroyed my fence from envy and I chose to install a fence on his property for free out of my own goodwill in response, that is certainly not a duty—it is benevolence. There is no ground in the person or object for such an action. The ground of the good is prior to and independent of others. It is entirely within the benevolent one.[57] With these distinctions in hand, we can say that God is both metaphysically and morally good to the greatest degree.

---

53. Katherin A. Rogers, *Perfect Being Theology* (Edinburgh University Press, 2000), 121.

54. Morris, *Our Idea of God*, 50.

55. Réginald Garrigou-Lagrange, *God, His Existence and His Nature: A Thomistic Solution of Certain Agnostic Antinomies*, trans. Bede Rose (B. Herder, 1936), 45.

56. Morris, *Our Idea of God*, 50–51.

57. Jonathan Edwards, "Dissertation II: The Nature of True Virtue," in *Ethical Writings*, vol. 8 of *Works of Jonathan Edwards Online*, ed. Paul Ramsey (Yale University Press, 2008), 542.

But there are further useful ways to think about divine goodness that can add clarity to its meaning. First, Thomas explains goodness in terms of desire. Goodness is what is to be *desired*.[58] Goodness is what *makes* something desirable or lovable.[59] Desire indicates a unique aspect of worth and goodness that is not clearly seen when one speaks of metaphysical or moral goodness. Metaphysical and moral likely appeal to the intellect, whereas desire appeals to the will. And so, God as goodness is also desirable. As the psalmist proclaims, "Oh, taste and see that the LORD is good!" (Ps 34:8). Examples like tasting, seeing, and feeling communicate the power of desire and the deep connection to goodness. It is no surprise that God has "pleasures forevermore" (Ps 16:11). As Sarah Coakley persuasively argues, desire is an ontological category that belongs *primarily* to God.[60] And what is supremely desirable about God is that he is supremely good. Sheer unadulterated power might inspire fear or reverence, unlimited knowledge might inspire awe, but unbounded goodness inspires desire and ultimately worship.

Second, goodness focuses on an *inclination* to do good. This is more than the simple propensity to do the right thing, even as a benevolent action. It is a self-diffusive good.[61] As Stephen Charnock explains, goodness (1) finds or makes an object to exercise its goodness and (2) communicates itself "not for its own interest but the good of the object it pitches upon."[62] Elsewhere he explains similarly, by arguing that "the goodness of God is the efflux of his will, whereby he is beneficial to his creatures."[63] So, more than having the propensity to *do* the "right" thing, he has the propensity to *communicate* his goodness to others for their own good. It is a superadded goodness of union.

Based on these general explanations of goodness, I'll take the below as a definitional starting point:

---

58. Aquinas, *The Treatise on the Divine Nature* I.6.1c.

59. Garrigou-Lagrange, *God, His Existence and His Nature*, 45.

60. Sarah Coakley, *God, Sexuality and the Self* (Cambridge University Press, 2013), 10.

61. Bonaventure, *Itinerarium Mentis In Deum*, ed. Zachary Hayes and Philotheus Boehner, rev. and exp. ed., vol. 2 (Franciscan Institute, 2002), 123.

62. Charnock, *The Existence and Attributes of God*, 1206.

63. Charnock, *The Existence and Attributes of God*, 1198.

> *Divine goodness:* God is good *if and only if* God is (1) supremely full, (2) supremely happy, (3) supremely morally upstanding, (4) supremely communicative/benevolent, and (5) supremely desirable.

It may well be possible to consolidate these conditions into a simpler hierarchy (such as the metaphysical and moral goodness categorization), but for now I've focused on five aspects of goodness, which I find to be within the tradition and reflective of the Scriptures. While others may quibble with aspects of this definition, one could remove what they find objectionable, and the account would still have a similar, though not full, effect on the classical attributes. For example, if someone thought God was not supremely happy because he felt all the sadness in the world and empathized with it to such a degree as to not be eternally blissful, God remains good, though his goodness does have a decidedly different shape. But this would be to beg the question by assuming the truth of passibility prior to understanding divine goodness.

Now, let me unpack this definition briefly. The goodness of God indicates (1) his fullness of being—he is metaphysically complete.[64] It indicates (2) his beatitude, for what else would be good without supreme delight in the good? Because of his completeness he is supremely happy in himself. God is also (3) morally upstanding, always doing what is right in every circumstance. Further, goodness by its very nature is (4) benevolently communicative or diffusive. God goes beyond what is obligated in situations. He shows mercy to sinners, forgives them, and rescues them from despair. There is an immensity to the eternal goodness of God that cannot be contained. Such eternal goodness existed in bliss in eternity past among the members of the Trinity. And thus, supreme goodness by its nature as communicative "demands necessarily" the Trinity, according to Bonaventure.[65] Finally, God as good is (5) supremely desirable. This is the external evaluation by others—they desire God because of his goodness. Because of his metaphysical and

64. I take it that this clause by itself does not imply aseity in total since aseity also includes complete independence. But I wonder if it would be possible (or preferrable) to trace the derivation of the attributes back to goodness alone.

65. Bonaventure, *Itinerarium Mentis in Deum*, 125.

moral goodness, others desire God. No one desires what they do not judge as good. All intrinsically desire what they evaluate to be good.

Given this definition of goodness it remains relevant to compare goodness to other, similar attributes to best understand why I consider it as fundamental compared to others, like love. First, consider the theological tradition's own categorization. It is a relatively common approach to explain that goodness, depending on the context, is understood to be love, mercy, patience, and so on.[66] And so it, in a way, contains the qualities of love, grace, mercy, and so on.[67] God's goodness is manifested variously depending on the circumstances. For example, as Bavinck explains, "The goodness of God appears as *love* when it not only conveys certain benefits but God himself."[68] Descriptions of love like these are common throughout the tradition. They are also indicated by Scripture itself. As God passes before Moses to show him his glory, prior to describing his grace and mercy he states that he will make all his "goodness pass before you" (Exod 33:19). Love, mercy, and grace just are goodness communicative of itself.[69] To show the point further, Charnock offers an extended illustration worth reading in full:

> When it confers happiness without merit, it is grace; when it bestows happiness against merit, it is mercy; when he bears with provoking rebels, it is long-suffering; when he performs his promise, it is truth; when it meets with a person to whom it is not obliged, it is grace; when he meets with a person in the world, to which he has obliged himself by promise, it is truth; when it soothes a distressed person, it is pity; when it supplies a destitute person, it is bounty; when it helps an innocent person, it is righteousness; and when it pardons a penitent person, it is mercy—all summed up in this one name of goodness.[70]

---

66. Bavinck, *Reformed Dogmatics*, 2:213; Mastricht, *Theoretical-Practical Theology*, 2:325; Gill, *A Body of Doctrinal Divinity*, 162.

67. Francis Turretin, *Institutes of Elenctic Theology*, ed. James T. Dennison, trans. George Musgrave Giger (P&R, 1994), 3.20.1–2.

68. Bavinck, *Reformed Dogmatics*, 2:215.

69. Mastricht, *Theoretical-Practical Theology*, 2:345.

70. Charnock, *The Existence and Attributes of God*, 1201.

What this means is that goodness is the main category from which we make sense of other attributes like love. Goodness is the transcendental.

BIBLICAL EXEGESIS

While divine goodness is intuitive and likely one that most Christians assume is biblical without need for proof, it remains relevant to consider what Scripture says beyond simple Anselmian perfect being musings and several proof texts. However, I will not provide the level of extended exegesis as offered for divine aseity because of its wide intuitive support. Christianity without a good God is no longer Christianity. All Christian models of God believe that God is properly and completely good.

First, consider the Psalms. There is a reason the psalmists ubiquitously ascribe goodness to God. While goodness is an important attribute for our own trust and faith in God, it is also most fundamentally true about who God is. As the psalmist repeats, "Give thanks to the Lord, for he is good" (Ps 106:1; 107:1; 118:1, 29; 136:1). We are continually reminded of his goodness. He is "good and upright" (Ps 25:8). He is "good to all, and his mercy is over all that he has made" (Ps 145:9). If that isn't proof enough of the profound importance of God's goodness, we are invited to "taste and see that the Lord is good" (Ps 34:8). His goodness functions for both the psalmist and the Christian as a sort of dogmatic control for our theorizing about God. Whatever else we say is a series of footnotes compared to the purpose of magnifying the intensity of God's goodness.[71]

Second, Matthew 19:16–17 provides a profound statement regarding God's goodness: "And behold, a man came up to him, saying, 'Teacher, what good deed must I do to have eternal life?' And he said to him, 'Why do you ask me about what is good? There is only one who is good. If you would enter life, keep the commandments.' " The reply from Jesus is striking. There is *only one who is good*. Goodness here does not admit of degrees. It is all-encompassing. Only God is good. No one else is. Nothing else is. It is standard to understand Jesus's claim as not a properly literal idea that truly nothing can be good. How else would we then understand that God does good, and his works and creation are described as good? However,

71. I am thankful for my friend Ryan Hurd, who has always been incredibly quick to point out the fundamentality and all-surpassing nature of God's goodness and the fierceness of his love.

the implication is clear: The goodness of God transcends whatever created goodness there is. As such, he exceeds the goodness of mere moral duty keeping. God exceeds whatever natural idea of goodness that we have. As Jesus ends his explanation of this story, he concludes by indicating that "everyone who has left houses or brothers or sisters or father or mother or children or lands, for my name's sake, will receive a hundredfold and will inherit eternal life" (Matt 19:29). God's goodness is rich. It gives a hundredfold and ultimately offers eternal life in union with himself.

Third, texts like Genesis 50:20 speak of God's work as good: "As for you, you meant evil against me, but God meant it for good, to bring it about that many people should be kept alive, as they are today." God here acts to do good, to save many lives. Similarly, Numbers 10:29 mentions the "good things" God has promised to Israel. As such, God is the source of all good things, benevolently bestowing on underserving people. As James 1:17 teaches, "Every good gift and every perfect gift is from above, coming down from the Father of lights." God is the source of innumerable goods. And he is pleased to bestow them. He never begrudgingly gives. He never gives out of a limited storehouse. He gives from unending abundance and joy.

THE CONTEXTUAL NECESSITY

Now it is important to explain why divine goodness is foundational for the classical attributes. As hinted at several times, the negative attributes of God cannot live in a vacuum and properly describe God. And an unhealthy fixation on them to the exclusion of God's plentiful divine life will warp our knowledge and worship of God. It is divine goodness, more than any other description of God, that brings balance and warmth to the divine life. When we contemplate the spirituality of God and conclude that he is simple, without body or parts, we must remember that this is because he is good. For the supreme good would not be supremely desirable if he were dependent on parts for his existence. The supreme good would lack fullness within himself to distribute benevolently for all eternity. And it is goodness that calls us to worship the simple God as wholly and exhaustively good.

But the necessity of goodness for the classical attributes is more than mere wordsmithing with theological categories. It has *real* practical relevance for the Christian life. Divine goodness teaches us that God never acts for his own profit but only for the benefit of his creation. He eternally shares his wealth without any lack or addition to himself.[72] God's goodness means he is bountiful and benevolent. God as immutable and impassible is not meant to communicate a frozen and rigid God. Indeed, his goodness reminds us of the purpose of these attributes—to extol his inexhaustible and unchangeable goodness. His goodness acts not for self but for others. This divine goodness inspires love and trust. God doesn't need to exploit his creation because there is nothing he could even gain from it if he tried! Goodness is also connected with divine aseity. As *a se* God receives nothing in addition by sharing his goodness because he lacks nothing. This bountiful disposition allows him to be incredibly good to his entire creation. He need not pick and choose his gifts lest he run out.

Inversely, God's goodness is also safeguarded by the classical attributes. What is it that inspires confidence that God will actually remain steadfastly good? Divine immutability. As James 1:17 explains, "Every good gift and every perfect gift is from above, coming down from the Father of lights, *with whom there is no variation or shadow due to change*" (emphasis added). James grounds God's goodness in his unchangeability. It is because God cannot change that we know every good gift comes from him.

While divine goodness is a contextual necessity, I do not always spell out the relations to it. Instead, I invite you, the reader, to make further connections that I don't for either space considerations or for my own lack of insight. Divine goodness is like an endlessly deep mine full of rich treasure. Even if one were to spend an eternity hewing from it, there would still be infinitely more. And so, there is great wisdom and understanding to be gained by enlisting an entire community as miners of goodness.

CONCLUSION

The classical attributes are not understood in a vacuum. The careful student of Christian theology must pay careful attention to the doctrines that generate and contextualize the classical attributes. Therefore, I've sought to provide a brief dogmatic and exegetical explanation of two key

72. Charnock, *The Existence and Attributes of God*, 1200.

concepts for classical theology in divine aseity and divine goodness. As we progress through the following chapters related to the specific divine attributes, these two attributes will be seen to play a major role. Divine aseity grounds the classical attributes metaphysically, and divine goodness grounds the classical attributes in a different, sort of moral, manner. Both are reasons for delight in themselves, and we will see how they unfold even greater doctrinal treasures to come.

6

DIVINE SIMPLICITY: THE WHOLLY DIVINE GOD

Divine simplicity is no longer presupposed in the task of theology. In ages past divine simplicity was taken as axiomatic. Not so today. While it is true that some popular segments of Reformed Protestantism are seeking to retrieve and defend divine simplicity in large numbers (relatively speaking!) once more, the doctrine has experienced an onslaught of critique. As Alvin Plantinga now famously laments, the traditional doctrine of divine simplicity is a "dark saying indeed."[1] Even worse, William Hasker describes divine simplicity as a "cognitive black hole that swallows up everything positive we might want to say about God."[2] To suggest that God is simple, lacking different parts, seems obviously false to most today. And yet the church catholic has confessed a version of divine simplicity throughout the ages. While simplicity doesn't feature explicitly in an ecumenical creed, it was assumed and deployed by the church fathers and has been codified in numerous magisterial Protestant confessions.

The main motivation for maintaining divine simplicity throughout the history of the church has been to confess God *as God*. The church has sought to safeguard the otherness and complete divinity of God, which is essential to Christian worship. For example, Boethius argues that "God is the very thing that God is; he is nothing other than what he is, and *for*

1. Alvin Plantinga, *Does God Have a Nature?* (Marquette University Press, 1980), 27.

2. William Hasker, *Metaphysics and the Tri-Personal God* (Oxford University Press, 2017), 61.

this very reason, he is God."[3] Because God is "nothing other than what he is," he is God and not a creature. Apart from simplicity God begins to depend on things outside of himself for his existence and divinity, which strips him of his "Godness." Suddenly God is no longer the majestic and transcendent being who overflows in perfection. Slowly but surely, he becomes dependent on his creation for his existence.[4] But no doctrine of divine simplicity is acceptable that jeopardizes the Trinity or incarnation, both of which are essential to the nature of the gospel itself. Therefore, in what follows I survey what divine simplicity means before engaging the motivations for it and challenges to it (especially that of the Trinity), and its practical relevance for the life of the church.

APPROACHING A DOGMATIC DEFINITION

Ask an average churchgoer if God is simple, and you'll likely receive a negative answer: "Of course God isn't simple! I'm simple, but not God! He is far beyond my simple little level of intelligence and power." Such a reply is indicative of a different understanding of what "simple" means. Today simple means "easy to understand." And who would ever think that God is *easy* to understand? But theologians have a far more technical meaning when they speak of simplicity. Typically, when theologians say God is simple, they mean it in relation to *composition*. God isn't *composed* of parts. He isn't like a home that is composed of bricks, wood, insulation, and the like. In God there isn't something more basic than him that makes him the way he is. So, he isn't complex in a mereological sense.[5] He therefore must be identical with himself rather than having any constituents apart from himself.

Simplicity, on this definition, relates to a type of unity beyond a mere aggregate (such as a pile of sand on the beach, which has no principle of

---

3. Boethius, "On the Holy Trinity," in *The Cambridge Edition of Early Christian Writings*, ed. Andrew Radde-Gallwitz (Cambridge University Press, 2017), 354, https://doi.org/10.1017/9781107449596.026. Emphasis mine.

4. This isn't to say there aren't sophisticated and legitimate ways to reject simplicity without turning God into a creature. There is a multitude of new criticisms of simplicity that develop alternative accounts of God's independence. I do not mean to suggest anyone that denies or revises divine simplicity is propping up an idol (a common trope today), though I do think they are wrong and must plug the leaking holes left in the ship of Christian theology when they toss simplicity overboard. The point here is to highlight the motivation for simplicity among the church catholic.

5. Stephen R. Holmes, "The Attributes of God," in *The Oxford Handbook of Systematic Theology*, ed. Kathryn Tanner, John Webster, and Iain Torrance (Oxford University Press, 2007), 63.

internal order that would make it an organism), ordered object (such as my hand being united to my arm and my arm to my torso), or essentially united object (such as my body to my soul). Simplicity is a unity beyond these unions. As Scotus explains, the unity of simplicity thinks "each of what exists is *really the same as any other*."[6] There is a relation here of identity. The supreme unity of simplicity, then, implies a negation of division.[7] God cannot be divided into anything smaller than himself. Whereas I have arms, legs, cells, mercy, and justice, God has nothing that is divisible. His love and mercy cannot be split. Therefore, God has no parts—metaphysical, physical, or otherwise.[8]

In recent times, popular-level works have sought to retrieve this vision of divine simplicity but have unnecessarily narrowed the tradition.[9] Divine simplicity is *simply* not monolithic in the tradition. While it is true that the church catholic has confessed the simple God, it has done so with various models. As Gavin Ortlund says, "It is a doctrine both enduring and elastic—standard and yet slippery."[10] Instead, I argue that it is better to begin with a shared baseline—a *mere* divine simplicity—from which various models make further claims and entailments rather than jumping to a sophisticated and contentious medieval model as the sole arbiter of orthodoxy from the start. Now, certainly there are models that utilize

---

6. John Duns Scotus, "Ordinatio," trans. Peter L. P. Simpson, I, d. 2, pars 2, q4, n. 403, https://www.aristotelophile.com/Books/Translations/Ordinatio%20I.pdf. Emphasis mine.

7. Francisco Suárez, *On the Various Kinds of Distinctions*, trans. Cyril Vollert (Marquette University Press, 2007), 16.

8. John Chrysostom, *On the Incomprehensible Nature of God*, trans. Paul W. Harkins (Catholic University of America Press, 2013), IV.19; John Gill, *A Body of Doctrinal Divinity* (George Keith, 1769), 75.

9. As a classical theist myself, I think any attempt to breathe fresh life into classical doctrines ought to be honored. Efforts to defend classical doctrines deserve our admiration. Unfortunately, some of the more recent reconstructions can become confused and sometimes even border on propaganda. By that I mean their retelling of the history of some classical doctrines like divine simplicity and their vision of orthodoxy are either revisionary or far too exclusive. In other words, some recent defenses ought to be categorized as projects of repristination instead of retrieval. And the person committed to a Reformed catholicity need not succumb to rhetoric that limits the theological and philosophical options for a classical theist. For example, Matthew Barrett has recently sought to reconcile Christian orthodoxy with a Thomistic account in a way that narrows the actual history. Differences are smoothed over, ignored, or misunderstood. Whatever differences exist are merely refinements on the road to the "fulfillment" of Thomism. Therefore, any deviation from the Thomistic version of divine simplicity is highly problematic for him. See Barrett, *The Reformation as Renewal*, 144. See also my forthcoming essay, "Plundering the Moderns."

10. Gavin Ortlund, *Theological Retrieval for Evangelicals*, 119.

the language of "simplicity" and yet are inconsistent even with a mere divine simplicity and should be considered non-classical, just as there are models that outright reject divine simplicity. Yet it is not the case that a strict Thomistic thesis is the only model available to the classical theologian. Or so I hope to prove.

These are important claims, so I ought to explain further. For example, as I referenced earlier, some like James Dolezal have argued that the divine simplicity of those in the early church like Basil and Gregory is "entirely repugnant to the later version of simplicity" and "entirely nonsensical."[11] Claims like this reduce the available orthodox positions on simplicity to one and cast off some of the church's greatest theologians and pastors. Certainly, Basil and Gregory ought not be considered unorthodox or, at least, theologically naive! Those interested in defending and participating in the catholicity of the church should not reject as entirely repugnant those luminaries of the catholic faith in the early church. But I suggest there is no need to reduce orthodoxy to one specific version of divine simplicity. Protestants ought to look to creeds and confessions as the boundary markers and not any one individual or school—even an influential school like Thomism, right as it may be!

I should note that an additional worry to my proposal might be that the various conceptions of divine simplicity that "differ" from Thomas in the Christian tradition (like Gregory or Basil) aren't simplicity at all but merely pay lip service to it. But as I intend to show throughout the remainder of this chapter, without the authority of an ecumenical council to arbitrate, we look to the important theological masters who do address it and the content of the Protestant confessions, both of which provide a spectrum of views. Some of these views may well be minority, but given the limits provided by these theological "authorities" there is room within the Christian tradition to nuance divine simplicity. We needn't let Thomism (or other theological and philosophical schools) disproportionally dominate the doctrine. This skewed narrowing of simplicity is in part due to the rise of Thomistic dominance but also in part due to reading the Christian tradition through some isolated segments

11. James E. Dolezal, "Review of Basil of Caesarea, Gregory of Nyssa, and the Transformation of Divine Simplicity," *Westminster Theological Journal* 73 (2011): 387.

of history, appealing to the no true Scotsman principle anytime deviation is found. While it is true that many in the medieval tradition (especially the Arabic tradition) crystalized an absolute version of simplicity, Russell Friedman remains instructive when he says "no medieval university theologian thought that any distinction he posited to be in God compromised divine simplicity. Nevertheless, simplicity can be something of an elastic concept, admitting of degrees ..."[12]

MERE DIVINE SIMPLICITY

Before I embark on sketching the various models of divine simplicity, as hinted at above, I take the following to be a *mere* divine simplicity:

> *Mere divine simplicity:* God is simple *if and only if* God is (1) *a se*, (2) necessary, (3) an indivisible unity, and (4) self-consistent.

Each of these deserves some further outworking. (1) By *a se*, I mean to especially key in on God's ungroundedness. In other words, there is no metaphysical or physical priority or explanation for his being. He exists, and nothing explains that besides himself. It is not as if God is made up of something that he then must *depend* on for his existence or his being the way that he is. He is entirely *a se*. In contrast, all of creation lacks such aseity. For example, I depend on my parents for my origin and on food, water, and oxygen for my continued existence. God, on the other hand, has no such dependence. (2) By necessary I mean to say that God cannot lack anything that he has—he is necessary in every respect. He exists necessarily but also his nature and attributes exist necessarily. Therefore, his attributes are inseparable from himself. For example, there is not a future time wherein God could suddenly lack love or justice. These are necessary to his being God. (3) By invisible unity I mean that God, as a unity, cannot be divided in any sense. Nothing can separate from his nature. This claim is slightly more expansive than his necessity, since his unity denies division. (4) By self-consistent I mean that God as simple is wholly consistent with himself—nothing in his nature is contrary to anything else in it, nor disrupts its unity.

---

12. Friedman, *Medieval Trinitarian Thought*, 100. See also David Bradshaw, *Aristotle East and West: Metaphysics and the Division of Christendom* (Cambridge: Cambridge University Press, 2007), 224–25, 40. Bradshaw likewise describes an Augustinian *version* which is in contrast to Gregory Palamas, implying there are multiple versions of simplicity.

These claims appear somewhat pedestrian on their face, even for some other models of God. Some neo-classical theists, for example, would generally affirm all four. But even other models will affirm some of these. For example, most all Christian theists confess God as a necessary being with necessary properties (e.g., 2). Even neo-process theist Thomas Jay Oord is willing to admit of God having his attribute of love necessarily.[13] Therefore, each part of this definition is necessary though not sufficient. The real debate relates to (1) and how it is explained. (1) is supposed to arise from any standard account of divine aseity since any dependence is outlawed by God's independence. But neo-classical thinkers affirm divine aseity and yet deny divine simplicity. Why? Because of the metaphysics packed into (1). Let me explain.

When one surveys the traditional doctrine of divine simplicity, the assertion that God is *a se* and thus ontologically basic means that God is independent and without explanation, which entails he must be *without composition*. As Gilles Emery explains, "God is exempt from the internal composition that characterizes the whole domain of the created order."[14] Likewise, Matthias Scheeben (1835–1888) defines divine simplicity as a lack of composition "of any kind whatsoever." Indeed, no composition can occur, nor is it even conceivable.[15] The composition denied of God is "everything that results from the joining or assembly of several elements or moments that are not essentially included in one another, one of which completes the other or which are mutually complementary."[16]

Since God is without composition, he lacks parts. But it is not wholly clear if *all* composition is outlawed by divine simplicity, or what counts as a part. For example, as discussed in chapter 4 on metaphysics, composition typically refers to material objects and doesn't have a specific correlation to immaterial objects. So, does this mean God lacks *every* conceivable kind of composition or that he just isn't a material object? Or does it allow for a sort of composition but define it differently so that it no longer counts as

13. See Thomas Jay Oord, *Open and Relational Theology* (SacraSage, 2021).

14. Gilles Emery, "The Immutability of the God of Love and the Problem of Language Concerning the 'Suffering of God,' " in *Divine Impassibility and the Mystery of Human Suffering*, ed. James F. Keating and Thomas Joseph White, trans. Thomas Joseph White (Eerdmans, 2009), 59.

15. Matthias Joseph Scheeben, *Handbook of Catholic Dogmatics* (Emmaus Academic, 2019), 2:83.

16. Scheeben, *Handbook of Catholic Dogmatics*, 2:81.

composition as we might think of it? Does simplicity mean God is strictly identical with his goodness, justice, and mercy so that there really aren't different attributes? Does it entail that there can be no Trinity of persons? And so on.

To best understand what kind of composition is denied by divine simplicity, we must utilize the distinctions found in chapter 4. As explained, while mereology and composition usually are only applied to material objects, it is not only integral parts like physical or spatial that can "compose" something.[17] There are metaphysical parts, temporal parts, and even logical parts depending on the object too. Naturally, any Christian doctrine will deny physical parts of God. He does not have a body. And hence he doesn't have any spatial parts. And the classical theologian objects to temporal parts because God is eternal. But what about metaphysical parts? Is God made up of essence *and* existence, or is he a species in a genus? Or what about logical parts? Is God's justice distinct from his love? There are a variety of answers to these questions. For example, medieval theologians took divine simplicity with the utmost seriousness but posited various distinctions, though none of them thought their distinctions compromised simplicity.[18] Therefore, these models I sketch must answer four related and important questions:

1. Can God be *a se* and yet be composed of parts?
2. Is there complexity that doesn't entail composition?
3. Are there grounds in God for any distinctions?
4. Are there any distinctions *in* God?

The first question asks whether there is a sort of composition that does not entail dependence. While divine simplicity, across the entire Christian tradition, clearly denies composition of God, it isn't always clear what *sort*

---

17. Martinus Becanus (1563–1624) gives a glimpse into the various kinds of composition we must consider: "Simplicity is opposed to composition, just as unity is to multitude. For what is simple is not composed: just as what is one is not multiple. But there are various kinds of composition, as the Scholastics rightly teach. One kind of composition is of genus and differences. Another is of form and matter. A third is of integral parts. Fourth, of essence and existence. Fifth, of nature and suppositum, or as others call it, of nature and subsistence or personality. Sixth, of a subject and accidents." Martinus Becanus, "Summa Theologiae Scolasticae," trans. Michael Lynch (Lyon, 1620), II.1.

18. Friedman, *Medieval Trinitarian Thought*, 100.

of composition is being denied. What is required is a close reading of a wide number of so-called theological masters and confessions to approximate an answer. The remaining questions relate largely to the various sorts of distinctions discussed in chapter 4: real, mental, virtual, and formal, and whether any are applicable to God. Another way of asking the fourth question is whether there is more than one truthmaker (e.g., there is more than one portion of reality in virtue of which something is true) for the distinctions we mentally conceive. If there is more than one, then there are distinctions *in* God. But this doesn't necessarily mean there is metaphysical composition.

MODELS OF DIVINE SIMPLICITY

As with any attempt to systematize the various doctrinal positions in the history of Christian dogma, both oversimplification and anachronism are nearly impossible to avoid. While we don't find historical thinkers discussing "models" of simplicity, it is part of the job of the constructive historical theologian to offer synthesized categories of explanation. Therefore, I've sought to categorize five broad approaches to divine simplicity exemplified in the Christian tradition before examining the historical witness to see which models are viable for the Christian committed to catholic Christianity. Others have created different organizations of these—some fewer and some greater.[19] I make no claim to provide the definitive categorization, but I've found these senses to be helpful. If you are a reader that is not regularly involved in these more technical discussions, some of the material may appear obtuse and require re-reading. Don't fret! As I've periodically suggested throughout this work, the journey can be arduous at times, but so is any great climb to a mountain peak. Once one has scaled the mountain, the views of the whole are well worth whatever arduous difficulty one endured along the way. So, if the going gets tough remember that the various nuances in the debates are about safeguarding God as totally, completely, irreducibly, and indestructibly God and thus are truly relevant to our

19. For example, Richards has given at least seven various senses of simplicity. McCall offers three. See Jay Wesley Richards, *The Untamed God* (InterVarsity Press, 2003), 217; McCall, "Trinity Doctrine, Plain and Simple," in *Advancing Trinitarian Theology: Explorations in Constructive Dogmatics*, ed. Oliver Crisp and Fred Sanders (Zondervan, 2014), 54–55.

own lives and worship. The fancy words and sometimes microscopic distinctions are just part of explaining how God remains fully himself while also remaining for us and our salvation. So, we should expect these technical debates to be necessary for exploring the sublime mystery of God himself.

As a note, when I speak of "properties" or "attributes" throughout this chapter I intend to use it in a neutral way that doesn't beg the question. "Property" or "attribute" here are just terms to pick out whatever it is we mean when we say God is good or God is love. It doesn't intend to assume that God has distinct properties or anything else. It is purely about the semantics unless noted otherwise. Further, when I use the term "extramental" I mean to communicate distinctions that exist prior to the working of the intellect. Finally, I invoke the terminology of "*ad intra*" in some of these definitions since it is standard in most theological literature as a term to pick out that which is internal to God rather than external (*ad extra*).

> *Maximal divine simplicity:* God is simple *if and only if* God lacks (1) all composition, (2) all extramental grounds for distinctions, and (3) all extramental distinctions.
>
> *Virtual divine simplicity:* God is simple *if and only if* God lacks (1) all composition and (2) all *ad intra* extramental distinctions.
>
> *Formal divine simplicity:* God is simple *if and only if* God lacks (1) all composition and (2) all *ad intra* extramental distinctions *except for the formal distinction.*
>
> *Parsimonious divine simplicity:* God is simple *if and only if* God lacks (1) all composition and (2) *ad intra* real distinctions.
>
> *Apophatic divine simplicity:* God is simple *if and only if* God is wholly himself.

For the sake of clarity, before exploring each of these models in greater detail, on the next page are the general answers to each of the four important questions.

Table 6.1. Four Important Questions

Model	**Can God be *a se* and yet be composed of parts?**	**Is there complexity that doesn't entail composition?**	**Are there grounds in God for any distinctions?**	**Are there any distinctions *in* God?**
Maximal	No	No	No	No
Virtual	No	No	Yes	No
Formal	No	No	Yes	Yes
Parsimonious	Yes	No	Yes	Yes
Apophatic	No analogue	No analogue	No analogue	No analogue

What is immediately noticeable is that the apophatic definition isn't structured in the same format as the others. That is intentional because the definition is supposed to eschew philosophical examination. It merely attempts to claim that God is wholly himself and not stake a claim on more definitive issues of philosophy. Therefore, it does little to positively explain what is meant by mere divine simplicity. But it does little to define what doesn't count as simplicity too. Must one commit themselves to the claim that God is only half himself to deny simplicity? Despite the conceptual ambiguity I suggest it is helpful to maintain this "model" for the sake of providing the various options that have been suggested in the Christian tradition. From these definitions, I argue that all are viable options—except certain construals of the parsimonious model—for the catholic Christian.

On the maximal version of divine simplicity, since God lacks all composition, all grounds for extramental distinctions, and all extramental distinctions, he is strictly *identical* to himself. There are no distinctions in the divine nature to be made whatsoever. There are no physical, metaphysical, or logical parts.[20] All that God has God is, in the strictest possible sense. And so, the only distinction we can draw in God about any of his attributes is purely mental. In no way do our distinctions map onto reality. When I think of God as love and then think of him as wisdom, these distinctions I am making and applying to God are entirely on "my side" as

20. James E. Dolezal, *God Without Parts: Divine Simplicity and the Metaphysics of God's Absoluteness* (Pickwick, 2011), 31.

a creature. They both correspond to the exact same referent. So, wisdom and love really aren't different in God. God's attributes are strictly speaking "really identical with each other."[21] It is not even that omnipotence and omniscience result in different effects in the world, but that power and knowledge are different ideas under which we variously conceive the absolutely one divine act (whether *ad extra* or not). This is *not* to say that the maximal model outlaws real distinctions with reference to the divine persons, lest modalism be the result (though, it might very well require one to do this).[22] These Trinitarian distinctions are usually described as non-identical to the divine nature since the personal relations are between the persons and not the nature.[23]

As a further example of the maximal model, consider the 1473 Parisian defense of nominalism:

> Those doctors are called nominalists who do not multiply things principally signified by terms in accord with the multiplication of terms. Realists, on the other hand, are those who contend that things are multiplied in accord with the multiplication of terms. For example, nominalists say that deity and wisdom are entirely one and the same thing, because everything that is in God is God. Realists, however, say that divine wisdom is divided from deity.[24]

The area of dispute, shown here, is on the structure of language and how it corresponds to reality. The Parisian defense argues that our language *doesn't* correspond to a really distinct thing in reality when it comes to God. His wisdom just is God, and there is no distinction.[25]

The virtual model of divine simplicity tracks very closely to the maximal model. Depending on the thinker these two models may collapse into one another. However, I think they should be kept distinct both for pedagogical reasons and for conceptual clarity. Furthermore, important thinkers like Scheeben have even called such accounts of simplicity

---

21. James Dolezal, *All That Is in God* (Reformation Heritage, 2017), 42.
22. See Friedman, *Medieval Trinitarian Thought*.
23. Dolezal, *All That Is in God*, 119.
24. Quoted in Robert Pasnau, *Metaphysical Themes: 1274–1671* (Clarendon, 2011), 86.
25. Pasnau, *Metaphysical Themes*, 86.

"exaggerated."[26] I take it that the virtual model is the proper and pure Thomistic form (though some Thomists such as Cajetan allow for more latitude, such as the formal version).[27] As Thomas says, "Although names said of God signify the same reality, they are yet not synonyms because they do not signify the same notion."[28] He likewise argues in his earlier commentary on the *Sentences*:

> The plurality of these names is not only on the side of our intellect forming the diverse conceptions about God, which are called the "diverse accounts," as is clear from things said in the previous article. Rather, it is also on the side of God himself, insofar as there is something in God corresponding to all these conceptions, that is, his full and total perfection, according to which it arises that each of the names signifying these conceptions is said truly and properly of God. However, this is not in such a way that any diversity or multiplicity is placed in the reality that is God by reason of such attributes.[29]

Therefore, the main difference is that the virtual model is committed to a virtual or eminent distinction, which has a single ground or foundation *in* God that accounts for the distinction of "notion."[30] So, there is a foundation in God for the distinction of the attributes that we see *ad extra*. However, there is no real extramental distinction in God.

The virtual distinction applied to God indicates that the wisdom and justice of God are the same in that they refer to the same reality (i.e., God) but with respect to different concepts, accounts, or notions (i.e., wisdom and justice).[31] The reason for this is due to the wealth of divine perfection by which we apprehend his single, simple essence through different notions.[32] As Steven Duby argues, "Divine simplicity signifies that God

---

26. Scheeben, *Handbook of Catholic Dogmatics*, 2:95.

27. Andreas J. Beck, *Gisbertus Voetius (1589–1676) on God, Freedom, and Contingency: An Early Modern Reformed Voice* (Brill, 2022), 260.

28. Thomas Aquinas, *Summa Contra Gentiles: Book One; God*, trans. Anton Charles Pegis (University of Notre Dame Press, 1975), 1.35.1.

29. Thomas Aquinas, *Commentary on the Sentences, Book I, Distinctions 1–20*, trans. Christopher Decaen (Green Bay, WI: Aquinas Institute, 2025), Sent.I.d2.q1.a3.c.15.

30. Scheeben, *Handbook of Catholic Dogmatics*, 2:96.

31. See also Aquinas, *Commentary on the Sentences*, Sent.I.d2.q1.a3.sc5.2.

32. Scheeben, *Handbook of Catholic Dogmatics*, 2:97.

is not composed of parts but is identical with his own essence, existence, and attributes, each of which is identical with God's whole being viewed under some particular aspect."[33] Drawing on the common illustration of light, it is similar to how heat and light are virtually distinct yet not distinct in reality in the rays of the sun.[34] And so any distinction in God is not real or formal—it is only virtual or relative.[35]

The formal version of divine simplicity takes its name from John Duns Scotus. Scotus and those that roughly follow him think there is not only a ground for distinctions in God alongside the virtual model with mental distinctions but also a ground for distinction itself *in* God. However, they do not admit of just any real extramental distinction in God. Only the formal distinction is admitted as a sort of real and extramental distinction. The formal distinction means that prior to any act of the intellect on our part, there is a distinction *in* the thing itself and thus there is an extramental distinction *in* God.[36] Therefore, there are distinct truthmakers for the various predications we make of God. While God is a single and simple subject, wholly identical with himself, identity does not entail complete sameness.[37] The differing truthmakers, say God's goodness and God's infinity, are formally distinct when they really are identical—they are both identical to God—and yet they have different essential characteristics rooted in some aspects of themselves.[38]

Given this, formal simplicity agrees with maximal simplicity and virtual simplicity in most respects. God lacks composition. He has no spatial, temporal, metaphysical, or temporal parts. He doesn't have accidents. So, it may appear that the difference between the virtual and formal is merely terminological, but I suggest this would be a mistake. I argue that the formal model goes beyond the virtual model by not only suggesting

---

33. Steven J. Duby, *Jesus and the God of Classical Theism* (Baker Academic, 2022), 31.

34. Richard Muller, *Post-Reformation Reformed Dogmatics* (Baker Academic, 2003), 3:292.

35. Steven J. Duby, *Divine Simplicity: A Dogmatic Account* (T&T Clark, 2016), 226.

36. Friedman, *Medieval Trinitarian Thought from Aquinas to Ockham*, 108.

37. Peter King, "Scotus on Metaphysics," in *The Cambridge Companion to Duns Scotus*, ed. Thomas Williams (Cambridge University Press, 2006), 22.

38. Jeff Steele and Thomas Williams, "Complexity without Composition: Duns Scotus on Divine Simplicity," *American Catholic Philosophical Quarterly* 93, no. 4 (2019): 6, https://doi.org/10.5840/acpq2019920185.

there is a foundation in the divine essence for the distinction but that it is present "actually."[39] It seeks a sort of middle ground between real and mental distinctions whereas the virtual sees no middle. Therefore, God is *not* strictly identical in the Leibnizian sense with his attributes, and those attributes are not strictly identical with each other.[40] Even if there are no minds thinking about God, there is a distinction between his attributes.

While it is true that the formal distinction is rather hard to understand, consider an analogy of light refracted through a prism. As children we stand in awe at how a single white ray of light can enter a prism and exit as a rainbow of colors. We may be tempted to think there is nothing intrinsic to the ray of light that causes such a wide display. However, all the colors are intrinsically within the single ray of light, and when they are refracted through a prism the wavelengths of colors travel at different speeds and exit in such a way that we can see the distinct colors in what previously we had no capacity to see. In an analogous way, though certainly different in very important respects, all of God's attributes are intrinsically in God and "one" and yet are formally distinct, and through creation and mental abstraction we can see the distinct colors.

The parsimonious model, as a discrete *model*, is relatively new compared to the others. Published originally in 2019 by Oliver Crisp, it argues that God is metaphysically simple but mereologically complex. In other words, God is similar to an electron or a soul. He is metaphysically primitive (i.e., lacks dependence on any subject) with no composition or physical or logical structure, though he can have different parts or properties that he exemplifies. For example, electrons or souls are simple, as in primitive, and yet can have different properties like mass or spin or conscious states.[41]

Finally, the apophatic model, as indicated above, eschews formal definition. The main claim is simply that God is entirely himself and there is no further definition to be had. Any attempt to make sense of the mystery is seen as cantankerous theological speculation. There is some appeal to such an approach. At least in the early church, divine simplicity functions as theological "grammar" intended to regulate our speech about

39. Beck, *Gisbertus Voetius (1589–1676) on God, Freedom, and Contingency*, 260.

40. Richard Cross, *Duns Scotus* (Oxford University Press, 1999), 29.

41. Oliver Crisp, *Analyzing Doctrine* (Baylor University Press, 2019), 66.

God without giving precise metaphysical accounts of his nature. But the apophatic model naturally lacks the same level of explanatory power as the other models that give more specific explanations.

CREEDAL AND CONFESSIONAL AFFIRMATION

Divine simplicity is latent within the creedal tradition but does not find explicit mention or explanation.[42] Part of the rationale for its omission is due to the occasional nature of the creeds and councils themselves. They were designed to discuss debated issues. And divine simplicity was not debated. Everyone agreed. Reaching as far back, at least, as Plato, simplicity was viewed as a given for the divine. In fact, it was the shared assumption of simplicity that generated other doctrinal puzzles that would lead to christological heresies. Therefore, most of the expansion on divine simplicity in the format of creed and confession finds itself in later confessional tradition.

While divine simplicity *does* feature in Protestant confessional tradition, it would be dishonest to claim that it is explicitly confessed universally—or even found in the majority of Protestant confessions in the sixteenth and seventeenth centuries. However, it is explicitly present in many and, more important, the most influential. The Second Helvetic Confession (1566) says God is without a "body," which typically is a nod to at least part of divine simplicity, but then launches into other descriptions "infinite, eternal," and the like. The Waldensian Confession (1560), French Confession (1559), and Confession of La Rochelle (1571), however, explicitly say that God's being is "simple." The Belgic Confession (1561) likewise in article 1 confesses God as a "single and simple spiritual being." The Forty-Two Articles (1552/53), Thirty-Nine Articles (1563), and Irish Articles (1615) all say God is "without body, parts, or passions." This phrase then gets repeated in the Westminster Confession of Faith (1644), Savoy Declaration (1658), and Second London Confession of Faith (1677/89). From these alone, the main expressions of the Reformed faith

42. I should note that this is so far as I am aware. We have no procedural documentation or notes from the council of Nicaea or Constantinople I, for example. We only have the final products: the creeds and canons. However, for the Roman Catholic church there *are* "ecumenical" councils that address simplicity in Lateran 4 and Vatican I. See Richard Price and Michael Gaddis, *The Acts of the Council of Chalcedon* (Liverpool University Press, 2007), 1:5–7; Tim Pawl, "The Incarnation of a Simple God," in *Classical Theism: New Essays on the Metaphysics of God*, ed. Robert C. Koons and Jonathan Fuqua (Routledge, 2022), 303–17, https://doi.org/10.4324/9781003202172-19.

all self-consciously confess that God is *simple*. However, these do not provide explanation beyond the negative phrasing of *without* body or parts.

Two important documents, however, do provide further elaboration on divine simplicity. The first is the Baptist *An Orthodox Creed* (1678). In article 1 it says God is "without matter or form, body, parts, or passions." Then in article 2 God "is simplicity, one meer ... and perfect act, without all composition." These descriptions are far more explicit and limiting compared to most Reformed confessions. While this creed does repeat the common "without body, parts, or passions," it adds a level of composition that is to be denied "matter or form" and confesses God as pure act.

The second important document is *not* strictly a confession. It was designed as a university textbook. Therefore, no church maintained it as a doctrinal standard. However, it came on the heels of the Synod of Dort and sought to elaborate its teaching. It was written by four professors who were trained by some of the Reformed "greats" like Beza, Daneau, Zanchi, and Ursinus. Therefore, it carries more consensus weight than typical individual authors. This document is the 1625 *Synopsis of Purer Theology*. Two sections stand out as illuminating for the doctrine of divine simplicity. In section 6.21, it states:

> Although this essence applies to God in an absolute way so that there is not one thing and another thing in God, but all what He is, is his essence, we nevertheless rightly assign to Him various properties or attributes, which are classified under the title of divinity (Rom 1:20), suggesting that there is a difference between essence and properties and between properties themselves. Yet this is not a real distinction, but a relational or rational distinction.[43]

Here the *Synopsis* is elaborating on divine simplicity—there is no real distinction or composition in God. He is wholly himself. It then provides two forms of distinctions that *are* authorized for the simple God.[44] In section 6.24, these are elaborated further:

---

43. Willem Arie den Boer and Riemer A. Faber, *Synopsis of a Purer Theology* (Davenant, 2023), 60.

44. It seems right to mention the work of Ryan Mullins here. He claims in his first monograph that divine simplicity requires a rejection of all distinctions in God whatsoever. He has repeated this claim elsewhere. So, "even conceptual distinctions are repugnant." But such a claim is either ignorant of the Christian tradition or ignorant of the use of words and concepts within the tradition. The *Synopsis of Purer Theology*,

> Simplicity is an attribute of God's essence of the first type, and certainly one of the more general attributes, indicating that the divine essence is altogether without any composition, whether that composition be from material and integral parts, or from the essential parts of matter and form, from genus and difference, subject and accident, act and potency, and finally, essence and existence.

Herein is one of the more robust consensus statements regarding divine simplicity and the parts that are removed by it. God is free from material, integral, and essential parts, doesn't stand under categories of genus, has no accidents, lacks all potency, and cannot be distinguished into essence and existence. So, while some of these more explicit documents *may* exclude some versions of simplicity, none of the five models appear to be properly excluded from classic Protestant doctrine. In fact, most Protestant confessions either elude the language of simplicity or leave it undefined, allowing the confessional church and individual a significant degree of latitude. Divine simplicity is certainly part of confessional dogma, but the particular model appears to be up for debate. Though, if there is one model with confessional support, it appears to be the maximal model as noted by *An Orthodox Creed.*

THE WITNESS OF THE CLASSICAL TRADITION

Throughout the classical tradition theologians and pastors make use of divine simplicity. It is called upon as a tool for explaining God's unity and aseity and protecting monotheism. And throughout the tradition it is often given significant explanation, offering us a better window into what models should be considered appropriate for the confessional and classical thinker. In what follows I provide extended explanations from

---

as quoted here, explicitly endorses a relational or rational *distinction.* And the *Synopsis* is not an outlier document. Thomas Aquinas, as shown earlier, admits of conceptual distinctions. So do modern authors like Steven Duby. So, while Mullins has demonstrated an adequate command of some historical sources in his work, he has not proven strong in engaging the full breadth of writing among the authors, especially those of the Reformation and Post-Reformation period. He has not always demonstrated a command of the overall theological logic and rationale the various traditional thinkers employed when using terms and concepts. While he often brings "receipts" in the form of quotes from various authors that appear to prove his point, on further inspection, within the larger flow of arguments, many of his judgments are far too quick. His recourse may be that these are distinctions without a difference, but that requires far more of an argument than an assertion, especially when the authors he seeks to disagree with beg to differ. See R. T. Mullins, *The End of the Timeless God* (Oxford University Press, 2016), 53.

several thinkers in each period, beyond what I provide in other chapters, primarily because divine simplicity is possibly *the* most contested classical doctrine today, and understanding the general theological logic of thinkers can be of immense value.

As we explore the classical tradition, especially the patristic tradition, there is a special danger that I should warn about. Especially as it relates to divine simplicity, there can be an impulse to employ what I call a "Where's Waldo" approach. *Where's Waldo?*, if you aren't initiated, is a classic children's puzzle book from the 1980s and 1990s where author Martin Handford paints crowded scenes with a character named Waldo hidden within the crowd. Waldo is always dressed the same, in a red and white striped shirt. The point is that he is supposed to be hard to find, which makes for entertainment as you search different crowds for Waldo. But what is a fun children's game can be a dangerous approach to historical theology. What can happen in theology (and all other disciplines too) is that we look for certain key words and extract them from their context once they are found. When this is done, a set of assumptions is brought in search of validation. We are on a scavenger hunt to find what we want to prove our own points. Once a word or phrase is found, we assume its congruence with other thinkers. But this is not responsible exegesis of historical or contemporary texts. Each work has an inner logic that can impact the way it uses certain words or phrases. Moreover, each work can define the same words in different ways. The advent of Google and other tools that allow us to quickly search for the key words we need can tempt us to this sort of methodology, short-circuiting a proper listening posture.

The main example of a *Where's Waldo?* approach for divine simplicity is the language of "identity." Throughout the tradition we find various thinkers employing the language of God being "identical" to himself or his attributes. But much of the more robust metaphysical analysis found in the later scholastic tradition and exemplified by the maximal, virtual, and formal models of divine simplicity are not present in the early church, though they deploy the language of identity. Depending on the thinker and context they may not be using identity in a strict sense like Leibniz's law. But to understand this one must pay careful attention to the inner logic of arguments and the context of the claims. And one must realize that while simplicity is ubiquitous in the tradition, it is often left undefined.[45] We can do our best to reconstruct the meaning but must avoid anachronistic reconstructions.

The Patristic Witness

Before referring to some of the patristic record, we should remember that Plato's *Republic* (especially 380d–383c) serves as the "paradigmatic background" to simplicity for much of the early church.[46] It is the background template many work from, expand on, and deviate from. Here Plato has a short dialogue glossing simplicity in ways that make simplicity a concept of self-constancy. God as simple is connected to the idea of immutability. He asks, "Is he really simple and never leaves his own form at all?"[47] Likewise, in the *Symposium*, Plato reflects on the form of the beautiful:

> Suddenly he will behold a beauty marvelous in its nature, that very Beauty, Socrates, for the sake of which all the earlier hardships had been borne: in the first place, everlasting, and never being born nor perishing, neither increasing nor diminishing; secondly, not beautiful here and ugly there, not beautiful now and ugly then, not beautiful in one direction and ugly in another direction, not beautiful in one place and ugly in another place. Again this beauty will not show itself to him like a face or hands or any bodily thing at all, nor as a discourse or a science, nor indeed as residing in anything, as in a living creature, or in earth or in heaven or in anything else, but being by itself with itself always in simplicity.[48]

The patristics place a similar emphasis on God's perfect and pure self-consistency, like Plato.[49] But the patristic record goes beyond Plato and deploys simplicity in ways that say God is incomposite, indivisible, and

---

45. Lewis Ayres, *Nicaea and Its Legacy: An Approach to Fourth-Century Trinitarian Theology* (Oxford University Press, 2009), 281.

46. Pui Him Ip, *Origen and the Emergence of Divine Simplicity before Nicaea* (University of Notre Dame Press, 2022), 19.

47. Plato, "The Republic," in *Great Dialogues of Plato: Complete Text of The Republic, The Apology, Crito, Phaedo, Ion, Meno, Symposium*, trans. W. H. D. Rouse (Signet, 2008), 380d.

48. Plato, "Symposium," in *Great Dialogues of Plato: Complete Text of The Republic, The Apology, Crito, Phaedo, Ion, Meno, Symposium*, trans. W. H. D. Rouse (Signet, 2008), 210B–212A.

49. Ip, *Origen and the Emergence of Divine Simplicity before Nicaea*, 9.

unique.[50] The main impulse is to ensure God is essential without participation in something else.

Now, hear directly from the patristic tradition. Origen calls God a "simple intellectual being."[51] Elsewhere he explains how God alone possesses his attributes essentially whereas others possess them as an accident that can be lost.[52] Saint Basil explains, "Though our Lord is one in substrate, and one substance, simple and not composite, he calls himself by different names at different times, using designations that differ from one another for the different conceptualizations."[53] Elsewhere he assumes that God is free from any and all composition.[54] What Basil provides are the ingredients for later developments, particularly what looks similar to the maximal or virtual models wherein distinctions are different mental conceptualizations and do not relate to anything *real* in God.

Both John Chrysostom and John of Damascus repeat the same phrasing about God. He is simple and not composed of parts.[55] Damascene adds that God is non-composite "since the whole is wholly everywhere and is not divided into parts in a corporeal fashion."[56] Augustine likewise explains that God is identical to himself. It is the same thing for God to be powerful as it is to be just or to be anything else. These are not distinct parts in him. His simplicity grounds a "multiplicity" for Augustine, but this multiplicity reflects how we understand the varied operations of the simple God.[57]

---

50. Lewis Ayres and Andrew Radde-Gallwitz, "Doctrine of God," in *The Oxford Handbook of Early Christian Studies*, ed. Susan Ashbrook Harvey and David G. Hunter (Oxford University Press, 2009), 874, https://doi.org/10.1093/oxfordhb/9780199271566.003.0043.

51. Origen, *Origen: On First Principles*, trans. John Behr (Oxford University Press, 2019), 1.1.6.

52. Origen, *On First Principles* 1.6.2.

53. Basil, *Against Eunomius*, trans. Mark DelCogliano and Andrew Radde-Gallwitz (Catholic University of America Press, 2011), 1.6–7.

54. Basil, *On the Holy Spirit*, trans. Stephen M. Hildebrand (St. Vladimir's Seminary Press, 2011), 8, 21.

55. John Chrysostom, *On the Incomprehensible Nature of God*, trans. Paul W. Harkins (Catholic University of America Press, 1984), IV.19; John of Damascus, *On the Orthodox Faith*, trans. Normal Russell (St. Vladimir's Seminary Press, 2022), 83.

56. John of Damascus, *On the Orthodox Faith* 92.

57. Augustine, *The Trinity*, trans. Edmund Hill (New City, 2015), VI.1.4, 6.

Nicene hero Athanasius also appeals to divine simplicity throughout his works. In his *Defense of the Nicene Definition,* he says: "But if God be simple, as He is, it follows that in saying 'God' and naming 'Father,' we name nothing as if about Him, but signify his essence itself."[58] In his *Orations Against the Arians* when he discusses divine simplicity, he is explicit that it means God cannot be composed of parts. God is not passible, partitive, or merely capable of instantiating something like wisdom. He doesn't participate in something external to himself. He is wisdom itself because it is proper to him.[59] The reason God cannot be composed is because God is immaterial, indivisible, and participates in nothing.

Gregory of Nyssa explains divine simplicity along these same sorts of lines. In *Against the Macedonians,* he says God is "simple, uniform, and non-composite, and no interweaving or composition from dissimilar things is considered in connection with it."[60] Later he says:

> The simplicity of the subject ensures that it does not possess these names by participation. ... If the formula of its nature is simple, it does not possess goodness as something acquired. Rather, the very thing it is, is goodness, wisdom, power, holiness, justice, eternity, incorruptibility, and all the names that are sublime and elevating.[61]

Gregory here is developing a corollary of aseity. God does not participate in something else when he has an attribute. It is not something he acquires from outside himself. He is the sum total of all his perfections by himself.[62] These descriptions echo the concept of mere divine simplicity. Gregory does not give details on the distinctions between the attributes. Instead, he makes blanket ontological claims about the independence of God, his self-constancy, his infinity, and his moral purity.

Two other important definitions of simplicity come from Irenaeus and Boethius. Irenaeus gives an exhaustive account in his *Against Heresies*:

---

58. Athanasius, "Defence of the Nicene Council," in *Select Works and Letters,* ed. Archibald Thomas Robertson and Philip Schaff, Nicene and Post-Nicene Fathers, 2nd ser., vol. 4 (Hendrickson, 2004), 5.22.

59. Athanasius, "Against the Arians," in *Select Works and Letters,* ed. Archibald Thomas Robertson and Philip Schaff, 4 (Hendrickson, 2004), 1.28.

60. Cited in Andrew Radde-Gallwitz, "Gregory of Nyssa and Divine Simplicity: A Conceptualist Reading," *Modern Theology* 35, no. 3 (2019): 459, https://doi.org/10.1111/moth.12504.

61. Cited in Radde-Gallwitz, "Gregory of Nyssa and Divine Simplicity," 460.

62. Radde-Gallwitz, "Gregory of Nyssa and Divine Simplicity," 453–54.

> He is a simple, uncompounded Being, without diverse members, and altogether like, and equal to himself, since He is wholly understanding, and wholly spirit, and wholly thought, and wholly intelligence, and wholly reason, and wholly hearing, and wholly seeing, and wholly light, and the whole source of all that is good.[63]

Several aspects are worth noting here. Irenaeus tracks with the same idea regarding simplicity as lacking composition. But he expands by explaining how God is *wholly* whatever he is. The idea explained here isn't a strict identity but that there is nothing "at variance" with himself.[64]

Boethius, throughout his works, also gives important notions of simplicity. He explains that "the divine substance is form without matter and thus is one thing, namely, its essence."[65] Again, "In God there is no diversity, no plurality that results from diversity, no multiplicity that results from incidental features and thus no number. ... God differs from God in no respect."[66] Finally, he explains that "it is the same thing to be God as it is to be just" and "it is the same thing to be God as it is to be great."[67] These claims largely correspond to the ideas from Irenaeus—God is not composite and he is wholly himself. In other words, there is nothing besides God that makes up God, and he isn't divided in such a way as to be partly wise or partly intelligent. He is wholly whatever he is. Therefore, when God's attributes are called identical to who God is, the main idea, at least for the early church, is that his attributes are inseparable from him and indivisible.[68]

The Medieval Witness

While the patristic era often lacks sophisticated taxonomies for divine simplicity, the medieval era, in typical fashion, explores divine simplicity in far greater depth. As was true of the patristic era, medieval theologians nearly universally assent to divine simplicity, though the concept

63. Irenaeus, *Against Heresies*, ed. Alexander Roberts and James Donaldson (Ex Fontibus, 2010), II.13.3.

64. Irenaeus, *Against Heresies* II.13.8.

65. Boethius, "On the Holy Trinity," in *The Cambridge Edition of Early Christian Writings*, ed. Andrew Radde-Gallwitz (Cambridge University Press, 2017), 351.

66. Boethius, "On the Holy Trinity," 352.

67. Boethius, "On the Holy Trinity," 354.

68. Ip, *Origen and the Emergence of Divine Simplicity before Nicaea*, 66.

remains somewhat elastic. Whatever model of simplicity was preferrable, no medieval theologian was willing to say anything about God that would suggest composition and compromise simplicity.[69] Unfortunately, there is not space to cover every important medieval figure or even the main ideas behind each figure mentioned here. The medieval period is too rich with metaphysical inquiry and insight to properly summarize. Even so, I do want to offer a somewhat broad engagement with several of them to give a sense for the unity and diversity of thought.

Anselm in his *Proslogion* meditates on the non-composite nature of God, asserting that "whatever is made up of parts is not absolutely one." And since God is absolutely one, being totally indivisible, he has no parts but exists wholly himself.[70] Other medieval authors relatively track with this Anselmian logic. Bonaventure says that God as "utterly simple" entails that he is "completely undivided."[71] But even more, God lacks not only actual composition but potential composition.[72] The reasoning for Bonaventure is that God is first and eternal and therefore cannot be composed from anything else.[73] Scotus argues in the same vein that God is supremely simple and that his simplicity is opposed to composition from essential parts, quantitative parts, and subject and accident.[74] But Richard of Saint Victor (d. 1173) goes much further, claiming, "Every theologian knows with indubitable reason that there is a supremely simple being in the true divinity. Therefore, it will be necessary that in the divinity being omnipotent is identical to having omnipotence, and that omnipotence is nothing other than the divine substance."[75] His rationale for his strong stance on identity is that he thinks if God's attributes weren't entirely

69. Friedman, *Medieval Trinitarian Thought from Aquinas to Ockham*, 100.

70. Anselm, *Proslogion*, ed. Brian Davies and G. R. Evans, Oxford World's Classics (Oxford University Press, 1998), 18.

71. Bonaventure, *Breviloquium*, trans. Dominic Monti (Franciscan Institute, 2005), 34.

72. Bonaventure, *Disputed Questions on the Mystery of the Trinity*, trans. Zachary Hayes (Franciscan Institute, 2000), 3.1.

73. Bonaventure, *Itinerarium Mentis In Deum*, vol. 2 (Fransciscan Institute, 2002), 117.

74. John Duns Scotus, "Ordinatio," trans. Peter L. P. Simpson, 8.1.1.6, https://www.aristotelophile.com/Books/Translations/Ordinatio%20I.pdf.

75. Richard of St. Victor, "On the Trinity," in *Trinity and Creation*, ed. Boyd Taylor Coolman and Dale M. Coulter, trans. Christopher P. Evans (New City Press, 2011), 4.19.

identical, then God would have his attributes like power and wisdom from a source besides himself.[76]

Thomas is one of the most well-known and formidable defenders of divine simplicity. He argues for simplicity in several places, but for the sake of space and clarity, I will only note the two arguments in question 3 of the *Summa* and part of his defense in the *Summa Contra Gentiles*. In the *Summa* Thomas prepares his explanation of simplicity by indicating that it is part of the *via negativa*—it is something that God is not like rather than a positive perfection. Divine simplicity is how we deny of God that which is not fitting to him, namely composition.[77] He then divides the question of God's simplicity into eight questions, ranging from the more obvious, "Does God have a body?," to more difficult notions such as, "Is there composition of genus and difference in God?" Thomas denies composition of all types herein. God lacks composition of (1) form and matter, (2) nature and subject, (3) essence and existence, (4) genus and difference, and (5) subject and accident. He is absolutely simple, identical to all that he is.[78]

In the *Summa Contra Gentiles*, Thomas dedicates several sections to topics that relate to divine simplicity, but chapter 18 on composition is especially relevant. He argues flatly: There is no composition in God.[79] His reasoning has several steps. First, he follows a broadly Anselmian line of logic, arguing that if God were to have parts, then he wouldn't be absolutely one, since nothing that is absolutely one can be bound or joined together.[80] Second, he argues that every composite is subsequent to its components. And since God is subsequent to nothing, he surely cannot be composite.[81] Third, every composite is potentially separable. And since God is necessary and inseparable, he cannot be composite.[82] Fourth, every composite needs a composer. And since God is the first and necessary being he cannot

76. Richard of St. Victor, "On the Trinity," in *Trinity and Creation*, ed. Boyd Taylor Coolman and Dale M. Coulter, trans. Christopher P. Evans (New City, 2011), 1.13.

77. Thomas Aquinas, *The Treatise on the Divine Nature*, trans. Brian J. Shanley (Hackett, 2006), I.3.

78. Aquinas, *The Treatise on the Divine Nature* I.3.7c.

79. Thomas Aquinas, *Summa Contra Gentiles: Book One; God*, trans. Anton Charles Pegis (University of Notre Dame Press, 1975), 1.18.1.

80. Aquinas, *The Treatise on the Divine Nature* 18.2.

81. Aquinas, *Summa Contra Gentiles: Book One; God* 1.18.3.

82. Aquinas, *Summa Contra Gentiles: Book One; God* 1.18.4.

have a composer and thus cannot be composite.[83] Fifth, in every genus, the simpler a being (in contrast to complex), the more noble it is. For example, in the genus of "hot" fire is the peak of nobility because there is no coldness. Thus, God is not composite.[84] Sixth, in every composite the good belongs to the whole and not the parts. Therefore, if God is composite, he lacks goodness in total—he isn't the highest and best good.[85] Seventh, every composite requires a multitude and cannot be wholly unified. Therefore, since God is wholly unified, he cannot be composite.[86] It is worth noting here that Thomas's list is not exhaustive. Hence, it doesn't exclude *all* composition whatsoever. Rather, it excludes only specific kinds. For example, substantial composition *is* allowed given the incarnation.[87] As Thomas explains, the incarnation requires Christ to be a "composite person" though this is not a composition "on account of parts, but by reason of number."[88]

Much more could be said of the Thomistic doctrine of divine simplicity, but such a summary exemplifies some of the highlights of his thinking. Henry of Ghent, a contemporary of Thomas, defends divine simplicity with even more fervent rhetoric. He asserts that "it must be absolutely stated that God lacks all composition and that he is utterly simple in the ultimate degree of simplicity and unity."[89] The idea of unity plays a central role for Henry, who sees a twofold unity in God: (1) God is one of singularity, which is opposed to multiplicity or plurality. In this sense, God is one numerically. (2) God is simple, which is opposed to many or to composition.[90] Therefore, God lacks composition *from other things* and *with something else*. He lacks composition from quantitative parts, matter and form, genus and difference, nature and suppositt, essence and being, potency and act.[91] Henry also deploys many of

83. Aquinas, *Summa Contra Gentiles: Book One; God* 1.18.5.

84. Aquinas, *Summa Contra Gentiles: Book One; God* 1.18.6.

85. Aquinas, *The Treatise on the Divine Nature* 18.7.

86. Aquinas, *Summa Contra Gentiles: Book One; God* 1.18.8.

87. Michael Gorman, *Aquinas on the Metaphysics of the Hypostatic Union* (Cambridge University Press, 2017), 54.

88. Thomas Aquinas, *The Summa Theologiæ of St. Thomas Aquinas*, trans. Fathers of the English Dominican Province, 2nd rev. ed. (Burns Oates & Washbourne, 1920), III.2.4.

89. Henry of Ghent, *Henry of Ghent's Summa: The Questions on God's Unity and Simplicity (Articles 25–30)*, trans. Roland J. Teske, Dallas Medieval Texts and Translations 6 (Peeters, 2006), 28.8.

90. Henry, *Henry of Ghent's Summa* 28.1.

91. Henry, *Henry of Ghent's Summa* 28.

the same arguments that have been mentioned before. For example, since God is the first being he cannot have anything by participation. Therefore, God must lack composition since composition entails participation.[92] Likewise, what is composed has its unity from its component parts. Therefore, it doesn't have its unity from itself but from something that belongs to it. And since God is absolutely unified, he cannot be composed.[93]

Henry further gives an extended treatment on the sorts of composition that ought to be denied of God and admitted. He argues, in standard fashion, that "actual composition" cannot be predicated of God because nothing in God is really distinct from his nature, nor is there any efficient cause that unites them. However, Henry suggests that there *is* a virtual composition in God because God has component properties that are virtually or eminently distinguished among themselves. He gives examples such as essence and existence, essence and attributes, and nature and personality. From this he interestingly argues that "there is even actual composition given through the operation of our intellect." The idea is that since the operation of our intellect distinguishes between things like goodness and justice, there is an actual composition in our intellects.[94] But this third composition depends totally on the operation of the intellect, which is both the ground and cause for distinguishing.[95]

The Witness of the Reformation

The Reformation saw little change from the medieval era in the doctrine of divine simplicity. The confession that God is not composed of parts remained largely axiomatic, though the outworking of such a claim continued to contain some varying degrees of nuance.[96] As with the medieval era, it is impossible to give a survey of *every* possible Reformation figure and their thoughts on simplicity. Therefore, I take a sampling of some of the more important figures, focusing especially on those that wrote more extensively on simplicity.

The early Reformed theologian Franciscus Junius assumes an account of simplicity that appears to mirror either the maximal or virtual model. In his

---

92. Henry, *Henry of Ghent's Summa* 28.4.
93. Henry, *Henry of Ghent's Summa* 28.8.
94. See, for example, Becanus, "Summa Theologiae Scolasticae," II.5.
95. Henry, *Henry of Ghent's Summa* 28.4.
96. Richard Muller, *Post-Reformation Reformed Dogmatics* (Baker Academic, 2003), 3:276.

discussion of the archetypal knowledge of God, he considers how wisdom might be predicated of God and whether any distinction is possible to be made in God, but he concludes that no "specifying characteristic" can be predicated of God because he is simple. He goes on to define simplicity as the dogma that removes every form of composition from God—as much as possible. For "God is so completely simple in His essence that not even by a plausible thought experiment can any composition be attributed to Him: not material and form, not of parts, not of essence and being, nor of subject and accidents. Because whatever exists in God is God."[97]

The Dutch Reformed theologian Gisbertus Voetius (1589–1676) is of great importance for understanding simplicity in Reformed contexts because he was trained in Leiden during a time of great humanist-styled interest in philosophy and theology. During his studies the theological students requested the school to organize public lectures in metaphysics to better grasp the polemical context. Because of this some of the most important and dense metaphysical manuals were being read, especially those like Suárez's. But even beyond metaphysics, there was great interest and training in logic, rhetoric, mathematics, and the like. Such training greatly aided Voetius and his later career as a professor and author.[98] For my purposes, I focus on his disputation on God's absolutely simple essence, which was clearly helped by his extensive training in metaphysics.

Voetius throughout this disputation focuses on the shared confession of what I call mere divine simplicity. According to Voetius, despite the varying metaphysics of Thomists and Scotists, "Everybody certainly aims at this: removing all composition from God."[99] It is from the quest to remove such imperfections from God that simplicity is understood. Therefore, simplicity excludes "from God all dependence, posteriority, lesser-status, composition, and multiplicity and division."[100] He expands on the negative scope of simplicity later by explaining that simplicity allows "neither multiplicity nor division and separating, not to mention opposition, priority,

97. Franciscus Junius, *A Treatise on True Theology*, trans. David C. Noe (Reformation Heritage, 2014), 108.

98. Beck, *Gisbertus Voetius (1589–1676) on God, Freedom, and Contingency*, 31–32.

99. Gisbertus Voetius, "God's Single, Absolutely Simple Essence," trans. R. M. Hurd, *The Confessional Presbyterian* 15 (2019): 21.

100. Voetius, "God's Single, Absolutely Simple Essence," 11.

posteriority, or succession, dependence of cause and effect, or any other order of whatever sort."[101] But simplicity does have a positive quality of sorts, as an aspect of divine unity.[102]

Throughout his disputation Voetius is careful to mediate between the Thomists and Scotists, which I have broadly categorized under the virtual and formal models of divine simplicity. But even more, Voetius tends to accommodate Scotist elements much more freely than some might assume, so much so that Voetius expert Andreas Beck has called his incorporation "quite significant."[103] Matthew Baines likewise has recently argued that while Voetius begins more Thomistic, he ends far more Scotist.[104] For example, Voetius says there is a

> virtual or eminent distinction or (to accommodate to Scotist terms) a formal distinction "according to the nature of the thing," not as that thing is in act but as it is virtually or eminently, so that there is some foundation for this second distinction on the part of the thing—but, not in God himself, but in his effects.[105]

Therefore, Voetius is seeking to incorporate the Scotist model within the fold of the Reformed orthodox, though he sides with the virtual model.

Voetius defines the virtual (or eminent) distinction, which is said to have a foundation in God, as a distinction "in the effects, outworkings, and terminations" of things.[106] He gives the example of the sun's light as singular but containing drying and heating power "virtually or with respect to its effects."[107] And as seen, he seems to assume that the Scotist formal distinction is either compatible with or reducible to the virtual distinction.

What is of special interest is Voetius's definition of composition. He argues that "composition requires the union of distinct things and also

---

101. Voetius, "God's Single, Absolutely Simple Essence," 31.

102. Voetius, "God's Single, Absolutely Simple Essence," 11.

103. Beck, *Gisbertus Voetius (1589–1676) on God, Freedom, and Contingency*, 266.

104. Matthew C. Baines, "Gisbertus Voetius's (1589–1676) Doctrine of Participation: Its Scholastic and Mystical Sources" (PhD diss., University of Edinburgh, 2023), 99–100.

105. Voetius, "God's Single, Absolutely Simple Essence," 22.

106. Voetius, "God's Single, Absolutely Simple Essence," 22.

107. Voetius, "God's Single, Absolutely Simple Essence," 23.

something that has transitioned from potency to act."[108] He expands even further on the nature of composition as follows:

> The things composition requires are these. First, you have to have opposites that are naturally distinct—namely, they are distinct either really, formally, or modally. Second, these opposites must be united or must have been united. Third, they must presuppose and include potentiality or potency. Fourth, you have to have some efficient cause for this union. Fifth, the following logical consequents have to follow from all these last essential, constitutive requirements for composition: dependence, multiplicity and division, resolution and change.[109]

When we come to the doctrine of divine simplicity that denies composition, we can tend to assume we know what composition means. But here Voetius clarifies what counts as the composition that should be excluded from God. It is not merely having a distinction that constitutes composition. Such descriptions allay worries like those about the Trinity. The Trinity doesn't introduce composition because God is not a single person that that is being united. The persons of the Trinity are three and not united in a formal sense.[110]

Petrus van Mastricht, a similarly important Dutch Reformed theologian, studied under Voetius and follows in his steps on simplicity. However, Mastricht in his main work attempts to be more transparently biblical in his approach to simplicity. Exodus 33:18–23 drives the entire discussion. But Mastricht follows the example set before him. Simplicity means God is free from all composition. He provides a very standard list of composition denied of God: (1) quantitative corporeal parts, (2) essential parts, matter and form, (3) substance and accident, (4) essence and existence, and (5) genus and difference.[111] Mastricht then describes simplicity as analogous to the horizon. We can contemplate the entire horizon, seeing east, west, south, and north, but the whole isn't in parts. As he explains,

---

108. Voetius, "God's Single, Absolutely Simple Essence," 28.

109. Voetius, "God's Single, Absolutely Simple Essence," 28.

110. Beck, *Gisbertus Voetius (1589–1676) on God, Freedom, and Contingency*, 257.

111. Petrus van Mastricht, *Theoretical-Practical Theology*, ed. Joel E. Beeke, trans. Todd M. Rester (Reformation Hertiage, 2018), 1.2.6.22.

"This hodge-podge of attributes arises not so much from God's perfection as from our imperfection."[112]

Francis Turretin is an exemplary Reformed theologian who has exercised a towering influence on the Reformed tradition. Like Calvin before him, Turretin garners near universal respect from those that agree and even those that disagree with his conclusions. Turretin was the son of professor and pastor Benedict Turretin in Calvin's Geneva. His family is traced to Lucca, Italy, where Peter Martyr Vermigli was affected by the Reformation. In 1644 Turretin began his academic travels, commonly called "academic wandering," including Leiden, Utrecht, and Paris before returning to Geneva in 1647. He later took a brief pastoral role before taking the chair of theology in Geneva, which he held from 1653 to 1687. His biographical sketch is relevant to show, once again, the varied intellectual contexts these Reformed thinkers were trained and served in. They are not merely academics but also pastors. They read and debated the widest range of ideas too.

Turretin's dogmatic sketch of divine simplicity is found in topic three of his *Institutes,* within questions five and seven. He utilizes and applies divine simplicity frequently elsewhere in his corpus like most classical thinkers, but these two sections form the heart of his doctrinal explanation. Turretin's definition of simplicity is captured well by his assessment of unity among the Reformed on the doctrine. He says the "orthodox constantly taught that the essence of God is perfectly simple and free from all composition."[113] It is this freedom from all composition that forms the heart of divine simplicity for him.

But it is not mere freedom from composition that forms the basis for simplicity for Turretin. Elsewhere he clarifies that it is an *incapability* of either composition or division.[114] We are to remove all composition, whether of quantitative parts, subject and accident, logical parts, metaphysical composition of act and power, or essence and existence.[115] As seen, such a claim is standard fare. While others may categorize compositional

112. Mastricht, *Theoretical-Practical Theology,* 1.2.5.5.

113. Francis Turretin, *Institutes of Elenctic Theology,* ed. James T. Dennison, trans. George Musgrave Giger (P&R, 1994), 3.7.1.

114. Turretin, *Institutes of Elenctic Theology,* 3.7.3.

115. Turretin, *Institutes of Elenctic Theology,* 3.7.5.

relationships differently, they are arguing for the same fundamental claim. Turretin's contemporaries, Mastricht and Wilhelmus à Brakel (1635–1711), both follow nearly the same categorization.[116] Turretin later summarizes the Reformed position on simplicity as understanding the divine attributes as "really the same with his essence, but are to be distinguished from it virtually and eminently."[117] This proclamation is a strong indication that the virtual model is widely accepted during his time. Mastricht similarly navigates how the attributes are to be distinguished. He says:

> The Reformed, although they admit that the essence does differ from the attributes, nevertheless do not admit that they differ really, in God himself, but by reason, in our conception, insofar as sometimes it conceives of the essence simply and abstractly from the attributes, and sometimes conceives of the same essence with various relations and operations in creatures.[118]

Mastricht is clear that there is no distinction "in God himself" but merely one "by reason, in our conception." All distinction is relegated to the relations and operations *in creatures*.

Later Reformed figures like John Gill and Herman Bavinck do not depart from the foundation laid. Gill argues that since God is spiritual, he is simple, which means he does not consist of parts. He lacks physical parts (e.g., matter and form or integral parts like soul and body), metaphysical parts (e.g., essence and existence, act and power), and logical parts (e.g., substance and accident).[119] Gill largely recounts the standard arguments in favor of divine simplicity as well. Gill quickly moves to various objections to simplicity, answering the worry of the Trinity by asserting that the persons only distinguish or modify and do not divide or compose the divine nature.[120] Herein he also gives clarity on how the attributes are distinct. He says, "They are no other than God himself, and neither differ from one another, but with respect to their objects, and

116. Mastricht, *Theoretical-Practical Theology*, 1.2.6.22; Brakel, *The Christian's Reasonable Service*, 1:96–98.

117. Turretin, *Institutes of Elenctic Theology*, 3.5.5.

118. Mastricht, *Theoretical-Practical Theology*, 1.2.5.10.

119. John Gill, *A Body of Doctrinal Divinity* (George Keith, 1769), 75.

120. Gill, *A Body of Doctrinal Divinity*, 76.

effects, and in our manner of conception of them."[121] Descriptions like this track, once again, with the virtual model.

Bavinck likewise argues that God as simple means he is "sublimely" free from composition and that there is no real ontological distinction between his being and attributes. God is all that he has.[122] The reason for simplicity is to keep the divine attributes from being treated as independent of God or opposed to him.[123] But Bavinck also is clear: Just because there is no distinction between God's essence and attributes doesn't mean that there are no distinctions between the attributes with a basis in reality.[124] On the contrary, while the attributes do not differ in substance, they do differ in more than just our conceptions of them. We *really* entertain different ideas.[125] Bavinck does not explain this in great detail, but he does indicate that "God is called by different names on account of the varying effects he produces in his creatures by his ever-constant being."[126] Elsewhere he suggests that Scotus differs from the consensus on simplicity.[127] Therefore, it appears that Bavinck is at minimum a species of the virtual model of simplicity.

Later Reformed thinkers like James P. Boyce (1827–1888), trained under the late Charles Hodge (1797–1878), argued that while composition is banned by divine simplicity, this does not mean God's attributes were "simply our different conceptions of God. They have existence independently of creatures. There is some foundation in God himself for the distinction between them."[128] In this way, Boyce is providing a model that would eschew both the maximal and virtual and align more closely with something akin to the formal model. Again, he says God's "attributes essentially inhere in that nature and are not capable of separation from it, which really makes them one with that nature."[129] For Boyce, the key aspect of divine simplicity is the *inseparability* of the divine attributes.

---

121. Gill, *A Body of Doctrinal Divinity*, 76.

122. Herman Bavinck, *Reformed Dogmatics*, ed. John Bolt, trans. John Vriend (Baker Academic, 2003), 2:118.

123. Bavinck, *Reformed Dogmatics*, 2:118.

124. Bavinck, *Reformed Dogmatics*, 2:124.

125. Bavinck, *Reformed Dogmatics*, 2:125.

126. Bavinck, *Reformed Dogmatics*, 2:127.

127. Bavinck, *Reformed Dogmatics*, 2:174.

128. James Petigru Boyce, *Abstract of Systematic Theology* (Founders, 2006), 65–66.

129. Boyce, *Abstract of Systematic Theology*, 67.

As has been seen from these several Reformed figures, all agree that there are *grounds* for distinctions in God, though they differ on what they are and how consistently they hold that they actually are in God or not. What one should *not* derive from this overview is that some figures are "bad" or theological "villains" that should be rejected. Instead, we should see the diversity of opinion on how divine simplicity should be worked out and yet the resolute commitment to denying composition of God.

THE DOGMATIC DEFINITION

Based on this overview from the classical tradition and the creedal and confessional formulas, we know that God cannot have parts, or at least creaturely parts that amount to creaturely composition. God is inseparable, unbreakable, and ontologically foundational. Even so, several thinkers are explicit that it is not composition or distinction *simpliciter* that is denied by divine simplicity.[130] Therefore, those like R. T. Mullins that claim simplicity means there are no distinctions whatsoever, even mental, are simply wrong.[131] So, I think it is wise to follow Gilles Emery, who explains divine simplicity as God lacking all forms of "composition *that characterize creatures*."[132] The idea, then, is not that God is like a simple monad without any distinction whatsoever. Instead, divine simplicity is designed to exempt God from *creaturely* forms of composition. He transcends such composition. And as he transcends composition, he does so because he is only constituted by himself. He is wholly and consistently himself.[133] He is the fullness of each of his divine attributes.[134]

So, it seems to me that mere divine simplicity is a sufficient definition to capture the consensus of the Christian tradition. However, some models may be insufficient or beyond the bounds of a mere classical theism. Models like Crisp's parsimonious model appear at times to transgress mere divine simplicity, admitting of composition that could jeopardize the ontological status of God. While he denies complexity in God,

130. Duby, *Jesus and the God of Classical Theism*, 162.

131. See Mullins, *The End of the Timeless God*, 52–53.

132. Gilles Emery, *The Trinity: An Introduction to Catholic Doctrine on the Triune God*, trans. Matthew Levering (Catholic University of America Press, 2011), 90. Emphasis mine.

133. Wittman, *God and Creation in the Theology of Thomas Aquinas and Karl Barth*, 12.

134. Duby, *Jesus and the God of Classical Theism*, 162.

when his model is expanded, he is content in admitting of some complexity. The reason he is willing to admit of complexity is that he argues that simplicity is mainly about lacking *separable* parts. As long as an object's parts are inseparable from it, and the whole is more fundamental than its parts, it counts as simple. So, a metaphysical simple can still be complex for Crisp since it isn't necessarily mereologically simple. But the entire thrust of a mere divine simplicity account is to avoid mereological parts.

Now, to be fair, the model can be confusing. And Crisp admittedly calls his approach a "cut-down" model that lacks the robust details of some of the others we've covered.[135] He constructs the model with a desire to avoid the metaphysical baggage of God as pure act.[136] And he positively wants to guard the real distinctions in the persons of the Trinity, which he thinks entails God being composite in some sense.[137] From these two commitments he attempts to approximate to a more apophatic mode, seeking to maintain as much of simplicity as he can, though his model is more metaphysically committed than what I have properly termed the apophatic description here, which would remain non-committal on doctrines such as pure act.[138]

DOGMATIC MOTIVATIONS

THE EXEGETICAL FOUNDATION: HOLY SCRIPTURE

It is now almost standard in many theological and philosophical works to claim that divine simplicity has no biblical support.[139] It is a doctrine of the Greek philosophers of ages past that was mistakenly imported into Christianity. And such critics are right. There is no text in holy Scripture that says: "Lo! Behold! Our God is simple and not complex. He has no parts and is not composed of anything: matter and form, essence and existence, or otherwise." Or as Mullins cheekily suggests, "Isaiah never says, 'Thus sayeth the Lord, all of my attributes are identical to each other.' Paul

135. Crisp, *Analyzing Doctrine*, 54.

136. Crisp, *Analyzing Doctrine*, 62.

137. Crisp, *Analyzing Doctrine*, 65.

138. Crisp, *Analyzing Doctrine*, 62.

139. See for example: Peckham, *Divine Attributes*, 241.

never writes to a church, 'This is the mystery expressed unto you: God is pure act.' "[140] But such a standard for theology is naive. No one could ever apply this consistently. The Bible simply doesn't speak to everything explicitly and formally. *All* doctrines require elaboration beyond the text alone.[141] Even the very life of Christ couldn't be contained word-for-word in Scripture, as Saint John reminds us: "Now there are also many other things that Jesus did. Were every one of them to be written, I suppose that the world itself could not contain the books that would be written" (John 21:25). But surely those acts are true and could be recounted as such without having been explicitly recorded.

As the classical tradition has understood the task of theology, Scripture is the supreme generative and authoritative foundation for all true theology (e.g., it is the *norming norm*, at least for Protestants). However, our theological developments *always* require wrestling with Scripture and its meaning and implications. It requires employing the tools of logic, history, rhetoric, and the like. It requires philosophy as a handmaiden. There is no theological doctrine that can be read straight off the page of Scripture and understood in its fullness. Jesus's own description is apt: "Therefore every scribe who has been trained for the kingdom of heaven is like a master of a house, who brings out of his treasure what is new and what is old" (Matt 13:52). God calls us to wisdom in exploring and mining the riches of Scripture, which is pregnant with meaning beyond the literal surface level. We are compelled to draw out the implications as wise and careful guides. Therefore, no doctrine, even more abstract ones like divine simplicity, should be required to provide texts that *explicitly provide every single detail.*

While all of this is true, none of this should be understood as an excuse for any doctrine, be it divine simplicity or otherwise, to forsake the task of careful exegesis of holy Scripture. It is not a trick by a used car salesman to avoid the lack of clear scriptural explanation of simplicity. Instead, the classical tradition implores us to recognize the nature of holy Scripture as

140. R. T. Mullins, "Simply Impossible: A Case against Divine Simplicity," *Journal of Reformed Theology* 7, no. 2 (2013): 190, https://doi.org/10.1163/15697312-12341294.

141. See Jordan L. Steffaniak, "The God of All Creation."

a narrative about God and his works that invites us to a divine wrestling match akin to Jacob. Scripture is not, by divine design, a scholastic theology manual devised to explicate the finer points of dogma.

Now, despite what the popular record may tell you, there *are* several "classic" proof-texts for divine simplicity. The *real* dispute is not if divine simplicity has scriptural warrant but whether these texts teach a classical doctrine of divine simplicity. The classical tradition has never been content assuming the truth of simplicity from the likes of Plato, Aristotle, or anyone else. It is understood as grounded in Scripture. For example, it is nearly universally accepted in the classical tradition that the name Jehovah in Exodus 3:14–15 implies simplicity. God's divinely revealed name "I am who I am" conveys a mere divine simplicity. It implies God as (1) ontologically basic, (2) necessary, (3) an indivisible unity, and (4) self-consistent. As Voetius explains, "He who is what he is, and for whom whatever is in him, is himself—he is one who has no parts, accidents, modes, or principles that are something other than himself."[142]

There are also the classic "God is" texts that imply a doctrine of divine simplicity. John 4:24: "God is spirit." First John 1:5: "God is light." First John 4:8: "God is love." In each of these texts Scripture predicates a particular attribute to God with no qualifications. God is love—wholly, completely, fully. It is not merely that God is lov*ing*. He is love. We would never say this of anyone else—even those we found most loving in our lives. Surely, they were not maximally loving at all times! But for God, love is not an appendage to his being or something he is partly made of. It is not something he is one day and then isn't the next. God *is* love since there is no real distinction between God and his love. Unlike us, who are sometimes loving and sometimes not, because we are not intrinsically love, God is always completely and fully loving because love is most fundamentally just what God is.

But there are other texts like Deuteronomy 6:4, which says: "The Lord our God, the Lord is one." The reason this text supports divine simplicity is because of what simplicity is supposed to guard—the utmost unity of the Trinity. Instead of the Trinity becoming three distinct individuals,

142. Voetius, "God's Single, Absolutely Simple Essence," 14.

the Trinity remains numerically *one* God. And this is so because of divine simplicity. Apart from divine simplicity the Trinity would collapse into three gods.

Or consider Isaiah 40:18, which says, "To who then will you liken God, or what likeness compare with him?" The idea behind this claim is that God is not in a class of beings. He is not like an individual human person that is one of many humans. But more than transcending genus, God is incomparable. But what would make God incomparable? Certainly, some of that has to do with his maximal greatness, his steadfastness, and his self-constancy. But there must also be a deeper explanation given the context of this text. Hear from the prophet in greater detail to see:

> Who has measured the waters in the hollow of his hand
> and marked off the heavens with a span,
> enclosed the dust of the earth in a measure
> and weighed the mountains in scales
> and the hills in a balance?
> Who has measured the Spirit of the LORD,
> or what man shows him his counsel?
> Whom did he consult,
> and who made him understand?
> Who taught him the path of justice,
> and taught him knowledge,
> and showed him the way of understanding?
> Behold, the nations are like a drop from a bucket,
> and are accounted as the dust on the scales;
> behold, he takes up the coastlands like fine dust.
> Lebanon would not suffice for fuel,
> nor are its beasts enough for a burnt offering.
> All the nations are as nothing before him,
> they are accounted by him as less than nothing and emptiness.
> To whom then will you liken God,
> or what likeness compare with him? (Isa 40:12–18)

Herein Isaiah is building a case against the Israelites that God is demonstrably *not* like anything in the world or any imagined conception of deity.

He transcends every possible category that they attempt to domesticate him with. He begins this section by contrasting the waters and the heavens and the earth and the mountains in such a way as to communicate the totality of which God transcends.[143] And the section builds to verse 18, where even the term used for God is, according to Alec Motyer, "the most transcendent of God-words."[144] And the question to be asked is this: What is it that makes God so unique and transcendent? Certainly, any of the classical attributes could explain this. No one else is immutable, impassible, or eternal. And yet, even they have a level of analogy in created being, whereas divine simplicity has less commonality to draw analogies from. God without parts makes him unique in a way that removes comparability. Nothing else exhibits such unity.

PHILOSOPHICAL ARGUMENTATION

Throughout the tradition there have been numerous motivations for divine simplicity. Some of these are more properly meditations on supernatural theology, like exegesis of the "God is" texts or exploring the theological and metaphysical entailments of the Shema in light of the clarity of Trinitarian disclosure of the New Testament. But others are better classified as natural theology, like defining and debating what counts as a relation of dependence. It is no secret that many of the most powerful defenses for divine simplicity come from philosophical argumentation that may be best classified as natural theology. This doesn't mean they are less biblical. It only means they require sustained attention to the patterns of biblical themes and to logical and theological entailments.

Depending on which thinker you read, you'll find a range of arguments for divine simplicity. For example, Francis Turretin provides four main arguments. First, God is independent, and since whatever is composed must be composed by another, he is simple. Second, God is unified, and since he who is one cannot be divided or composed, he is simple. Third, God is perfect, and since composition implies imperfection, passive power, dependency, and mutability, he is simple. Fourth, God is pure act, with no passive admixture, and since composition entails passive potency, he is

143. J. A. Motyer, *The Prophecy of Isaiah* (InterVarsity Press, 1993), 303.

144. Motyer, *The Prophecy of Isaiah*, 304.

simple.[145] Each of these draws on similar themes: There is nothing above or behind God that makes him who he is.[146]

There are many other arguments, but two things should be noted before exploring some of the more important ones in greater detail. First, while these are more philosophical arguments, they are expanding on biblical ideas and seeking to understand their entailments. Those that defend divine simplicity are not doing so by closing their Bibles. They are not ignoring divine revelation. They are doing so by meditating on the implications of other biblical doctrines. Second, the methodological process for arriving at divine simplicity is a mixture of the *via negativa* and *via eminentiae*. Much of it depends on removing what God is not like. God is not dependent, for instance. But it also requires positive ascription of his perfection.

The Argument from Aseity

The chief and greatest argument for simplicity by my lights is the argument from divine aseity. As we explored in chapter 5 on the theological foundations for classical theism, divine aseity is about God's independence and fullness. As totally independent of *everything*, God cannot depend on anything. This has caused the classical tradition to ascribe simplicity to God since it is designed, in part, to prohibit any relations of dependence, such as parts. The idea is that whatever is composed of parts depends on those parts.[147] Parts, by their nature, are prior to wholes.[148] And if something depends on something else, it is neither independent nor self-existent. Everyone from Bonaventure and Henry to Mastricht and Bavinck utilize such argumentation.[149] For example, Voetius explains: "If God were composed from parts, accidents, or modes of being, he would not then be first absolutely. This is because parts are prior to the composite, and principles (on which modes of being or accidents would depend) are

145. Turretin, *Institutes of Elenctic Theology*, 3.7.4.

146. Duby, *Jesus and the God of Classical Theism*, 31–32.

147. Dolezal, *All That Is in God*, 40.

148. Bonaventure, *Disputed Questions on the Mystery of the Trinity*, trans. Zachary Hayes (Franciscan Institute, 2000), 3.1.

149. Bonaventure, *Disputed Questions on the Mystery of the Trinity*, 3.1; Henry, *Henry of Ghent's Summa* 29.8; Bavinck, *Reformed Dogmatics*, 2:176; Mastricht, *Theoretical-Practical Theology*, 1.2.5.6; 1.2.5.10.

prior to what they principled."[150] The idea of "first absolutely" and being "prior to" something are abstractions from divine aseity. God cannot be second or subsequent to anything else without violating his status as *a se*.

So, the argument formally goes like this:

1. If something is composed of parts, then it depends on those parts.
2. God depends on nothing.
3. Therefore, God isn't composed of parts.

It should be uncontroversial for any Christian theist that God is *a se* and does not depend for his existence on anything else. He necessarily exists and does not gain perfections through anything external to himself. But there have been challenges to premise 1 of this argument, suggesting that wholes are prior to their parts in some cases. Therefore, something may be composed of parts and yet *not* depend on those parts. This objection will be explored in the following section. However, suffice to say that if parts are ontologically prior to the whole, or even if wholes merely depend on their parts in some fashion, God cannot be *a se* if he is not simple.

The Argument from Participation

Similar to the argument from aseity, the argument from participation claims that God is simple because he participates in nothing. For example, Henry of Ghent says: "Because God is the first being, he can have nothing in himself by participation from something else, because whatever has something else by participation necessarily has it from what has it through its essence and, in that way, prior to and more essentially than it."[151]

Therefore, God is simple because he cannot stand in a relation that would implicate him in participation. *Really* distinct attributes, then, would entail that they exist apart from him, which means God would "participate" in them if he were to possess them. The argument could be put formally as follows:

---

150. Voetius, "God's Single, Absolutely Simple Essence," 13.

151. Henry, *Henry of Ghent's Summa* 29.4.

1. If x is composed of parts, then x is part of a greater whole (e.g., participates in something greater).
2. God participates in nothing.
3. Therefore, God isn't composed of parts.

This argument is not available to the nominalist, who denies any form of participation, but since most of the classical tradition leans away from such naked nominalism, it can remain quite persuasive. What is debated by those that deny classical theism is whether God must be simple in any respect to lack "participation." Why assume that composition entails "participation"? And most in the tradition simply presuppose agreement with the conclusion, and thus do not defend the further claims about the nature of participation.

The Argument from Spirituality

A further argument for simplicity comes from God's spirituality. As John 4:24 indicates, God is spirit. Since something of a spiritual nature cannot be material, it cannot have any accidental properties since those inhere in matter. And therefore, if God is immaterial, he lacks parts.[152] The argument is formalized easily:

1. If something is immaterial, then it is simple.
2. God is immaterial.
3. Therefore, God is simple.

Of course, this argument does not arbitrate between the various models of divine simplicity. Nor does it defend the premise that immaterial things lack parts. Many today would deny premise 1. But even if premise 1 isn't denied, there is vagueness here since there are many immaterial objects on most Christian accounts: angels, demons, human souls, and so on. But what the classical theologian intends to convey about God's simplicity is not *merely* that of lacking material parts like angels, demons, and human souls. Therefore, this argument appears to lack full justification for divine simplicity.

152. Mastricht, *Theoretical-Practical Theology*, 1.2.6.7; 1.2.6.20.

The Argument from Unity

Divine simplicity has also been defended based on divine unity because the highest manner of unity depends on it.[153] As Henry has argued, "Since the proper notion of unity is the notion of indivision, it follows from the fact that he is supremely simple that he is supremely one and thus supremely undivided."[154] Thomas argues similarly: For something to be supremely one "it must be both supreme in being and supremely undivided."[155] This is so because nothing that is absolutely one can be bound or joined together.[156] Likewise, Anselm in his *Proslogion* meditates on the non-composite nature of God, asserting that "whatever is made up of parts is not absolutely one." And since God is absolutely one, being totally indivisible, he has no parts but exists wholly himself.[157]

Based on these arguments, it seems that the formal idea is as follows:

1. If something is truly one (e.g., has the highest degree of unity), then it is simple.
2. God is truly one.
3. Therefore, God is simple.

As for the other arguments, the area of debate is around premise 1. Should we assume that the highest degree of unity requires or entails simplicity? Thomas's thought suggests that every form of unity requires a "binding" or "joining" except that of simplicity. Therefore, since God isn't bound or joined in any sense, he must be simple.

POTENTIAL PROBLEMS AND SOLUTIONS

The gritty details of divine simplicity are often fleshed out when one encounters the bewildered questions of those unfamiliar with the doctrine. For example, if God is simple, then are his attributes properly *identical* (e.g., his love *is* his justice, his immutability *is* his eternality, and vice versa, etc.)? If the divine attributes are properly identical to one another

153. Aquinas, *The Treatise on the Divine Nature* I.11.3c.

154. Henry, *Henry of Ghent's Summa* 25.1.

155. Aquinas, *The Treatise on the Divine Nature* I.11.4c.

156. Aquinas, *The Treatise on the Divine Nature* I.18.2.

157. Anselm, *Proslogion*, ed. Brian Davies and G. R. Evans (Oxford University Press, 1998), 18.

(i.e., God is all that God has), then how can there be a Trinity of persons? When these sorts of questions are answered, you'll find the metaphysical machinery that makes simplicity tick. In what follows I engage some of the more important and popular objections to divine simplicity. These are not exhaustive. There are many more objections, some of which have been roundly criticized, but space limits our ability to sufficiently engage every possible one. Therefore, I focus only on those I think are most relevant.

BIBLICAL PROBLEMS

Most of the so-called "problems" for divine simplicity end up getting classed as more philosophical and theological than "biblical." And yet the common refrain that divine simplicity isn't in the Bible or that it contradicts it remains a poignant worry. As John Feinberg claims, "In consulting various systematic theologies, one is hard pressed to find one that offers biblical support for the notion. There is no verse that explicitly teaches that God is simple."[158] For example, some think that divine simplicity is incompatible with divine revelation, wherein God is called Creator, Redeemer, and Lord. The reasoning is that these are supposedly accidental properties that are not admitted by divine simplicity.[159] If divine simplicity did reject God as Creator, surely this *would* be a problem. But it doesn't.

The titles of Creator and Redeemer are not additions to God's being but descriptions of changes in his creation. As Augustine explains: "Thus when he is called something with reference to creation, while indeed he begins to be called it in time, we should understand that this does not involve anything happening to God's own substance, but only to the created thing to which the relationship predicated refers."[160]

For example, when God created the crocodile, what changes is not that God metaphysically adds a new property of "Creator of the crocodile" but that the crocodile changes from not existing to existing. God merely adds a relation to creation but not a real relation that is metaphysically robust enough to impact his ontological status. His actions are ontologically innocuous relations between objects rather than properties

158. John S. Feinberg, *No One Like Him: The Doctrine of God* (Crossway, 2001), 327.

159. Mullins, "Simply Impossible," 200.

160. Augustine, *The Trinity*, trans. Edmund Hill (New City, 2015), V.4.16, 17.

that ontologically inhere in him. In this sense, it is wrong to think that "accruing relative attributes would entail accidents in God."[161] Instead, as Mastricht explains, "relation is not a being of any sort, nor does it imply composition in God (for things are related to something, not in something)."[162] So, it doesn't matter if God becomes Creator, Redeemer, and Lord, because these are not real substantial relations for him. Despite "adding" this relation, he does not change or add any being or properties. They are not accidents for him because accidents are only accidental of an object if they are a characteristic of the object *and* explained by some other characteristic of the object rather than being primitive.[163]

The philosophical concept of truthmakers offers great assistance in understanding why this is the case. A truthmaker for truth is just the fact that a truth is true *in virtue of* some portion of reality.[164] There is a certain metaphysical function or role that truthmakers perform. They necessitate the truth of predications.[165] The necessitation isn't necessarily causal. Nor is the necessitation relation something over and above the item. There is no addition of being.[166] For example, think about the truth that Napoleon Bonaparte was short (at least compared to our modern standards). The "truthmaker" for this is Napoleon himself and his height. It is true *in virtue of* his physical body. In the case of God as Creator, Redeemer, and Lord, the extramental truthmaker for these claims is not any real relation in God to his creatures. It is merely something intrinsic to the creatures.[167] So, the idea is that, yes, God does in some sense become Creator, but this isn't any sort of accidental inhering relation in God. What changes is the creation. For example, when my first son was born, I "became" a father. But there is no ontological change in me. I don't add a new ontological property. I gain a new relation. Analogously, God doesn't add any new degree of being when creation occurs. Of course, all talk of occurring,

161. Contra Richard C. Barcellos, *Trinity & Creation: A Scriptural and Confessional Account* (Resource, 2020), 63.

162. Mastricht, *Theoretical-Practical Theology*, 1.2.6.23.

163. Michael Gorman, "The Essential and The Accidental," *Ratio* 18, no. 3 (2005): 284.

164. D. M. Armstrong, *Truth and Truthmakers* (Cambridge University Press, 2004), 5.

165. Jeffrey E. Brower, "Making Sense of Divine Simplicity," *Faith and Philosophy* 25, no. 1 (2008): 18, https://doi.org/10.5840/faithphil20082511.

166. Armstrong, *Truth and Truthmakers*, 9.

167. Richard Cross, *Duns Scotus on God* (Ashgate, 2005), 103.

becoming, before, and after is not literal. God never "becomes" Creator or Redeemer in a literal sense. He is *eternally* Creator and Redeemer. As eternal, God wills creation and redemption timelessly.[168]

PHILOSOPHICAL PROBLEMS

God and Freedom: Modal Collapse

One of the most important contemporary challenges to divine simplicity is the problem of "modal collapse." Because of its force, I spend an abnormally large amount of space defending divine simplicity from it. Ryan Mullins, one of the chief antagonists of classical theism in the contemporary period, has recently forcefully articulated the problem. In its simplest terms, the idea is that divine freedom cannot coexist with divine simplicity. If divine simplicity is true, then divine freedom is false since everything becomes necessary (hence, modality collapsing into necessity). And since Christians want to preserve divine freedom, they must reject divine simplicity.[169]

Mullins's argument is more sophisticated than this initial summary. He begins by suggesting that freedom for God means he could have done otherwise. He wasn't *required* to create or give grace to anyone. He could have refrained. But divine simplicity seems to entail that God couldn't do otherwise since he is identical to all his attributes, including his eternal and immutable will, having no potential (ignore the fact that not all versions of simplicity entail a strict identity). If his will is immutable and eternal, in what sense could he *do otherwise*?[170] Moreover, Mullins asks if God *could* create another universe, different than the one he made. If the answer is yes (hence, preserving divine freedom), God has unactualized potential, which is supposed to be outlawed by divine simplicity.[171] If it is possible for God to exist without this world or that, he cannot be simple.[172] Why? Take a mereological simple, like an electron, as an example. Isn't it possible for that electron to exist without the rest of the world? Certainly, it

168. Bavinck, *Reformed Dogmatics*, 2:429.

169. Mullins, "Simply Impossible," 192. See also Bradshaw, *Aristotle East and West*, 268.

170. Mullins, "Simply Impossible," 193.

171. Mullins, "Simply Impossible," 195.

172. Mullins, "Simply Impossible," 195–96.

seems to me that it can. So, if that simple can do it, why not God? Mullins puts it baldly: "On simplicity, God's act of creating is identical to His act of willing Himself, so there cannot be two different modalities at play. Otherwise, the acts are not identical, and that is repugnant to divine simplicity."[173] So, Mullins thinks the only way to maintain divine simplicity is to affirm a "modal collapse" where everything is necessary.[174] But a modal collapse robs God of freedom, sovereignty, and aseity.[175]

To allow for the most precise form of argument, let's spell out his thinking as best we can:

1. Divine simplicity is true [assumption for *reductio*].
2. If God is simple, then he is identical to his act(s).
3. If God is identical to his act(s), then he is identical to his act of creation.
4. If God is identical to his act of creation, then creation is necessary.
5. If God is free, then his act of creation cannot be necessary.
6. God is free.
7. Therefore, God is not simple [*contradiction*].

The point is that divine freedom is impossible to reconcile with divine simplicity. If God is identical to his attributes and act(s) (including creation), then God's creation is *necessary*, which is contrary to divine freedom.

The argument fails for several reasons as Mullins fails to distinguish between absolute and hypothetical necessity. Armed with these distinctions, I argue that divine simplicity does not entail a modal collapse. Creation is *not* absolutely necessary even if it is hypothetically necessary. So, the argument trades on equivocations on necessity, ironically, collapsing necessity unnecessarily. Both premise 4 and 5 fail to properly distinguish between types of necessity. Instead, classical theists have often argued that while the willing of God is *absolutely necessary*, the *reference* of the willing is *hypothetically necessary*,

173. Mullins, "Simply Impossible," 199n66.
174. Mullins, "Simply Impossible," 196.
175. Mullins, "Simply Impossible," 196–97.

which does not lead to a modal collapse, at least not the devilish sort that is worried about.[176] The point is that God "hypothetically" could do otherwise—he was not bound by anything to make his decision. His freedom was in no way hindered because he *could* have chosen not to create as the simple God. There is nothing external to himself that would constrain his choice. But even if it did turn out that "modal collapse" was resultant, this *still* wouldn't undermine God's freedom. Some have argued that certain versions of divine simplicity, like Thomas Aquinas, cannot avail themselves of these distinctions because of divine simplicity.[177] However, this reading of someone like Thomas would categorize him along the maximal model as I've described, which I don't think he ultimately holds to. Either way, it is important to broadly summarize modal semantics before attempting to wield them.

The distinction between the absolutely and hypothetically necessary is rather common in the tradition. Absolute necessity means that something *must* be. It would be contradictory to be otherwise.[178] But within absolute necessity, things can be distinguished. There is a narrow sense in which things are *logically* necessary like the truths of logic, the truths of mathematics, that red is a color, and no numbers are human beings.[179] Hypothetical necessity, on the other hand, is a necessity that *depends* on something.[180] Therefore, the distinction between the two senses of necessity rests on the source or ground of a thing's necessity in relation to its concept.[181]

Take a few examples of these senses of necessity. While something may be naturally necessary given the physical laws of the universe (like for me to be unable to jump to the top of Mount Everest because of that pesky gravity), if the laws were changed, it very well *could* be possible.

176. Steven J. Duby, "Divine Simplicity, Divine Freedom, and the Contingency of Creation: Dogmatic Responses to Some Analytic Questions," *Journal of Reformed Theology* 6, no. 2 (2012): 133, https://doi.org/10.1163/15697312-12341234.

177. See Bradshaw, *Aristotle East and West*, 247, 268.

178. Richard A. Muller, *Divine Will and Human Choice: Freedom, Contingency, and Necessity in Early Modern Reformed Thought* (Baker Academic, 2017), 194.

179. Alvin Plantinga, *The Nature of Necessity* (Clarendon, 2010), 2–3; Alfred J. Freddoso, "Human Nature, Potency and the Incarnation," *Faith and Philosophy* 3, no. 1 (1986): 31, https://doi.org/10.5840/faithphil1986312.

180. Muller, *Divine Will and Human Choice*, 97.

181. Daniel J. Pedersen and Christopher Lilley, "Divine Simplicity, God's Freedom, and the Supposed Problem of Modal Collapse," *Journal of Reformed Theology* 16 (2022): 131, https://doi.org/10.1163/15697312-bja10028.

So, this is not a strictly logical necessity. It lacks absoluteness. There are conditions in which it *wouldn't* be necessary. Absolute necessity, on the other hand, is a necessity that *cannot fail* to be the case whereas hypothetical necessity is a necessity that cannot fail to be the case *given* some other proposition (or conjunction of propositions).

Applied to God, he wills his own goodness by absolute necessity, but he hypothetically wills creation since there is no logical necessity to God's creating *this* world and not another—even if the attributes of God are identical to one another.[182] Denying logical necessity (or absolute necessity) to God's creation relates to the distinction between God's absolute power (what God *could* will) and God's ordained power (what God *has* willed).[183] While divine simplicity would equate God's ordained power with his will, this does not remove the hypothetical ability of his absolute power to create a different world or to not create at all. Similarly, Turretin explains, "It is only an extrinsic necessity and from the hypothesis of the divine will, without interference with the liberty and contingency of things."[184] The idea is that God's acts are hypothetically necessary because they could have been otherwise. While he may be constrained by his own nature in certain respects (e.g., he couldn't will against his own goodness), he is not constrained by anything external to himself. Since God has the natural capacity to do otherwise (he could have *hypothetically* done otherwise), creation is contingent.

Consider two examples to make this plain. First, think about Socrates running at T1. If this is true at T1, it is necessary that he runs at T1 because it is impossible that he simultaneously be running and sitting at T1. However, it is not absolutely necessary. He could have been sitting at T1.[185] In another possible world, Socrates may have chosen to sit or to lay down. Or think about God's predestining of Jacob. Prior to God's decree, it was not necessary that Jacob be predestined. He could have been passed over. But once decreed, it's necessary relative to—or on the hypothesis of—the decree.[186]

So, Mullins's argument is unsound. Creation can be *hypothetically necessary* and yet God remains free. This is so because the necessity of God's will

182. Wittman, *God and Creation in the Theology of Thomas Aquinas and Karl Barth*, 266–67.

183. Muller, *Divine Will and Human Choice*, 21.

184. Turretin, *Institutes of Elenctic Theology*, 3.11.14.

185. Muller, *Divine Will and Human Choice*, 132.

186. Turretin, *Institutes of Elenctic Theology*, 3.14.5–10.

is absolutely necessary only in a natural sense. God is constrained by his own nature (being unable to will evil, etc., which is traditional on standard accounts of divine omnipotence). But God is free from obstacle and is completely self-directed.[187] So, God's will is free in the sense of having *no external cause*. There is no coercion or coaction.[188] There is no principle external to God, whether physical or metaphysical, that explains his action.[189] God is the sole source of his decree, and his creating is not logically necessary. It is not entailed by the laws of logic or the nature of deity.[190] So, creation is not necessary because had God not willed it, it would not have occurred. Even if God eternally wills something, it doesn't change its logical status.[191]

It is important to clarify that this move requires denying that acts take their objects essentially. In other words, God is identical to his will, and hence his decree, but his decree could have had a different object (e.g., God decrees to create a world that does not contain oatmeal, or where God decrees to not create at all). At least the Reformed tradition "nearly universally" observes this and defends the complete freedom of God.[192] If one denies object essentialism, then each of those acts can be identical to each other. The cost, though, is that object essentialism is extremely intuitive.[193] So, the classical theist will need to bite the bullet and deny what some have referred to as the difference principle (a difference in effect requires an intrinsic difference in the cause) to avoid modal collapse. This is certainly unintuitive, but it's not surprising that we'd encounter some unintuitive things in the context of divine simplicity. And given the choice between giving up simplicity and giving up object essentialism/the difference principle, I'm deferring to the Christian tradition and giving up object essentialism.[194]

---

187. Eleonore Stump and Norman Kretzmann, "Absolute Simplicity," *Faith and Philosophy* 2, no. 4 (1985): 364, https://doi.org/10.5840/faithphil19852449.

188. Muller, *Post-Reformation Reformed Dogmatics*, 3:448.

189. Paul Helm, *Eternal God*, 2nd ed. (Oxford University Press, 2010), 174.

190. Stump and Kretzmann, "Absolute Simplicity," 368; Helm, *Eternal God*, 187.

191. Helm, *Eternal God*, 177.

192. Richard A. Muller, *Understanding the Divine in Early Modern Reformed Theology* (Reformation Heritage Books, 2024), 202.

193. Timothy O'Connor, "The Unity of the Divine Nature: Four Theories," in *Classical Theism: New Essays on the Metaphysics of God*, ed. Robert C. Koons and Jonathan Fuqua (Routledge, 2022), 129.

194. Thanks to several friends for helping me to think through this, namely Joel Chopp and Matt Ntiros.

Now, it is true that on this account, freedom consists in freedom from external constraints and *not* absolute freedom.[195] God has natural freedom from *external* obligations though he does have *internal* obligations.[196] But such a way of thinking about freedom is well attested within the tradition and is compatible with both compatibilist and incompatibilist accounts of free will because freedom is not about leeway but about sourcehood. So, God's freedom doesn't guarantee his ability to do otherwise (i.e., leeway), but it does guarantee his freedom as sole source of his actions.[197]

Some may worry that the aforementioned distinctions do not remove the force of modal collapse. Everything is still necessary in one sense or another. And any sense of necessity is bad news for divine freedom. We'd at least hope that while God may not be able to change the past, he could still change his mind about the future, which divine simplicity quite clearly denies (at least on the A-theory of time—for those B-theorists, like myself, this problem shouldn't really occur because all times are equally real and "present," whether past, present, or future). If this is true, which I doubt, some argue that there can be good theological reasons to think it doesn't bear any serious consequence for traditional theology (including divine freedom).

There are several thinkers in the tradition that have accepted modal collapse at face value.[198] Peter Abelard is one such thinker that does just this. For Abelard it is necessary that God create because of his absolute goodness.[199] Similarly, Brian Leftow suggests that a necessary creation isn't a problem because God is perfectly good, which means he has the properties of generosity and creativity that lead to a necessary creation.[200] God as perfectly generous means he has a supremely generous disposition to give to others. God as perfectly creative means he is irrepressibly creative, thinking up creatures just by his own nature.

---

195. Muller, *Post-Reformation Reformed Dogmatics*, 3:433.

196. Muller, *Post-Reformation Reformed Dogmatics*, 3:447.

197. Brian Leftow, *God and Necessity* (Oxford University Press, 2015), 147.

198. For a recent contemporary example, see Pedersen and Lilley, "Divine Simplicity, God's Freedom, and the Supposed Problem of Modal Collapse."

199. Cited in Muller, *Post-Reformation Reformed Dogmatics*, 3:35.

200. Leftow, *God and Necessity*, 273–74.

Jonathan Edwards is also quite famous for this sort of thinking about God and creation. Consider his words at length to get the proper context for his argument:

> And as this fullness is capable of communication or emanation ad extra; so it seems a thing amiable and valuable in itself that it should be communicated or flow forth, that this infinite fountain of good should send forth abundant streams, that this infinite fountain of light should, diffusing its excellent fullness, pour forth light all around. And as this is in itself excellent, so a disposition to this in the Divine Being must be looked upon as a perfection or an excellent disposition; such an emanation of good is, in some sense, a multiplication of it; so far as the communication or external stream may be looked upon as anything besides the fountain, so far it may be looked on as an increase of good. And if the fullness of good that is in the fountain is in itself excellent and worthy to exist, then the emanation, or that which is as it were an increase, repetition or multiplication of it, is excellent and worthy to exist. Thus it is fit, since there is an infinite fountain of light and knowledge, that this light should shine forth in beams of communicated knowledge and understanding: and as there is an infinite fountain of holiness, moral excellence and beauty, so it should flow out in communicated holiness. And that as there is an infinite fullness of joy and happiness, so these should have an emanation, and become a fountain flowing out in abundant streams, as beams from the sun.[201]

So, Edwards thinks there is a disposition in God's own nature to emanate his infinite fullness. He thinks it is precisely this disposition that is the aim of creation.[202] Edwards likens it to the nature of a tree and the sun. The tree, by nature, puts forth buds, shoots out branches, and brings leaves and fruit. It has an internal disposition or causal power to do these things naturally and it terminates in itself. The same with the sun. It has an irrepressive disposition to shine and diffuse its fullness, warmth, and brightness, which is its

---

201. Jonathan Edwards, *Dissertation I: Concerning the End for Which God Created the World*, in *Ethical Writings*, vol. 8 of *Works of Jonathan Edwards Online*, ed. Paul Ramsey: Yale University, 1749), 433.

202. Edwards, *Dissertation I: Concerning the End for Which God Created the World*, 8:435.

completed state. In the same way, God emanates and communicates himself as the completeness of himself.[203]

But accounts like these give off hints of neo-Platonic emanation which would appear to violate divine aseity. It seems the tradeoff here to protect simplicity isn't worth it, at least by my lights. But there are reasons to think necessary attributes may not violate aseity because if God is necessarily generous, diffusive, or creative, these do not *cause* God to be *dependent* in any way. Generosity isn't a need, it's a willful volition. The same is true of creativity. These are willful independent acts of God. Consider an example. Think of your favorite artist, maybe Van Gogh or Michelangelo. When Michelangelo painted the Sistine Chapel, he wasn't in need of his creation. He expressed his skills in a willful act of creativity, totally independent of the creation itself. There was no dependence relation. He simply wanted to do it. Therefore, for those unafraid of modal collapse, denying significant freedom to God, there is nothing wrong with positing a *willful* absolute necessity of sorts. However, most of the tradition has not thought along these lines about divine freedom, and I believe the resources provided to parry against modal collapse apart from such an account are both sufficient and persuasive. God, for the vast majority of classical thinkers, has free choice, willing without necessity.[204] Therefore, I think it is better to avoid positing such strong necessities as there may be other theological consequences that are worse than the cure. No distinction? No Trinity.

A further supposed problem for divine simplicity relates to the Trinity (and similarly the incarnation, but I will explore some of the classical challenges to the incarnation in the following chapter on divine immutability in more detail). Many have wondered, *If God is simple, how can the Trinity be affirmed?* In other words, if there are no distinctions because of divine simplicity (at least in the maximal model), doesn't this mean there can be no distinctions between the persons of the Trinity?[205] Tom McCall, a defender of divine simplicity, has mused that on a maximal (or what he calls strict) model of divine

203. Edwards, *Dissertation I: Concerning the End for Which God Created the World*, 8:439.

204. See, for example: Aquinas, *Summa Contra Gentiles: Book One; God* 1.88.

205. Richards, *The Untamed God*, 229.

simplicity, the "doctrine truly may be inconsistent with trinitarian theology."[206] The argument could be stated formally:

1. If the Trinity is true, then there must be distinctions between the persons of the Trinity.
2. If divine simplicity is true, then there are no distinctions.
3. Divine simplicity is true.
4. Therefore, there are no distinctions in God.
5. Therefore, the Trinity is false.

How else could we make sense of the Father *alone* having the property of paternity and yet affirming divine simplicity? As Richards concludes, "If one wishes to retain trinitarian distinctions, one must deny that every essential divine property or relation is strongly equivalent."[207] If true, this is a devastating objection to simplicity. A Christian has far stronger commitments to upholding the Trinity than divine simplicity given the content of the ecumenical creeds (not to even mention the biblical witness). What are we to make of this problem, then?

The problem could be spelled out along the lines of identity. *Strict identity*, as Leibniz would suggest, is symmetric (e.g., if a=b, then anything true of a is true of b and vice versa), reflexive (e.g., everything is identical to itself), and transitive (e.g., if a=b and b=c, then a=c).[208] So, if divine simplicity is true, then the Father is identical to the divine essence, and the Son is identical to the divine essence. Therefore, if the Father is unbegotten, then the Son also must be unbegotten. Based on standard accounts of divine simplicity where God lacks all composition due to divine simplicity, it is not clear how defenders can then say God is "really identical with each of the persons of the Trinity" with the belief that the persons are different.[209]

---

206. McCall, "Trinity Doctrine, Plain and Simple," 57.

207. Richards, *The Untamed God*, 230.

208. Tim Pawl, "Conciliar Trinitarianism, Divine Identity Claims, and Subordination," *TheoLogica: An International Journal for Philosophy of Religion and Philosophical Theology* 4, no. 2 (2020): https://doi.org/doi.org/10.14428/thl.v4i2.23593.

209. Duby, *Divine Simplicity: A Dogmatic Account*, 83.

But there are several ways to difuse this problem. First, one could deny any model of simplicity that rejects real extramental distinctions. Divine simplicity, then, does not amount to what premise 2 claims. There *are* distinctions in God. This is the route well summarized by Martinus Becanus (1563–1624), who says:

> For we do not ask here whether there is in God some real distinction which effects a real multitude or plurality (about which no one doubts except Sabellius), but instead, whether in God there are some real components which effect real composition. The divine persons are indeed really distinguished; but they are not external components which concur with the composition of some thing.[210]

In other words, divine simplicity doesn't mean there are no distinctions altogether, or at least it *shouldn't* mean that. Divine simplicity only denies "real components which effect real composition." Its main focus is to deny *composition* and not *distinction*. Therefore, the divine persons are really distinct, and this does nothing to violate the maxim of divine simplicity.[211]

One could also argue along the lines of *relative identity*. Relative identity is a thesis in metaphysics that says it is possible for *x* and *y* to be the same *F* but different *G*'s. That's a technical way of saying that identity doesn't need to be exclusively used in the strict sense where everything must be super-duper identical. It is fine to say I am identical to my younger self (*F*, in this instance) even though I have all sorts of differences (*G*, in this instance, most notably less hair on my head). Therefore, relative identity denies transitivity, which is the move Thomas seems to make.[212] So, while the Father and the Son both have the identical divine nature (they are the same *F*), they are different persons (they are different *G*'s), and this still counts as being "identical" as divine simplicity would have us want to say. On this account, there is something hidden in this argument that makes it invalid. There are identity claims at work, assuming a strict account, wherein it is possible to accept a relative account of identity to make sense of simplicity and the Trinity.

Third, we could develop an account like Tim Pawl's, who argues that

---

210. Becanus, "Summa Theologiae Scolasticae," II.6.

211. See for example, Scott Williams, *The Trinity* (Cambridge University Press, 2025), 60–64.

212. Mark K. Spencer, "The Flexibility of Divine Simplicity: Aquinas, Scotus, Palamas," *International Philosophical Quarterly* 57, no. 2 (2017): 126, https://doi.org/10.5840/ipq201731682.

simplicity has less to do with extravagant maximal claims and more do to with concrete natures. So instead of something being simple only if it has no parts whatsoever in a maximal sense, being simple means having a concrete nature that does not have parts. So, then, the Father is simple just in case he has a nature that has no parts. Likewise, the Son and the Spirit are simple if they have a nature that has no parts. This also has the advantage of explaining how the Son can *also* be complex while still being simple, which he certainly is in the incarnation (he has a body with parts, after all). The Son has *two natures*, one of which is simple and the other of which is complex.[213]

SIMPLICITY FOR THE CHURCH

Classical theism is for the church. Its *telos* is doxology. Therefore, even when engaging the finer points of doctrine, the goal of worship is always in view. And the classical doctrine of divine simplicity is designed to disclose the foundation of every perfection.[214] There is a story to be told here. There is an aesthetic and not merely an abstract philosophical ideal. Simplicity gives grounds for God's pure goodness, universal goodness, and limitless goodness.[215] As pure, universal, and limitless good, God must be simple. No other account of God's being could preserve and maximize the extensive goodness of God. As John reminds us, "This is the message we have heard from him and proclaim to you, that God is light, and in him is no darkness at all" (1 John 1:5). Apart from divine simplicity wherein God is identical to light, there is no firm and unshakeable ground for his lack of darkness.

But God's simplicity also grounds other perfections like his generosity. Instead of simplicity being a boring or entirely abstract doctrine, it has pastoral warmth and explanatory power. In short, it can soothe, and it can preach! As simple, he gives "simply." In fact, this is just what James says in James 1:5. The word often translated "generosity" is ἁπλῶς and can be fairly translated as "simple." Those like Mastricht pick up on this meaning and argue that because God is simple, he gives simply, which means he gives himself completely. It is impossible to only give part of himself. We cannot only get his mercy but not his love. Therefore, he is entirely and wholly devoted to us in his giving.[216]

---

213. Pawl, "The Incarnation of a Simple God."

214. Mastricht, *Theoretical-Practical Theology*, 1.2.6.25.

215. Mastricht, *Theoretical-Practical Theology*, 1.2.6.26.

216. Mastricht, *Theoretical-Practical Theology*, 1.2.6.26.

Generosity of this degree, because of God's simplicity, ought to conjure worship. There is not one aspect of God he withholds from us in his pursuit of union with us. He doesn't hide a portion of himself. When he offers himself, he offers quite literally *everything*.

Church members and pastors should find these explanations of divine simplicity refreshing. When counseling the fatherless, it is good news that God is simple, giving all of himself to us and never hiding any part. There is never a moment when we will be tricked and find out there is another "god" behind God. The God we find in Jesus—the one who is the same yesterday, today, and forever—just is God. When feeling the pain of the Lord's restorative discipline, we can know that God's justice is his love. In his commitment to discipline, he loves us like a father. But in loving us like a father, his discipline is never apart from his tender care and love. He is not like our own fathers who are incited to rage and cannot see through the boiling of their blood in those moments. God, in his discipline, is patient, kind, and controlled. Divine simplicity provides stability in our faith. It gives us confidence that we receive all of who God is and that we receive his very best.

CONCLUSION

Divine simplicity, whether one is keen to follow a maximal, virtual, formal, or apophatic model, remains essential to confessing God as God for the classical tradition. As simple, God is wholly God. There is nothing that contributes to his being. The simplicity of God is an entailment from his independence from everything, including parts. Yet, while God lacks all creaturely forms of composition, he maintains distinctions on the virtual, formal, and apophatic models. The persons of the Trinity are distinguished as well as his attributes, depending on what model is defended. While simplicity is admittedly a difficult doctrine to understand, I submit that it's less daunting than supposed. And it has significantly more pastoral value than is assumed at first glance. We need more Christians to take the doctrine of divine simplicity seriously again. However, in our zeal, we should avoid limiting the various senses of divine simplicity. We must remain generous in our theological pronouncements. The creedal and confessional traditions simply do not allow for such dogmatism.

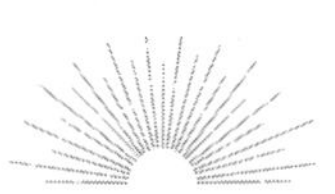

7

DIVINE IMMUTABILITY: THE UNCHANGEABLY GOOD GOD

Only six chapters into Genesis, and the reader is confronted with a startling narrative:

> And the Lord regretted that he had made man on the earth, and it grieved him to his heart. So the Lord said, "I will blot out man whom I have created from the face of the land, man and animals and creeping things and birds of the heavens, for I am sorry that I have made them." (Gen 6:6–7)

The reader has barely forgotten the creation of the world as *good* and humans as *very good*. But now we are confronted with God regretting his creation and changing course to destroy it. There is a cognitive dissonance built into the story designed to shock us. Creation is so bad that God has already changed his mind. Creation was actually a *very bad* idea. *Every* intention of the thoughts of humankind's heart was *continually* evil (Gen 6:5). Therefore, God changed his mind, which means he quite obviously is "mutable." He became sorry, he changed his mind, and he decided to destroy his creation, which he originally deemed good. Case closed: God changes.

Yet the Christian tradition from the patristic fathers through the seventeenth century universally call God immutable.[1] They claim that God's

1. Thomas G. Weinandy, *Does God Change? The Word's Becoming in the Incarnation* (St. Bede's, 1985), xxi.

inability to change is an essential divine perfection.[2] They think that despite the strong claims of Scripture that would appear to indicate God changes, like his grieving in Genesis 6, God actually *doesn't* change. He *doesn't* regret his decisions. He *doesn't* grieve to his heart and change course.

For those unfamiliar with the classical tradition, this likely appears dubious on its face. It is impossible to ignore Genesis 6! Moses narrates at the very beginning of Scripture that God is influenced and changes. To say that God is immutable in the face of both the literal meaning *and* the priority of placement is to do violence to the text of holy Scripture. Those that argue for God's immutability defy Scripture.

While it may appear obvious to say that God changes and that any alternative is foreign to the world of the Bible, this would be far too hasty. Knowing God requires patience. It requires wrestling with the entirety of divine revelation. It is after this patient wrestling that the classical theologian claims that contrary to first impressions, God is immutable. In fact, Scripture itself leads us by the hand to make the interpretive judgments that render God as unable to change. Without an immutable God our very hope, trust, and faith are wholly destabilized. We have no firm foundation or confidence without the immutable God of classical theism. We no longer can rest in the promise that the Lord "knows who are his" (2 Tim 2:19) as there is no ground for our trust. It is to this very ground of hope that we now turn.

APPROACHING A DOGMATIC DEFINITION

Many theologians today argue along the lines of Emil Brunner (1889–1966), who criticizes classical theism for allowing a "philosophical ideal" to take the place of the living God. It is the philosophical ideals of classical theism, like immutability, that sideline and make biblical ideas, like divine faithfulness, imaginative expressions rather than truths to which we cling.[3] But whatever immutability means, no one in the tradition allows it to reject or mythologize biblical characterizations of divine character. Instead, immutability is meant to safeguard and further explain how and why God is the way he is. There is a ground for his faithfulness when he is

2. Richard Muller, *Post-Reformation Reformed Dogmatics* (Baker Academic, 2003), 3:308.

3. Emil Brunner, *The Christian Doctrine of God*, trans. Olive Wyon (Westminster, 1949), 271.

immutable in a way that doesn't exist apart from it. And yet, there remains a variety of accounts of immutability that require careful delineation.

MERE DIVINE IMMUTABILITY

To best evaluate various models of immutability and which ones can properly be defined as within the fold of classical theism, I begin with the following account from which we can build:

> *Mere divine immutability*: God is immutable *if and only if* God cannot change.

As expected, such a definition leaves much to be desired, especially given the contemporary worries and modifications of divine immutability. After all, nearly everyone in the Abrahamic faith (Christianity, Judaism, Islam) confesses some sort of immutability in God. Everyone wants *something* about him not to change. At minimum there is a desire for God's promises not to change—at least his promise to *me* and those I care about. Despite the laments of those like Brunner to the contrary, everyone wants an immutably faithful God. So, in *what* sense does God not change? I suggest that by asking only two questions, we can determine three senses in which God can be immutable:

1. Can God change intrinsically?
2. Can God change extrinsically?

How one answers these two questions will determine in what sense God is immutable. As a reminder, these concepts, intrinsic and extrinsic, are explained further in chapter 4. Intrinsic properties are those something has independently of everything else, whereas extrinsic properties are dependent on something else.

MODELS OF IMMUTABILITY

When categorizing the various senses of immutability that are generated from answering the two aforementioned questions, there is a natural spectrum. There is a maximal sort of immutability that denies *all* changes of God. Whatever change you can think of is denied. Period. On the opposite end of the immutability spectrum could be a wide array of options.

There are those who outright deny most any immutability—God changes in most every respect. But for our purposes, I limit the extent to which change is admissible since we are discussing variations of divine *immu*tability. Therefore, I've chosen to extend the models of immutability at this point to a weak immutability that denies any changes to God's essential properties. God can change intrinsically on this account, but he still cannot change in ways that would jeopardize his love, moral character, or perfection.

With these ends in mind, the below three categories are the most relevant for understanding immutability from my perspective. There are other variations that could be parsed here, but these capture the main opinions.[4] I begin with the strongest form of immutability and move to the weakest.

> *Global divine immutability:* God is immutable *if and only if* God cannot change (1) intrinsically and (2) extrinsically.

> *Local divine immutability:* God is immutable *if and only if* God cannot change intrinsically.

> *Weak divine immutability:* God is immutable *if and only if* God cannot change in his essential characteristics.

I argue that the first two definitions (global and local) form the bedrock of the classical tradition. They are both *strong* versions of immutability. Those motivated to remain within the classical tradition will need to accept one of them. However, I think there is much room for creativity in understanding this doctrine within the dogmatic consensus. Moreover, the tradition has often not been clear on the distinction between these two versions. Therefore, depending on the thinker, they may oscillate between these categories at times.[5] But depending on how strong the first version is, it may very well be flatly inconsistent with conciliar teachings that teach of Christ suffering, dying, and rising.[6] So careful examination

4. For example, John Feinberg has offered *eight* senses in which God could change. John S. Feinberg, *No One Like Him* (Crossway, 2001), 267–69.

5. Saint Anselm may be an example of someone that could be read as advocating for global immutability and local immutability, depending on the passage.

6. Tim Pawl, "Conciliar Christology and the Consistency of Divine Immutability with a Mutable, Incarnate God," *Nova et Vetera* 16, no. 3 (2018): 920.

of each model is important. Each of them answers the previously mentioned questions as follows.

Table 7.1. Two Important Questions

Model	**Can God change intrinsically?**	**Can God change extrinsically?**
Global	No	No
Local	No	Yes
Weak	Yes	Yes

The first two versions (global and local) are strong accounts of immutability because they both claim that God cannot change intrinsically. He cannot change in any *real* respect, though they differ over what constitutes a *real* change. Global immutability suggests that God cannot change intrinsically *or* extrinsically since both would constitute a change in his being (hence its global nature). Local immutability suggests extrinsic changes have no impact on his ontology and thus can be attributed to him. Scheeben is characteristic of this approach when he defines immutability as an exclusion of "every *inner* change" and not change wholesale.[7]

The now-commonplace terminology for acceptable extrinsic changes is "Cambridge change." These changes are changes "in" a thing but not ontologically speaking. They are changes in the descriptions borne by the thing. For example, prior to my first son being born I was not a father, but after his birth I became a father, though nothing ontologically changed about me. While a new predication was true, it did not indicate any actual change in me intrinsically.[8] Only a local account of immutability finds these "changes" acceptable. A global account, on the other hand, denies them. For example, Paul Helm claims that "an individual is immutable in the required sense if no temporal or spatial changes apply to that thing, not even temporal or spatial 'merely Cambridge' changes."[9] As Helm says, there are no Cambridge changes. Alternatively, Brian Leftow argues for

7. Matthias Joseph Scheeben, *Handbook of Catholic Dogmatics*, trans. Michael J. Miller (Emmaus Academic, 2019), 2:109.

8. See Peter Geach, *God and the Soul* (St. Augustine's, 2001), 71–72.

9. Paul Helm, *Eternal God*, 2nd ed. (Oxford University Press, 2010), 19.

the weaker local immutability when he claims that "God cannot undergo real or intrinsic change in any respect."[10]

As can be seen, the distinction between intrinsic and extrinsic properties or predications is very relevant. The reason is because the local immutability model thinks there needs to be a way to distinguish between the predications concerning God, which can change in truth-value without precluding divine immutability, and those that can't. For global immutability, no predications concerning God can ever change in truth-value without implicating God ontologically in some sort of change. If God were to not have a predication true of him at one time and then have one true at another time, he would be mutable—even if that predication was a Cambridge change.

For local immutability, the reason that predications concerning God can change in truth-value is *not* because of a change in God. God remains intrinsically immutable. Instead, it is because of some other change in something else. Immutability *would* be compromised if a proposition such as "God is planning to redeem creation" changed in truth-value. But it is not compromised if a proposition such as "God is being praised by Fred" changes in truth-value. And so, things like God's plans are intrinsic to him, but his being praised is extrinsic to him (unless he is praising himself). I speak here of a proposition changing its truth-value, though it is not essential for divine immutability that propositions can change truth-values. If the reader holds a view where propositions have their truth-values eternally, the reader may substitute in his or her preferred paraphrase for apparent change in the truth-value of propositions.[11]

The third model, weak immutability, has gained significant support in recent years from those amiable to the classical tradition. The basic claim is that God *does* change intrinsically and extrinsically. But those changes are limited in extent. God remains immutable in his "essential" characteristics, whatever those are. Typically, this is understood to be that his nature and character are changeless.[12] Conversely, his relationships, his knowl-

---

10. Brian Leftow, "Immutability," in *The Stanford Encyclopedia of Philosophy*, ed. Edward N. Zalta, Winter 2016, https://plato.stanford.edu/archives/win2016/entries/immutability/.

11. I am especially indebted to Tim Pawl for parsing out the importance of these distinctions here. Where I have failed to capture his ideas, the fault is my own.

12. John C. Peckham, *Divine Attributes* (Baker Academic, 2021), 45.

edge of certain things like temporal indexicals, and his way of working in the world changes.[13] Therefore, real properties can be added or subtracted from God.[14] Since God is a real "agent in history," the "historical process" for God must change.[15] Any number of accounts can fit under this model. So long as the account thinks God has some essential characteristic, it is a version of weak immutability. For example, those like Isaak Dorner, who further strip down what is changeless in God to "ethical immutability" alone, remain within the definitional bounds of weak immutability.[16] He simply differs on what characteristics are essential to God.

It should be noted that those with more classical intuitions that fall under the weak immutability umbrella often speak of ontological categories as very limited in nature. A change in non-essential characteristics, like the knowledge of temporal indexicals (what time it is *now*, etc.) does not count as an "ontological" change. God remains ontologically immutable despite such changes.[17] The reason adherents to this model say this is because they assume only essential properties are ontological. So long as God remains changeless in his essential characteristics, he can freely change in other respects. But it should be noted from the start that this use of "ontological" is indicative of a misunderstanding of *ontology*. Ontology includes the study of properties, whether essential or non-essential. I suggest that much of the bewilderment of those that defend weak accounts in contrast to strong accounts stems from this misunderstanding. Regardless, as we explore the creedal, confessional, and classical tradition, it will be clear that no weak account of immutability can be considered "classical," even if some find it attractive for other reasons.[18]

---

13. Feinberg, *No One Like Him*, 267–69.

14. Jay Wesley Richards, *The Untamed God* (InterVarsity Press, 2003), 209; Bruce Ware, *God's Greater Glory* (Crossway, 2004), 39, 139.

15. John M. Frame, *Systematic Theology: An Introduction to Christian Belief* (P&R, 2013), 377.

16. Isaak August Dorner, *Divine Immutability: A Critical Reconsideration*, trans. Robert R. Williams and Claude Welch (Fortress, 1994), 176.

17. Ware, *God's Greater Glory*, 140.

18. Again, I think it is important to note that while I strongly argue that no version of weak immutability is compatible with classical theism, this does not mean that those who argue for weak immutability (at least some versions) are therefore unorthodox. There are arguments to be made in favor of it, though I find them unpersuasive and in contrast to classical Christianity. However, some of them, I think, are simply constructed out of an ignorance of the older ways of thinking and speaking and in reaction to some of the sloppier contemporary claims about immutability. Of course,

CREEDAL AND CONFESSIONAL AFFIRMATIONS

Before examining the diversity and uniformity within the classical tradition's individual thinkers, it is best to examine those documents that are confessed by all orthodox Christians and those that are confessed by a significant segment of the Christian tradition.[19] Consider first the Council of Nicaea (325). All orthodox Christians affirm the creed that resulted from this council. It is axiomatic for the Christian faith. However, few realize that hidden within the anathemas of the creed is a claim about immutability. It says: "But those who say ... that he is mutable or alterable—the Catholic and Apostolic Church anathematizes."[20] This is an anathema directed at those who suggest the Son is mutable, and hence that God is mutable too. To deny immutability, then, is to deny the Nicene Creed.

The Council of Antioch in the same year as Nicaea has a similar declaration. It says, "We anathematize those who supposed that He is immutable by His own act of will, just as those who derive His birth from that which is not, and deny that He is immutable in the way the Father is."[21] Again, this is speaking of the Son. It is rejecting the belief that the Son could be immutable based on his own will and not due to his nature. It requires immutability of all the persons of the Godhead. Now, as has been seen with the initial definition of immutability, it isn't specific enough to account for the granularity at which the discussion has moved.

The first session of Chalcedon is especially clear about the doctrine of divine immutability when the entire council jointly read and "made the same declaration" as the letter of Cyril to John of Antioch:

> But I am so far from thinking such a thing that I count them insane who can for a moment suppose it is possible for a "shadow of turning" to take place in respect of the nature of God the Word; for

some may quip that classical theism is a necessary condition for orthodoxy. But the nature of theological "orthodoxy" is a topic for another book. My minimal suggestion is that orthodoxy relates to the ecumenical creeds, the Ten Commandments, etc. and not to some of the more fine-grained theological distinctions here.

19. For more in-depth treatment of some of these conciliar texts see the work of Tim Pawl: Tim Pawl, "Divine Immutability," in *Internet Encyclopedia of Philosophy*, n.d., https://iep.utm.edu/divine-immutability/; Tim Pawl, *In Defense of Conciliar Christology* (Oxford University Press, 2016); Pawl, "Conciliar Christology and the Consistency of Divine Immutability with a Mutable, Incarnate God."

20. Leo Donald Davis, *The First Seven Ecumenical Councils (325–787)* (Liturgical Press, 1990), 60.

21. Davis, *The First Seven Ecumenical Councils (325–787)*, 55.

> he remains for ever what he is and has not been altered, neither, indeed, could he ever be altered or be capable of change.[22]

According to the council, it is *insane* to posit any sort of change in the incarnation. The Son, even though he assumes a human nature, remains unchanged. In the face of one of the most potent contemporary objections to divine immutability, the fathers at Chalcedon unashamedly affirm a strong immutability. If ever there was an opportunity to give some degree of latitude, this would be it. And yet there is no room for a weak account of immutability. He is incapable of change.

Even if one seeks to evade the force of these creedal formulas and acts of the councils by requiring them to carry less metaphysical baggage than the framers intended, there are other creedal claims that direct us toward a global or local account. For example, the Fourth Council of Constantinople (869–870) confesses that God suffers no change or alteration. It makes no mention of any potential for change whatsoever. It, like Nicaea and Antioch, is a blanket statement.[23] But there is more significant evidence in Cyril's third letter to Nestorius, which was read and approved by the Council of Ephesus and given formal synodal approval at Constantinople in 553. Herein Cyril claims that God is "entirely unchanging and immutable" even as the Son is incarnate and swaddled in clothes.[24] For the creedal tradition, therefore, God is immutable in every respect.

The confessional tradition likewise defends the immutability of God. The blanket ascription of immutability is made in numerous Protestant confessions including the Belgic Confession, the Confession of Varadiensis/Nagyvárad (1569), the Confession of La Rochelle (1571), the Westminster Confession of Faith, the Midlands Confession (1655), the Canons of Dort (1619), and the French Confession (1559). Yet many of these confessions go further. For example, Theodore Beza's Confession (1560) says that "God is immutable in his counsels." The Strong Declaration of the Formula of Concord XI.75 says that God "cannot deny Himself, because He is

22. Richard Price and Michael Gaddis, trans., *The Acts Council of Chalcedon* (Liverpool University Press, 2007), 1:181–82.

23. However, this council is not accepted by the Eastern church.

24. Cyril of Alexandria, "Third Letter to Nestorius," in *The Cambridge Edition of Early Christian Writings*, ed. Mark DelCogliano, trans. Matthew R. Crawford (Cambridge University Press, 2022), 628.

unchangeable in will and essence." The Second London Confession section 2.1, patterned on Westminster and Savoy, also confesses that God is immutable in essence and will.

The additional clarity provided by the Protestant confessional tradition that immutability requires an immutability not only of essence but of will effectively eliminates weak immutability from the realm of dogmatic possibilities. Since weak immutability requires mutability of will, it cannot comport with the confessional consensus. However, the confessional tradition, like the creedal tradition, is compatible with either local or global immutability.

THE WITNESSES OF THE CLASSICAL TRADITION

In what follows I provide a general survey of the main claims regarding divine immutability throughout the Christian tradition. I conclude that, like the creedal and confessional consensus, the dogmatic shape of the individual thinkers within the tradition remains open to either local or global immutability but is closed to weak immutability. While versions of weak immutability may be more prevalent today, they would be rejected by the classical tradition.

The Patristic Witness

First, consider several thinkers within the patristic era. Augustine by any standard holds pride of place given his downstream influence on the generations that followed him. He references immutability throughout his works, assuming its truth and putting it to theological work. This is characteristic of the period as there are few extended treatments of the doctrine, most of the references being occasional in nature. Extracting the development of immutability from these larger contexts is dangerous business, however. We must be careful not to overlook the overall flow of the argument from which the claims are made. For example, one of Augustine's characteristic definitions of immutability comes from his treatise on the Trinity:

> There is nothing changeable about it; not changeable in time and space like bodies, nor changeable only in time and quasi-space, like the wandering fancies of our spirits, nor only in time and not even

> in imagined space, like some of the reasonings of our minds. For God's essence, by which he is, has absolutely nothing changeable about its eternity or its truth or its will.[25]

For Augustine, *absolutely nothing* is changeable about God. His claim comes amid an existential reflection, meditating on how God as immutable guarantees "unchanging joy."[26] For Augustine, immutability is a key to happiness and not merely a logical tool with which to bludgeon others. He offers three modifiers for what is immutable: eternity, truth, and will. The first two are noncontroversial. Even those that hold a very weak account of divine immutability still think truth doesn't change and that God exists eternally (though how eternity is understood is a matter of debate). But the fact that God's will doesn't change in any respect is quite important. The unchangeable nature of his will plays an especially important role in the later development of Protestant confessional theology. It is not merely that God's overarching purpose to redeem doesn't change. There is *absolutely nothing* changeable about his will—even to the smallest detail.

It is also important to see that Augustine is assuming a strong sense of divine simplicity. God's essence is that "by which he is," and therefore nothing about God is changeable. His knowledge and his will cannot change since they are identical to him. For example, elsewhere he says, "His nature will never vary at different times, and his will is not external to his nature. It follows that he does not will one thing at one time, and another thing at another time. Once and for all and simultaneously, he wills everything that he wills."[27]

Augustine is blending several classical doctrines together here to explain the nature of immutability. A strong doctrine of eternity and simplicity are presupposed and weaved throughout. One cannot make sense of what he says about immutability without also assuming the truth of these doctrines. As he makes use of these various doctrines God is shown to be immutable in every respect. His knowledge, his will, his action, and everything else is wholly unchangeable—it never varies. Augustine's description does appear to favor a global version

---

25. Augustine, *The Trinity*, trans. Edmund Hill (New City, 2015), IV.prol.
26. Augustine, *The Trinity* IV.1, 2.
27. Augustine, *Confessions*, trans. Henry Chadwick (Oxford University Press, 2008), XII.xv (18).

of immutability more than a local version, though nothing is explicitly at odds with a local account.

Augustine is not alone in positing a strong account of immutability. Gregory of Nyssa is a close contemporary and says that God is "incapable of changing to worse or changing to better."[28] This rationale for immutability is replete throughout the tradition. All change is either for the better or the worse. So, if God is perfect, he cannot change lest he become less than perfect or prove that he wasn't as perfect as he was prior to the change. Gregory of Nazianzus echoes him, saying that God is free from change.[29] Likewise, Cyril argues in numerous places that God is immutable and unchanging.[30] As noted, in his *Third Letter to Nestorius*, which received synodal affirmation at the second Council of Constantinople (553), he argues that "the one who abides eternally, according to the scriptures, is entirely unchanging and immutable."[31] Likewise, Pope Leo's Tome, which received approval at Chalcedon, argues for a strong account of immutability.[32] Leo later provided a more mature reflection, his *Second Tome*, in which he asserts that the divine essence is immutable, impassible, and timeless.[33] Athanasius also describes Christ as immutable since, if he could change, he would no longer be divine.[34] Leo also calls God immutable, in part, because his will cannot be severed from his goodness.[35] While none of these claims

---

28. Quoted in Bruce Ware, "An Evangelical Reexamination of the Doctrine of the Immutability of God," PhD diss., Fuller Theological Seminary, 1984, 40.

29. Gregory of Nazianzus, *On God and Christ*, trans. Frederick Williams and Lionel R. Wickham (St. Vladimir's Seminary Press, 2002), 28.9.

30. Cyril of Alexandria, "First Letter to Succensus," in *The Cambridge Edition of Early Christian Writings*, ed. Mark DelCogliano, trans. Matthew R. Crawford (Cambridge University Press, 2022), 738, https://doi.org/10.1017/9781107449640.052; Cyril of Alexandria, *Letters 51–110*, trans. John I. McEnerney (Catholic University of America Press, 1987), 24.

31. Cyril of Alexandria, "Third Letter to Nestorius," 628.

32. Fairbairn, "Interpreting Conciliar Christology," *Journal of Analytic Theology* 10 (2022): 376–77; Price and Gaddis, *The Council of Chalcedon*, 1:67.

33. Leo of Rome, "The Second Tome (Letter to Emperor Leo)," in *The Cambridge Edition of Early Christian Writings*, ed. and trans. Mark DelCogliano (Cambridge University Press, 2022), 120–21.

34. Athanasius, "Defence of the Nicene Council," in *Select Works and Letters*, ed. Archibald Thomas Robertson and Philip Schaff, Nicene and Post-Nicene Fathers, 2nd ser., vol. 4 (Hendrickson, 2004), 165.

35. Leo the Great, *Sermons*, trans. Jane Patricia Freeland and Agnes Josephine Conway (Catholic University of America Press, 1995), 81.

are robust in the contemporary philosophical sense, they are indicative of the consensus of the period: God is wholly immutable.

The Medieval Witness

The mature expressions of immutability flower within the medieval era. Immutability remains axiomatic but articulations of the doctrine bring greater depth and insight. Peter Lombard (1100–1160) offers a standard description that tracks neatly with the patristic witness. God "neither does, nor can, change."[36] But it is not merely God's generic essence that is unchangeable. Lombard is emphatic that even God's knowledge is wholly unchangeable as well.[37] Hugh of Saint Victor (1096–1141) confesses a similar opinion that God "cannot be altered and changed at all." He goes on to explain that this means God cannot change in nature, knowledge, will, or disposition.[38] Bonaventure, following Hugh in many respects, explains that "without a doubt, the divine being is completely unchangeable." He tracks with the arguments of Hugh by explaining that all change can be reduced to form, place, or time. But since God is simple, immense, and eternal, he cannot change.[39] The idea is simply that there are other divine attributes we are already committed to that remove the possibility of change.

Saint Anselm says that God is "supremely unalterable." However, Anselm considers an important question for the distinction between what I have called global and local immutability. He allows for "accidents" that "do not entail any change in a substance." Here he contrasts between two sorts of accidents, which roughly amounts to the intrinsic and extrinsic property distinction explained in chapter 4. Any property "whose presence or absence implies some change in the subject" is intrinsic and cannot be predicated of God. However, properties that don't cause change (e.g., for Anslem, "some relations") are allowed to be predicated

36. Peter Lombard, *The Sentences*, trans. Giulio Silano (Pontifical Institute of Mediaeval Studies, 2007), VIII.2 (22).

37. Lombard, *The Sentences*, XXXIX.1 (175).

38. Hugh of Saint Victor, *On the Sacraments of the Christian Faith (De Sacramentis)*, trans. Roy Deferraro (Ex Fontibus, 2016), 1.3.13.

39. Bonaventure, *Disputed Questions on the Mystery of the Trinity*, trans. Zachary Hayes (Franciscan Institute, 2000), 229.

of God. Anselm offers the example of birth. Prior to someone's birth it is impossible to be taller than or shorter than them, since they don't exist. Yet once they are born, suddenly, it is possible to obtain these qualities "without my changing at all." The father, mother, and delivery doctor do not change in any respect and yet "add" a new relation. But they do not "change" their ontology. These accidents, then, "do not take away inalterability in any respect whatsoever." However, these accidents are improperly accidents since they do not entail any ontological change.[40] Therefore, for Anslem, some relational predications change truth value and do so without some intrinsic constitutive part of God beginning or ceasing to exist. I take this to be the core claim of a local immutability, which allows for extrinsic change.

Some, like Bruce Ware, have attempted to describe their weak accounts of immutability as identical to Anselm's (e.g., God can remain immutable in his essence while changing in other respects). However, I am not aware of any reading of Anselm that would accept this.[41] Weak immutability allows for *real* changes to God, whereas Anselm does not.[42] So, for weak immutability, while God is essentially immutable in his nature, he is "relationally" mutable.[43] These relational changes are those like God's pursuing, establishing, and developing relationships with those whom he has made.[44] God changes in his attitudes, conduct, and relationships.[45] Proponents of this view usually recognize this as a departure from the classical tradition but do not worry because it is clear that God changes according to the scriptural testimony.[46]

Thomas Aquinas likewise argues that God is "completely immutable" because he is "pure actuality without any tincture of potentiality."[47] But

---

40. Anselm, *Monologion*, ed. Brian Davies and G. R. Evans (Oxford University Prerss, 1998), 25.

41. Ware, "An Evangelical Reexamination of the Doctrine of the Immutability of God," 425–26. While Ware invokes Anslem, I suggest that his usage is quite contrary to Anselm's point. Anselm speaks of Cambridge changes being predicable of God whereas Ware intends to predicate *real* changes and not mere Cambridge ones.

42. Anselm, *Monologion* 25.

43. Ware, *God's Greater Glory*, 28, 37.

44. Ware, "An Evangelical Reexamination of the Doctrine of the Immutability of God," 425.

45. Ware, "An Evangelical Reexamination of the Doctrine of the Immutability of God," 430.

46. Ware, *God's Greater Glory*, 142.

47. Thomas Aquinas, *The Treatise on the Divine Nature*, trans. Brian J. Shanley (Hackett, 2006), I.9.1c.

Thomas elsewhere offers indication that he would admit of "Cambridge changes," which would indicate his account is like a local immutability. In question 13, article 7 of his *Summa* he considers whether certain names are attributed to God at *points in time*. Thomas argues that some *do* begin at a certain point in time and *not* from eternity. But these names do not cause any change in God, only in creatures. Consider how an animal can move from the left to the right of a column, and thus there is a sense in which the column "changes" from having something on its left to now its right, though in a strictly ontological sense nothing about the column changes. The change is entirely extrinsic.[48] And so, names such as Savior and Creator are attributed to God temporally and not eternally.[49] This doesn't mean that God becomes something new in an ontological sense. To think in these terms is to flatten out the distinction between intrinsic and extrinsic changes.[50]

The Reformation Witness

The Reformation and post-Reformation periods unsurprisingly follow the patristic and medieval consensus. As has become more apparent in historical scholarship over recent decades, the Reformation was not an iconoclastic deconstruction of every received dogma from Rome. Instead, it was a purifying movement, casting off what the Reformers understood as faulty soteriology and ecclesiology while continuing to receive and confess the same doctrine of God and Christ. The Reformers and those after them depend on the church catholic—even those within the church of Rome—to articulate a healthy doctrine of God. While the church needed reform, it wasn't in need of resurrection.

Francis Turretin is representative when he explains that "immutability is an incommunicable attribute of God by which is denied of him not only all change, but also all possibility of change, as much with

48. Aquinas, *The Treatise on the Divine Nature* I.13.7c.

49. Aquinas, *The Treatise on the Divine Nature* I.13.7 ad 3.

50. For example, James Dolezal appears to be loose in his defense of an eternal Creator, saying that "the belief that God *became* Creator is the foundation for this insistence upon ontological becoming in God." But one must be more careful than this and allow for many important distinctions, such as the relevant distinction between intrinsic and extrinsic or other scholastic categories, to have their full say. See Dolezal, *All That Is in God*, 103.

respect to existence as to will."[51] This strong affirmation of immutability in a universal respect is echoed throughout the Reformed tradition from Wilhelmus à Brakel to Thomas Ridgeley (1667–1734) to Jacob Arminius to Petrus van Mastricht.[52] With each thinker we find the same phrasing and same rationale for immutability with respect to existence, knowledge, will, and the like. Mastricht summarizes well that God has an "omnimodal immutability."[53]

These descriptions continue in later Reformed thinkers. For example, William Shedd (1820–1894) says that "the immutability of God is the unchangeableness of his essence, attributes, purposes, and consciousness."[54] This stacking of terms for God that goes beyond essence or nature alone is instructive and remains common for traditionally Reformed thinkers even into the early modern era. Louis Berkhof likewise removes all change from God not only in his essence but also in his purposes and promises.[55] Herman Bavinck follows these as well, claiming that "God is as immutable in his knowing, willing, and decreeing as he is in his being."[56]

These are but a small sampling of the universal defense of immutability throughout the Reformed period. Other Protestant traditions join the witness as well. Lutherans like Johann Gerhard offer strong accounts of immutability. He explains that a rational nature can change in five ways: (1) existence, (2) place, (3) accidents, (4) knowledge, and (5) will. But none of these are possible for God, who is unchangeable in every respect. For example, he never ceases to exist and never changes place.[57] We find early modern Baptist pastors like John C. Ryland defending immutability too. He explains:

---

51. Francis Turretin, *Institutes of Elenctic Theology*, ed. James T. Dennison, trans. George Musgrave Giger (P&R, 1994), 3.11.1.

52. Wilhelmus à Brakel, *The Christian's Reasonable Service*, ed. Joel R. Beeke, trans. Bartel Elshout (Reformation Heritage, 1992), 1:100; Petrus van Mastricht, *Theoretical-Practical Theology*, ed. Joel R. Beeke, trans. Todd M. Rester (Reformation Heritage, 2018), 2:155; Thomas Ridgeley, *A Body of Divinity* (Robert Carter & Brothers, 1855), 89–90; Jacob Arminius, *The Works of James Arminius*, trans. James Nicholes and William Nicholes (Baker Book House, 1996), Oration 2.

53. Mastricht, *Theoretical-Practical Theology*, 2:153.

54. William G. T. Shedd, *Dogmatic Theology*, 3rd ed. (P&R, 2003), 284.

55. Louis Berkhof, *Systematic Theology* (GLH, 2017), 37.

56. Herman Bavinck, *Reformed Dogmatics*, ed. John Bolt, trans. John Vriend (Baker Academic, 2003), 1:154.

57. Johann Gerhard, *On the Nature of God and on the Most Holy Mystery of the Trinity*, ed. Benjamin T. G. Mayes, trans. Richard J. Dinda (Concordia, 2007), 148.

> The divine immutability consists in a freedom from all kind of change or inconstancy as to his nature, purposes, and happiness. God is immutable in his essence or nature—immutable in his knowledge, and all his other perfections—in his will and purposes—and he is equally unchangeable as to place, i.e. he is eternally and immutably omnipresent.[58]

For Ryland and Gerhard, there is no aspect of God that can change. He cannot change relationally. He cannot change in knowledge. He cannot change in any respect. But there are more witnesses. General Baptists like Dan Taylor and Anglican Francis Hall (1857–1932) offer the same descriptions that sound repetitive by now. It is impossible for God to change.[59] No matter what classical Protestant tradition we encounter, we find the same confession of God as wholly unchangeable.

Depending on how these thinkers understand change, they could be compatible with either global or local immutability. But it is abundantly clear that no weak account of immutability is admissible from any period or strand of the Protestant tradition (at least through the early modern period). God is immutable in every respect. To admit of relational changes in God is to sharply contrast with the heritage of Reformed Protestant thought.

THE DOGMATIC DEFINITION

With this brief historical exploration in view, I suggest that weak immutability has no historical precursor within the major thinkers of the church catholic. Therefore, it should not be classified as a classical view of God. Of course, this doesn't mean it is *wrong*. History alone does not have the power to declare that. However, it should cause us to pause, and to pause with significant weight. It is not merely individual thinkers through the tradition that sing in concert of divine immutability in a strong sense but the Protestant confessional tradition alongside the creedal tradition. Those that would admit of mutability were anathema to the holy fathers. True—Christians are called to charity and generosity.

---

58. John C. Ryland, *Contemplations on the Beauties of Creation and on All the Principal Truths and Blessings of the Glorious Gospel; with the Sins and Graces of Professing Christians* (Thomas Dicey, 1779), 2:347.

59. Dan Taylor, *Fundamentals of Religion in Faith and Practice* (Leeds, 1775), 8; Francis J. Hall, *The Being and Attributes of God* (Longmans, Green, 1909), 256.

The wisdom from above is peaceable, gentle, and full of mercy (Jas 3:17). And the fathers did not have the same sophisticated taxonomy that is available to us. They may have seen some of these later distinctions as less threatening. Even so, the Christian is called to standing firm in the faith and defending "the faith that was once for all delivered to the saints" (Jude 3). This faith that was once for all delivered includes immutability, which forms part of the core dogma of the catholic faith about God that should be defended.

While weak immutability is non-classical, there *is* significant divergence on whether global or local immutability is *the* classical doctrine. Most often it is not clear at all whether someone is confessing one or the other. Therefore, I suggest that either option is viable for a classical thinker. God in his freedom from all change is, at minimum, incapable of intrinsic change. But regardless of which model one accepts, God cannot change ontologically in any respect. His knowledge, will, power, decrees, and perfections all admit of no change whatsoever.

For those that find the strong accounts of divine immutability unsavory or confusing, the church catholic encourages patience and prayer. Maybe it's true that the mystery of the divine nature has been accurately discerned throughout the ages, and through a posture of humble curiosity and dependence on divine guidance those that find differing interpretations more plausible may find themselves *changing* their minds.

DOGMATIC MOTIVATIONS

When considering *why* someone would want to affirm a strong account of immutability, it is important to canvas the various motivating sources. The classical tradition, like all orthodox Christian traditions, affirms the supremacy of Scripture. While there may be nuance regarding its nature, it is assumed to be a genuine, serious, and authoritative revelation of the divine. No classical doctrine of God can be motivated apart from scriptural warrant. However, the classical tradition is not beholden to a form of biblicism. It also uses the tools of nature, such as philosophical contemplation, to construct further doctrinal formulations. It is from these various philosophical or dogmatic arguments that much of the motivation for a strong account of immutability is supplied.

THE EXEGETICAL FOUNDATION: HOLY SCRIPTURE

The classical Christian tradition has not affirmed immutability simply because of philosophical contemplation. It begins with Scripture. And it seeks to respect the wisdom from God in the order of disclosure. As a divine *drama* there is a narrative arc that should be respected with its twists and turns. Yet, throughout the divine drama we are reminded that while Scripture speaks of God in terms that make us naturally assume he is mutable, in reality he is radically unlike us and doesn't change. As Numbers 23:19 reminds us, "God is not man, that he should lie, or a son of a man, that he should change his mind." While we see narratives like Genesis 6 that would make us think God changes, this isn't the rock-bottom truth. God is not a man that he should change.

We should keep this interpretive "key" with us as we read Scripture. God is always teaching us about himself and about ourselves, but he often does so in ways that speak to our hearts more than to our philosophical abstractions. And so, he teaches us in poetic ways and in enchanting stories—poems and stories that are undoubtedly *true*. But the poems and stories are deliberately metaphorical to draw us into communion with his intention. These intentions, though, are not to describe how he literally and ontologically is in his being. God in his kindness reminds us of this at important junctures. For example, he does so again in 1 Samuel 15:29. God "is not a man, that he should have regret." Instead of letting us read narrative texts like Genesis 6 in woodenly literalistic manners, God is giving us guidance that this is not the point of those texts of holy Scripture. They are not designed to give us ontological maps to his being. God is not a creature, and while Scripture describes him in ways that make him appear as such, he reminds us that this is not literally the case. If our hermeneutic is unable to account for these important elements, it is to our own detriment, dethroning the Creator to the status of a creature.

Besides these interpretive keys there remain important biblical expositions of divine immutability. Malachi 3:6 stands atop the many proof texts for immutability, which says, "For I the Lord do not change." As Saint Basil comments on this text, Malachi teaches that "the divine substance is always the same and unchanging."[60] This is not a mere aside or a commentary by

60. Basil, *Against Eunomius*, trans. Mark DelCogliano and Andrew Radde-Gallwitz (Catholic University of America Press, 2011), 1.8.

a creature but divine disclosure from the voice of God himself. He does not change. There is "no variation or shadow due to change" in God (Jas 1:17). Likewise, Jesus "is the same yesterday, today, and forever" (Heb 13:8). But it is not only a generic lack of change that God possesses. Even his purposes are unalterable, as Hebrews 6:17–18 describes.

Psalm 102:25–27 beautifully portrays God as immutable in a strong sense as well:

> Of old you laid the foundation of the earth,
> and the heavens are the work of your hands.
> They will perish, but you will remain;
> they will all wear out like a garment.
> You will change them like a robe, and they will pass away,
> but you are the same, and your years have no end.

The psalmist compares God to the longest-lasting objects that we could imagine. No one knows when the earth and heavens began. No one knows when they will end. But they've existed and will exist far longer than any other passing object. And yet God is even greater than they. In comparison, they will pass away quicker than a used T-shirt. The psalmist doesn't even dignify the earth or the heavens with a relatively long-lasting comparison. They are like clothing, here today and gone tomorrow. But God is the *same* throughout all ages. God's sameness is pregnant with meaning. As Stephen Charnock wisely comments, God's sameness means he is "the same in essence and nature, the same in will and purpose. You do change all other things as you please, but you are immutable in every respect and receive no shadow of change."[61]

PHILOSOPHICAL ARGUMENTATION

Within the classical tradition there are various theological and philosophical "arguments" for a strong version of immutability. Some of the arguments are unique to specific thinkers, while others carry a minority report. However, others are nearly universal within the classical tradition. I intend to focus largely on those with strong consensus throughout the tradition before providing three additional reasons for why alternative versions are unworkable.

---

61. Stephen Charnock, *The Existence and Attributes of God*, ed. Mark Jones (Crossway, 2022), 474.

The Argument from Perfection/Infinity

The argument from perfection/infinity is likely the most common argument within the classical tradition for immutability. Thomas sums up the argument well, saying, "But God, since his infinity comprehends in itself every plentitude of perfection of all of existence, cannot acquire something or extend itself toward something he had not previously attained."[62] So the argument is formally as follows:

1. If *x* changes, *x* changes for the better or the worse.
2. God cannot become better or worse (e.g., he is perfect/infinite).
3. Therefore, God cannot change.[63]

On this argument God is immutable because God is both perfect and infinite, lacking nothing whatsoever. If God were to add any new intrinsic property, whether a new fact of knowledge or a new desire of the will, he would be changing either for the better or the worse and thus would be either less perfect or more perfect than he was before.

No orthodox Christian denies the second premise. God is perfect, and God is infinite. He lacks nothing and so cannot become better or worse. However, other models of immutability attempt to redefine perfection. Rather than perfection being infinite fullness with no need to respond or change, perfection consists in the ability to change because being the *most* responsive is a good thing—a perfect thing.[64] Of course, this denies both the nature of perfection and infinity that the classical tradition, and most of the orthodox Christian tradition,

---

62. Aquinas, *The Treatise on the Divine Nature* I.9.1c.

63. For several representative examples, see Katherin A. Rogers, *Perfect Being Theology* (Edinburgh University Press, 2000), 47; Terry L Johnson, *The Identity and Attributes of God* (Banner of Truth Trust, 2019), 54; Dolezal, *All That Is in God*, 19; Thomas, *Compendium of Theology*, trans. Richard J. Regan (Oxford University Press, 2009), 23; John Gill, *A Body of Doctrinal Divinity* (George Keith, 1769), 80; Bonaventure, *Disputed Questions on the Mystery of the Trinity*, 225; Richard of St Victor, "On the Trinity," in *Trinity and Creation*, ed. Boyd Taylor Coolman and Dale M. Coulter, trans. Christopher P. Evans (New City, 2011), 2.3; Charnock, *The Existence and Attributes of God*, 480; Ridgeley, *A Body of Divinity*, 89; Réginald Garrigou-Lagrange, *God, His Existence and His Nature*, trans. Bede Rose (B. Herder, 1936), 51.

64. Richard Swinburne, *The Coherence of Theism*, 2nd ed. (Oxford University Press, 2016), 234; Gregory A. Boyd, *God of the Possible: A Biblical Introduction to the Open View of God* (Baker Books, 2000), 78.

has affirmed. Moreover, it is not clear why such a state would be *more* perfect. It seems that a God who was so perfect that he had no need to respond or change would be more perfect than one who needed to respond or change.

The most serious potential objection comes from those that want to reject premise one. While there is a common intuition throughout the classical tradition that there is no change that could be neutral (i.e., all changes are either positive or negative), other versions of immutability reject this axiom. They claim that not all changes violate perfection because there are such things as neutral changes.[65] The most common example relates to a change in God's knowledge of times. So, consider changes like knowing it is 12:00 p.m. versus knowing it is 12:01 p.m. or that I was born in Wichita, Kansas (where I was actually born!), versus Raleigh, North Carolina (where I live now and my children were born). These seem like value-neutral changes. They wouldn't detract or add to God's being. Why would such a change in knowledge be better or worse? There are at least four problems with this contention. First, these aren't strictly *changes*. These would be differences in knowledge and not changes in knowledge. God would know whichever is true and would never need to change in knowledge. It is not possible for me to be born in Wichita and then be born in Raleigh. Only one is true. Second, the "changing" (if it is indeed change!) knowledge of what time it is would require God to be in time. If one rejects that God is in time, this is impossible. Third, if God is infinite, he wouldn't need to change. He has every good at once already.[66] Fourth, many simply accept premise one at face value. There is good and bad in *every* change. Even eating chocolate ice cream instead of strawberry isn't value neutral.[67] So, knowing that it is 12:00 p.m. versus 12:01 p.m. actually isn't value neutral. The reason no change is value neutral is because every change entails a movement through cessation, defection, or destruction.[68]

---

65. Richards, *The Untamed God*, 201; Ware, "An Evangelical Reexamination of the Doctrine of the Immutability of God," 430–31.

66. Rogers, *Perfect Being Theology*, 48.

67. Rogers, *Perfect Being Theology*, 47.

68. Scheeben, *Handbook of Catholic Dogmatics*, 2:108.

The Argument from Aseity

The argument from aseity is the second most fundamental argument for a strong account of immutability. There is near-universal acceptance that God is perfect and infinite. Likewise, all orthodox Christians affirm God is *a se*—dependent on nothing. Given this shared assumption, various thinkers have suggested that change in God would violate aseity. Change would indicate that he is dependent on something, whether that is some unrealized potentiality within himself or some fuller actuality beyond himself. Thus, he would be dependent if he changed.[69] Petrus van Mastricht exemplifies this approach, arguing that "whatever is changed is changed by something prior."[70] The argument is roughly as follows:

1. If *x* changes, then *x* depends on something prior to cause the change.
2. God is *a se* and thus independent and uncaused.
3. Therefore, God cannot change.[71]

Since all change amounts to dependence on something external, God cannot change. As Thomas explains it: "What is present in a thing accidentally has a cause of its presence, since it is outside the essence of the thing in which it is found."[72] The idea is that every change requires a prior cause.

The key question is whether premise 1 is true. Does *all* change require dependence on something *else*? It makes sense that external causation from something else would indicate dependence, but what about self-causation? If I will myself to change, does that mean I am dependent on something outside myself? If I will to think of something besides divine immutability at this time, say the latest half-ton pickup truck, does that mean I am dependent on something else for this change? It doesn't seem that this is true. But Thomas suggests it would be impossible for God

---

69. David Bentley Hart, *The Experience of God* (Yale University Press, 2013), 135.

70. Mastricht, *Theoretical-Practical Theology*, 2:155.

71. Matthew Barrett, *None Greater: The Undomesticated Attributes of God* (Baker Books, 2019), 98.

72. Thomas Aquinas, *Summa Contra Gentiles: Book One; God*, trans. Anton Charles Pegis (University of Notre Dame Press, 1975), 1:23.

to do this because then "one and the same thing would make itself to be actual in the same respect."[73] What exactly does Thomas mean by this? He means that self-causation of this sort would violate divine simplicity. So, while it may be true for composite objects that they can self-cause and not be dependent on something else, it is impossible for a simple object. Therefore, if one accepts divine simplicity, as the classical tradition does, they will find this argument persuasive.

Others instead limit the meaning of divine aseity in premise 2. Divine aseity, then, does not have a universal scope. It does not require complete independence. It only means that he doesn't "depend on anything with respect to his existence or essential nature."[74] But as I've argued in chapter 5, this is not at all what aseity requires. It requires far more than a mere independence of essential nature.

The Argument from Simplicity

Naturally now, we move to the argument from divine simplicity. As is common through the classical tradition, the classical attributes are mutually entailing. If one is true, the others are true as well.[75] I consider this argument to be roughly identical to the argument from *actus purus*.[76] It roughly goes as follows:

1. If *x* changes, then *x* is composed of something.
2. God is uncomposed (i.e., simple).
3. Therefore, God cannot change.[77]

God is unchangeable in a strong sense because all change requires a denial of simplicity. Change needs to add or subtract a property, which entails composition. But composition is outlawed by divine simplicity.

---

73. Aquinas, *Summa Contra Gentiles: Book One; God* 1:23.

74. Peckham, *Divine Attributes*, 46.

75. Charnock, *The Existence and Attributes of God*, 495–99.

76. Aquinas, *The Treatise on the Divine Nature* I.9.1c; Samuel D. Renihan, *Deity & Decree* (independently published, 2020), 53; Eleonore Stump, *The God of the Bible and the God of the Philosophers* (Marquette University Press, 2016), 20; Craig A. Carter, *Contemplating God with the Great Tradition* (Baker Academic, 2021), 63.

77. Aquinas, *The Treatise on the Divine Nature* I.9.1c; Rogers, *Perfect Being Theology*, 46; Renihan, *Deity & Decree*, 51.

The strength of this argument depends on premise two: divine simplicity. If someone rejects divine simplicity (such as many who affirm weak immutability), they will likely find little reason to accept a strong immutability because of it. However, it also depends on which version of simplicity one affirms. It is possible to reject this argument while accepting a version of simplicity such as the *parsimonious* model.[78] However, most of the classical tradition has utilized the stronger models, as we saw in the previous chapter, which would keep the argument sound.

The Argument from Eternity

The argument from eternity is like the argument from simplicity in that it requires the prior affirmation of another classical doctrine, in this case eternal timeless eternity. It goes like this:

1. If *x* changes, then *x* exists at T1 and T2.
2. God does not exist at either T1 or T2 (i.e., he is timelessly eternal).
3. Therefore, God cannot change.[79]

So, if God is timeless, he cannot change because change requires existing in time. Since the classical tradition affirms that God is timelessly eternal, he necessarily must also be immutable in a strong sense.

The Revisionary Oddness of Weak Immutability

There are further reasons to find a strong account of immutability (besides historical consensus) preferrable for the classical tradition compared to other options like weak immutability. This is because versions like weak immutability require a revision of essential properties such as omniscience and eternity. For example, Jay Richards admits that "God cannot be essentially immutable in knowledge, since a contingent creation entails—or perhaps presupposes—counterfactual possibilities."[80] God's knowledge *must*

---

78. See Oliver D. Crisp, "A Parsimonious Model of Divine Simplicity," *Modern Theology* 35, no. 3 (2019): 558–73, https://doi.org/10.1111/moth.12520.

79. Johnson, *The Identity and Attributes of God*, 54; Edward R. Wierenga, *The Nature of God: An Inquiry into Divine Attributes* (Cornell University Press, 1989), 172.

80. Richards, *The Untamed God*, 206.

be changing. Now, Richards would deny that God's knowledge is changing for the better or for the worse—it remains maximally perfect. However, this is hard to square with the Christian tradition's understanding of omniscience. The classical tradition has typically understood omniscience to mean that God's knowledge is not obtained *a posteriori* by observation but *a priori* from eternity by his own creative will. It is not susceptible to either increasing or decreasing.[81] Therefore, it cannot change. Not only does it not comport with typical definitions of omniscience, it would be really weird at times too. God would keep learning and unlearning things. For example, he would know that it is *now* raining at T1. Then he would know it is *now* raining at T2, having unlearned the first fact.[82]

A second reason to find weak immutability objectionable is because it doesn't say anything unique about God. Most who defend an account of weak immutability do so by recourse to philosophical "essentialism."[83] Essentialism is a doctrine that can be applied to *anything*. In fact, that's just what essentialism is for most things.[84] Thus, it is *trivial* to attribute weak immutability to God. If weak immutability is what it means for God to be immutable, then persons, animals, trees, and the like are all immutable too. But this isn't what the tradition has wanted to say about God. Nor is it what we even intuitively want to say about God—there is something deeper about him that is unchangeable compared to creation. There has been a desire to communicate something unique about God's steadfastness that isn't true of created things. It is true that weak immutability might be able to accommodate for this fact by adding additional properties as essential, such as God's will. But then, if consistent, it will end up becoming a strong version of immutability.

A third reason to find weak immutability problematic is due to its equivocation on "ontology." As noted earlier, its adherents seem to think that changes in God, such as his ongoing relationship with others, aren't ontological. But it is not clear why such changes *aren't* ontological. As James Dolezal has correctly asserted, "Every state of being, whether

81. Bavinck, *Reformed Dogmatics*, 2:192; Hart, *The Experience of God*, 137.

82. Helm, *Eternal God*, 86.

83. My usage of "philosophical" here is not pejorative but technical. Essentialism is primarily a philosophical doctrine.

84. Dolezal, *All That Is in God*, 26n38.

essential or nonessential, is an ontological state."[85] If these changes aren't ontological, they aren't a real change in any sense, which would mean that local immutability would be a better fit.

POTENTIAL PROBLEMS AND SOLUTIONS

The strength of the classical understanding of immutability is not without its potential costs. No one can seriously affirm the classical tradition without understanding these objections. So, like the section before, I begin with the biblical worries before moving to the more philosophical arguments. It is necessary to count the cost if one is to affirm the classical tradition in today's context.

BIBLICAL PROBLEMS

While the Bible clearly ascribes some level of immutability to God, detractors of immutability quickly locate alternative texts that suggest God clearly *does* change. Several examples are Genesis 6:6 and God's regret; Exodus 32:14, which tells of God "relenting" from his action; and Jeremiah 18:8–10 and 26:2–3, where God considers that he may relent from his action *if* repentance comes from the people. These sorts of texts could be significantly multiplied. But the point is clear: The Bible literally says God changes. He relents, changes his mind, and changes his actions. If we are to take Scripture seriously, how can we say that these claims are false?

Noted open theist Greg Boyd takes these passages as conclusive that God is not immutable. These texts don't even "remotely imply" that God is unchanging. They speak in the "plainest possible terms" that he changes.[86] But while these texts are no doubt of the same authoritative status as those in favor of immutability, the classical tradition has seen no reason to assume these must be *strictly literal* descriptions of God. Quoting a proof-text like this is not an argument. These texts require interpretation, like all Scripture. And since there is significant agreement that some other texts about God are non-literal, it is not out of the realm of possibility that these too are non-literal.

85. Dolezal, *All That Is in God*, 25–26.

86. Boyd, *God of the Possible*, 77.

Therefore, the traditional classical reply has been to explain these texts as anthropomorphic. This is what Augustine meant by saying, "We must not allow ourselves to be so befogged by literal-minded materialism."[87] So, when things such as hands and feet are ascribed to God in the Bible, these are not to be interpreted as meaning he has a literal body but as metaphors. It is a legitimate interpretive strategy to explain these texts about God repenting or changing as metaphors as well. We are given this very license in Numbers 23:19 and 1 Samuel 15:29.[88]

PHILOSOPHICAL PROBLEMS

In my view, the most serious challenges to the classical version of immutability are not from Scripture itself but from potential philosophical problems. I consider four of the most pressing problems below, though this is by no means an exhaustive list. Some of the problems that could be listed here I defend in other chapters, whether simplicity, eternity, or impassibility. In many ways, where to place some of these objections is difficult to determine since they relate to multiple classical attributes.

The Problem of Divine Freedom

One of the most important problems for a classical account of immutability is God's freedom. The problem is this: A perfectly free being cannot be immutable in a strong sense.[89] The argument goes like this:

1. If *x* is free, then *x* can do otherwise.
2. God is free.
3. If *x* is immutable, *x* cannot do otherwise.
4. Therefore, God is not immutable.[90]

While this argument is valid, it is unsound. The argument assumes a specific version of libertarian freedom, which is by no means the consensus

---

87. Augustine, *The Trinity* II.6.31.

88. Duby, *Divine Simplicity: A Dogmatic Account*, 137.

89. Swinburne, *The Coherence of Theism*, 214.

90. Richards, *The Untamed God*, 200–202.

view. To assume this as axiomatic is to beg the question. If by freedom it is meant that God has free will and is not "forced" or determined to make any action, it remains false that God must have the ability to do otherwise. Such a conception of free will requires a *leeway* account of free will, whereas many (even libertarians about free will) suggest a *sourcehood* account of free will, where someone is free if they are the proper source of their actions, is true. So, God's freedom is just the freedom to do what he most wants (which never changes) without any hindrance or dependence on external things.[91] Therefore, if the objection from freedom is to work, there is a significant amount of metaphysical work regarding the nature of free will that must first be argued for and proved. Without this, the argument lacks force.

The Problem of Immobility/Loving Relationship

Emil Brunner complained that classical theism, especially divine immutability, removes "personal correspondence" from God. He becomes the isolated "divinity of abstract thought" rather than the personal "living God."[92] This objection, though masked by effusive language, roughly goes like this:

1. If *x* acts (e.g., loves, responds, etc.), then *x* changes.
2. God acts.
3. Therefore, God changes.

This is often buttressed by the straightforward texts of Scripture where God repents, changes his mind, and so on.[93] But the classical tradition rejects the metaphysical assumptions within premise 1. Neither action nor love require change. Love at its core is *always* willing the good to another rather than being affected by others. It is an action that need not be characterized as a property that requires change.[94] Action also doesn't need to change. As Ed Feser explains, "The essence of action is bringing about an effect in another thing. There is nothing necessarily part of action that requires the actor to

91. James E. Dolezal, *God Without Parts: Divine Simplicity and the Metaphysics of God's Absoluteness*, (Pickwick, 2011), 204.

92. Brunner, *The Christian Doctrine of God*, 269.

93. Brunner, *The Christian Doctrine of God*, 268–69.

94. William E. Mann, "Simplicity and Properties: A Reply to Morris," *Religious Studies* 22 (1986): 349.

change in its act."[95] God, then, can timelessly will a single, simple act that is unchangeable and yet has an outward working and relation to creation.[96]

Consider a relatively banal example. There are plenty of times where my young sons think they are wily and changing my mind. They might want to go for a walk outside, play baseball in the backyard, or sneak a few extra "gummies" from the pantry. They conjure up elaborate little plans and make "deals" with me to get what they want. I play along and let them think they are brokering the greatest deal known to man. But in reality, I had planned all along to do what they wanted. They didn't change my mind or course of action in any respect. This doesn't lessen our relationship or love in any way. Analogously, God's inability to change his mind has no impact on our intimate relationship with him. Intimacy, love, and relation are not grounded upon *change*. This assumption goes unexamined by many in the modern period and is simply false.

The Problem of Temporal Indexicals

Another argument against a strong account of immutability comes from "temporal indexicals." The problem of temporal indexicals is not unique to immutability. It similarly plagues eternity. But I've chosen to treat it here. The main idea is roughly that some sentences contain "now," and that varies in truth status over time. For example, I know that it is raining *now* but not *later*. Once it stops raining, while I knew that it rained then, I no longer know that it is raining now. Therefore, God must know some things that are "now" and then pass out of existence. Hence, he must change.[97] In short, the argument is this:

1. If God is omniscient, then he always knows what time it is *now*.
2. God is omniscient.
3. Therefore, God changes in knowledge.[98]

95. Edward Feser, *Five Proofs of the Existence of God* (Ignatius, 2017), 198.

96. Scheeben, *Handbook of Catholic Dogmatics*, 2:113.

97. Wierenga, *The Nature of God*, 175; Anthony Kenny, *The God of the Philosophers* (Clarendon, 2001), 48.

98. Leftow, "Immutability."

But it is possible to reformulate all of these tensed facts in neutral terms along a static account of time within the B-theory of tenseless time discussed in chapter 4.[99] So, premise one is not necessarily true. God can know that it is raining at 12:35 p.m. on Saturday (instead of *now*). In fact, God is not omniscient as is traditionally understood on this version of the problem because he loses knowledge no longer knowing what was happening *now* once time *now* passes. God keeps on learning and unlearning facts.[100] Though, some retort that this doesn't compromise omniscience because he isn't *really* learning. If these facts don't exist yet to know, then there is no intellectual deficiency.[101] But this defense begs the question and requires that God be temporal.

The Problem of the Incarnation

The final worry strikes at the heart of the Christian message. The idea is this: God *becomes* incarnate. If this is true, how can he *not* change? Formally the argument would go like this:

1. If *x* becomes *y*, then *x* changes.
2. God becomes incarnate.
3. Therefore, God changes.

The argument is straightforward. But throughout the classical tradition none has thought that the "becoming" of the incarnation entails a change. While there are various accounts of what becoming amounts to and why it doesn't require change in God, I think the following two are the most persuasive.

First, the argument assumes a particular meaning of "becoming" that is foreign to the historical witness. As Thomas Weinandy has explained, *become* doesn't mean *change*.[102] The incarnational becoming is a personal/existential becoming. It is a new mode of existence and not an ontological change.[103] Consider, for example, the classical rendition of the incarnation from Cyril of Alexandria, who says:

---

99. Helm, *Eternal God*, 73–94.
100. Helm, *Eternal God*, 86.
101. Feinberg, *No One Like Him*, 273.
102. Weinandy, *Does God Change?*, 45.
103. Weinandy, *Does God Change?*, 54.

> He became flesh not because he turned into the nature of the flesh according to a transition, or a change, or an alteration, nor because he underwent a confusion, or a blending, or the fusion of essences being babbled about by some, for that is impossible since he is by nature unchangeable and is unalterable, as I said, but because he took flesh animated with a rational soul from a virginal and undefiled body and made it his own.[104]

Here Cyril is giving a metaphysically opinionated account of what it means for the Word to become flesh. Cyril argues that *become* doesn't mean "turn into." A "turning into" could be taken as transition, change, or alteration. None of these, for Cyril, properly explains the nature of the incarnation. Instead, there is a "making one's own" that accounts for the becoming flesh. It is a "taking" wherein the Son now owns a human nature.

However, the reply is then that this *isn't* a true *personal* union. It is a mere Cambridge change.[105] But as has been suggested via the metaphysics of relations, there are alternative ways to account for *real* relations that don't metaphysically amount to *real* accidents that would indicate a change in being. God the Son can have a *real* union without having any sort of *real* change. The metaphysics under the hood can become very complex very quickly, but there is no necessary incoherence here.

For those not satisfied with this reply, there is a second explanation worth considering (one which I find most agreeable personally!). Tim Pawl has denied the validity of the argument in multiple publications. He does so because the incarnation does not require change of the divine *nature*. While it requires change of the person, the divine nature remains unchanged, and immutability only requires that the divine nature remains unchanged.[106] So, the argument *does* show that God *the Son* changes. He really changes, really is one way, then another. But this is all true "qua human" or according to his human nature. His hand really, honestly, goes from being unpierced to being pierced. He is different at different times. He is okay with all of that. But none of this requires us to deny

104. Cyril of Alexandria, *Letters 51–110*, 24.

105. Richards, *The Untamed God*, 210.

106. Pawl, *In Defense of Conciliar Christology*, 205; Pawl, "Conciliar Christology and the Consistency of Divine Immutability with a Mutable, Incarnate God."

immutability. It only requires us to understand that immutability is a property of natures, and in the case that someone has two natures, they then can truthfully be said to be immutable and mutable if they have a divine and human nature.[107]

IMMUTABILITY FOR THE CHURCH

Immutability is not a dry or dusty doctrine. It is full of vitality for the life of the church. It should bring comfort. It should impel worship. It should incite fire within the bones of God's people. Because of immutability there is no reason to be suspicious of God. We are suspicious of those we do not trust to consistently do the best for us. We are suspicious of our employers, of our neighbors, maybe even of our spouse. But God has an impeccable record, and beyond his track record his own being makes it impossible. He cannot change, and so we cannot be suspicious. There is only comfort and trust.

Therefore, immutability comforts, fuels, and motivates in life and death because we know that God is gracious, good, wise, caring, and loving. And we know this is not temporary. It is eternal and necessary. God could not be otherwise even if he tried. Divine immutability, then, is "indicative of his plenitude of being, love, and beatific life."[108] As Stephen Charnock warmly reminds us: "His goodness could not be distrusted if his unchangeableness were well apprehended and considered. All distrust would fly before it, as darkness before the sun; it only gets advantage of us when we are not well grounded in his name."[109] For those of anxious heart, consider God's utter unchangeableness. Unchangeably loving and unchangeably good. Forever willing the best toward his people. What delight there is in his immutability!

Church members and pastors should regularly reflect on God's immutability, as the psalmists so frequently do, reminding us of God's constant shelter as our rock. When our world is chaotic and continually changing,

---

107. He really is! This is simply my edited quotation from his commentary on my initial manuscript draft, which I hopefully have captured correctly.

108. Gilles Emery, "The Immutability of the God of Love and the Problem of Language Concerning the 'Suffering of God,' " in *Divine Impassibility and the Mystery of Human Suffering*, ed. James F. Keating and Thomas Joseph White, trans. Thomas Joseph White (Eerdmans, 2009), 63.

109. Charnock, *The Existence and Attributes of God*, 526.

we can take shelter in the one who never changes. We may even worry that those closest to us will someday change their minds about us and no longer love us. Maybe our spouse won't love us if we gain weight. Maybe our children won't love us if we don't tell them "yes" enough. Maybe our parents won't love us if we don't follow their career path. But God never changes in his love and mercy. He has covenanted with us and will eternally love us and seek our good. Those whom he foreknew he ultimately justifies and glorifies—and that never changes. Whether it is for the grieving widow or the preacher in the pulpit, there are few greater anchors than God as never-changing.

CONCLUSION

In conclusion, I argue that a mere classical theist doctrine of divine immutability requires, at minimum, that God doesn't change intrinsically, though he can "change" extrinsically. While there are those within the tradition that argue for a more robust doctrine of immutability, I think this is beyond the requirements for a mere classical theism. The reason the classical tradition has found immutability as crucial to preserve is that God's reliability and faithfulness depend on his inability to change in any real respect. Destabilizing God's immutability ultimately destabilizes our trust in him. The tradition has not found this to be at odds with the incarnation, God's love for creation, or anything else. While it can sometimes appear counterintuitive based on certain biblical texts, this tension largely is resolved upon philosophical contemplation in the classical mode. For the classical tradition, God is the unchangeably good God. His delight and bliss are never-ending, and they never fluctuate.

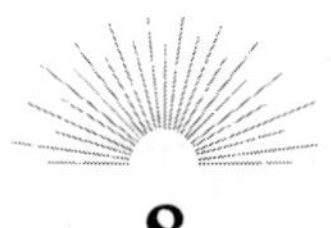

8

DIVINE ETERNITY: THE FOREVER PRESENT GOD

Time is money. Or so goes the saying goes. We may not have a good grasp for what time physically or metaphysically is, but we intuitively recognize the value of time. We know that we can never regain lost time and have no power over how much time remains. We can "revisit" times past through memories, photos, and other means. But we cannot "go back" and re-*live* those moments. Nor can we experience the future, as much as we might try. But this is about the extent to which most of us understand time. Begin asking questions like, "How fast does time go?" or why it feels like there is only one direction for time—forward—and we will run into dense and confusing territory. And as was seen in the philosophical debates about the metaphysics of time, there remains no strong consensus on what time is.

To make matters worse, when we add our idea of God to an already difficult concept—that of time—it is wholly unsurprising that the literature on God's relationship to time is vast and dense. One demanding subject added to the most demanding subject is bound to generate numerous views. For example, when the apostle Paul calls God the "King of ages" and immortal in 1 Timothy 1:17, does this only mean he has boundless duration and exists forever? Is it like how I am promised eternal life wherein I have a beginning but no end? Or does it entail that God relates to time in a different way altogether? Does he have control, in some sense, over time? What would that even mean? To these questions we now turn.

APPROACHING A DOGMATIC DEFINITION

The claim that God is eternal likely won't strike most as radical. In fact, all traditional Christian models of God will at least pay lip service to the term *eternity*. Boethius was so confident that he claimed that the belief in an eternal God is "the common view of all living creatures endowed with reason."[1] The point is clear. Everyone believes God is eternal because if you thought otherwise, you would be an irrational beast. John Ryland even found eternity so wonderful that, for him, it is the most "venerable" of all the attributes of God. He described it as the very "life of all the attributes of God."[2] But the devil is once again in the details. There are a multitude of ways the concept of eternity can be understood, some of which are decidedly non-classical. Given the potential confusion, it is wise to once again explore a mere definition of eternity followed by expanding on various models.

MERE DIVINE ETERNITY

Divine eternity is designed to explain God's mode of possessing life.[3] He is not simply another created being with no control over what time it is. He is never stressed that he has too little time to accomplish his purposes. His control of time and by extension history, then, is grounded in his transcendence of time. It is not merely because God is meticulously efficient that he never worries about being "late." It is because he is eternal. He is unbounded by the traditional "limits" of time that we experience. But he remains *with* us throughout all our lives. He hears our cries for help and delivers us from trouble and remains near to us (Ps 34:17–18). In this way, God must possess the whole of time in a special manner to both exist beyond it and yet within it in some mysterious manner. Therefore, a baseline definition to begin our exploration of eternity could be described as follows:

> *Mere divine eternity:* God is eternal *if and only if* God (1) lacks beginning, (2) lacks end, (3) transcends time, and (4) wholly possesses time.

1. Boethius, *The Consolation of Philosophy*, trans. Scott E. Goins and Barbara H. Wyman (Ignatius, 2012), 5.6.

2. John C. Ryland, *Contemplations on the Beauties of Creation and on All the Principal Truths and Blessings of the Glorious Gospel; with the Sins and Graces of Professing Christians* (Thomas Dicey, 1779), 2:333–34.

3. Paul Helm, *Eternal God*, 2nd ed. (Oxford University Press, 2010), 17.

The mere account of eternity assumes God's life extends infinitely to the "past" and "future." There is no point at which he doesn't exist. But there is more to the story than mere eternal duration. God also transcends and wholly possesses time. Now, both of these concepts, *possessing* and *transcending*, are vague ways to gesture at many of the more robust accounts of God and time. The reason I've chosen such a vague way to characterize divine eternity at this point is to allow for explication of the various models and yet to limit the meaning of eternity. It must be beyond infinite duration alone. It also includes a peculiar relationship to time that is beyond it but also intimately present with it.

To clarify what this peculiar relationship to time is, it is useful to consider Johann Gerhard's description of God's transcendence of time: "He is interminable because it excludes beginning and ending limits, indivisible because it excludes all succession of time, independent because it excludes every imperfection and change."[4] From his description, there are three aspects of eternity that we should subject all models to. (1) Is God interminable in existence? (2) Is God indivisible in existence? (3) Is God independent in existence? But it is useful to add two further questions about God's potential temporal relations: (4) Does God have temporal extension? (5) Does God have temporal location? So, these five questions will clarify what a fully worked-out theory of God and time looks like:

1. Is God interminable in existence?
2. Is God indivisible in existence?
3. Is God independent in existence?
4. Does God have temporal extension?
5. Does God have temporal location?

An important note before proceeding is that the ubiquitous terminology of "duration" can cause confusion. Most intuitively assume that duration entails temporal extension by necessity. But the Latin term for "duration" has two senses and not just one. It can mean *either* temporal

4. Johann Gerhard, *On the Nature of God and on the Most Holy Mystery of the Trinity*, ed. Benjamin T. G. Mayes, trans. Richard J. Dinda (Concordia, 2007), 139.

extension *or* a non-temporal existential experience.[5] So, while many in the Christian tradition may use the terminology of duration, this does not automatically entail temporal extension. One must pay careful attention to the overall flow of the argument and the general context from which the author is working. It is insufficient to merely search for key words to determine what someone thinks about God's life. It is a constant reminder that knowing how Christians have thought about issues requires careful and patient listening.

MODELS OF DIVINE ETERNITY

There are several models that have sought to explicate God as eternal. The views may expand to a significant list if I nuanced each one to the greatest detail, but for our purposes, these should help guide our exploration. Therefore, I do not develop some of the more niche models like those of William Lane Craig or Alan Padgett. Each expands on what I have called transcending and wholly possessing time in mere divine eternity.

> *Timeless eternity*: God is eternal *if and only if* God lacks (1) beginning, (2) end, (3) succession of moments, (4) temporal extension, and (5) temporal location.
>
> *Timeless present*: God is eternal *if and only if* God (1) lacks beginning, (2) lacks end, (3) lacks succession of moments, (4) lacks temporal extension, (5) lacks temporal location, and (6) wholly possesses time as an eternal now.
>
> *Omnitemporal eternity*: God is eternal *if and only if* God (1) lacks beginning, (2) lacks end, and (3) is present at every point in time.
>
> *Everlasting eternity*: God is eternal *if and only if* God (1) lacks beginning and (2) lacks end.

For the sake of clarity, before exploring each of these models in greater detail, below are the general answers to each of the five important questions.

5. Rory Fox, *Time and Eternity in Mid-Thirteenth Century Thought* (Oxford University Press, 2006), 35.

Table 8.1. Five Important Questions

Model	Is God interminable?	Is God indivisible?	Is God independent?	Does God have temporal extension?	Does God have temporal location?
Timeless Eternity	Yes	Yes	Yes	No	No
Timeless Present	Yes	Yes	Yes	No	No
Omnitemporal Eternity	Yes	No	Maybe	Yes	Yes
Everlasting Eternity	Yes	No	No	Yes	Yes

The timeless eternity view is most distinctive by its claim that God's manner of existence lacks all temporal relations whatsoever.[6] God thus lacks both temporal location and temporal extension since he is wholly infinite.[7] As Francis Hall explains, "He utterly transcends in essence, life, and action the relations of time."[8] Real eternity, then, is not only infinite but *non-temporal.*[9] The lack of temporal extension is especially important as it means God properly has no duration, where duration is defined as an interval of time through which something endures.[10] As Nelson Pike explains, "It is not just that the life of God lacks temporal limits: the point is that it has no temporal spread at all."[11] This usage of duration is the first sense that was attributed to the term in medieval literature, whereas these thinkers would be theoretically free to use duration language in the second existential sense, though such usage is absent.

---

6. Helm, *Eternal God*, 27.

7. Edward R. Wierenga, *The Nature of God* (Cornell University Press, 1989), 170; Delmas Lewis, "Eternity, Time and Timelessness," *Faith and Philosophy* 5, no. 1 (1988): 74–75.

8. Francis J. Hall, *The Being and Attributes of God* (Longmans, Green, 1909), 253.

9. Hall, *The Being and Attributes of God*, 254.

10. Alan G. Padgett, "Eternity as Relative Timelessness," in *God and Time: Four Views*, ed. Gregory E. Ganssle (InterVarsity Press, 2001), 94; Nelson Pike, *God and Timelessness* (Wipf & Stock, 2002), 7; Matthew Barrett, *None Greater* (Baker Books, 2019), 146.

11. Nelson Pike, *God and Timelessness* (Wipf & Stock, 2002), 7.

Such claims have led many to think God as "timeless" is "very strange."[12] Some, like Anthony Kenny, have even argued that it is "incoherent, theologically unimportant, and inessential to the tradition."[13] Even historian Richard Muller has claimed that "the historical sources do not offer a doctrine of 'timeless eternity.' "[14] Yet, while Muller has forcefully claimed that there is not a doctrine of timeless eternity in the tradition, he has thought of it as a doctrine that requires God to be "unrelated to time and incapable of dealing with temporal events as temporal."[15] And he is right in this sense: No classical theologian argues for a God that is unrelated to time in the sense that he is incapable of dealing with temporal events. But that is not what contemporary thinkers mean when they ascribe *timelessness* to God. Timelessness does not deny God's lordship over time or his ability to work within it. Rather, it denies created temporal *relations*. God has no temporal location or temporal extension.[16]

The second timeless model, what I call the timeless *present*, is designed to explicate the Boethian view more fully in a positive direction. Instead of a purely negative claim, like the timeless eternity model, it is focused on how God possesses his life positively too (though, there is some matter of debate about what exactly Boethius thought). So, the main difference between these two timeless views is that for the timeless present model, God is not *merely* timeless. He is *more* since he embraces all times in an eternal present.[17] While God may have no temporal location, he still possesses all times *as present* to himself.[18]

On this model, God has no succession of time, but he has a duration *of sorts*. However, this is not necessarily a duration of temporal extension where God is somehow "spread out" across time. It is not Bilbo Baggins feeling thin and stretched, like butter scraped over too much

12. William Hasker, *God, Time, and Knowledge* (Cornell University Press, 1998), 146.

13. Anthony Kenny, *The God of the Philosophers* (Clarendon, 2001), 40.

14. Richard Muller, *Post-Reformation Reformed Dogmatics* (Baker Academic, 2003), 3:354.

15. Muller, *Post-Reformation Reformed Dogmatics*, 3:354.

16. See a similar, though slightly different, reading in Stump and Kretzmann, who explain eternity as "two separate modes of real existence": Eleonore Stump and Norman Kretzmann, "Eternity," *The Journal of Philosophy* 78, no. 8 (1981): 434.

17. Ortlund, *Theological Retrieval for Evangelicals*, 94; Eleonore Stump, *The God of the Bible and the God of the Philosophers* (Marquette University Press, 2016), 57.

18. Wierenga, *The Nature of God*, 170.

bread. The semantic range of his duration is expanded beyond our general conceptual usage to a significant degree. For example, Gerhard says that "the duration of the divine essence is nothing else but the ever-enduring divine essence."[19] Gerhard uses duration in a very elastic way that does not entail temporal extension. It is designed to communicate something of the divine experience of the eternal present.

However, sometimes duration does appear to entail some sort of temporal extension. For example, Stump and Kretzmann argue for God's duration to be one of infinite *extension* that is "fully realized" and "all present at once."[20] Instead of God's life being the interminability of a single point or instant, it is of "unending duration of some sort."[21] So, in a sense, this model does allow for temporal *extension*. But it is not a standard temporal extension or one that would admit of parts. Even if the terminology of extension is used, it is in a highly analogical context: a "duration of *some sort*." It might be akin to the contemporary philosophical debates about extended simples, which have no parts and yet are "spread out" in space.[22] But even if there were an analogue with extended simple, when duration is used, even by those like Stump and Kretzmann, God does not persist through time. Instead, he has a non-temporal existential experience.[23] He has an infinite "atemporal duration, where 'duration' is understood analogically with temporal duration."[24]

What binds these two timeless models together, then, is their resolute commitment to rule out all succession.[25] My distinction between the two may be somewhat artificial, but it is designed to distinguish between two approaches: one that is purely negative and one that seeks to provide a constructive account of how God is present in time. Neither view necessarily requires any particular ontology of

---

19. Gerhard, *On the Nature of God and on the Most Holy Mystery of the Trinity*, 146.

20. Stump and Kretzmann, "Eternity," 441.

21. Stump, *The God of the Bible and the God of the Philosophers*, 58.

22. For literature on extended simples in philosophical contexts, see Peter Simons, "Extended Simples: A Third Way Between Atoms and Gunk," *The Monist* 87, no. 3 (2004): 371–84; Kris McDaniel, "Extended Simples and Qualitative Heterogeneity," *The Philosophical Quarterly* 59, no. 235 (2009): 325–31, https://doi.org/10.1111/j.1467-9213.2008.589.x.

23. Stump and Kretzmann, "Eternity," 446.

24. Stump, *The God of the Bible and the God of the Philosophers*, 59.

25. T. J. Mawson, *The Divine Attributes* (Cambridge University Press, 2019), 24.

time. There are those that assume a dynamic theory of time, especially theologians that are unaware of the philosophical debates. However, it is increasingly common to argue that a timeless view, particularly one like the timeless present where all is *present* to God, entails a static eternalism about the nature of time.[26]

The model of God as "omnitemporal" eternity has been championed by theologians such as John Frame and Bruce Ware. God as omnitemporal does not deny succession in God. Instead, it focuses on God's infinite spread over time. What distinguishes God is that he transcends the "limits" of time so that he experiences no change over time, no ignorance of the future or past, and no frustration.[27] And yet, God is wholly present at each point in the temporal timeline in a rather literal way. As Ware explains, God becomes "omnitemporal" by fully entering the "temporal dimension."[28] This is so because Scripture requires "that we understand God literally in the space and the time of creation, with the difference from creaturely experience being that God (alone) inhabits *all* of space and *all* of time."[29]

In an odd sense, the omnitemporal model claims that God's transcendence of time entails being *both* outside *and* inside time. Therefore, he is apparently temporal, though he is not merely temporal.[30] God is temporal because he knows temporally indexed expressions like "it is dark outside *now*." He feels the flow of time from one moment to the next and reacts in a "significant sense" to events on the temporal timeline.[31] Therefore, it is entirely "misleading" to say there is no succession in God.[32] As Henri Blocher has similarly said, God has a "kind of succession in his own life."[33] There is no indication that "God's permanence and lordship over the ages

26. Katherin A. Rogers, *Perfect Being Theology* (Edinburgh University Press, 2000), 59.

27. I should note that it is not at all clear to me what it means for God to not experience change over time if he experiences the passage of time. That is a rather straightforward admission of *change*. John Frame, *Systematic Theology* (P&R, 2013), 363–65.

28. Bruce Ware, *God's Greater Glory* (Crossway, 2004), 136.

29. Ware, *God's Greater Glory*, 138.

30. Frame, *Systematic Theology*, 367.

31. Frame, *Systematic Theology*, 366–67.

32. Frame, *Systematic Theology*, 364.

33. Henri Blocher, "Yesterday, Today, Forever: Time, Times, Eternity in Biblical Perspective," *Tyndale Bulletin* 52, no. 2 (2001): 199.

rules out the reality of succession for him."[34] But God is in some sense atemporal because he is not subjected to its "limitations."

The final model is God as everlasting eternal, which amounts to him being temporal since there are no further negations of his relationship to time. On this model God is eternal because he is without beginning or end. There is no further need to define what it means to be eternal.[35] This then entails that God exists in a straightforward, temporal way. What other sort of existence could there be? Therefore, he *ages* as time progresses, though without deterioration, and he experiences the "flow" of time as it marches on. He has a history like everyone else. He responds to events in time and acts successively throughout time. Therefore, there are changes in God's actions, responses, and knowledge.[36] In this sense, God is everlasting. The distinguishing characteristic between God and creation is not the experience of time but the lack of any beginning or ending in God. What makes this view distinct from the omnitemporal model is that the omnitemporal model attempts to claim there is no change in God (whether it achieves that is another matter).

CREEDAL AND CONFESSIONAL AFFIRMATION

The creedal formulas and creedal tradition both affirm and depend on the eternity of God. The Nicene Creed and Chalcedonian Definition both speak of the Son being begotten *before all ages*. God exists infinitely in the past and infinitely to the future. The Athanasian Creed explicitly attributes eternity to the Trinity. Each person of the Trinity is uncreated, immeasurable, and *eternal*. But it further claims, in elaborating on the nature of the incarnation, that the Son was begotten "before time." This is the same sort of locution as "before all ages" and yet strikes a decidedly clearer explanation for us modern readers. Time is part of creation, and prior to creation there was no such time to measure God.

34. Blocher, "Yesterday, Today, Forever: Time, Times, Eternity in Biblical Perspective," 194.

35. Interestingly, self-proclaimed classical thinker Craig Carter defines eternity as existence that has "no beginning or end and thus is atemporal." But lack of beginning and ending by themselves is traditionally attributed to a temporal God. See Craig A. Carter, *Contemplating God with the Great Tradition* (Baker Academic, 2021), 61–62.

36. Nicholas Wolterstorff, "Unqualified Divine Temporality," in *God and Time: Four Views*, ed. Gregory E. Ganssle (InterVarsity Press, 2001), 187–88.

Depending on how one understands the nature of time, one may also see creedal dogma about eternity within the Nicene Creed in a further respect. It says that God is the "maker of heaven and earth, of all things visible and invisible." If time is understood in a substantival manner rather than relational, where it is a real "thing" that only comes to existence with creation, then the creed in a real sense requires us to believe that time is a creation. It is not merely an eternally existing relation dependent on individual objects. It is part and parcel of the doctrine of *creatio ex nihilo*. God creates the entire world out of nothing. He uses no matter, no space, and no time to do so.[37]

While the creedal tradition is unanimous in requiring the predication of eternity to God, it does not develop to a significant extent the various models that may be appropriate for understanding *how* God is eternal. The later confessional tradition, especially in the period of the Protestant Reformation, is once again of great use here. There is unanimous agreement with the creedal tradition that God is eternal. You find this language in the Scottish Confession (1560), the Waldensian Confession (1560), the Second Helvetic Confession (1566), the Confession of Varadiensis/Nagyvárad (1569), the Sandomierz Consensus (1570), the Confession of La Rochelle (1571), the Westminster Confession (1646), the Savoy Declaration (1658), and the Midlands Confession (1655). Interestingly, the Thirty-Nine Articles calls God *everlasting* rather than eternal.

The Confession of the Synod of Csenger (1570) expands further in thesis 43 by stating that eternity with reference to God "means eternity without beginning, end, or change." Not only does God infinitely extend to the past and future, but he is immutable, which implies no succession. Likewise, the Orthodox Creed (1679) in article II says God is "the only Eternal Being, everlasting without Time." Here we have a clear affirmation that God exists "outside" of time. He is time*less*.

The Synopsis of Purer Theology in section 6.28 elaborates in a characteristically useful way: "Eternity is an attribute of the duration assigned to the essence of the infinite God, whereby his being is exempt from a temporal *terminus a quo*, a beginning, and a *terminus ad quem*, an ending; it is also free of any succession (i.e., former and latter), of bygone and future time."

37. Janet Martin Soskice, *Naming God* (Cambridge University Press, 2023), 68.

Therefore, eternity for the creedal and confessional tradition is *at least* a lack of beginning, ending, and temporal succession. However, it is not clear if that means there is no extension or duration. The Synopsis readily attributes duration to God, but it does not appear to suggest temporal extension.

THE WITNESS OF THE CLASSICAL TRADITION

Eternity is replete throughout the classical tradition, as we will find. And there is a surprising level of continuity on this dogma of the faith. It will be seen that a purely temporal account of God and time, like that of the everlasting eternity view, is not to be found in the tradition. Nor is any model that allows for succession, such as the "omnitemporal" God of John Frame and Bruce Ware. While there are some groups and individuals in history that do argue that God is purely temporal, they are rejected. For example, the Socinians stand well outside the classical tradition, indeed the *Christian* tradition on a host of matters, including God's eternity. While the Racovian Catechism of 1652 *does* attribute eternity to God, it describes it in *purely* temporal terms: God's eternity just is to be "without either beginning or end." For the Socinians, the lack of temporal succession is incoherent and non-scriptural. But the Socinian characterization of God's eternity is roundly rejected.

As we move to the early modern and modern period, the classical vision of God's eternity does slowly lose its primacy among theologians and churches. No longer must you be an anti-trinitarian Socinian to find God's eternity in a classical sense utterly confused. Now, one can be a mainstream evangelical. But hearing from the tradition can and should reshape and redirect our minds. It should cause us to reconsider our presuppositions and draw us to a deep heritage of thinking about God. While the Christian tradition is not infallible for the Protestant, it is more authoritative than any of us as individuals. The universal chorus of the church from different eras dwarfs any of us—even large groups that lack historical rootedness. Without an obviously true biblical case for a matter of doctrine, we ought to defer to the wisdom of those before us. And even if we do have a biblical case, we are called to honor those before us.

The Patristic Witness

The patristic witness contains two of the most important figures for thinking about God and time: Augustine and Boethius. These two representatives have been received and retrieved throughout the tradition and play a crucial role in the development of the doctrine. Nearly everyone appeals to the classical definition of Boethius when expanding on the nature of God and time. Therefore, it is natural to spend most of our time sitting with them to understand their claims and theological logic. Of course, others in the patristic era speak of God's eternity. John of Damascus says God is timeless.[38] He says God is "without beginning, without end, eternal and everlasting."[39] Origen likewise indicates that God's existence surpasses "every idea of a sense of time."[40] But it is the Augustinian and Boethian shadow that is cast across much of medieval and Reformed reflection.

For Augustine, God exists in an eternal present. As eternal, "he knows events in time without any temporal acts of knowledge, just as he moves events in time, without any temporal motions in himself."[41] Augustine, thus, is denying temporal relations that would entail temporal succession or temporal location. Therefore, "there is no past and future, but only being, since it is eternal. For to exist in the past or in the future is no property of the eternal."[42] On this account, God lacks beginning and end but also lacks temporal location and temporal succession. But on these statements, it is not wholly clear what it means for God to be "eternally present." In the *City of God*, Augustine gives further clarity:

> It is not with God as it is with us. He does not look ahead to the future, look directly at the present, look back to the past. He sees in some other manner, utterly remote from anything we experience or could imagine. He does not see things by turning his attention from one thing to another. He sees all without any kind of change. Things which happen under the condition of time are

---

38. John of Damascus, *On the Orthodox Faith*, trans. Norman Russell (St. Vladimir's Seminary Press, 2022), 74.

39. John of Damascus, *On the Orthodox Faith* 61.

40. Origen, *Origen: Contra Celsum*, trans. Henry Chadwick (Cambridge University Press, 1980), 1.3.4.

41. Augustine, *Concerning the City of God against the Pagans*, trans. Henry Bettenson (Penguin, 2003), XI.21.

42. Augustine, *Confessions*, trans. Henry Chadwick (Oxford University Press, 2008), IX.x (24).

> in the future, not yet in being, or in the present, already existing, or in the past, no longer in being. But God comprehends all these in a stable and eternal present.[43]

Augustine's logic here begins with God's transcendence. His relationship to time is not like ours. We cannot merely assume that God relates in the same way and is thus just *older* than we are. Instead, God "sees" the entire temporal spread as a single vision. He "comprehends" it in a stable instant. There is no change. Further, Augustine refrains from using "experiencing" sort of language that would indicate a duration of temporal extension. God knows and sees the temporal framework in a single moment.

Boethius, in his *Consolation of Philosophy*, provides a similar explanation and rationale. He explains that an infinitely long life *isn't* eternal in the sense that classical theologians have meant. God is not merely temporal. God does not only extend infinitely in either direction since that mode of existence "doesn't comprehend and embrace the entire space of the time it lives."[44] Instead, God transcends time and "embraces" the entire timeline in one single instant. God, therefore, is not another being within time. He is outside of time and immutably comprehends the entire timeline at once.

But the most important claim from Boethius is that "eternity is total and perfect possession at one time of unlimited life." Boethius comments further that "whatever comprehends and possesses all at once the complete fullness of unlimited time and also possesses all of the future and has lost none of the past, this is rightly claimed to be eternal."[45] Throughout the Christian tradition, this idea is reflected on, commented on, and expanded. For Boethius, to be eternal is not merely the ability to *comprehend* the fullness of time at once but the *possession* of it. Eternity, then, is not simply a cognitive ability attached to omniscience. It includes a further quality, what Brian Leftow has called "co-possession," which could be likened to the unextended center of a circle that is equally present to all points of its circumference. It could also theoretically be analogous to being "stretched

43. Augustine, *Concerning the City of God against the Pagans* XI.21.

44. Boethius, *The Consolation of Philosophy* 5.6.

45. Boethius, *The Consolation of Philosophy* 5.6.

out" alongside the whole of time, but Boethius likens God to the center point earlier in the *Consolation*.[46] Bavinck picks up this sort of illustration later in history, likening eternity to the "immutable center that sends out its rays to the entire circumference of time."[47]

While the classical statement from Boethius comes from his *Consolation*, his extended explanation in his work on the Trinity is more illuminating by my lights:

> As to the saying that God "always is," this signifies just one thing: that he *was* in every past, that he *is* in every present, in whatever manner, and that he *will be* in every future. Although according to the philosophers the same can be said of the heaven and of other immortal bodies, the sense is not the same as in the case of God. For he always is, since "always" is in him in the present tense, and there is such a great difference between the present—that is the "now"—for our realities and for divine realities that our "now," like a running time, constitutes sempiternity, whereas the divine "now," which is permanent, immobile, and stable, constitutes eternity.[48]

Therefore, God lacks succession because there is no before and after. Everything is *present*. God possess all times *at once*.[49] On this explanation, it appears Boethius is assuming a dynamic conception of time, at least for creatures who experience time as a constant *becoming*, whereas he is positing a second mode of temporal existence for God that is static—"permanent, immobile, and stable"—and is the experience of pure *being*. However, there remains no succession. Succession would require that God *not* wholly possess life because he would be acquiring something new with the passage of time, even if ever so small.[50] Instead, God does not experience change with the passage of time because he experiences

---

46. Brian Leftow, "Boethius on Eternity," *History of Philosophy Quarterly* 7, no. 2 (1990): 125.

47. Herman Bavinck, *Reformed Dogmatics*, ed. John Bolt, trans. John Vriend (Baker Academic, 2003), 2:429.

48. Boethius, "On the Holy Trinity," in *The Cambridge Edition of Early Christian Writings*, ed. Andrew Radde-Gallwitz (Cambridge University Press, 2017), 355.

49. Stump and Kretzmann, "Eternity," 433.

50. Lewis, "Eternity, Time and Timelessness," 74.

no passage of time whatsoever. His experience of the past and future is not as "past" or "future" but entirely and wholly present.

The Medieval Witness

The medieval period sees a continued development from Augustine and Boethius on eternity. The common theme across the period is that eternity lacks extension, and if there is "duration" it is an "instant-like" element. It is akin to the "eternal now" or "eternal present" found in both Augustine and Boethius.[51]

Anselm provides a characterization of time that sounds similar to a pure timelessness, though cryptic in other respects. In his opening to section 22 of his *Monologion* he muses that "perhaps ... God can exist as a whole in individual places and times, without there being lots of wholes, and without its life span (which is nothing other than true eternity) being divided into past, present and future." God, instead, lacks "time" because time does not "delimit" his duration or measure him. As can be seen here, Anselm oscillates between a sense in which God is in time—he exists in times—and yet is wholly without it. As he concludes, God is "always and everywhere and never and nowhere."[52] While this likely sounds contradictory on its face, Anselm has a deep logic to his weaving of these two themes.

His rationale is made clearer when he explains that to be "in time" according to ordinary language is to be present and contained by it. This is quite natural since it is how we intuitively think about time. However, when applied to the divine, his being "in time" *only* indicates his presence. It does not indicate "containment." Therefore, given the nature of ordinary language, Anselm prefers to use the locution that God is "with" time rather than "in" it to avoid the unsavory conclusion that he is limited in any sense. And so, he agrees that if we speak "properly" then God strictly "is in no time" because he is not contained by anything. He has no temporal location. And yet, God is still present in or with every time because he is absent from none.[53] But his presence with time is not temporal because

51. Rory Fox, *Time and Eternity in Mid-Thirteenth Century Thought* (Oxford University Press, 2006), 303.

52. Anselm, *Monologion*, ed. Brian Davies and G. R. Evans (Oxford University Press, 1998), 22.

53. Anselm, *Monologion* 22.

it lacks the transitory character that is common to our experience of the present. Therefore, for Anselm "eternity is life unending, simultaneous, whole, and perfectly existing."[54]

Bonaventure gives an exhaustive treatment of eternity, providing numerous reasons for its truth and potential objections, along with specific replies to each and every objection. At bottom for Bonaventure eternity is total simultaneity and total interminability.[55] Therefore, there is "no succession whatsoever" in the life of God.[56] This is because simultaneity refers to a simple and undivided presence without any intrinsic diversity.[57] Despite this, he does speak of an eternal *duration* of sorts. But he is clear that "eternal duration cannot be understood correctly by anyone who does not first lay aside his imagination."[58] Duration, applied to the eternal, is a highly analogical and qualified term that is due to our mode of knowing. And yet, there is a real sense in which we can predicate it of God as his mode of existence.[59] His rationale for this is because he understands duration to not entail extension. He explains: "Extension always involves parts outside of parts, and hence corporality, quantity, and the possibility of division, while duration refers to undivided being which is found not only in composite beings but in simple beings as well."[60] Duration, then, indicates an undivided experience of life and not necessarily an extension of life.

Other medieval thinkers like Richard of St. Victor argue forcefully that there is a distinction between everlasting and eternal. An everlasting being, like God, "lacks any beginning, is uncreated."[61] However, God is more than *merely* everlasting. God is eternal. And eternity means that God "lacks a beginning, end, and any mutability." Eternity, then, is the "duration of time without a beginning and end, and the absence of all

---

54. Anselm, *Monologion* 24.

55. Bonaventure, *Disputed Questions on the Mystery of the Trinity*, trans. Zachary Hayes (Franciscan Institute, 2000), 208.

56. Bonaventure, *Disputed Questions on the Mystery of the Trinity*, 208.

57. Bonaventure, *Disputed Questions on the Mystery of the Trinity*, 212.

58. Bonaventure, *Disputed Questions on the Mystery of the Trinity*, 208.

59. Bonaventure, *Disputed Questions on the Mystery of the Trinity*, 210.

60. Bonaventure, *Disputed Questions on the Mystery of the Trinity*, 212.

61. Richard of St Victor, "On the Trinity," in *Trinity and Creation*, ed. Boyd Taylor Coolman and Dale M. Coulter, trans. Christopher P. Evans (New City, 2011), 2.2.

mutability."[62] Thomas, in a similar way, explains that eternity has two main components: (1) it is illimitable, meaning it has no beginning or end, and (2) it lacks succession, meaning it exists all at once.[63] Therefore, there is no before and after in God.[64] As eternal he has "His whole being at once."[65] Scotus calls this idea a "perfect stationary" now.[66] On each of these accounts, God must be more than everlasting to be eternal. God must lack change, which entails no succession. God is not like us creatures who experience and know successively. He experiences and knows "at one and the same time."[67]

The Reformation Witness

The Protestant Reformers once again build upon the foundation laid in the patristic and medieval period. However, it is not a monolithic period. There are different approaches to the concept of eternity, some taking a more negative and apophatic approach and others taking a positive approach.[68] These two approaches are mirrored by my distinction between the pure timeless model and the timeless present model. Whatever approach, there is agreement that God as eternal exists infinitely but also lacks change and succession. For example, Turretin, Bavinck, Arminius, Junius, Ridgeley, Bénédict Pictet (1655–1724), Ryland, and later figures like James P. Boyce and John Dagg (1794–1884) all define eternity in this way. Turretin says that infinity with reference to duration is called eternity from which God is without beginning, end, *and succession*.[69] So, like the patristic and medieval

---

62. Richard of St Victor, "On the Trinity," 2.4.

63. Thomas Aquinas, *The Treatise on the Divine Nature*, trans. Brian Shanley (Hackett, 2006), I.10.1.c.

64. Aquinas, *The Treatise on the Divine Nature* I.10.1c.

65. Thomas Aquinas, *Summa Contra Gentiles: Book One; God*, trans. Anton Charles Pegis (University of Notre Dame Press, 1975), 1.15.3.

66. John Duns Scotus, "Ordinatio," trans. Peter L. P. Simpson, 1.9.1.11, https://www.aristotelophile.com/Books/Translations/Ordinatio%20I.pdf.

67. John Duns Scotus, *Philosophical Writings*, trans. Allan B. Wolter (Hackett, 1987), 69.

68. Muller, *Post-Reformation Reformed Dogmatics*, 3:346.

69. Francis Turretin, *Institutes of Elenctic Theology*, ed. James T. Dennison, trans. George Musgrave Giger (P&R, 1994), 3.10.1; Herman Bavinck, *Reformed Dogmatics*, ed. John Bolt, trans. John Vriend (Baker Academic, 2003), 2:160; Richard Muller, *Post-Reformation Reformed Dogmatics* (Baker Academic, 2003), 3:347; Jacob Arminius, *Works of Arminius*, trans. James Nicholes and William Nicholes (Baker, 1996), disputation 4.XIV; Thomas Ridgeley, *A Body of Divinity* (Robert Carter & Brothers, 1855), 85; James Petigru Boyce, *Abstract of Systematic Theology* (Founders, 2006), 74;

period, the Protestant Reformers are resolute that God also lacks succession. Indeed, eternity entails not only that God does not experience succession but that he *cannot*. This is *the* Reformed view.[70]

Some proceed further, like Boyce, arguing that "with God there is no time and no relation of time."[71] Similarly, Bavinck says that "in God's eternity there exists not a moment of time."[72] These track well with the timeless eternity model. However, Richard Muller has forcefully argued against the concept of timelessness and views that posit God as "outside" of time. For example, he has defended the concept of eternal *duration* at significant length:

> Eternal duration is *beyond* time in the sense of transcending temporal limitations, but is not descriptive of God as being *without* time, and certainly not as *outside* of time—as if time were an objectively existent container around things. According to the scholastics, God is without change and without succession, but not without duration.[73]

While Muller is no doubt the leading expert on the Reformation period, he makes a rather odd argument here. First, it is by no means universal to deny a substantival account of time in favor of a relational account. Thinkers can and do think of time as an "objectively existent container around things." But it is also far too hasty to claim that God *with duration* is *the* scholastic view. As has been shown, it very much depends on the figure and the usage of the terminology of duration since the term is highly elastic and often obscures more than it clarifies. For example, the explanation of Henry More (1614–1687) is unusual in comparison with the definitions provided thus far. For More, God is not properly and formally successive but only

Franciscus Junius, *A Treatise on True Theology*, trans. David Noe (Reformation Heritage, 2014), 109; John C. Ryland, *Contemplations on the Beauties of Creation and on All the Principal Truths and Blessings of the Glorious Gospel; with the Sins and Graces of Professing Christians* (Thomas Dicey, 1779), 2:333; John L. Dagg, *Manual of Theology* (Southern Baptist Publication Society, 1859), 65.

70. Petrus van Mastricht, *Theoretical-Practical Theology*, ed. Joel R. Beeke, trans. Todd M. Rester (Reformation Heritage, 2018), 1.2.11.

71. Boyce, *Abstract of Systematic Theology*, 75.

72. Bavinck, *Reformed Dogmatics*, 2:158.

73. Muller, *Post-Reformation Reformed Dogmatics*, 3:355.

> virtually and applicatively; that is to say, it contains in it *virtually* all the successive duration imaginable, and is perpetually *applicable* to the succeeding parts thereof, as the channel of a river to all the water that passes through it but the channel is in no such successive defluxion though the water be.[74]

While More's explanation doesn't appear to be outside some of the standard accounts since he denies succession to God properly, his language of virtually containing successive duration is obscure and not in line with how other patristic and medieval thinkers explain eternity. While his account may well be true, it doesn't fit neatly with either timeless model of eternity. It doesn't fit with any of the other more temporal models I've proposed either, however. In any case, there are far clearer accounts of God and time, and we shouldn't stake our flag on terms or concepts that are inherently flexible. This is not to say that accounts of God's duration are absent, or even a minority (they appear rather frequently in the Reformed period), but that the terminology is slippery and should be handled carefully. So, when terms that indicate the same concept without the same dangers are available, I propose that wisdom calls us to avail ourselves of them.

Other Protestant Reformers like Stephen Charnock, in his massive work on the existence and attributes of God, argues that eternity is fundamentally about priority and, interestingly, "extension of duration."[75] However, extension of duration is used in a highly analogical sense, not entailing temporal extension. As he explains:

> Eternity is a perpetual duration, which has neither beginning nor end; time has both. Those things we say are in time that have beginning, grow up by degrees, have succession of parts; eternity is contrary to time and is therefore a permanent and immutable state, a perfect possession of life without any variation.[76]

---

74. Henry More, *Divine Dialogues, Containing Sundry Disquisitions & Instructions Concerning the Attributes and Providence of God* (James Elesher, 1668), 62.

75. Charnock, *The Existence and Attributes of God*, 414.

76. Charnock, *The Existence and Attributes of God*, 417.

Whatever perpetual duration means, it is clear for Charnock that God lacks beginning, end, and succession. He is utterly immutable and cannot vary as the change of time would require. God, therefore, cannot be measured by time.[77]

Bavinck says that God "transcends" time, which means he can be neither measured nor defined by it.[78] Time for Bavinck is not a real substance. It is a mode of existence rather than an actual real container. Therefore, without creatures there would be no time.[79] Time for Bavinck, like many in the classical tradition, is bound up with motion, change, limitation, and measure.[80] These descriptions of time appear to indicate the assumption of a dynamic theory of time. Bavinck likens God's eternity to that of a "cheerful laborer, for whom time barely exists and days fly by."[81]

But Bavinck goes further, explaining that "God's eternity does not stand, abstract and transcendent, above time, but is present and immanent in every moment of time."[82] In it, "in every second throbs the heartbeat of eternity."[83] While such language may sound unusual if God is time*less*, similar phrasing is found in various other thinkers. Richard Muller explains that "eternity, given that it is a duration, coexists with all times without disrupting or confusing times of individual things."[84] Mastricht likewise says that "God with his eye, because he is by his eternity above time, coexists invariable with the past, the present, and the future, and with the whole flow of things, such that nothing either flows from him or to him."[85] God, then, "coexists with all types of time, as he is in eternity."[86] So, God as eternal, despite lacking beginning, ending, succession, and the like remains abundantly present in every moment of time in his eternal present.

77. Charnock, *The Existence and Attributes of God*, 418.
78. Bavinck, *Reformed Dogmatics*, 2:161.
79. Bavinck, *Reformed Dogmatics*, 2:162.
80. Bavinck, *Reformed Dogmatics*, 2:163.
81. Bavinck, *Reformed Dogmatics*, 2:163.
82. Bavinck, *Reformed Dogmatics*, 2:163.
83. Bavinck, *Reformed Dogmatics*, 2:164.
84. Muller, *Post-Reformation Reformed Dogmatics*, 3:348.
85. Mastricht, *Theoretical-Practical Theology*, 1.2.10.
86. Mastricht, *Theoretical-Practical Theology*, 2:82.

DOGMATIC DEFINITION

Throughout this brief exploration what has been made clear, I hope, is that God lacks beginning, end, and succession. Therefore, only the two timeless models can account for the classical vision of God and time. The omnitemporal and everlasting accounts both run afoul of the non-successive nature of God's being. Therefore, since eternity has such a wide semantic range, I have adopted, like many others, the modifying terminology of *timelessness* to clarify what is meant by eternity.

This is not meant to suggest that *eternal* by itself is a term that shouldn't be used or that is inadequate to describe God's relationship to time, *if described appropriately*. Eternity intuitively suggests many of the aspects of divine timelessness that may not be as apparent to the common church member when they hear a word like *timelessness*. In this sense, it is a very good word! But I find clarity to be a feature of generous and wise theology. Clarity is generous because it serves readers by sparing them needless vexation and confusion. It explains *exactly* what is and isn't meant and what areas might be grey. But it is also wise because it limits confusion, misrepresentation, and fundamentally, misunderstanding. Therefore, I utilize the term *timeless* eternity as constitutive of the classical view, encompassing both the pure timeless and timeless present models.

It is God's non-successive nature that, in part, explains how he "transcends" time according to the mere definition I provided initially. It is not just that he lacks beginning and end but that he has an entirely different mode of existence. And this mode of existence, if parsed out positively, includes an eternal present—an immutably static state. While most figures appear to hold to a dynamic view of time for creatures, their descriptions of eternity appear to posit a static account of time. For example, Mastricht argues that God cannot have the past or future because they are "nonbeing," as they don't exist, which is disallowed for God.[87] Regardless, God is understood as without beginning, end, or succession by virtually everyone. And as such, God transcends time and possesses each moment *always*. He is, therefore, closer to each moment in the temporal timeline than anyone else despite not being "in" time.

87. Mastricht, *Theoretical-Practical Theology*, 1.2.11.

The question of God's *duration*, on the other hand, is a difficult matter. There are those like Muller that vehemently argue in favor of it. There are others like Bonaventure that appear to favor the terminology but only if the appropriate qualifiers are given prior to using it. Then there are those like Paul Helm who argue that "if there is duration, then presumably it is possible to denote points along that duration. But then any such point will have temporal relations to the points of temporal duration and another such point will have different temporal relations to temporal duration."[88] But if the terminology of duration can mean *either* temporal extension *or* an existential experience of the eternal now, then it appears innocuous to attribute duration to God, if done in a highly qualified sense. However, given my prioritization of clarity, I prefer to avoid positing duration of God.

DOGMATIC MOTIVATIONS

As with all the classical doctrines, God's timeless eternity is not merely a philosophical dogma. Nor is it merely the heritage of the church. It is first and foremost a doctrine of holy Scripture. Therefore, I begin once again with exegesis prior to considering the theological and philosophical arguments for and against the classical understandings of eternity.

THE EXEGETICAL FOUNDATION: HOLY SCRIPTURE

Throughout Scripture, God is described as eternal or by terms that appear to equate to eternity. For example, God is the "Ancient of Days" (Dan 7:9, 13) and the "King of the ages" (1 Tim 1:17). He is the everlasting God, according to Abraham (Gen 21:33). Deuteronomy 33:27 describes God as "the eternal" who has "everlasting arms." The number of his years is "unsearchable" (Job 36:26). "From everlasting to everlasting" he is God as he was before the mountains and before the formation of the world (Ps 90:1–2). God is the same, as his "years have no end" (Ps 102:27). He inhabits eternity (Isa 57:15). He is the "Alpha and Omega," the one "who is and who was and who is to come" (Rev 1:8). God's glory is not only forever to the future but "before all time" (Jude 25). His promises were made "before the ages began" (Titus 1:2–3). He is the living and everlasting king

88. Paul Helm, "Divine Timeless Eternity," in *God and Time: Four Views*, ed. Gregory E. Ganssle (InterVarsity Press, 2001), 37.

(Jer 10:10). These proofs, taken together, form a coherent picture of the God who is not only everlasting but prior to any time ever existing. Time is not its own eternally and necessarily existing entity. Instead, it is part of God's own creative design as he puts it to use in the Levitical codes and displays its various uses throughout scriptural texts such as Ecclesiastes 3.

Of special biblical interest is Peter's assertion that "with the Lord one day is as a thousand years, and a thousand years as one day" (2 Pet 3:8). Here he draws on the language of Psalm 90:4 to make an important theological point that is assuming a certain metaphysical account of God.[89] His claim comes in the context of defending the immanent return of the Lord and his powerful creation of the world by his word and the impending judgment the world will experience by the same word. God, then, is not *slow* to fulfill his promise and complete his work. The reason he is not slow is because he does not experience time as we do. He is not bound by successive days, weeks, months, and years. As Tom Schreiner exposits, "The marking of time is irrelevant to God because he transcends it."[90]

But Scripture further speaks to God's boundless eternity in great detail. The prophet Isaiah reminds the Israelites at length of the greatness of their God, including his eternity:

> Have you not known? Have you not heard?
> The Lord is the everlasting God,
> the Creator of the ends of the earth.
> He does not faint or grow weary;
> his understanding is unsearchable.
> He gives power to the faint,
> and to him who has no might he increases strength.
> Even youths shall faint and be weary,
> and young men shall fall exhausted;
> but they who wait for the Lord shall renew their strength;
> they shall mount up with wings like eagles;
> they shall run and not be weary;
> they shall walk and not faint. (Isa 40:28–31)

89. Mastricht, *Theoretical-Practical Theology*, 1.2.11.

90. Thomas R. Schreiner, *1, 2 Peter, Jude* (Broadman & Holman, 2003), 379.

God, here, is described as everlasting or eternal. As eternal he never grows tired, since time does not successively wear him down. His understanding is unsearchable because the past and future are entirely present before him. And the beautiful news of God's eternity is his boundless generosity. God, as eternal, continually refreshes and renews his people who are bound to time.

PHILOSOPHICAL ARGUMENTATION

There are countless arguments for a timeless eternity. I will not recount many of these here as I focus on the most powerful and persuasive by my lights. Many of the arguments for timelessness are bound up with other attributes of God, assuming that if God is like *that* then he must also be like *this*. In fact, most historical arguments in favor of timelessness depend on the classical attributes of simplicity and immutability. But there are several arguments made apart from the classical attributes, which I attempt to prioritize for the sake of persuasion.

Time as Measure of Change

A common argument in favor of eternity is concisely explained by Thomas in the *Summa Contra Gentiles*. He argues that time, by its very nature, is the measurement of change or motion. Therefore, if something is measured, then it can change or move. God, because he is immutable, cannot change or move. Therefore, God is not measured by time and hence not temporal.[91] The ideas is roughly this:

1. If something is measured by time, then it moves or changes.
2. God cannot move or change.
3. Therefore, God is not measured by time (and hence, is not temporal).

The argument is valid and sound for those already convinced of the doctrine of divine immutability. But for those unconvinced already of immutability, the argument may be valid, but one of the premises is false. Therefore, while arguments like these are persuasive if one is committed to

---

91. Aquinas, *Summa Contra Gentiles: Book One; God*, 1.15.3; Ridgeley, *A Body of Divinity*, 86–87.

the theological premise, I leave most of these underdeveloped to prioritize arguments that do not depend on other classical doctrines in great detail.

Time Requires a Cause

Another argument for divine eternity parallels the cosmological argument that defends the existence of God since if everything has a cause then we have an infinite regress. Since infinite regresses are things we want to avoid, we need a first uncaused cause. Likewise, if time is just the measure of change (like Aristotle would have it), then if time exists (which we intuitively know that it does) we need one immutable (and hence timeless) object lest we run into another infinite regress since every change requires a cause.[92] This assumes a dynamic view of time so it may only be persuasive to those that already agree with it.

Goodness as Luck

An interesting modern argument in favor of divine eternity comes from T. J. Mawson. He explains that goodness is an objective property. As an objective property, it could be understood in either consequential, deontological, or virtue ethics frameworks. And whichever framework one accepts, it is true that if God is good, then he must *do* good. On no framework can God be good apart from good action. But if this is true, God's goodness for a temporalist about God is a matter of luck since God's goodness is then dependent on future things outside his knowledge and control. If this understanding of goodness is accurate, according to Mawson, then a temporal God could not have his goodness *essentially*. It would be a matter of luck as it would require the best-case scenario, which may still not provide the fullness of divine goodness.[93] The argument, then, goes something like this:

1. If x is essentially good, then x's goodness is not dependent on future contingents.
2. God is essentially good.

92. Robert C. Koons, "Does the God of Classical Theism Exist?" in *Classical Theism: New Essays on the Metaphysics of God*, ed. Robert C. Koons and Jonathan Fuqua (New York: Routledge, 2022), 129.

93. Mawson, *The Divine Attributes*, 47–48.

3. Therefore, God's goodness is not dependent on future contingents.
4. If x is not dependent on future contingents, then x is not temporal.
5. Therefore, God is not temporal.

The concept of "luck" is built into the concept of essential for Mawson. If God is to truly be essentially good, he must be intentionally good. In other words, he must be *a se*. His goodness must depend on nothing outside of himself. If this is true, then God cannot depend on the best-case scenario occurring in time for his goodness.

Time Is Created

One of the main arguments for God being timeless is that time is a creation. The rationale is that since God is *a se* he cannot be dependent on creation, which includes time. If it can be proven that time is a creation, then it is much easier to defend the notion that God is timeless, since time isn't necessarily existing. A recent defense of time as being created has been argued forcefully by Alexander Pruss and Josh Rasmussen. They have several cogent arguments in their work, one of which I find rather persuasive here:

1. If time exists independently of creation, then time is an independent substance or reality.
2. If time is an independent substance or reality, then nothing causes time to begin.
3. If nothing causes time to begin, then there is an infinite past.
4. It is impossible to have an infinite past.
5. Therefore, time does not exist independent of creation.[94]

94. Alexander Pruss and Joshua Rasmussen, "Time Without Creation?," *Faith and Philosophy* 31, no. 4 (2014): 402–5, https://doi.org/10.5840/faithphil201412819.

The only challengeable premise is the fourth about the impossibility of an infinite past. However, an infinite past has few defenders and is intuitively implausible. To posit a succession of moments with a before and after, there must be a beginning. An infinite past, then, requires an infinite regress. Therefore, time is created, whatever it is. And if it is created, then God cannot be a temporal being since he existed without time. And this is true no matter what account of time one is committed to. Even if presentism about time is true, there is no reason to think time existed without creation unless time is no longer the measure of change but is about sheer existence.[95]

God as Author of Time

Another relatively new argument defending God's eternity comes from Gavin Ortlund, who appears to be riffing on C. S. Lewis in some ways. Ortlund likens God analogously to an author. In this sense, God is beyond, outside, and above the temporal timeline of his story. He surrounds it and penetrates it.[96] But as author of the story, it is impossible for him to experience temporal succession in the way his creation does. He simply doesn't live in the story like any character does. He can write the story and "act" within it. He can even write himself into the story. In all these ways, he can be intimately "with" the characters in his story. He knows their minds, thoughts, and actions. Indeed, he created them all! So, in this sense, he is far "closer" to them than they are to themselves, for it is his own creativity that gives them life. But he still cannot experience time in the way that they do. This argument isn't a standard syllogism but one of analogy. The point is to give a relevant and coherent model of how God could be timeless from an example in life that we accept naturally as plausible.

The Special Theory of Relativity

A further argument in favor of timeless eternity comes from modern physics and relativity theory. Einstein's two theories, the Special Theory of Relativity (1905) and General Theory of Relativity (1915), both construct

95. Pruss and Rasmussen, "Time Without Creation?," 407.

96. Ortlund, *Theological Retrieval for Evangelicals*, 97.

accounts of time that make timelessness a rather coherent and plausible belief. Indeed, it potentially undermines all accounts of temporality.[97] However, I proceed cautiously as I am not a physicist and am wholly dependent on others for proper explanations of these theories. But from my understanding, the basic idea, which is indeed revolutionary, is that time and space are relative concepts. This means that there is no absolute privileged time. Time is relative to our frame of reference.[98] Therefore, given relativity, if God is in time, whose time is he in? There is no universal or global "now" for him to exist in. And since God is not a physical object from which to have a frame of reference, the question is impossible to answer.[99] The argument, then, might go something like this:

1. If God is temporal, then he knows everyone's "now."
2. If the theory of relativity is true, then there is no universal "now."
3. The theory of relativity is true.
4. Therefore, God is not temporal.

The basic idea, again, is to undercut much of the motivation for a temporal God. If anyone is temporal it is impossible to know anything as "now" universally. My "now" is distinct from your "now," and so on. If part of the motivating factor for the temporal God is to know my "now," and if relativity is true, then he cannot know my "now." It is no longer clear that God is responding to my prayer *after* I pray, and so on.[100] And if he can't know my now or respond truly after my prayers, there is no motivation for a temporal God.

---

97. William Lane Craig, *Time and Eternity: Exploring God's Relationship to Time* (Crossway, 2001), 32.

98. Craig, *Time and Eternity*, 43.

99. Craig, *Time and Eternity*, 43.

100. Brian Leftow, *Time and Eternity* (Cornell University Press, 1991), 272.

POTENTIAL PROBLEMS AND SOLUTIONS

BIBLICAL PROBLEMS

Timeless eternity is criticized on several grounds in the contemporary literature, not least of them for being unbiblical. For example, where does Scripture explicitly call God *timeless*? And if it doesn't, why think that's what the Bible teaches? As William Hasker muses, "If the doctrine of timelessness is true, then a great many of the things believers are accustomed to say about God will be strictly and literally false."[101] In other words, a timeless God would render false much of what ordinary Christians think the Bible teaches. Alvin Plantinga is even more forceful, surmising that "there is nothing in Scripture or the essentials of the Christian message to support this utterly opaque addition."[102] Put simply, the Bible says God does stuff a timeless God can't do. He intends to do things. He remembers things and forgets. He responds to prayers. He becomes angry and later rejoices. And so, a timeless God is wholly inconsistent with the biblical portrait of God.[103] And since Scripture *alone*, apart from any other resource, can resolve the issue of God and time, according to thinkers like Frame, we are at an impasse.[104]

For example, Galatians 4:4 speaks of "when the fullness of time had come, God sent forth his Son." How else are we to understand this than God temporally existing, since there is a distinct moment, a *when*, that God acts? But the classical tradition has the resources to explain these biblical texts in a different way. Rather than texts like Galatians 4:4 suggesting temporal relations, they speak to God's transcendence over time. His control over time is so great that he executes his plans with exact precision. And any temporal language is affixed to the human nature of Christ or is understood in a metaphorical way to describe timeless realities to creatures that naturally lack the ability to understand a timeless existence. Such an interpretive approach is not ignoring the Bible, relativizing the Bible, or anything else. It is taking the Bible with seriousness, examining

101. Hasker, *God, Time, and Knowledge*, 162.

102. Alvin Plantinga, *Does God Have a Nature?* (Marquette University Press, 1980), 45.

103. John S. Feinberg, *No One Like Him* (Crossway, 2001), 399–400.

104. Frame, *Systematic Theology*, 362.

the entire canon and the overall logic of the text for how individual texts fit appropriately. One cannot simply extract a single text from Scripture and assume that its literal force *must* be the meaning. Exegesis of Scripture is not a mathematical equation we can memorize. It requires deep wrestling with the God of Scripture to find the beauty and richness of its meaning.

PHILOSOPHICAL PROBLEMS

For my money, the philosophical challenges for a classical account of God and time are far more persuasive than the biblical arguments that rest on anemic interpretive practices. The hermeneutical practice of those seeking to deny classical doctrines rests on a thin biblicism wherein interpreters become enamored with literal words and descriptions and lack the ability to rise above to the context of the whole canon and the entire theological logic of Scripture. Instead, the philosophical challenges are wide.

Some philosophical problems have little force, like Emil Brunner's simplistic claim that eternity depreciates and denies time and ultimately all of creaturely reality.[105] More important challenges are like those that suggest that if God has a "life" as we understand, it then he must have different instants or points in his life that entail a temporal existence.[106] Of course, many of these charges, like this one, assume rather than defend a strictly univocal account of life between God and creatures.[107] But there is no good reason to think that the concept of life is strictly identical between God and creatures. Why not think that God's life is different in relevant respects from ours? His life is indestructible, for example. This is very much unlike our life. In any case, to several of these important challenges I now turn.

---

105. Emil Brunner, *The Christian Doctrine of God*, trans. Olive Wyon (Westminster, 1949), 266.

106. Padgett, "Eternity as Relative Timelessness," 94.

107. I've sought to avoid the terminology of univocal as much as possible throughout this work as there are numerous caricatures of univocity that, in the tradition, are more often semantic theses than ontological ones. Therefore, when I invoke it, like I do here, I affix the terminology of "strictly" to indicate I mean a one-to-one correlation in every detail.

Time Is Dynamic

One of the main arguments against timeless eternity is that it requires a static account of time and the tenseless B-theory. Since many assume dynamic accounts and the A-theory of tense are true, naturally timelessness is false.[108] The argument, then, is very simple:

1. If God is timeless, then the dynamic theory of time is false.
2. The dynamic theory of time is true.
3. Therefore, God is not timeless.

This "problem" coincides with the argument against divine immutability from tensed facts. It assumes the dynamic theory of time as well. However, there is no reason to assume the dynamic theory of time must be true. In fact, the static account of time is the most popular among philosophers and physicists today.[109] So it's not an *ad hoc* move to deny premise 2. And further still, the static and B-theorist have rather plausible ways to account for time that even match up to our intuitions about time. It turns out that it's not really that hard to account for tensed facts without tense since we can give truthmakers for them without tense. Tense doesn't refer to some ontologically "special" fact about a bit of reality any more than other kinds of indexical language and belief (spatial indexicals, personal indexicals, etc.) refer to some ontologically "special" fact about a bit of reality. "I am here" cannot be translated as "I am in my office," but "being here" is not a special fact over and above "being in my office." They are the same thing. "I am blue" cannot be translated as "Jordan is blue," but "being me" is not a special fact over and above "being Jordan." They are the same thing. So, the fact that indexicals pertaining to space ("here," "there"), time ("past," "present," "future"), and persons ("I," "you," "we") cannot be eliminated from our language does not mean that they refer to realities over and above that picked out by non-indexical language.[110]

Applying the dynamic ontology of time to God's knowledge creates further problems. If God were to know that it was happening at the indexical *now* rather than the non-indexical on Monday, August 23, 2021, God

108. Padgett, "Eternity as Relative Timelessness," 95; Natalja Deng, *God and Time* (Cambridge University Press, 2018), 42–43, https://doi.org/10.1017/9781108653176.

109. Barry Dainton, *Time and Space* (McGill-Queen's University Press, 2001), 27.

110. My thanks to conversations with Greg Welty about time for some of these insights.

would not be omniscient because he loses knowledge by no longer knowing what was happening *now* once time *now* passes. God keeps on learning and unlearning facts.[111]

The even bigger problem I see is with the A-theory's ability to make sense of truth. I would say most assume there are such things as truthmakers for what makes something true. So, it would be weird to say that Abraham Lincoln signed the Emancipation Proclamation and yet there be *nothing* that makes this claim true. If the past (and future) are not real, how is it that Abraham Lincoln makes it true that he signed the Emancipation Proclamation? At any rate, the point is clear enough. There is no reason a classical theologian couldn't simply deny premise 2 in order to affirm God as timeless.

But some thinkers like R. T. Mullins balk at such a defense because no classical theist in history rejected the dynamic conception of time.[112] This is wrong for two reasons. First, ironically, while he criticizes contemporary thinkers that attempt to construct classical thinkers as eternalists on the ontology of time as "anachronistic," his argument in favor of presentism as a required belief is itself an anachronistic presupposition. Take the work of Katherin Rogers alone who has argued that luminaries like Anselm are eternalists as a case in point.[113] But even if Anselm wasn't an eternalist, the tradition did not have the same fine-grained distinctions or categories as we do, and so we must be careful to not read back our own precise categories back into earlier thinkers who might simply be sloppy with their language (at least sloppy given today's categories and standards). Second, Mullins seems to think that classical doctrine and every jot and tittle of metaphysics is a package deal. One must accept the entire metaphysical package over and above the dogma. But this is no serious worry for the theologian committed to a research program of reformed catholicity that is eclectically opportunistic. Former classical theologians very well could uncritically accept a dynamic conception of time without any damage being done to the dogma of timeless eternity. Now, whether classical thinkers did or not is a matter of serious debate

111. Helm, *Eternal God*, 86.

112. R. T. Mullins, *The End of the Timeless God* (Oxford University Press, 2016), 74–75.

113. Katherin A. Rogers, "Anselmian Eternalism: The Presence of a Timeless God," *Faith and Philosophy* 24, no. 1 (2007): 3–27, https://doi.org/10.5840/faithphil200724134.

(I tend to think many would accept static ontologies of time). But even if they were all presentists, it is wholly irrelevant to the truth of the doctrinal claim of divine timeless eternity.

Divine Action Is Impossible

One of the most potent objections to timeless eternity is that divine action of all sorts is rendered impossible. The reason for this is because actions take *time*. If God is to become incarnate and be raised from the dead or even answer prayers, all of these require time. Without successive stages, one cannot *answer prayers*.[114] As Stephen T. Davis explains, "The obvious problem here is to understand how a timeless being can plan or anticipate or remember or respond or punish or warn or forgive. All such acts seem undeniably temporal."[115] So, one way of construing the argument is this:

1. If prayer is real, then God must have a before and after the prayer.
2. Prayer is real.
3. Therefore, God has a before and after the prayer (and hence, is temporal).

But there is no reason to think actions like prayer require any sort of temporal before and after. Instead, an answer to prayer needs to be given *because* of the prayer. The temporal relation of before and after is not a necessary ingredient to prayer, though it is common to our own existence.[116] And since God is timeless and infallibly knows the future as present he can know our prayers "before" (not in a temporal sense) we even ask them. For example, my oldest son loves chocolate milk. It's his first request every morning when he wakes up. But it wouldn't be the case that I wasn't "answering" his request if I woke up before him and prepared it for him before he even asked. This would remove the "before" and "after" temporal sequence, but it would be no less an "answer" to his request.

---

114. Feinberg, *No One Like Him*, 400.
115. Stephen T. Davis, *Logic and the Nature of God* (Eerdmans, 1983), 14.
116. Stump, *The God of the Bible and the God of the Philosophers*, 66.

God Isn't a Person

Many critics of divine timelessness think that a timeless being wouldn't be a person, or at least wouldn't be personal. And if God lacks the necessary conditions for personhood, then God becomes more akin to pagan deities that are aloof and inert. For a timeless being, it seems impossible to have typical characteristics like memory, purpose, and knowledge. He needs to reflect, deliberate, anticipate, intend, and the like. And these all require time. So, if these are essential to personhood, then God is not a person. And if God is not a person, he can't be our friend or care about us.[117] We could spell out the argument something like this:

1. If *x* is a person, then *x* has mental acts like reflection, deliberation, and memory.
2. Mental acts like reflection, deliberation, and memory require temporal succession (before and after).
3. God is a person.
4. Therefore, God experiences temporal succession (before and after).

But this argument is dubious. Just because humans need to reflect, deliberate, or remember in a temporal manner doesn't entail all persons must do so.[118] The argument relies on assuming certain qualities we find in human persons are necessary for other natural kinds. It also has unsavory implications for humans that lack proper function. But more seriously, it relies on a strictly univocal account of knowledge between Creator and creature. But no classical theologian thinks of God's knowledge like a creature's knowledge. God doesn't need to remember facts if he is omniscient in the traditional sense of lacking any need to recall information at all—everything is wholly present to him as an immediate vision. God's mental acts are wholly different than how we experience mental acts. Therefore, God can timelessly know the whole temporal series in an instant without any need for before and after. God knows *at a glance* the whole of his temporally ordered creation.

117. Pike, *God and Timelessness*, 121–29.

118. Leftow, *Time and Eternity*, 283.

ETERNITY FOR THE CHURCH

God's timeless eternity is not simply for the philosophers. It grounds numerous ecclesial doctrines and fuels the worship of God. It is in many cases the "metaphysical underpinning" for God functioning as we see him in Scripture.[119] The covenant-keeping God of Scripture is grounded in his eternity. Apart from his eternity, there is no solid foundation for his covenant promises or his unending faithfulness. They are grounded in his eternal existence.[120] The church ought to be encouraged and assured that God will never fail because he is eternal. He will forever keep his promises and remain faithful to his people. In so doing, he will be ever present to them. God is more intimately *with* us as timelessly eternal than he ever could be as a temporal or omnitemporal being. God's timelessness allows him to transcend and penetrate every instant of time in a way that is impossible for one experiencing the flow of time. All times are eternally present before him.

There is a great joy and beauty in God's eternity that cannot be captured apart from it. Charnock once again marvels at the wonders of eternity:

> The enjoyment of God will be as fresh and glorious after many ages as it was at first. God is eternal, and eternity knows no change; there will then be the fullest possession without any decay in the object enjoyed. ... That infinite fullness of perfection that flourishes in him now will flourish eternally, without any discoloring of it in the least by those unnumerable ages that shall run to eternity, much less any despoiling him of them.[121]

God's eternal timelessness is for our joy, as Charnock shows. It is not merely abstract doctrine but practical divinity that leads us to the throne. Again, Charnock inflames our hearts through the doctrine of eternity: "When the glory of the Lord shall rise upon you, it shall be so far from ever setting that after millions of years are expired, as numerous as the sands on the seashore, the sun, in the light of whose countenance you shall live, shall be as bright as at the first appearance."[122] There is no superlative that adequately

---

119. Helm, *Eternal God*, 21.

120. Charnock, *The Existence and Attributes of God*, 441.

121. Charnock, *The Existence and Attributes of God*, 443.

122. Charnock, *The Existence and Attributes of God*, 443.

captures the heart-swelling wonder of God's eternity quite like meditating on his eternal love being poured into our hearts, day after day, forevermore. Each passing day is another for God to give himself to us without end.[123]

CONCLUSION

While a timeless eternity or timeless present may appear strange to some, they are the standard views of the Christian tradition, and for good reason. God transcends every created reality, including time itself. And his transcendence allows him to be wholly present to each moment of time. He is forever present to each of us throughout time. God as timelessly eternal is nearer to us than we are to ourselves. And his divine eternity grounds his unending love for us. While there are numerous objections to a timeless eternity in today's literature, there remain defeaters for each objection. And the rationale for holding to timeless eternity remains undefeated. Throughout the Christian tradition, while some vary on certain respects like using the language of duration, we see a unified voice that God is without beginning, without ending, and without succession.

---

123. Ephraim Radner, *Time and the Word: Figural Reading of the Christian Scriptures* (Eerdmans, 2021), 89.

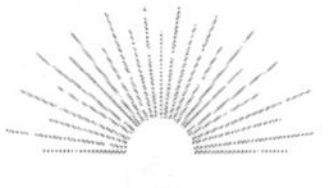

9

DIVINE IMPASSIBILITY: THE INDESTRUCTIBLY RICH GOD

Jesus once said: "Do not lay up for yourselves treasures on earth, where moth and rust destroy and where thieves break in and steal, but lay up for yourselves treasures in heaven, where neither moth nor rust destroys and where thieves do not break in and steal. For where your treasure is, there your heart will be also" (Matt 6:19–21). Many hear this and think of the call to forsake material possessions in favor of good works that will be rewarded in the life to come. True as this may be, there is a deeper reality behind Jesus's sage wisdom. The place where moth and rust do not destroy and thieves do not break in and steal is but a faint reflection of the God who is above destruction and theft: *the impassible God.*

But as a common thread among all the classical attributes, such an image of the divine has largely been rejected in favor of the infinitely feeling God—the God who experiences the height and depth of every conceivable emotion, the God who deeply experiences our pain, loss, and suffering. He shares it in his own being. He knows what it is like when philosopher Nicholas Wolterstorff laments over the tragic death of his son:

> It's the *neverness* that is so painful. *Never again* to be here with us—never to sit with us at a table, never to travel with us, never to cry with us, never to embrace us as he leaves for school, never to

> see his brothers and sister marry. All the rest of our lives we must live without him. Only our death can stop the pain of his death.[1]

Surely no one is left without deep feeling over such grief. And it was mass grief in locations like Auschwitz that became the guiding interpretive experience for many theologians over the last century.[2] If the impassible God lacks the grief accompanied by tragedy, what God is he really? So, the impassible God is made out to be terribly unfeeling, harsh, and cold. Impassibility, then, is designed precisely to minimize rather than maximize "the intimacy of God's cognitive contact with his creation."[3] At the recounting of Wolterstorff's lost son or the horror of Auschwitz there is nothing but silence—piercing darkness. Such a God is a cosmic warlord that is infinitely obsessed with himself with no such care for his creation. He is of no help in times of need. No comfort in times of pain. And certainly not worthy of worship. This has led some to remark that we "live in a golden age of divine suffering."[4] But no classical theologian worth his salt has described God in this way. It is but a cheap caricature of the true doctrine of divine impassibility that is found throughout the tradition of the church.

So, it is not shocking why those that have rejected impassibility have done so as a recoiling against such an image. Certainly, a dark and aloof deity that has no care is to be rejected. But such an image is false. Rather than treating God as unfeeling, harsh, and cold, classical impassibility has aimed to say that God cannot be robbed or destroyed and that such invincibility actualizes his ability to be nearer to the brokenhearted than they even are to themselves. He is, as divine aseity would remind us, infinitely full. And because he is full, he is indestructibly rich. And as the generous, good God that he is, he shares his wealth with all. No one can rob him of the eternal bliss that he gladly shares with us. But such a picture doesn't answer a host of questions generated by the older theological language of God without passions. Does a God without passions entail a God with no

---

1. Nicholas Wolterstorff, *Lament for a Son* (Eerdmans, 1987), 15.

2. Thomas G. Weinandy, *Does God Suffer?* (University of Notre Dame Press, 2000), 3.

3. William Hasker, "The Absence of a Timeless God," in *God and Time*, ed. Gregory E. Ganssle and David M. Woodruff (Oxford University Press, 2001), 185, https://doi.org/10.1093/acprof:oso/9780195129656.001.0001.

4. R. T. Mullins, *God and Emotion* (Cambridge University Press, 2020), 2, https://doi.org/10.1017/9781108688918.

emotion? Does he not see, hear, or feel my pain? Such existential questions deserve to be taken seriously. Therefore, while I seek to cast a vision for a *mere impassibility* as a dogmatic pillar for classical theology, it is not mere doctrine alone. Impassibility serves as a great pastoral comfort, or so I intend to demonstrate.

APPROACHING A DOGMATIC DEFINITION

The classical theologian confesses God as impassible. In fact, impassibility is used more often of God than almost any other comparable word in the tradition.[5] But the terminology of impassibility is cause for great confusion to the untrained modern mind. While the concept itself is not shrouded in dark mystery, being the negation of passions, the terminology of passions is opaque to us today. Many unfamiliar with the terminology quite naturally assume passion is a *good* thing. They understand it in a similar way to zeal. The passioned person is excited, motivated, and *zealous* for something. Why would we want to deny this of God? Surely God is passionate about his creation and even his own glory. But the devil is in the details. Passions for the older tradition are unruly, unwanted forces introduced after the fall.[6] They are not mere zeal. They are properly about *suffering*.[7] They imply a loss of power and self-control.[8] As such they are not identical to what we now call emotion, which is why it is crucial to properly distinguish between these terms: Impassibility does not necessarily imply that God lacks a passionate love, mercy, or compassion.[9]

It was during the mid-nineteenth century that there was a "wholesale change in established vocabulary" in psychology. Through the desire to secularize the discipline there was a concerted effort to remove terminology that necessarily embedded itself within Chrisitan concepts, and so the terminology of emotions was born.[10] No longer were older theories

5. Gerald Lewis Bray, *The Attributes of God: An Introduction*, Short Studies in Systematic Theology (Crossway, 2021), 35.

6. Thomas Dixon, *From Passions to Emotions: The Creation of a Secular Psychological Category* (Cambridge University Press, 2006), 29; Robert C. Solomon, *The Passions: Emotions and the Meaning of Life* (Hackett, 1993), 10.

7. Solomon, *The Passions*, 67.

8. Richard Muller, *Post-Reformation Reformed Dogmatics* (Baker Academic, 2003), 3:553.

9. Weinandy, *Does God Suffer?*, 39.

10. Dixon, *From Passions to Emotions*, 4.

that trafficked in terms like *passion, affection, sentiment,* and *appetite* palatable. This change, though, was not merely substituting new words for older ones, where if we simply knew the relevant "translation" we could make sense of older and newer theories.

Modern theories of emotion are defined in amoral ways as a sort of autonomous mental state that are described by vivid feelings and physical responses. They include feelings, sensations, and physiological reactions categorized by several older terms like *appetites, affections,* and *sentiments—but not passions. Passion* is a technical term that refers to disobedient and morally dangerous movements of the soul (a concept most moderns reject from the start—we are all basically moral people and any feeling we experience is by definition good and authentic). It is primarily moral and theological in scope rather than describing a more generic mental state. It is a disturbance wherein the one acted upon is shaped and conformed to an external agent. As such passions are irrational motions of the soul. Emotions simply don't map onto this idea in any coherent way.[11] They are much broader than passion, affection, appetite, and so on.

For example, consider how Thomas speaks of a "passion." He says, "In every passion of the appetite the patient is somehow drawn out of his usual, calm, or connatural disposition."[12] Passions, then, are passive potencies. They are things that happen *to us* rather than things we actively cause.[13] In fact, as Charnock says, they are "signs of weakness and impotence."[14] Such a definition doesn't relate well to our modern broad category of emotion. So, when the classical theist speaks of God as impassible (literally negating *passions*), they are not immediately arguing that God has no *emotions.* Maybe he doesn't have emotions, but denying the narrower category of passion does not immediately negate the broader category of emotion.

Similarly, consider how Richard Muller explains the consensus on defining affections in the Reformed period. He explains that they are "a

11. See Dixon, *From Passions to Emotions*, 18; Augustine, *Concerning the City of God against the Pagans*, trans. Henry Bettenson (Penguin, 2003), VIII.17; Duby, *Jesus and the God of Classical Theism*, 326.

12. Thomas Aquinas, *Summa Contra Gentiles: Book One; God*, trans. Anton Charles Pegis (University of Notre Dame Press, 1975), 1.89.4.

13. Peter King, "Emotions in Medieval Thought," in *The Oxford Handbook of Philosophy of Emotion*, ed. Peter Goldie (Oxford University Press, 2009), 179, https://doi.org/10.1093/oxfordhb/9780199235018.003.0008.

14. Steven Charnock, *The Existence and Attributes of God*, ed. Mark Jones (Crossway, 2022), 507.

condition, property, disposition, or desire; specifically, an intrinsic disposition or a disposition toward someone or something." Affections, thus, can be understood as a fundamental, even essential, positive characteristic *toward* something.[15] Contemporary accounts of emotion locate affections as cognitive emotions in contrast to the non-cognitive passions.[16] Therefore, affections are also a far smaller subsegment within the larger category of emotion. And so, if one denies affections of God, this likewise does not entail that God lacks emotions. Further argumentation is required.

But it is not merely confusion of the terminology of emotions compared to older terms like *passion* and *affection* that can create problems. Even the older terms themselves, like *affection*, can create problems. Even the older authors themselves do this at times, some calling terms affections and others calling them passions. Some categorize affections in ways that mirror passions and others do not. As a modern example, Sam Renihan in his short volume on impassibility defines affections as "motions of the soul worked out through the body, relative to perceived good or evil. They depend on an external object."[17] Therefore, affections are "inherently *creaturely* and eminently inconsistent with a most pure spirit" and thus, "*properly defined*, then, God does not and cannot have passions or affections."[18] Since affections are creaturely and "worked out through the body" according to Renihan, God lacks them necessarily as a pure spirit. But such a definition assumes a very particular sense of affection that is not at all universal. For example, Puritan William Fenner (1600–1640) argued that since angels desire (1 Pet 1:12) and demons believe and tremble (Jas 2:19), affections are not necessarily bodily. They can exist in purely spiritual beings.[19] Further, Muller baldly argues that the Protestant orthodox "assume that God has affections"

15. Richard A. Muller, *Dictionary of Latin and Greek Theological Terms: Drawn Principally from Protestant Scholastic Theology*, 2nd ed. (Baker Academic, 2017), 19.

16. Anastasia Philippa Scrutton, *Thinking Through Feeling: God, Emotion, and Passibility* (Bloomsbury, 2013), 65.

17. Samuel Renihan, *God without Passions: A Primer* (Reformed Baptist Academic Press, 2015), 39.

18. Renihan, *God without Passions*, 68.

19. See the recounting of William Fenner's arguments in David Sytsma, "The Logic of the Heart: Analyzing the Affections in Early Reformed Orthodoxy," in *Church and School in Early Modern Protestantism*, ed. Jordan Ballor, David Sytsma, and Jason Zuidema (Brill, 2013), 477, https://doi.org/10.1163/9789004258297_035, 478.

with no caveat.[20] Therefore, without examining what one means by the various terms, it is nearly impossible to determine what one means by God's impassibility.

MERE DIVINE IMPASSIBILITY

It is once again appropriate to begin with a baseline definition that more specific models of impassibility can expand upon. When asked what divine impassibility means, there is common assent to a lack of divine suffering, which is an appropriate starting point:

> *Mere divine impassibility*: God is impassible *if and only if* God cannot suffer.

But a lack of suffering is a *very* broad definition to begin with and doesn't explicitly mention the terms of passion, affection, or even emotion. What does suffering mean or entail? For example, God as incapable of suffering doesn't tell us whether God can experience emotions. Can he be angry, anxious, or jealous? Nor does it tell us if his emotions (if he has them) fluctuate. Can he be angry at one moment, sad the next, and then happy after? Nor does it distinguish between emotions, passions, affections, and the like. So, the various models of impassibility are needed to explain just what it means for God to not suffer. It will be important that they answer four related and important questions:

1. Can God be moved?
2. Does God have emotions?
3. What kind of emotions does God have?
4. Can God's emotions change?

Each of these touches on important aspects of divine impassibility and whether God can suffer. The first question listed is likely the least straightforward given the general terminology of "movement." It attempts to capture the idea of whether God can be influenced or caused to do anything. In the older terminology, this question was posed by the terms

20. Muller, *Dictionary of Latin and Greek Theological Terms*, 163.

agent and *patient*. Agents are those that act on things—they are the source of change. Patients are those that are acted upon and undergo, or *suffer*, change.[21] You see, in older literature, and even contemporary philosophy of action, the idea of "suffering" is far broader than simply experiencing pain or torment—it indicates the entire spectrum of receiving action and undergoing change. As a simple example, if I enter a state of deep depression at the loss of a beloved family member, does this *move* God by influencing or causing him to share in sadness with me? Does it compel him to show compassion? Does he change based on my state of misery? Or does he have such control and knowledge that nothing can cause, influence, or compel him to change in any respect? This question is a corollary of divine aseity and immutability. To answer in the negative, that God cannot be moved, is to suggest that God is *unable* to be caused or receive anything because of his fullness, infinite beatitude, and unchangeableness. As the infinitely full and happy God that is unchangeable in every respect, even if he has emotions, he cannot be changed in them. Nothing can disturb his infinite happiness as the God who is "blessed forever" (Rom 9:5).

But before answering these questions, it is important to define with the utmost clarity what is meant by the terminology of *emotions*, at least as I use it. As explained, emotion is a broader category than that of passion, affection, and the like. It covers a wide range of conscious feelings like love, joy, sadness, grief, anger, and the like. But there are various models of emotion that explain what a conscious feeling is. Each of these models must answer at least three questions: (1) Is there a cognitive element to emotions? (2) Are emotions necessarily embodied? (3) Are emotions caused by external stimuli?

The jury is generally split on whether emotions are cognitive or not. Some argue emotions are purely non-cognitive feelings, and others argue they are cognitive evaluations of beliefs.[22] It is now far more common to describe emotions as judgments that are not merely blind and irrational

21. Sarah K. Paul, *Philosophy of Action: A Contemporary Introduction* (Routledge, 2021), 9.

22. Anastasia Philippa Scrutton, *Thinking Through Feeling* (Bloomsbury, 2013), 56.

feelings.[23] Emotions are *about* something.[24] Some do combine these two views, explaining emotion as a cognitive mental state that has an affective "what it feels like" aspect.[25] As an example, consider my younger days. I used to run cross country. I would log seventy to eighty miles per week during my peak. Running that much required running twice a day. But it was the late-night runs that I really loved. Sneaking out of my house after midnight to pound out a brisk twelve-mile jaunt was a delight. The crispness of the air and the calmness of the lonely pavement was serenity—except for when I would be running miles away from any general civilization and a car would begin to follow me or my brain began to conjure worries about mysterious shadows lurking near the trail. In those times, my anxiety heightened, my heart began to beat faster, and my mind began to race. I began to run much faster. It is this combination of the evaluative judgment of danger mixed with the bodily experience of blood pumping faster and the hair raising on my arms that constitutes an emotion. If I didn't make the cognitive judgment that there was danger, it wouldn't be an emotion but just a bodily reaction.

In this example, my emotion of anxiety is deeply embodied. What would my anxiety be while running without the throbbing of my heart? The enmeshment of my judgment with my body is what the founders of the modern science of emotions would argue is necessary for an emotion to be an emotion—bodily arousal.[26] For it is when my body is aroused and accompanied by a mental state that my experience becomes an emotion. So, emotions then are "embodied judgments."[27] Of course, for those with strong dualist intuitions, it may seem inconceivable that we could exist as souls apart from bodies and by virtue of our division be devoid of emotions. Surely, if disembodied souls are possible, they continue to feel joy, love, grief, and the like, or at least something comparable. What else does the rich man feel in Luke 16 but anguish and pity for his family, whom he begs Abraham to warn? And if angels and demons both

23. Solomon, *The Passions*, 15.

24. Solomon, *The Passions*, 111.

25. Mullins, *God and Emotion*, 4.

26. Thomas Dixon, *The History of Emotions: A Very Short Introduction* (Oxford University Press, 2023), 13.

27. Dixon, *The History of Emotions*, 14.

experience emotions, then emotions need not have corporeal bodies to be true emotions.

But my example of anxiety appears to also be necessarily understood in responsive terms. It is a feeling *caused* by something external.[28] I wouldn't have experienced anxiety apart from the vehicle that appeared to be following me or the rustling of the trees in the dead of night. And so my emotion is properly caused by external stimuli.

Given this brief foray into the nature of emotions, when I speak of a *proper* emotion, I mean a traditional account of embodied judgments wherein someone has (1) a mental state (2) that is caused by *something* and (3) leads to an affective bodily response. However, there are two important remarks to be made here. First, on any standard Christian account, God is not a body. Therefore, God cannot have proper emotions even if he were mutable and desired to feel a wide range of emotions. It is impossible (at least qua God—the divine nature is incapable). Yet, second, it is possible to speak *improperly* of emotions to designate merely a mental state of some sort—love, joy, peace, anxiety, and the like—apart from the embodied and responsive elements. So much is clear, I think, from simple conceivability experiments like those of disembodied souls and from exploring the entailments of scriptural claims like those in Luke 16. But it is also clear from a broadly Augustinian account of emotions that is later picked up by thinkers like Anslem, Abelard, and later Scotus, wherein emotions are bound up with the will and thus can be understood without the need to be caused by something external.[29] For the sake of clarity, when I speak of emotion henceforth, I intend to use it improperly. If I intend to refer to proper emotions, I denote it as such.

MODELS OF DIVINE IMPASSIBILITY

Categorizing the various models of impassibility in the tradition and contemporary period is no easy task. Beyond the general agreement on the incapability of divine suffering, it can become rather fuzzy. As such, I've offered four models of divine impassibility below.

---

28. John C. Peckham, "Qualified Passibility," in *Divine Impassibility: Four Views of God's Emotions and Suffering*, ed. Robert J. Matz and A. Chadwick Thornhill (InterVarsity Press, 2019), 88.

29. Peter King, "Emotions in Medieval Thought," in *The Oxford Handbook of Philosophy of Emotion*, ed. Peter Goldie (Oxford University Press, 2009), 168–71.

Maximal divine impassibility: God is impassible *if and only if* God (1) cannot be moved, (2) lacks emotions, and (3) is immutable.

Qualified divine impassibility: God is impassible *if and only if* God (1) cannot be moved, (2) lacks some emotions, and (3) is immutable.

Apophatic divine impassibility: God is impassible *if and only if* God (1) cannot be moved, (2) transcends emotion, and (3) is immutable.

Kenotic divine impassibility: God is impassible *if and only if* God (1) lacks immoral emotions and (2) experiences emotion by choice of the divine will.

Immediately, it should be apparent that the kenotic account of divine impassibility differs markedly from the first three approaches, lacking a commitment to divine immutability and God's inability to be caused by something external to himself. For kenotic impassibility, God's lacks suffering in a much narrower sense since God can be acted upon and experience change. In fact, he *can* suffer, and so it is typically understood as a version of *passibility*. But for the sake of argument, I treat it as a version of impassibility until further exploration is complete. In contrast, the maximal, qualified, and apophatic models deny God's status as a patient. There is no agent that can determine him to experience love, joy, or anything else.[30] Each of these accounts, however, no matter their theological commitments, assume the sheer goodness of God. Whatever emotions he might have, he doesn't experience morally objectionable ones. No matter the account, for such models, God is not like a moody teenager, moved by the slightest events to radically different emotional states. We needn't walk on eggshells in fear of angering him.

For the sake of clarity, before exploring each of these models in greater detail, below are the general answers to each of the four important questions

30. James E. Dolezal, "Strong Impassibility," in *Divine Impassibility: Four Views of God's Emotions and Suffering*, ed. Robert J. Matz and A. Chadwick Thornhill (Downers Grove: InterVarsity Press, 2019), 17.

Table 9.1. Four Important Questions

Model	Can God be moved?	Does God have emotions?	What kind of emotions does God have?	Can God's emotions change?
Maximal	No	No	N/A	N/A
Qualified	No	Yes	Some affections	No
Apophatic	No	Yes	No analogue	No
Kenotic	Yes	Yes	Any moral emotion	Yes

On the maximal account, God lacks all emotion whatsoever. As Spinoza (1632–1677) explains, "God is without passive emotions, and he is not affected with any emotion of pleasure or pain." The translation here of "passive emotions" is literally *passions*. But the key for Spinoza is the universality of God's lack. As he notes, "Strictly speaking, God does not love or hate anyone."[31] In no sense does God have love, joy, or any emotion whatsoever. All such emotions require instability, brevity, change, and so on. Therefore, he not only lacks passions but lacks affections. Instead of affections being permanent dispositions of virtue, they are merely figurative attributions based on God's operations.[32] When we read of God loving David or Abraham, for the maximal impassibility model, there is *nothing* real that corresponds to what we understand and experience as love, joy, or anger in the being of God—it is purely figurative. Descriptions like this lead many thinkers, such as William Shedd, to characterize such an approach to impassibility as an absolutely indifferent God that is reduced to blind force, since "it could not even concede happiness to the deity, because this is a species of feeling."[33]

It is relevant to note that the maximal model is also held by heretical groups like Arians and Nestorians. God is categorically excluded from

---

31. Benedictus de Spinoza, *The Essential Spinoza: Ethics and Related Writings*, ed. Michael L. Morgan, trans. Samuel Shirley (Hackett, 2006), V.17.

32. See Muller, who notes the variety of approaches in the Post-Reformation period on whether such affections are figurative or literal: Muller, *Post-Reformation Reformed Dogmatics*, 3:552.

33. William G. T. Shedd, *Dogmatic Theology*, 3rd ed. (P&R, 2003), 166.

emotion, feeling, or suffering.[34] Including these groups is not an attempt to "poison the well." Rather, it is to show a broadly shared intuition that God cannot feel an emotion on pain of violating dearly held beliefs about God. As Paul Gavrilyuk explains:

> The Nestorians could not allow the thought that God could act in a way that might impinge upon his impassibility; that he could genuinely participate in the human experiences to the point of suffering, without ceasing to be what he is. To admit this would be to abrogate the fundamental division between creator and creation.[35]

While upholding the Creator/creature distinction is a shared goal by all Christians, for the maximal version of impassibility it potentially comes at the expense of other traditional Christian doctrines. But the maximal model needn't be encumbered by such heretical theological entailments, though it is the specter next door.

But there is a further problem with the maximal model. As I've indicated, the language surrounding the discussion of impassibility can cause relative confusion. Emotion, passion, and affection are all used variously. So, for some, the language of maximal impassibility is a common framework. Sam Renihan is an example of a prominent contemporary Reformed figure that denies both passions *and* affections in God. For Renihan passions and affections are both creaturely modes that are necessarily embodied and thus cannot be said of God.[36] Therefore, God does not have any emotions, even love and joy, *as emotions*. Instead, God loves but it is neither affection nor passion.[37] The reason love as emotion is denied to God is because it would result in a caused love, which cannot be the case for God. Even good affections require dependence on an external object.[38] God's love must be completely uncaused and altruis-

34. Paul Gavrilyuk, "God's Impassible Suffering in the Flesh: The Promise of Paradoxical Christology," in *Divine Impassibility and the Mystery of Human Suffering*, ed. James F. Keating and Thomas Joseph White (Eerdmans, 2009), 143.

35. Paul L. Gavrilyuk, *The Suffering of the Impassible God: The Dialectics of Patristic Thought* (Oxford University Press, 2004), 143.

36. Renihan, *God without Passions*, 67–68.

37. Renihan, *God without Passions*, 69–71.

38. Renihan, *God without Passions*, 39.

tic.[39] But given how I've defined the terminology of passion, affection, and emotion, there is terminological slippage here that may cause talking past one another. Their point is not that God doesn't love but that God doesn't love as the result of an external causal agent.[40] Affection *toward* something does not entail affection being *dependent* on something. And so, while the terminology they use (denying both passions and affections) may suggest these thinkers are a "maximal" model, I think given their explanations they better fit with the following qualified model.

The qualified account of divine impassibility takes its name from the seminal work of Paul Gavrilyuk, which has explained the patristic theology of impassibility as the idea that God is in total control and has no morally objectionable emotions.[41] Because he is in complete control and is immutable, he experiences no suffering or emotional fluctuation.[42] Therefore, on a qualified account, God *does* have emotions. He experiences the positive emotions of love and joy to an infinite degree.[43] But these emotions that God experiences are typically called affections in the older literature. Whereas passions have their foundation or beginning *ad extra* and terminate *ad intra*, affections have their foundation or source *ad intra* and terminate *ad extra*. Therefore, affections like love can properly be predicated of God.[44] Thomas Weinandy gives a characteristically useful explanation of this model:

> No, God in himself as God does not suffer. To say that God does not suffer means not only that he does not feel any physical pain, since he is not corporeal, but also that he does not undergo some passible changes of state whereby he experiences some form of divine emotional agitation, anguish, agony, or distress. God is never in a state of inner *angst*.[45]

Therefore, the main thrust of a qualified sense of impassibility is to rule out the possibility of God being harmed or compromised by anything

39. See Dolezal, "Strong Impassibility."

40. Dolezal, "Strong Impassibility," 17.

41. Gavrilyuk, *The Suffering of the Impassible God*, 51.

42. Matthew Barrett, *None Greater* (Baker Books, 2019), 113–14.

43. Rogers, *Perfect Being Theology*, 51.

44. Muller, *Post-Reformation Reformed Dogmatics*, 3:554.

45. Weinandy, *Does God Suffer?*, 153.

outside himself.[46] However, God remains immutable and impervious to external movement.

Even so, there are many contemporary thinkers that, in arguing for divine impassibility, slip between a maximal and qualified model for various reasons. Some fail to properly define terms. Others are overly zealous for divine insulation. Whatever the reason, David Bentley Hart, though impassioned, offers an important caution:

> In many cases it is those who adhere most fiercely to the traditional language of impassibility who often prove most oblivious to the true logic of transcendence, and that their maladroit devotion to a principle they only partially understand frequently leads them to conclusions that cannot help but bring that principle into disrepute.[47]

There is a real danger for those new to impassibility of entering a sort of theological "cage stage" that flattens out necessary distinctions. So, while God lacks all passions, on a qualified model this does not negate all emotions whatsoever. And emphasizing his lack of passions shouldn't negate the fullness of his affection properly defined.

The apophatic model of divine impassibility differs only slightly from the qualified account by refusing to demarcate what sort of emotions God might or might not have. There is no possible analogue for explaining exactly what it is that God experiences. So, it *could* be that these two models collapse into one another, but there is an insistence that we shouldn't attempt to explicitly demarcate these details. Instead, the general idea of God transcending such created realities is deployed. As Michael Allen has argued, impassibility is an "analogical qualifier" and is "meant to keep us from interpreting divine emotions as mere counterparts to human emotional experience." This is why divine emotions *are* affirmed alongside divine impassibility.[48] As *a se*, immutable, good, and spiritual (i.e., incorporeal), he transcends our created

---

46. Gerald L. Bray, *The Attributes of God* (Crossway, 2021), 37.

47. David Bentley Hart, "Impassibility as Transcendence: On the Infinite Innocence of God," in *Divine Impassibility and the Mystery of Human Suffering*, ed. James F. Keating and Thomas Joseph White (Eerdmans, 2009), 302.

48. Michael Allen, "Divine Attributes," in *Christian Dogmatics: Reformed Theology for the Church Catholic*, ed. Michael Allen and Scott R. Swain (Baker Academic, 2016), 73.

emotional categories and states altogether. So, God is not merely incapable of suffering like a rock. He is *beyond* it.

On the kenotic model God *could* lack all emotion, yet he chooses to divest himself of such properties and experiences various emotions. He can experience joy, grief, anxiety, pain, and suffering—but only voluntarily. No one can force any emotion on God. They are all deliberate choices by God himself. And he remains completely emotionally stable. He never departs from the golden mean of emotion. Now, while I call this a kenotic model, those I categorize as such may or may not appreciate the language of kenoticism given its baggage in other christological discussions. However, the general idea of the ability to change based on divine choice is apparent and makes such a term apt.

For example, evangelical Calvinist biblical scholar D. A. Carson has argued for something along these lines, though without the terminology: "Closer to the mark is the recognition that all of God's emotions, including his love in all its aspects, cannot be divorced from God's knowledge, God's power, God's will. If God loves, it is because he chooses to love; if he suffers, it is because he chooses to suffer."[49]

For Carson, impassibility means a lack of vulnerability. God experiences a range of emotions. He even suffers apart from the incarnation, experiencing what John Frame calls "negative emotions," but only by divine choice.[50] Similarly, Daniel Castelo indicates that "God's nature is passible but only to the degree that God allows Godself to be."[51] And so God *can* be affected by agents outside himself, but only by divine permission.[52] In other words, God voluntarily becomes passible. His emotions remain perfectly rational and holy, yet he experiences emotions of pain, suffering, and the like by his own choice.[53]

Rob Lister similarly explains impassibility primarily in terms of God's inability to be surprised, manipulated, or overwhelmed by others. But he too is quite clear: God *is* impassioned *and* can be affected by

49. D. A. Carson, *The Difficult Doctrine of the Love of God* (Crossway, 2000), 60.

50. John M. Frame, *Systematic Theology* (P&R, 2013), 415.

51. Daniel Castelo, "Qualified Impassibility," in *Divine Impassibility: Four Views of God's Emotions and Suffering*, ed. Robert J. Matz and A. Chadwick Thornhill (InterVarsity Press, 2019), 54.

52. Castelo, "Qualified Impassibility," 66.

53. John C. Peckham, *Divine Attributes* (Baker Academic, 2021), 65.

his creatures.[54] The main idea behind impassibility for him is what he calls invulnerability.[55] As such, God can experience a range of emotions but does so only based on his permission. In fact, Lister, in a strikingly kenotic explanation, argues that God must become incarnate to "overcome *natural* divine impassibility."[56]

Given the senses of these models, I suggest from the outset that the kenotic model is not a "classical" doctrine. Instead, it is better understood as a version of passibility. A necessary condition for any version of impassibility is a denial of suffering. But the kenotic model willingly admits suffering. So, since they are unable to affirm the maxim of God not suffering, while the view may be the truth of the matter, it is not a classical version.

CREEDAL AND CONFESSIONAL AFFIRMATION

The creedal and confessional traditions give common assent to the doctrine of divine impassibility. However, it frequently leaves the doctrine underdefined. For example, at Chalcedon, the gathered bishops exclude from the priesthood "those who dare to say that the divinity of the Only-begotten is passible."[57] It further criticizes those "fantasizing that the divine nature of the Only-begotten is passible."[58] At the first session of Chalcedon it was noted that *all* "confess the Word of God to be impassible." The logic was that "according to the all-wise Peter ... Christ suffered for us in the flesh and not in the nature of the ineffable Godhead."[59] As can be seen here, there is an incredibly strong belief that God is impassible, though it is not explicated with great detail, nor is all suffering removed from God as he *does* suffer in and through his human nature. Therefore, those that find the proclamations made at an ecumenical council like Chalcedon as either authoritative or strongly suggestive of true theology have ample reason to confess God as impassible.

---

54. Rob Lister, *God Is Impassible and Impassioned: Toward a Theology of Divine Emotion* (Crossway, 2013), 36.

55. Lister, *God Is Impassible and Impassioned*, 190.

56. Lister, *God Is Impassible and Impassioned*, 37.

57. Christopher A. Beeley, *The Unity of Christ: Continuity and Conflict in Patristic Tradition* (Yale University Press, 2012), 281.

58. Richard Price and Michael Gaddis, trans., *The Acts of the Council of Chalcedon* (Liverpool University Press, 2007), 1:72.

59. Price and Gaddis, *The Council of Chalcedon*, 1:182.

The Protestant confessional tradition regularly shares the creedal belief in the impassible God. It is a shared claim throughout the Thirty-Nine Articles (1562/63), Irish Articles (1615), Westminster Confession of Faith (1646), Savoy Declaration (1658), and Second London Confession (1677/1689) that God is *without passions*. While these confessional documents do not expand on the precise nature of passions, they do ascribe without reservation to God that he is loving, gracious, merciful, and the like. Therefore, based on the juxtaposition of such claims, it appears difficult to understand them as subscribing to a maximal model of impassibility.

However, the *Synopsis of Purer Theology* is once again elaborative on classical doctrines. In section 6.39 it states:

> God's good affections (which in human beings are the passions), and the virtues of his intellect and will (which in mortals are the ethical and moral qualities which designate regulation of the affections), are: truth, love, goodness, gentleness, charity, generosity, mercy, and long-suffering, anger, hatred, justice, and also holiness, etc., and are truly and properly said of God (of course with the removal of every imperfection from them) and they are nothing other than God's ardent will towards us, and its power and effect in creatures.

And later in section 6.40, "Compassion and mercy are whereby He wills, is able to provide, and actually does provide help." Therefore, the *Synopsis* attributes affections such as love and mercy to God *properly*. Such a definition conflicts with the maximal model and leaves only the qualified and apophatic model.

THE WITNESS OF THE CLASSICAL TRADITION

Impassibility is not commonly a separate locus of doctrine throughout Christian history. While it has universal assent it is typically folded under other headings such as immutability. This doesn't make the doctrine less relevant, though it does make it more difficult to follow the general logic of individual authors. Merely mining for the terminology of impassibility does little to explain what the authors think impassibility really is.

The Patristic Witness

The patristic period explodes with references to divine impassibility. Even as early as Justin Martyr we find God being called impassible with no hesitation.[60] There is a shared logic throughout the period that passion is to be denied of God in full.[61] Such beliefs pervade conciliar declarations and traditional preaching. As Leo proclaimed, God is "incapable of suffering."[62] He is not subject to any passion whatsoever.[63] Those that ascribe such human passions to God, along with their "mental tendencies," prove themselves "ignorant of God."[64] But pastor-theologians like Cyril and Augustine give greater detail to divine impassibility.

For Cyril, Christology offers the most important lacuna for understanding divine impassibility. As the divine Word he is completely impassible.[65] As he explains, "The Word of God is impassible confessedly as far as pertains to his own nature as the Word of God. No one is so thunderstruck as to think that the nature which is over all things is able to be receptive of suffering."[66] Apparently, no one was so bold or confused to think that God could suffer. The reasoning is that God is incorporeal and therefore "lies entirely outside suffering."[67] However, Cyril doesn't reject all suffering, for through the incarnation God suffers in his human nature.[68] And through the *communicato idiomatum*, God does suffer. As David Bradshaw explains:

> It is important to note that, in thus interpreting the biblical references to divine jealousy and anger, Cyril does not deny that God

60. Justin Martyr, *The First and Second Apologies*, trans. Leslie W. Barnard (Paulist Press, 1997), 1, 25.

61. Basil, *Against Eunomius*, trans. Mark DelCogliano and Andrew Radde-Gallwitz (Catholic University of America Press, 2011), 2.24.

62. Leo the Great, *Sermons*, trans. Jane Patricia Freeland and Agnes Josephine Conway (Catholic University of America Press, 1995), 81.

63. John of Damascus, *On the Orthodox Faith*, trans. Norman Russell (St. Vladimir's Seminary Press, 2022), 60, 73.

64. Irenaeus, *Against Heresies*, ed. Alexander Roberts and James Donaldson (Ex Fontibus, 2010), 2.13.3.

65. Cyril of Alexandria, "Second Letter to Succensus," in *The Cambridge Edition of Early Christian Writings*, ed. Mark DelCogliano, trans. Matthew R. Crawford (Cambridge University Press, 2022), 743, https://doi.org/10.1017/9781107449640.053.

66. Cyril of Alexandria, *Letters 51–110*, trans. John I. McEnerney (Catholic University of America Press, 1987), 30.

67. Cyril of Alexandria, *On the Unity of Christ*, trans. John Anthony McGuckin (St. Vladimir's Seminary Press, 2000), 121.

68. Cyril of Alexandria, *On the Unity of Christ* 130.

> experiences something like human emotion. In fact, his explanation hinges on attributing to God concern and tender love (φιλοστοργία) for His creatures. Cyril even goes so far as to say that God is pained (οὐκ ἀνάλγητως ἔχων) by His creatures' sin.[69]

Cyril offers an illustration of how this might work. It is like when someone puts iron in contact with a raging fire to mold it and reshape it. The iron "receives" the fire into itself, and once heated thoroughly, it can be beaten into a myriad of shapes. It even appears like a form of malleable liquid. But no matter how hard the iron is beaten or how different it is molded from its original construction, only the iron is injured or changed. The fire, while it is in the iron, receives no such injury. In an analogous way, the Son of God suffers in his human nature while his divine nature suffers no such injury.[70]

Augustine's theory of emotion and impassibility is one of the earliest and most well-developed theories that is transmitted throughout the tradition. For Augustine, God neither suffers nor undergoes anything.[71] Therefore, he is impassible according to a maximal or qualified model. As for many theologians, anger and repentance serve as an ideal test case for divine impassibility. Both terms are frequently predicated of God in Scripture, and yet classical theologians have been unwilling to literally predicate them of God. Augustine comments at length in his *City of God*:

> God's anger is not an agitation of his mind; it is a judgement by which punishment is inflicted on sin. And his consideration and reconsideration are his unchanging plan applied to things subject to change. For God does not repent of any action of his, as man does, and his decision on any matter whatsoever is as fixed as his foreknowledge is sure. But if Scripture did not employ such words, it would not strike home so closely, as it were, to all mankind. For Scripture is concerned for man, and it uses such language to terrify the proud, to arouse the careless, to exercise the inquirer, and to nourish the intelligent.[72]

---

69. David Bradshaw, "The Philosophical Theology of St Cyril's Against Julian," *Phronema* 29, no. 2 (2014): 33.

70. Cyril of Alexandria, *On the Unity of Christ* 130–31.

71. Augustine, *The Trinity*, trans. Edmund Hill (New City, 2015), V.2.8, 9.

72. Augustine, *Concerning the City of God against the Pagans*, trans. Henry Bettenson (Penguin, 2003), XV.25.

Herein we find standard classical logic on divine emotions in Scripture. The Bible speaks of God as angry and repenting to communicate something that transcends what we commonly understand by the terms. Anger is not designed to indicate a bloodthirsty God with a fast-beating heart and a red face. Instead, it is designed to show forth his judgment on sin. And these images are not empty metaphors in Scripture. They are designed with the purpose of pedagogy in mind. They teach readers of Scripture about God.

But elsewhere in the *City of God* Augustine offers commentary that is also consistent with a more qualified model of impassibility. He distinguishes between disordered passions and virtuous emotions that "spring from love of the good and from holy charity" and "are the consequence of right reason when they are exhibited in the proper situation." Therefore, he argues that divine impassibility is understood as "a life without the emotions which occur in defiance of reason and which disturb the thoughts."[73]

The Medieval Witness

The medieval era tracks similarly with the patristic period yet often with greater detail and sophistication. In many respects the medievals' development of complex psychological systems allows them to provide characteristically nuanced explanations of the nature of divine impassibility. Thomas Aquinas is exemplary here with a mammoth treatise on emotion and several sections on impassibility.

For Thomas, as for many thinkers, human passions cannot be predicated of God from the very start. There is no need to offer sophisticated exegetical explanations because passions by definition require a body.[74] And since passions are necessarily embodied, any bodiless being *cannot* possess passions by necessity. But this is not the end of the story. God is not simply understood as totally aloof and distant, experiencing "zero" emotion. Thomas deploys a tremendously important distinction to make sense of how emotional terminology ranging from wrath to delight applies to God. The theologian and wise reader of Scripture must distinguish what

73. Augustine, *Concerning the City of God against the Pagans* XIV.9.

74. Thomas Aquinas, *Summa Contra Gentiles: Book One; God*, trans. Anton Charles Pegis (University of Notre Dame Press, 1975), 1.89.1.

is said *properly* of God and what is said *metaphorically*.[75] No one doubts that Scripture calls God angry or jealous. Neither the patristic authors nor the medieval thinkers ignore the clear biblical descriptions of God. But to theologically understand the meaning behind the descriptions requires theological judgments on whether terms like *anger*, *wrath*, and *sadness* are properly said of God or whether they metaphorically communicate something beyond the literal semantic meaning.

For example, anger is metaphorically used for God. He is not properly angry because God, in his "anger," is not affected with sadness, nor does he have an "appetite for revenge arising from sadness due to injury."[76] Instead, "God is at times called *angry* in so far as, following the order of his wisdom, He wills to punish someone."[77] Like how a judge punishes from justice or an angry man punishes from anger, God punishes from anger. The point is to draw out the minimal similarity while removing the creaturely imperfections of such anger. God's anger is analogically related to these creaturely realities. They are small windows into the divine perfection of God's justice. Similarly, God *is* sad too. But he is not properly sad. He is sad "*in so far as* certain things take place that are contrary to what He loves and approves; just as we experience sadness over things that have taken place against our will." The "in so far as" language is critical to understanding the exegetical and theological logic deployed by Thomas. He *is* angry or sad *in so far as* certain aspects reflect truly of God and other aspects are removed. Therefore, biblical texts such as Isaiah 59:15, according to Thomas, directly apply to God. He *is* "displeased" and saddened. But his sadness does not correspond with our own sadness that results from injury, lack, confusion, and betrayal.[78] Therefore, God is angry, sad, jealous, and the like metaphorically. But metaphorically applying these terms does not remove their force or importance. They simply are the means to understanding what God intends to communicate through human language about himself. As should be seen, there is a deep exegetical

75. Aquinas, *Summa Contra Gentiles: Book One; God* 1.91.18.

76. Aquinas, *Summa Contra Gentiles: Book One; God* 1.89.14.

77. Aquinas, *Summa Contra Gentiles: Book One; God* 1.91.16.

78. Aquinas, *Summa Contra Gentiles: Book One; God* 1.91.17. Emphasis added.

logic at work. Thomas is reasoning biblically about the text of holy Scripture and making theological judgments about how the entirety of the canon works together to speak of God.

And yet Thomas argues that there are passions that can still *properly* be predicated of God in some cases. There are passions like love and joy that are *properly* predicated of God.[79] The reason for this is that "there are certain passions which, though they do not befit God as passion, do not signify anything by the nature of their species that is repugnant to the divine perfection."[80] These are appetitive acts that bear the same name as some of the passions have. As such, joy and delight are both properly in God because their object and disposition are not repugnant to the divine nature. Delight is of a present good. Its object is good, and its disposition is possessed as joy.[81]

Scotus, similarly, offers a characteristically clear explanation that impassibility is about *not receiving*. For example, there are active and passive principles. Active principles make something whereas passive principles receive something.[82] Therefore, God as impassible cannot be moved to receive anything. But Scotus, unlike Aquinas, conceives of emotions as being apart from the body since they are connected to the will, including the intellect, and not merely the sensible appetite, which is necessarily embodied.[83]

But there are also claims to the effect of a strong maximal model in the medieval period. For example, Anselm explains: "You are merciful according to our way of looking at things and not according to Your way. For when You look upon us in our misery it is we who feel the effect of Your mercy, but You do not experience the feeling."[84] On such a rendering, it appears that no model but the maximal would be able to account for an impassible God.

79. Aquinas, *The Summa Theologiæ of St. Thomas Aquinas*, trans. Fathers of the English Dominican Province, 2nd rev. ed. (Burns Oates & Washbourne, 1920), I.20.1 ad 2.

80. Aquinas, *Summa Contra Gentiles: Book One; God* 1.90.1.

81. Aquinas, *Summa Contra Gentiles: Book One; God* 1.90.1-3.

82. John Duns Scotus, *Selected Writings on Ethics*, trans. Thomas Williams (Oxford University Press, 2017), I, d. 17, pars1, q1, n55.

83. Duns Scotus, *Selected Writings on Ethics* III, d. 33, q. un.

84. Anselm, *Proslogion*, ed. Brian Davies and G. R. Evans (Oxford University Press, 1998), 8.

The Reformation Witness

In the Reformation and post-Reformation period there remains a strong consensus on divine impassibility. They do not deviate from the received theological tradition of the church. Impassibility remains jointly confessed throughout the period in numerous shared confessions: God is without passions. He is incapable of suffering. As Calvin says, God is "beyond all disturbance of mind."[85] Arminius is no different, claiming that God is "devoid of all suffering or feeling; not only because nothing can act against this Essence, for it is of infinite Being and devoid of an external cause; but likewise because it cannot receive the act of anything, for it is of simple Entity."[86] John Gill similarly opines that God is "free from all passion and perturbation of mind."[87] Likewise, William Shedd resolutely states that "God has no passions. He stands in no passive and organic relations to that which is not himself. ... He is not operated upon and moved from the outside, but all his activity is self-determined."[88]

The logic of impassibility for the Reformed is much the same as prior periods. John Calvin's rationale is representative. When we read in Scripture of God being angry, sad, or repenting, as Calvin explains, "we ought not to imagine any emotion in him, but rather to consider that this expression has been taken from our own human experience."[89] In other words, we ought not imagine such disturbances truly represent the way that God is. As Luther explains of *locus classicus* Genesis 6:6, it should be "understood in accordance with the usage of Scripture. One should not imagine that God has a heart or that He can grieve." His grief and repentance refer to their effects and not the divine essence.[90] They are *accommodated* means of communicating something about the divine that far transcends our creaturely reality, though it does have some analogue to our human experience of emotions. In the language

85. John Calvin, *Institutes of the Christian Religion*, ed. John T. McNeill, trans. Ford Lewis Battles (Westminster John Knox, 2006), 1.17.13.

86. Jacob Arminius, *Works of Arminius*, trans. James Nicholes and William Nicholes (Baker, 1996), disputation 4.XVII.

87. John Gill, *A Body of Doctrinal Divinity* (George Keith, 1769), 152.

88. Shedd, *Dogmatic Theology*, 164–65.

89. Calvin, *Institutes of the Christian Religion*, 1.17.13.

90. Martin Luther, *Lectures on Genesis*, ed. Jaroslav Pelikan and Daniel E. Poellot, vol. 2, Luther's Works (Concordia, 1960), 49.

of Thomas, when we read of God being angry, sad, or jealous, these words are metaphorical terms applied to God and not proper.[91] They apply to God in a rough sense once the various creaturely imperfections have been removed.

So, again, for Reformed thinkers, while Scripture certainly *does* speak of divine passions, they ought not be read back literally or properly into the nature of God. Terms like *mercy*, while they predicate something true about God, do not properly apply to God because mercy is naturally a passion in men, necessarily attended with grief, sadness, anxiety, misery, and the like. But none of these experiences can apply to the most blessed God![92] Therefore, God *does* have mercy. But he possesses it in a transcendent manner, experiencing and distributing mercy according to a distinctively divine mode that is far beyond the creaturely experience of sadness and sorrow. Whereas misery is the cause of mercy in us creatures, it causes nothing in God since he cannot "be moved and wrought upon as creatures are."[93]

And yet, while passions are purely metaphorical language for God, many Reformed thinkers predicate divine affections of God in a more straightforward manner given their nature as active acts of the will. However, they remain improper predications in the sense that they imply imperfections, for no creaturely term can truly properly be predicated of God without the analogical process of removing imperfections. For example, Mastricht and Edward Leigh (1602–1671) locate affections as acts of the will. As acts of the will, they sustain relations to creation and set operations in motion for creatures in an analogous way to affection in humans.[94] Therefore, God has affections, though he doesn't have them in the same way creatures have them. So, in this respect, they are what I've called *improper* emotions. They are predicated of God with greater similarity than the metaphorical terms, though they remain distinct from our creaturely modes of affection or emotion.

---

91. Edward Leigh, *A Systeme or Body of Divinity* (William Lee, 1654), 170.

92. Gill, *A Body of Doctrinal Divinity*, 152; Shedd, *Dogmatic Theology*, 166.

93. Gill, *A Body of Doctrinal Divinity*, 153.

94. Petrus van Mastricht, *Theoretical-Practical Theology*, ed. Joel R. Beeke, trans. Todd M. Rester (Reformation Heritage, 2018), 1.2.15.19; Edward Leigh, *A Systeme or Body of Divinity*, 167.

A consistent theme through numerous Reformed thinkers is to define affections properly as human emotions but improperly or metaphorically applied to God by reason of an analogical process. For example, Mastricht suggests that "almost the whole nature of affections consists" in disturbances. As he explains:

> Affections are attributed to him not without a grain of salt, namely, not according to the affections, or the emotions and disturbances of the soul, but only in relation to the effective operations that those affections customarily excite in creatures: that is, the affections that are attributed to God in a human way must not be understood except in a way worthy of God.[95]

John Owen is similarly negative toward affections at points. He argues neither affections nor passions are attributed to God properly but rather metaphorically "in reference to his outward works and dispensations."[96] Owen argues that "*to ascribe affections properly to God is to make him weak, imperfect, dependent, changeable, and impotent.*"[97] The reason for this is because affections in their proper nature are incomplete and imperfect acts of the will. And so, while they are more similar than passions, which are not acts of the will, in humans affections remain incomplete acts, lying "between the firm purpose of the soul and the execution of that purpose."[98] Therefore, affections, like passions, are not proper significations. Rather, they should be understood according to the rule of *theoprepos*, as discussed in chapter 3. All descriptions of God must be taken in a way that is fitting or worthy of him. The truth behind the affection is "interpreted in a suitableness to divine perfection and blessedness."[99] So, God is not properly affectionate because he lacks disturbance. He is never tossed to and fro by the waves or driven and tossed by the winds (Eph 4:14; Jas 1:6). He is eternally free from suffering.

95. Mastricht, *Theoretical-Practical Theology*, 1.2.15.32.

96. John Owen, *Vindiciae Evangelicae; or, The Mystery of the Gospel Vindicated and Socinianism Examined*, ed. William H. Goold (Banner of Truth Trust, 1966), XII:108.

97. Owen, *Vindiciae Evangelicae; or, The Mystery of the Gospel Vindicated and Socinianism Examined*, XII:110. Emphasis original.

98. Owen, *Vindiciae Evangelicae; or, The Mystery of the Gospel Vindicated and Socinianism Examined*, XII:109.

99. Owen, *Vindiciae Evangelicae; or, The Mystery of the Gospel Vindicated and Socinianism Examined*, XII:111; Gill, *A Body of Doctrinal Divinity*, 141.

THE DOGMATIC DEFINITION

As the creedal, confessional, and church traditions have taught us, God is without passions. He is free from suffering. While the language varies across thinkers, there is also consistency in his transcendence of emotion. To whatever degree he experiences emotions, it transcends all creaturely conceptions and lacks any creaturely aspect of imperfection, whether mutability, disturbance, weakness, or otherwise. Therefore, impassibility functions like an apophatic qualifier on emotions, reminding us of their unlikeness to creation.[100] God certainly has and experiences love *properly*. But he doesn't possess love in the incomplete way that humans do. He does not experience it as a rollercoaster of intense emotion. For God love is an eternal disposition of the will toward union. Similarly, God improperly has sorrow and grief. He doesn't have them by way of emotional changes or pain but by denoting his all-loving and good nature to care for his creation and act on their behalf.[101]

Therefore, when considering the nature of impassibility in the classical tradition, what is found is *not*, as Rob Lister confidently proclaims, a "shared recognition" for "the need for a dual affirmation of divine impassibility and divine passion."[102] It is not at all true that either Anselm or Aquinas have dual affirmation of divine passion and divine impassibility predicated of the divine nature.[103] Nor is it true that God is "unhesitatingly portrayed" as passionate and emotional by others like Irenaeus.[104] It does not follow that because there is a diversity of opinion on how to explain divine impassibility that versions properly categorized as passibility can cohere with the classical models of impassibility.[105] Rather, divine passion in the proper sense is completely outlawed by the patristic fathers and only affections are predicated of God, but even so, in a way that removes creaturely imperfections. And it is unacceptable to smooth over these important distinctions by using terms with a "degree of layman-like

100. Gavrilyuk, *The Suffering of the Impassible God*, 173.

101. Weinandy, *Does God Suffer?*, 169.

102. Rob Lister, *God Is Impassible and Impassioned* (Crossway, 2013), 101.

103. Lister, *God Is Impassible and Impassioned*, 112.

104. Lister, *God Is Impassible and Impassioned*, 68.

105. Contra Peckham, *Divine Attributes*, 45.

interchangeability" like Lister casually does.[106] The entire debate about impassibility *requires* precision in terminology. To ignore this necessity is to disqualify oneself from wise and careful theology.

Given the consensus of the tradition, it is difficult to accept a maximal version of divine impassibility since affections like love, joy, and delight are in God, even "properly" in God, according to the Thomistic linguistic framework.[107] There is a degree of difficulty here, though, given the significant variance in how language is deployed. But if taken as I have attempted to define the model with the definitions I have provided for the important terms, I take it that the maximal version is at minimum not preferrable, if not unacceptable. Therefore, either the qualified or apophatic models are sufficient to hold the weight of the classical confession of God as impassible. Both are resolute to deny suffering of God, as the mere doctrine of impassibility requires. And both lack entailments that would deny Scripture or be difficult to square with more traditional expositions of the doctrine. However, the kenotic model is straightforwardly non-classical, in my view. The kenotic model lacks any real grounding in creed, confession, or church. I think the maximal model is likely on similar shaky ground, depending on how it is articulated and what is really meant. The reason I am more reticent to cast it aside is because many can speak in less-than-careful ways that would seem to imply the maximal model. As such, there are a number of contemporary writers who argue in ways that *could* be categorized as a maximal model, though I remain unconvinced this is their true intention. Where theologians are more precise and informed, they avoid such characterization.

DOGMATIC MOTIVATIONS

The motivations for a God that is free from suffering are found in both Scripture and theological and philosophical reasoning. It is not merely an abstract concept from philosophers who have conjured up an idea of what God must be like untethered from his own self-disclosure.

106. Lister, *God Is Impassible and Impassioned*, 35.

107. Emmanuel Durand, *Divine Speech in Human Words: Thomistic Engagements with Scripture*, ed. Matthew K. Minerd (Catholic University of America Press, 2022), 54.

As Paul Gavrilyuk has conceded in his masterful study of patristic thought on impassibility:

> It must be admitted that the Bible ascribes to God a much wider range of human emptions than any philosophically minded pagan of the Hellenistic period would ever find appropriate. Let us note, however, that the biblical authors themselves see such descriptions as at once illuminating and problematic.[108]

Therefore, like the other chapters on the attributes in this book, I seek to provide the exegetical warrant for the doctrine before expanding on the more common arguments in favor of divine impassibility.

THE EXEGETICAL FOUNDATION: HOLY SCRIPTURE

The apostle Paul in his letter to the Romans offers several indications that God is impassible. In Romans 9:5, Paul calls God "blessed forever," which is the motivating logic for impassibility. If God is to be blessed forever, he could never experience suffering, for suffering is not the object of blessedness but torment. Similarly, in Romans 11:33–36, Paul's doxology of "the depth and riches and wisdom and knowledge of God" applies Job 41:11 to the divine. For "who has given a gift to him that he might be repaid? For from him and through him and to him are all things" (Rom 11:35–36). In context Paul is explaining why God's mercy is not a national prerogative for ethnic Jews. There is no presumption that God owes anyone anything based on any aspect.[109] Instead, God is wholly undomesticated and independent. He is self-sufficient and sovereign over all things.[110] Therefore, it is impossible to give God a gift or to make God our debtor. He is indescribably rich and cannot suffer a loss or lack of any sort. No one can act upon him to enrich him in any way. While Paul is not giving a metaphysical treatise, his exegetical logic maps onto what classical thinkers have sought to explain with the doctrine of impassibility.

James 1:13 likewise entails a doctrine of divine impassibility. God cannot be tempted. The reason he cannot be tempted is because he is beyond

---

108. Gavrilyuk, *The Suffering of the Impassible God*, 37.

109. James D. G. Dunn, *Romans 9–16* (Word, 1998), 703.

110. John Murray, *The Epistle to the Romans* (Eerdmans, 1968), 2:107.

suffering. He cannot be acted upon to receive any source of temptation. And James 1:17 offers the positive side of immutability. As James writes: "Every good gift and every perfect gift is from above, coming down from the Father of lights, with whom there is no variation or shadow due to change." As the benevolent source of all that is good and the one that cannot be tempted, God transcends all suffering as indescribably rich, sharing his goodness with all.

Acts 14:11–15 gives an overlooked defense of impassibility. In this story, while Paul and Barnabas are at Lystra working miracles, the crowds begin to worship them, thinking they are gods. But Paul corrects them. And in his correction in verse 15, he grounds his unlikeness to God by saying that he and Barnabas are "of like nature," which is a translation of ὁμοιοπαθής, quite literally, "of like passions." Elsewhere, παθής is used throughout Scripture to refer to divine suffering and divine passion. Indeed, it is the term we use for passions. The reason this is of great value is because when Paul seeks to ground a distinction between him and God, he immediately reaches for a lack of passion. God is impassible while humans are passible.

There is implicit logic for impassibility hidden within Hebrews 2:17–18 and 4:15. Both teach that God the Son had to become like us in every respect. Each explains that the Son became like us in all things with temptation and suffering. The implication from this necessity of becoming incarnate to experience such temptation and suffering is that God could not experience temptation and suffering apart from the incarnation.[111] The link here between suffering and temptation highlights further the importance of James 1:13. Hebrews 2:18 says "because he himself has suffered *when* tempted" (emphasis mine). The logic for the author of Hebrews is that suffering is a passive experience. It is an external action upon us, in this case, temptation. Therefore, James 1:13 and the lack of divine temptation is all the more powerful a reminder that God cannot suffer.

Hosea 11:8–9 is also an important text for classical theology, in particular divine impassibility:

> How can I give you up, O Ephraim?
> How can I hand you over, O Israel?
> How can I make you like Admah?
> How can I treat you like Zeboiim?

111. Steven J. Duby, *Jesus and the God of Classical Theism* (Baker Academic, 2022), 362n135.

> My heart recoils within me;
> my compassion grows warm and tender.
> I will not execute my burning anger;
> I will not again destroy Ephraim
> for I am God and not a man,
> the Holy One in your midst,
> and I will not come in wrath.

There is a juxtaposition of deep feeling, God's heart "recoiling" and his compassion growing "warm and tender." It appears on its face that such a text would mitigate against any form of divine impassibility besides a kenotic one since God is being acted upon from outside himself. The actions of Israel are causing him to feel deep internal turmoil. Yet, the following verse qualifies the divine description with the refrain that God is not a man—he is God. This qualifier is the same as Numbers 23:19: "God is not man, that he should lie, or a son of man, that he should change his mind." The point here is that these descriptions are designed to explain a true reality in the world, but the true meaning must be filtered through the way of negation and way of eminence. Rather than God truly changing his mind, the grief and compassion portrayed here are designed to teach of the experiences of Israel—how they perceive God's *action* toward them. They are designed to teach that God is present. He is near. He is in our midst. He cares. As Paul reminds us, "In him we live and move and have our being" (Acts 17:28). But these actions are grounded in his radical unlikeness—his divine holiness.

PHILOSOPHICAL ARGUMENTATION

There are various theological and philosophical arguments for why God is impassible throughout the tradition. Often the doctrine of divine impassibility has exclusively been drawn from them. Some are more common than others, but each is relevant for thinking about the validity of impassibility.

The Blessedness Argument

One of the main reasons that God cannot experience suffering is because he is blessed. God cannot grieve because as blessed, he is in eternal bliss. As Romans 9:5 confesses, God is over all and blessed *forever*. He is infinitely blessed.[112] To admit a disturbance of passion is to admit of a diminution of divine beatitude. It is to suggest that God is *not* blessed forever.[113] Therefore, as Owen argues, "If he be properly and literally angry, and furious, and wrathful, he is moved, troubled, perplexed, desires revenge, and is neither blessed nor perfect."[114] For Owen and others, then, the argument goes like this:

1. If someone is blessed forever, then they cannot experience suffering.
2. God is blessed forever.
3. Therefore, God cannot experience suffering.

Naturally, the question then becomes what exactly is required for such a divine beatitude. Some have misunderstood this argument as a binary competition wherein God must exclusively think of himself as the most valuable to truly be blessed. His value must "swamp" all others. Therefore, he couldn't possibly be moved by anything external to himself.[115] But such a critique of the blessedness argument misses the mark. It does not need to place the Creator and creation on opposite ends of a value scale. The point, rather, is that *suffering* inhibits blessedness. And suffering comes from being the receiver of any action as the patient.

Others might worry that texts like Matthew 5 mitigate against understanding the pinnacle of blessedness as a lack of suffering since Jesus calls the persecuted *blessed*. Certainly, they did not lack suffering! But if suffering is included in the ultimate concept of beatitude, and not simply a means to it for many of us fallen humans, then the final end state of humanity will also include mourning since the beatitudes likewise call mourning blessed. Indeed, we may well find persecution in the new heavens and new earth! But Revelation 21:4 promises that God will wipe away

112. Mastricht, *Theoretical-Practical Theology*, 1.2.15.32.

113. Charnock, *The Existence and Attributes of God*, 508.

114. Owen, *Vindiciae Evangelicae; or, The Mystery of the Gospel Vindicated and Socinianism Examined*, XII:112.

115. R. T. Mullins, "Why Can't the Impassible God Suffer? Analytic Reflections on Divine Blessedness," *TheoLogica: An International Journal for Philosophy of Religion and Philosophical Theology* 2, no. 1 (2018): 17, https://doi.org/10.14428/thl.v0i0.1313.

every tear from our eyes. No longer will we mourn. Therefore, the pinnacle of joy and beatitude lacks all suffering.

Spirit and Passions Unmixed

One of the most common arguments for divine impassibility is from the fact that God's nature is spiritual. For example, Charnock argues that even if God sought to experience passions, he couldn't because he is pure spirit and thus incapable of being disturbed in such a manner.[116] The reason spirituality entails a lack of passions is because passions, by definition, require the body.[117] So, the argument is rather simple:

1. If *x* is immaterial, then *x* cannot have passions.
2. God is immaterial.
3. Therefore, God cannot have passions.

The only real way to deny this argument is to argue that passions can be had by immaterial beings. But if passions are capable of being had by immaterial beings, then we would need to make significant conjectures about how the tradition would have responded to such argumentation since they denied such a possibility. Even so, denying this one argument would not close the case for impassibility.

Co-Suffering Is Less Virtuous

A common newer argument in favor of impassibility is to show that an impassible God is more virtuous in times of hurt and pain. Steven Duby has explained this well:

> Even in human situations, one's participation in the grief of another in and of itself is not what is virtuous. It is one's attentiveness to the well being of someone who suffers, one's readiness to remain present with them and help them in their suffering, that is virtuous. And sometimes when that propensity to help and comfort has no

116. Charnock, *The Existence and Attributes of God*, 507.

117. Gilles Emery, "The Immutability of the God of Love and the Problem of Language Concerning the 'Suffering of God,' " in *Divine Impassibility and the Mystery of Human Suffering*, ed. James F. Keating and Thomas Joseph White, trans. Thomas Joseph White (Eerdmans, 2009), 64.

> reference to alleviating any suffering of one's own, the benevolence involved is all the more brilliant.[118]

For Duby, the lack of need in oneself, which is entailed in impassibility, makes God's presence far superior. Grief, pain, loss, and co-suffering by themselves are not necessary features of love. Nor does their absence lessen love.[119] The only reason that being *moved* by another to co-suffer with them would be virtuous is if we *needed* that motivation to love them.[120] But God needs no motivation to love like we do. In fact, Paul Gavrilyuk suggests that a fellow-sufferer *cannot* help suffers. He claims that passibility trivializes suffering and falsely romanticizes suffering as intrinsically valuable and redemptive when it is not.[121]

The Goodness Argument

Another argument in favor of divine impassibility is based on the nature of good and evil. The general idea is that suffering is always caused by a privation of good (evil), and since God can never lack goodness of any sort, he cannot suffer.[122] The argument could be put roughly as follows:

1. If x suffers, then x lacks some good.
2. God never lacks any good.
3. Therefore, God cannot suffer.

The premise that is liable to be challenged is the first. Maybe there is a scenario in which something could suffer without having some privation of the good. But if suffering is inherently defective, or a lack, it is hard to imagine any example wherein someone could suffer and *not* lack something good. If true, some may challenge the second, that God never lacks any good. But if we accept the definition of goodness from chapter 5, this is not possible. One must revise not only traditional theism and common intuitions about God but the numerous scriptural claims that ascribe goodness to the greatest degree to God in whom

118. Duby, *Jesus and the God of Classical Theism*, 360.

119. Weinandy, *Does God Suffer?*, 160.

120. Duby, *Jesus and the God of Classical Theism*, 361.

121. Gavrilyuk, "God's Impassible Suffering in the Flesh: The Promise of Paradoxical Christology," 145.

122. Weinandy, *Does God Suffer?*, 157.

there is no variation or shadow. The reason God cannot perform evil acts like temptation and lying is because he is *good*. And to allow for a removal of his goodness is to destabilize the entire concept of God that arises from Scripture.

POTENTIAL PROBLEMS AND SOLUTIONS

As with each classical doctrine, divine impassibility has been subjected to significant critique over the last few centuries. But impassibility, more than some other classical doctrines, tends to be mocked: The impassible God is of no help in time of need. What sort of person could see God's acts in Scripture—he hears his people's cries, is moved to his heart, and responds to comfort—and conclude that the opposite is the case? God *isn't* moved by any of this! The impassible God is a frigid deity. Of course, these descriptions have been shown to be false. And yet there are challenges that *should* be addressed for any honest and fair thinker. Classical theism should never devolve into traditional*ism* that substitutes platitudes for clear thinking. Besides, if something is true, there should never be fear of genuinely hearing from critics.

BIBLICAL PROBLEMS

It is the Bible that motivates many of the critiques against divine impassibility, as has been hinted at throughout. There is a "complete lack of biblical evidence" according to some.[123] The simplest critique is simply that the literal text of Scripture is clear: God is passible. He is grieved in both Old and New Testaments (Gen 6:6; Eph 4:30). He gets very angry. Remember when his wrath burned hot against the Israelites, so much so that Scripture says his wrath would "consume them" (Exod 32:10)? What is an impassible God to say? Is this text not true? Does the impassible God really say that instead of being angry and having wrath he has no emotion? That what we see in the Bible isn't true? That there is some sort of deception? But it is not this text alone. God is constantly portrayed as engaging in "back-and-forth" relationships with his creation.[124] As John Peckham argues, "The God of

---

123. R. T. Mullins, "Classical Theism, Christology, and the Two Sons Worry," in *Impeccability and Temptation: Understanding Christ's Divine and Human Will*, ed. Johannes Grössl and Klaus von Stosch, Routledge Studies in Analytic and Systematic Theology (Routledge, 2021), 167.

124. Peckham, *Divine Attributes*, 41.

Scripture is repeatedly grieved and provoked."[125] To reinterpret these texts in the ways necessary for impassibility is to "impose alien presuppositions" on the text.[126] And the recourse to "accommodation" is meaningless because all language about God is accommodative.[127] As D. A. Carson has forcefully argued, "the price is too heavy" to deny "that God has an emotional life" and to insist "that all the biblical evidence to the contrary is nothing more than anthropomorphism." If divine impassibility is true,

> you may then rest in God's sovereignty, but you can no longer rejoice in his love. You may rejoice only in a linguistic expression that is an accommodation of some reality of which we cannot conceive, couched in the anthropopathism of love. Give me a break. Paul did not pray that his readers might be able to grasp the height and depth and length and breadth of an anthropopathism and know this anthropopathism that surpasses knowledge.[128]

The classical theologian disagrees with the entire premise. This is not how we read and interpret Scripture. Nor is it a fair representation of the classical God.[129] The idea that we can (1) simplistically assume everything said of God is literally true in the most wooden of senses, and (2) merely assemble various statements apart from context to construct sound theology is the real fool's errand. We must ask how texts *function* in the larger whole. To do so is not to relativize the force of Scripture and relegate God to an anthropopathism. Instead, it is to remember that the debate over impassibility cannot remain at the micro level where terms are used in Scripture. There is a "logic of broader doctrinal developments" and a "complex web of communal beliefs and practices" that are

---

125. Peckham, *Divine Attributes*, 43.

126. Peckham, *Divine Attributes*, 57.

127. Peckham, "Qualified Passibility," 94.

128. Carson, *The Difficult Doctrine of the Love of God*, 58–59.

129. While I am rather critical of Carson here, I should be clear that I owe him (as do many other evangelicals) a great debt. During my undergraduate studies he unlocked a love for Scripture and theology for me. Without his work I would not have progressed in my own understanding and knowledge of the divine mysteries. Further, as with many of the evangelicals I have been critical of at points, one should be as charitable to them (and to older saints who can no longer speak for themselves!) as one would be to a fellow church member one sees in worship every Sunday. Many of them did not have the benefit of the classical "revival" that many are seeing in Protestant and evangelical circles today.

necessary for a wise reading of Scripture.[130] Theology is not done merely by "counting verses" but by weighing them in light of the entirety of the canon. We cannot separate and isolate texts from the sequence of the biblical narratives and the overall theological development. Terms and descriptions receive their meaning *within* a broader narrative and not just the isolated paragraph or verse from whence we read.[131]

One cannot simply see God's "grief" in Genesis 6 and immediately conclude that God is passible. The reason is that later texts teach us that simplistic readings are not the divine intention. The grief *does* teach us something true, but it's not teaching a literal ontological lesson. God's grief and sorrow are properly manifested in his compassionate love.[132] Durand turns this objection on its head by arguing that "God alone can have endless sorrow lived solely for the other, without turning back to himself or experiencing pain for himself. ... God's sorrow is more than a passion. It is a pure affection of his loving will, entirely concerned for the other without itself being altered."[133] The idea, then, is that when we read grief in a purely human way, we are missing the deepest meaning of the text. We are forgetting to remove the imperfections of fallen human nature from our concepts.

But we also see later in Scripture, such as in Hebrews 4:15, that for God to sympathize with our weaknesses *as we experience and feel them*, he had to become human. Without the incarnation such human sympathy was impossible, hence impassibility. Therefore, from the perspective of the Son's human nature, suffering *is* proper to the Son and by virtue of the Son is predicated of God. Full stop. Every Chalcedonian Christian must affirm that God suffers, just like they must affirm that Mary is the mother of God.[134] As Thomas Joseph White explains, "All that occurs to Jesus by virtue of his human nature, from the time of his conception until the moment of his death, is properly ascribed to God himself."[135] This is why we can truly say that

130. Gavrilyuk, *The Suffering of the Impassible God*, 65.

131. Durand, *Divine Speech in Human Words*, 116–17.

132. Durand, *Divine Speech in Human Words*, 62.

133. Durand, *Divine Speech in Human Words*, 135.

134. James F. Keating and Thomas Joseph White, "Introduction: Divine Impassibility in Contemporary Theology," in *Divine Impassibility and the Mystery of Human Suffering*, ed. James F. Keating and Thomas Joseph White (Eerdmans, 2009), 17.

135. Thomas Joseph White, *The Incarnate Lord* (Catholic University of America Press, 2017), 64.

God purchased the church with his blood and that the Lord of glory was crucified (Acts 20:28; 1 Cor 2:8). But God the Son suffers *only* in virtue of his human nature and not his divine nature, which is properly impassible.[136]

Similarly, divine anger teaches us something. But it doesn't teach us God's literal ontological makeup. It doesn't teach us that God is volatile or prone to extreme mood swings. Uncontrollable, white-hot anger is a mark of the pagan deities. Instead, we must purify the concept of anger to see how or if it might improperly apply to God. In humans, anger motivates us and intensifies our passion to not merely passively suffer unjust situations. It enables us to fight against them.[137] But an omnipotent, omniscient, and maximally perfect God is never in need of motivation to reverse unjust situations. God has the perfect possession of justice. And so, when anger is attributed to God, it is not the *passion* of violent emotion that is being taught but God's intention to remedy an unjust situation.[138] Therefore, the wise exegete of Scripture understands that the proper sense of terms like *repent*, *grief*, *jealousy*, *anger*, and *mercy* do not "accord with the nature of the subject since God's wisdom includes all that will ever come to pass."[139]

PHILOSOPHICAL PROBLEMS

Beyond the biblical portrayals of God, there are further "philosophical" and theological challenges to divine impassibility. Many of these are relatively recent articulations that often relate to various human emotions that we intuitively ascribe goodness to. For example, it is good to be compassionate or empathetic. Therefore, based on what we naturally take these terms to mean, there appears to be an obvious conflict with an impassible God since he supposedly cannot be compassionate or empathetic. However, in times past, common criticisms often related to the improper importing of Greek thought. But numerous studies over the last several decades have proven this thesis wholly untenable, so much so that new arguments against impassibility rarely, if ever, deploy these strategies. Greek thought, rather than being what classical thinkers plagiarized, is widely variegated

136. Gill, *A Body of Doctrinal Divinity*, 615.

137. Durand, *Divine Speech in Human Words*, 87.

138. Durand, *Divine Speech in Human Words*, 96.

139. Duby, *Jesus and the God of Classical Theism*, 350.

on classical doctrines.[140] And early thinkers show little awareness of them as sources, anyway.[141] But even if they were to pillage exclusively from a monolithic Greek thought without baptizing it, this does not mean the view is wrong or poisoned. That is a genetic fallacy. Therefore, in what follows I survey some of the latest criticisms. Of course, my decision on which to include is necessarily highly selective given the range of objections. But I believe these at least give a fair sense for the intuitions at work for those that deny impassibility.

The Problem of Love

A common refrain from those uncomfortable with the impassible God is that it excludes true love from his being. Daniel Castelo is representative with his criticism that "the very idea of love requires an openness and vulnerability that creates necessary space for suffering."[142] He draws on those like Moltmann, who in the shadow of the pain and suffering in places like Auschwitz argues that we *must* understand God as passible. He must be suffering *there*:

> Any other answer would be blasphemy. There cannot be any other Christian answer to the question of this torment. To speak here of a God who could not suffer would make God a demon. To speak here of an absolute God would make God an annihilating nothingness. To speak here of an indifferent God would condemn men to indifference.[143]

Moltmann, thus, thinks there is no room for the impassible God. He would be a demon. Instead, "God takes man so seriously that he suffers under the actions of man and can be injured by them."[144] The basic idea behind these sort of arguments goes as follows:

1. If *x* is loving, then *x* suffers with those *x* loves.
2. God is loving.
3. Therefore, God suffers with those he loves.

---

140. Gavrilyuk, *The Suffering of the Impassible God*, 21–22.
141. Gavrilyuk, *The Suffering of the Impassible God*, 34–35.
142. Castelo, "Qualified Impassibility," 57.
143. Jürgen Moltmann, *The Crucified God* (SCM, 2015), 207.
144. Moltmann, *The Crucified God*, 204.

The argument is a valid one. The conclusion follows from the premises. However, there is no need for the classical theologian to accept that love necessarily includes suffering, or at least the "openness" to it. For the classical theologian, God's love is so strong, so powerful, and so wise that it never suffers. God is indestructibly rich. Without an overriding biblical or overpowering philosophical rationale for the necessity of suffering for true love, it is natural to reject this criticism.

The Problem of Knowledge

The basic issue here relates to divine omniscience. Some argue that since some aspects of knowledge are only possible through emotions, then God must be passible.[145] Linda Zagzebski's model of divine omnisubjectivity has been deployed in this argument more than probably any other, though she avoids weaponizing it against classical models of God and attempts to suggest a way to hold the two doctrines in tension.[146] In a nutshell, omnisubjectivity means that God not only knows all universals or all true propositions but all particulars, including the particularity of each human mind. He doesn't just know anxiety in the abstract. He knows *your* anxiety. Zagzebski therefore argues that "God's knowledge must include knowledge of our subjective experiences not only because our subjective states are part of everything and God knows everything, but because God is the ultimate cause of those states and keeps them in existence."[147]

It is impossible to lay out the entire argument that Zagzebski makes in defense of omnisubjectivity, but a general summary is captured by her here:

> Our desires and many of our feelings have intentional objects, and God's awareness of those states does not imply that God adopts the same intentional object. God's consciousness of my revulsion of snakes is not revulsion of snakes. God's consciousness of someone's desire to harm is not a desire to harm. But revulsion feels a certain way apart from its intentional object, and a desire feels a certain

145. Anastasia Philippa Scrutton, *Thinking Through Feeling* (Bloomsbury, 2013), 73.

146. For example, Mullins deploys Zagzebski's work against impassibility, but Zagzebski herself criticizes Mullins's arguments: R. T. Mullins, "Omnisubjectivity and the Problem of Creepy Divine Emotions," *Religious Studies* 58, no. 1 (2022): 162–79, https://doi.org/10.1017/S0034412520000220.

147. Linda Trinkaus Zagzebski, *Omnisubjectivity: An Essay on God and Subjectivity* (Oxford University Press, 2023), 35, https://doi.org/10.1093/oso/9780197682098.003.0002.

> way apart from its object. An omnisubjective God must be aware of the way those states feel, and that awareness cannot be perceptual.[148]

So, if God is omniscient for Zagzebski, he must be omnisubjective. And if he is omnisubjective, he must know what it *feels* like for me to experience life, which includes moments of pain, grief, and anguish. God's knowledge extends beyond perception. The argument then could go as follows:

1. If God is omniscient, then God is omnisubjective.
2. If God is omnisubjective, then God feels human emotions.
3. If God feels human emotions, then he is passible.
4. God is omniscient.
5. Therefore, God is passible.

But Zagzebski herself considers the possibility that God can fully grasp our feelings "without taking on the feeling itself" and thus maintain impassibility. Grasping a feeling, then, is not identical to "feeling it." And so, the classical theologian could deny premise 2. Omnisubjectivity does not entail an infinitely "feeling" God. This is precisely what Zagzebski argues: "If God is passible, it is not because of omnisubjectivity."[149] The defense here could mirror the sort of distinction used to explain how God can have pleasure in creation without "receiving" anything from it. Pleasure follows from a perfect act of "willing a good for its own sake."[150] In an analogous way, knowledge comes from this same act of willing that is creative and not "receptive" in a sense that would deny impassibility.

But the classical theologian could also deny premise 1 and reject omnisubjectivity as a perfection. Given that Zagzebski's account is not latent in the tradition, it is hard to determine what the classical tradition would think of omnisubjectivity, though I have strong intuitions that they would reject it. Either way, there are several ways to avoid any unsavory implications for divine impassibility here.

---

148. Zagzebski, *Omnisubjectivity: An Essay on God and Subjectivity*, 72.

149. Zagzebski, *Omnisubjectivity: An Essay on God and Subjectivity*, 102.

150. Duns Scotus, *Selected Writings on Ethics*, I, d. 1, pars 2, q1, n. 68; Aristotle, *Nicomachean Ethics*, trans. Terence Irwin, 3rd ed. (Hackett, 2019), 1174b14–23.

The Problem of Compassion and Empathy

A final possible problem for divine impassibility worth exploring is that of compassion and empathy. The basic idea is that compassion is quite literally *suffering with* and not just benevolence.[151] And since God has compassion, he must suffer. Similarly, empathy transfers an emotion from one subject to another and helps them better understand a person.[152] Since empathy is a virtue, then God must possess it. An empathetic God, then, must also be passible given the experience of emotion *from another*. We could formally state the argument as follows:

1. If *x* is compassionate or empathetic, then *x* suffers (or is moved by another).
2. God is compassionate or empathetic.
3. Therefore, God suffers (or is moved by another).

But there are reasons to deny premise 1. Before offering the rationale, it is wise to consider Paul Gavrilyuk's cheeky reminder that "to make God super-emotional and omni-relational" does not secure divine compassion. For "God may indeed be relational, but so is the Devil."[153] In other words, there is no intrinsic value to being maximally emotional *simpliciter*. Often, in many of these criticisms of impassibility there is an unexamined assumption that emotions are intrinsically valuable in a naive way.

Now, the classical theologian should reject the first premise. First, there is no reason to assume compassion entails suffering in this way. Emmanuel Durand is especially perceptive here:

> The divine compassion transcends emotion and empathy, though it takes up their positive outcome: engagement and action. God's ontological impassibility is the condition for pure compassion, without him needing to experience the mere affection of his own self before the sufferings undergone by his creatures.[154]

151. Scrutton, *Thinking Through Feeling*, 75–76.

152. Mullins, *God and Emotion*, 31.

153. Gavrilyuk, "God's Impassible Suffering in the Flesh: The Promise of Paradoxical Christology," 142.

154. Durand, *Divine Speech in Human Words*, 132.

The idea, then, is that compassion for God is not exactly like compassion for me as a limited human. The real beauty of compassion (or empathy) is the *outcome* and not the journey there. It is the action to absolve me of suffering.[155] And this is precisely what God provides. For example, when Jesus has "compassion" on the crowd in Matthew 14:14, his compassion leads to *action*. Jesus heals their sick. He doesn't merely evaluate their felt notion of suffering and pain. He *does* something. And it is the action that is the core of compassion. For us humans, we need to "feel" deep emotions in our compassion and empathy because we lack the internal motivation to act. The reason I am filled with a strong emotional experience, like sadness, when I see my children trip and scrape their knees is because I need to be moved to action. But God needs no such motivation.

However, R. T. Mullins has advanced this problem further by focusing on empathy. He suggests that for God to lack empathy is for God to be a psychopath, since those that lack empathy are clinically diagnosed as psychopaths. And psychopaths are "grandiose, manipulative, and deceitful" because they lack empathy.[156] But there are two problems here. First, it is not clear why God must be empathetic. Second, it is wholly unclear why a lack of empathy entails traits like deceit or manipulation. Mullins makes no argument for such an assertion. He merely states it and assumes it is true. But there is no good reason to think this. Why should we think that God is deceitful or manipulative if he doesn't experience my pain like me and yet loves me with an unending, pursuing, and perfecting love that rescues me from my pain? Surely, I am much more interested in God's power and kindness to eradicate my suffering than I am in him wallowing with me. I want his presence *and power*. I want a closeness that is defined by healing, comforting, and restoration—not co-suffering and anguish.

IMPASSIBILITY FOR THE CHURCH

The church should take comfort in God's impenetrable goodness that is his impassibility. He is indestructibly rich and deals bountifully with us all. There is a beauty to the classical doctrine of God that should

155. Emery, "The Immutability of the God of Love and the Problem of Language Concerning the 'Suffering of God,'" 56.

156. R. T. Mullins, "Closeness with God: A Problem for Divine Impassibility," *Journal of Analytic Theology* 10 (2022): 237–38, https://doi.org/10.12978/jat.2022-10.17-51-65122018.

not be ignored, sidelined, or marginalized. It is not simply abstract and theoretical reasoning. It has real-world impact. God's impassibility assures us of his kindness, care, and wisdom. It tells us the story of an all-wise God who can be present and love in a way that transcends any created reality. It promises real joy. It is a message of hope for those in desperate need.[157] Instead of God needing to feel alongside us at every moment in our deepest pain, we are assured of his goodness, commitment, presence, and mission to restore.[158] The impassible God can offer such care because he is not able to be robbed of himself.[159] God is where moth and rust do not destroy.

As David Bentley Hart reminds us, divine impassibility teaches us that God requires no "supplement of any external force in order to know and to love creation in its uttermost depths." Instead, it teaches us that God is infinitely active and eternally loving.[160] There is nothing at stake for God in our suffering. There is nothing he might add or lose. And so, he is able to perfectly love us, to be perfectly present, and to truly wipe away every tear from our eyes.[161] But what is even greater is that God *does* weep with us in the glory of the incarnation. God the Son in virtue of his human nature *feels*. Therefore, the church gets to have its cake and eat it too. It can sing of divine presence unhindered.

John Chrysostom also highlights the ecclesial value of divine impassibility. He exhorts:

> If the wrath of God were a passion, one might well despair as being unable to quench the flame which he had kindled by so many evil doings; but since the Divine nature is passionless, even if He punishes, even if He takes vengeance, he does this not with wrath, but with tender care, and much loving-kindness; wherefore it behooves us to be of much good courage, and to trust in the power of repentance. For even those who have sinned against Him He is not wont

157. David Bentley Hart, "No Shadow of Turning: On Divine Impassibility," *Pro Ecclesia* 11, no. 2 (2002): 185.

158. Durand, *Divine Speech in Human Words*, 41.

159. Duby, *Jesus and the God of Classical Theism*, 28.

160. Hart, "Impassibility as Transcendence: On the Infinite Innocence of God," 301.

161. Gavrilyuk, "God's Impassible Suffering in the Flesh: The Promise of Paradoxical Christology," 140–41.

> to visit with punishment for His own sake; for no harm can traverse that divine nature; but He acts with a view to our advantage.[162]

Without impassibility, we would be at the mercy of passion. We would be at the behest of fury. Anxiety would be warranted. But the impassible God, *because of his impassibility*, is guaranteed to deal tenderly with us. He always works to our advantage. Rather than being the frigid doctrine of the philosophers, impassibility is the comforting doctrine of the church. It is for the grandmothers and the toddlers. In times of fear, anxiety, and need, we call upon the impassible God.

CONCLUSION

Impassibility in popular contemporary discussions is often truncated. Too many assume it entails that God lacks all emotions, which makes for an easy target. But this is not the case for the classical tradition. God does have emotions. Therefore, the maximal model is inconsistent with both the tradition and Scripture. But God does lack passions. If God were to have passions, we would be unsure of his goodness. We would be unsure of his promises. His faithfulness would be cast in doubt. Therefore, it is good news that God is impassible.

But God's lack of passions is not license for us to passionately despise those that misunderstand or modify the classical doctrine of God. Especially as it relates to impassibility, there is difficulty and nuance. There are also many well-natured intuitions that arise from Scripture to worry about what might have poorly been taught as impassibility. As classical theologians, we should always praise intuitions, worries, and ideas that arise from Scripture. So, instead of repeatedly castigating those that question impassibility, the classical theologian should (and can!) take a positive approach. It is an opportunity to recast the vision for the wonder of the impassible God. It is an opportunity to invite weary travelers and skeptics alike to the feast found at the table of the indestructibly rich God who offers a bountiful meal.

---

162. John Chrysostom, "An Exhortation to Theodore After His Fall," in *Nicene and Post-Nicene Fathers*, ed. Philip Schaff, trans. W. R. W. Stephens (Parker, 1899), 9.4.

10

ENJOYING THE CLASSICAL FEAST

At long last we've reached the end of this brief tour of classical theism. I've attempted to cover a topic that is quite honestly impossible to summarize appropriately in the space of one book. I know sections of this work are underdeveloped due to space constraints—and due to my own limitations of knowledge as a finite human. Regardless, I hope it isn't the end of your exploration. In my attempt to retrieve an old and ever-new dogma of the church in a fresh way I've sought to invite you to continue laboring, cherishing, and wondering about the classical doctrine of God. There are treasures within the tradition, within Scripture, and within the life of the church awaiting us. These treasures are not merely abstract theoretical ideas to study as a scientist or physicist but spiritual food and nourishment to our souls. They are a feast from which we delight in God and commune with the church catholic. They are resources that heighten the true sacrament of ecclesiastical communion with our Triune God and the church whom he purchased with his blood.

Therefore, I urge you to take up and read. Read Scripture. Read the tradition. Read, dare I say it, philosophy. But don't just read. Share your discoveries with others, and most important, allow the classical doctrine of God to fuel your worship within the church to the praise of our good God. The classical doctrines are supposed to be gasoline for our experience of God. They are not merely academic tropes for debate or intellectual superiority. They are fire for the church's confession of God as God. The steadfastness of the immutable God is kindling for the word preached. The unbreakable richness of the impassible God is firewood for the Christian life. The nearness of the eternal God is tinder for the sacraments. The generosity of the simple God is a blow torch for our union with him. Of course, each dogma is fuel for every aspect of the Christian life. But they each impel Christian faith and ecclesial worship.

Therefore, my hope and aim are that the introduction to these dogmas will be of great comfort, joy, and delight for you. While they may not be of direct practical relevance for your morning routine, they remain essential to our lives as *human*. Too often we assume things are only valuable insofar as they lead to productivity, efficiency, and usually money. The refrain from most American churches is all too common. Why care about complicated theological debates? How does that help me be a better parent? How does that equip me to create a business case at work? And on the objections go. Academic theology—or at least theology that goes beyond simple platitudes—is stuck in an ivory tower, divorced from the life of the local church and totally ignorant of my normal life that requires me to pay the bills.

But these criticisms are all bark and no bite. True enough, the whole of the Christian life is not bound up with intellectual pursuits. We are not merely to know God intellectually. We are to love him with our hands, too, as we labor to serve. So, maybe there does exist a person that is too heavenly minded for any earthly good. But I have yet to meet them. And if I fail to find the value in fixing my eyes on the things above, the problem is with me and not the heavenly minded person. But whether or not ivory tower theologians exist (who coincidently, must also pay bills and live in the "real world"), our natural propensity to fail to see value in difficult theology is problematic for several more reasons.

First, as we've seen, a deep appreciation and articulation of the classical doctrine of God fuels our confession of God as God. All true theology leads to worship. And this is the most practical of ends that we could ever labor toward. Therefore, no matter how abstract the idea may appear, all of God's world is charged with his beauty and is intrinsically designed to lead us by the hand to worship.

Second, we, especially as a Western society, have often lost our vision for what is most fundamental to being *human*. The hunger for truth, goodness, and beauty is forgotten. But these are our deepest longings as *humans*. God has intrinsically designed us with these needs that cannot be met by more money, more power, or more influence. There is a reason the rich and famous remain empty. Truth, goodness, and beauty are goods that are ends in themselves and not merely means to another. We are not created as creatures for endless "productivity" that is measurable.[1] We are designed to know, savor, and experience God for eternity. Therefore, even difficult areas of theology are part of what fulfills our longings as human. In some deep and mysterious way, laboring to know difficult dogmas for no purpose other than experiencing God is very good. It makes us more human and lead us to deeper union with God. There is no "practical" justification needed.

Third, our churches are not made only of those uninterested in intellectual pursuits. The parishioners that fill the pews are not all content to know as little as possible. Many in our churches are salivating for robust, sound doctrine. They are pining for serious dogma. They are searching for the challenge of Mount Everest. Their minds cause their hearts to be stirred and inflamed. And even those that aren't actively seeking have the capacities to learn, though they must be inspired. While it is true that the church is not made purely of academic elites or those of ravenous desire, the demographic is probably true of the reverse as well—the church is not made purely of those unable or unwilling to exercise intellectual effort. Many of the members of our churches hold important careers that require serious intellectual abilities. They only need a compelling story to inspire them. What is needed is careful pastoral wisdom to unlock passion for the classical doctrine of God. So, we *should* speak to the life of the mind. And we should speak, and preach, vigorously. We may not be brains on sticks, but we certainly have brains for a reason.

Finally, for those that remain unconvinced of classical theism, I pray your heart still has been warmed. I also pray you've found yourself surprised. There is more to the Christian tradition and to theological defenses of classical theism than you may have thought. Maybe I've presented an argument in a different way or introduced a new and novel defense. Or maybe I've helped you to see why there are differences between the models of God, which often boil down to different interpretive paradigms

---

1. See Ross D. Inman, *Christian Philosophy as a Way of Life: An Invitation to Wonder* (Baker Academic, 2023), 116–18.

for Scripture. Whatever the case, I know better than to think I'll have convinced everyone, but I hope, if you remain distant from classical theism, that you feel welcome. Because you are. All are welcome at the table of our good God.

THESES OF MERE CLASSICAL THEISM

As a concluding summary, I provide nine theses of mere classical theism that can serve as a mini-instructive manual for classical theism as I've articulated it here.

1. Classical theism arises organically from the Bible.
2. Classical theism is most fundamentally concerned with articulating the coherence and foundation of God's everlasting love and covenant faithfulness.
3. Classical theism is undergirded by divine aseity and divine goodness.
4. The "classical" attributes are primarily negative in scope.
5. Classical theism has shared sensibilities about the epistemological process.
6. Classical theism is the consensus view of the church catholic.
7. The classical tradition and classical theism necessitate piety.
8. The *telos* of classical theism is doxology.

THESES OF MERE CLASSICAL THEISM EXPLAINED

1. Classical theism arises organically from the Bible.

Classical theologians are deeply committed to scriptural exegesis and the authority of divine revelation. Read the biblical commentaries of classical theologians. Read the polemical texts of classical theologians. Read the systematic theologies of classical theologians. In every example one will find a wide and deep commitment to and engagement with the sacred page. Because of the claims of Scripture itself, classical theism organically arises.

2. Classical theism is most fundamentally concerned with articulating the coherence and foundation of God's everlasting love and covenant faithfulness.

While many treatments of classical theism are highly technical and specialized, classical theism is ultimately focused on explaining God's love and care for us. Because God is simple, immutable, impassible, and eternal, he is always sure and trustworthy. This belief grounds his steadfast love and faithfulness. Because God is eternal, his love remains forevermore. Because God is immutable, his love never changes or vanishes.

3. Classical theism is undergirded by divine aseity and divine goodness.

Aseity and goodness should always be prioritized in any description of God. Because God's goodness is immutable, he always keeps his promises. He never changes! His promises are sure. As *a se* God is wholly independent and wholly full, which drives our beliefs that God is simple, impassible, and the like. God is wholly good in every respect. He never changes, and his promises are forever sure.

4. The "classical" attributes are primarily negative in scope.

The classical attributes are apophatic qualifiers on the nature of God and should not be turned into positive perfections. If we turn attributes like simplicity into a positive perfection they are no longer properly understood as the church catholic has articulated them. They also begin to cause logical and biblical problems for understanding who God is.

5. Classical theism has shared sensibilities about the epistemological process.

These shared sensibilities include a wide range of concepts, but six key loci in particular. First, those in the classical tradition understand that the community in the church is to exercise a primary interpretive voice. Second, they believe that natural theology is a God-given resource and exercise. Third, they argue that we should not confine ourselves to only one tradition for resources. Fourth, they regularly rely on the divine names that teach us about the nature of God in a special way. Fifth, the classical tradition believes that Scripture speaks in various modes, and we should be careful to not be overly literal. Finally, it is common throughout that classical tradition to think we can know God well through the ways of eminence, negation, and causality.

6. Classical theism is the consensus view of the church catholic.

We find classical theism in the ecumenical councils, the Protestant confessional developments, and in most of the great Christian theologians. We forsake it at our own peril. As such, the classical tradition exemplifies catholicity. This is why there is a *mere* classical theism. The tradition is variegated with numerous rich sub-traditions within. Each sub-tradition, whether Roman, Eastern, Lutheran, Presbyterian, or Baptist, offers unique resources and inflections that make the symphony of classical theism beautiful. Therefore, we should avoid overly narrow proclamations on what is and is not "classical."

The consensus of the classical tradition, with all its variegated beauty, invites us to both retrieve the ancient dogma and to explore, develop, and defend it in new ways. The classical tradition provides a theological culture that resources continued development and growth. The church through its worship and witness teaches us about the nature of God across time and space. Therefore, the classical tradition through time is both orthodox and modern, ruthlessly committed to the good deposit but eagerly explaining orthodoxy for our time. It does not fear the development of doctrine so long as it is done in an organic and faithful fashion.

The consensus of the classical tradition on the divine attributes is well summarized by "mere" definitions of simplicity, immutability, eternity, and impassibility. Mere classical divine simplicity means that God is wholly and fully himself, not constituted or composed by anything. Mere classical divine immutability means that God does not change ontologically in any respect. His knowledge, will, power, decrees, and perfections all admit of no change whatsoever. Mere classical divine eternity means that God lacks beginning, end, and succession. Mere classical divine impassibility means that God does not have passions and to whatever degree he experiences emotions, they transcend all creaturely conceptions and lack any creaturely aspect of imperfection, whether mutability, disturbance, weakness, or otherwise.

7. The classical tradition and classical theism necessitate piety.

The true and proper theologian is one of Christian virtue. We encounter God most clearly through the word and sacrament, which inflames and impels our faith. Christian habits of prayer, worship, evangelism, confession, and repentance all teach us about who God is.

8. The *telos* of classical theism is doxology.

Like all theology, classical theism is meant to lead us to praise of God. This is why it is an eminently ecclesial doctrine. It guides, guards, and fuels the worship of the church catholic.

"For from him and through him and to him are all things.
To him be glory forever. Amen."
—Romans 11:36

GLOSSARY OF TERMS

accident: Properties that inhere in or depend on substances.
apophatic theology: An approach to theology that avoids ascribing positive things to God. Instead, God is described in negative terms, denying predicates of him (e.g., he is *im*mutable, *im*passible, etc.).
classical theism: The family of views that claims that God is simple, immutable, impassible, and eternal.
divine aseity: God is completely independent of everything besides himself and completely full through himself.
divine eternity: God lacks beginning, end, and succession.
divine immutability: God cannot change.
divine impassibility: God cannot suffer.
divine simplicity: God lacks all composition that characterizes creatures. He is an indivisible unity and entirely self-consistent.
dogmatic theology: A theological method that exposits and defends the faith recognized and confessed by the church with its end goal as doxology.
dynamic theory of time: The passage of time is real and independent of our own conscious experience of it.
extrinsic predicate: A predicate a thing satisfies not purely in virtue of intrinsic features it has.
extrinsic property: Properties an object has that are dependent on things external to itself.
eternalism: The passage of time isn't real. The "now" of the present has no special privileged place.
intrinsic predicate: A predicate a thing satisfies in virtue of intrinsic features it has and not necessarily intrinsic properties it has.
intrinsic property: Properties an object has independent from everything else.

Leibniz's Law: For a thing to be identical it must be symmetric (e.g., if a=b, then anything true of a is true of b and vice versa), reflexive (e.g., everything is identical to itself), and transitive (e.g., if a=b and b=c, then a=c).
mereology: The study of parts and wholes.
natural revelation: God's objective revelation in nature.
natural theology: The task of utilizing the material content of natural revelation to understand God.
neo-classical theism: The family of views about God that denies one or more of the "classical" attributes (simplicity, immutability, impassibility, or eternity).
nominalism: The metaphysical view that denies abstract objects and/or universals.
open theism: The model of God that denies that God has exhaustive foreknowledge.
perfect being theology: The theological method that takes every discernable good, strips it of any imperfection, and predicates it of God to the highest possible degree by its proper proportion.
process theism: The model of God that claims God (1) is essentially involved in and affected by temporal processes, (2) not omnipotent, (3) not the creator from nothing.
real accident: An accident that is genuine, irreducible, and exists in its own right—even if it inheres in a substance.
real relation: The relation R of a to b is real for a if and only if: (1) a is related by R to b; (2) a and b are really distinct extra-mental things; (3) there is a real extra-mental foundation in a for R.
relative identity: *x* and *y* are the same A but different Bs. For example, the Father and Son are the same divine substance (A) but different persons (B).
substance: Something that stands under and possess properties. It has a unity that mere aggregates lack.
supernatural revelation: God's objective revelation in Scripture.
supernatural theology: The task of utilizing the material content of supernatural revelation to understand God.
temporal indexical: Perspectival words like *now* used to capture the first-person perspective.

BIBLIOGRAPHY

Allen, Diogenes, and Eric O. Springsted. *Philosophy for Understanding Theology*. 2nd ed. Westminster John Knox Press, 2007.

Allen, Michael. "Divine Attributes." In *Christian Dogmatics: Reformed Theology for the Church Catholic*, edited by Michael Allen and Scott R. Swain. Baker Academic, 2016.

———. *The Fear of the Lord: Essays on Theological Method*. T&T Clark, 2022.

———. *The Knowledge of God: Essays on God, Christ and Church*. T&T Clark, 2022.

Allen, Michael, and Scott R. Swain. "Introduction." In *Christian Dogmatics: Reformed Theology for the Church Catholic*, edited by Michael Allen and Scott R. Swain. Baker Academic, 2016.

———. *Reformed Catholicity: The Promise of Retrieval for Theology and Biblical Interpretation*. Baker Academic, 2015.

Alston, William P. *Divine Nature and Human Language: Essays in Philosophical Theology*. Cornell Paperbacks. Cornell University Press, 1989.

———. *Perceiving God: The Epistemology of Religious Experience*. Cornell University Press, 1995.

Alter, Robert. *The Book of Psalms: A Translation with Commentary*. W. W. Norton, 2009.

Anatolios, Khaled. *Retrieving Nicaea: The Development and Meaning of Trinitarian Doctrine*. Baker Academic, 2018.

Anselm. *Compendium of Theology*. Translated by Richard J. Regan. Oxford University Press, 2009.

———. *Monologion*. Edited by Brian Davies and G. R. Evans. Oxford World's Classics. Oxford University Press, 1998.

———. *Proslogion*. Edited by Brian Davies and G. R. Evans. Oxford World's Classics. Oxford University Press, 1998.

Aquinas, Thomas. *Commentary on the Sentences, Book I, Distinctions 1–20*. Translated by Christopher Decaen. Aquinas Institute, 2025.

———. *Summa Contra Gentiles: Book One; God*. Translated by Anton Charles Pegis. University of Notre Dame Press, 1975.

———. *The Summa Theologiæ of St. Thomas Aquinas*. Translated by Fathers of the English Dominican Province. 2nd rev. ed. Burns Oates & Washbourne, 1920.

———. *The Treatise on the Divine Nature: Summa Theologiae I, 1–13*. Translated by Brian J. Shanley. Hackett, 2006.

Ariew, Roger. "Modernity." In *The Cambridge History of Medieval Philosophy*, edited by Robert Pasnau. Cambridge University Press, 2009. https://doi.org/10.1017/CHOL9780521762168.

Aristotle. *Categories and De Interpretatione*. Translated by John L. Ackrill. Clarendon, 1994.

———. *Metaphysics: Zeta, Eta, Theta, Iota; Books VII–X*. Translated by Montgomery Furth. Hackett, 1985.

———. *Nicomachean Ethics*. Translated by Terence Irwin. 2nd ed. Hackett, 1999.

———. *Nicomachean Ethics*. Translated by Terence Irwin. 3rd ed. Hackett, 2019.

Arlig, Andrew. "Medieval Mereology." Edited by Edward N. Zalta and Uri Nodelman. *The Stanford Encyclopedia of Philosophy* (Fall 2023). https://plato.stanford.edu/archives/fall2023/entries/mereology-medieval/.

Arminius, Jacob. *The Works of James Arminius*. Translated by James Nicholes and William Nicholes. Baker Book House, 1996.

Armstrong, D. M. *Truth and Truthmakers*. Cambridge University Press, 2004.

Athanasius. "Against the Arians." In *Select Works and Letters*, edited by Archibald Thomas Robertson and Philip Schaff, Nicene and Post-Nicene Fathers, 2nd ser., vol. 4. Hendrickson, 2004.

———. "Defence of the Nicene Council." In *Select Works and Letters*, edited by Archibald Thomas Robertson and Philip Schaff, Nicene and Post-Nicene Fathers, 2nd ser., vol. 4. Hendrickson, 2004.

Augustine. *Concerning the City of God against the Pagans*. Translated by Henry Bettenson. Penguin, 2003.

———. *Confessions*. Translated by Henry Chadwick. Oxford University Press, 2008.

———. *On Christian Teaching*. Translated by R. P. H. Green. Oxford World's Classics. Oxford University Press, 2008.

———. *The Trinity*. Translated by Edmund Hill. New City, 2015.

Ayres, Lewis. *Nicaea and Its Legacy: An Approach to Fourth-Century Trinitarian Theology*. Oxford University Press, 2009.

Ayres, Lewis, and Andrew Radde-Gallwitz. "Doctrine of God." In *The Oxford Handbook of Early Christian Studies*, edited by Susan Ashbrook Harvey and David G. Hunter, 864–85. Oxford University Press, 2009. https://doi.org/10.1093/oxfordhb/9780199271566.003.0043.

Baines, Matthew C. "Gisbertus Voetius's (1589–1676) Doctrine of Participation: Its Scholastic and Mystical Sources." PhD diss., University of Edinburgh, 2023.

Barcellos, Richard C. *Trinity & Creation: A Scriptural and Confessional Account*. Resource, 2020.

Barrett, Matthew. *None Greater: The Undomesticated Attributes of God*. Baker Books, 2019.

———. *The Reformation as Renewal: Retrieving the One, Holy, Catholic, and Apostolic Church*. Zondervan, 2023.

Basil. *Against Eunomius*. Translated by Mark DelCogliano and Andrew Radde-Gallwitz. The Catholic University of America Press, 2011.

———. *On the Holy Spirit*. Translated by Stephen M. Hildebrand. St. Vladimir's Seminary Press, 2011.

Bavinck, Herman. "Herman Bavinck, 'Foreword to the First Edition (Volume 1) of the Gereformeerde Dogmatiek.' " Translated by John Bolt. *Calvin Theological Journal* 45 (2010): 9–10.

———. *Reformed Dogmatics*. Edited by John Bolt. Translated by John Vriend. Baker Academic, 2003.

Becanus, Martinus. "Summa Theologiae Scolasticae." Translated by Michael Lynch. Lyon, 1620. https://michaellynch.substack.com/p/martin-becanus-on-divine-simplicity.

Beck, Andreas J. *Gisbertus Voetius (1589–1676) on God, Freedom, and Contingency: An Early Modern Reformed Voice*. Brill, 2022.

Beeley, Christopher A. *The Unity of Christ: Continuity and Conflict in Patristic Tradition*. Yale University Press, 2012.

Berkhof, Louis. *Systematic Theology*. GLH, 2017.

Bigg, Charles. *The Christian Platonists of Alexandria*. AMS, 1970.

Billings, J. Todd. *The Word of God for the People of God: An Entryway to the Theological Interpretation of Scripture*. Eerdmans, 2010.

Blocher, Henri. *Original Sin: Illuminating the Riddle*. InterVarsity Press, 2004.

——. "Yesterday, Today, Forever: Time, Times, Eternity in Biblical Perspective." *Tyndale Bulletin* 52, no. 2 (2001): 183–202.

Block, Daniel L. "How Many Is God? An Investigation into the Meaning of Deuteronomy 6:4–5." *Journal of the Evangelical Theological Society* 47, no. 2 (2004): 193–212.

Bockmuehl, Markus. "A Commentator's Approach To the 'Effective History' of Philippians." *Journal for the Study of the New Testament* 18, no. 60 (1996): 57–88. https://doi.org/10.1177/0142064X9601806003.

Boer, Willem Arie den, and Riemer A. Faber, eds. *Synopsis of a Purer Theology*. Davenant, 2023.

Boethius. "On the Holy Trinity." In *The Cambridge Edition of Early Christian Writings*, edited by Andrew Radde-Gallwitz. Cambridge University Press, 2017. https://doi.org/10.1017/9781107449596.026.

——. *The Consolation of Philosophy*. Translated by Scott E. Goins and Barbara H. Wyman. Ignatius, 2012.

Bonaventure. *Breviloquium*. Translated by Dominic Monti. Franciscan Institute, 2005.

——. *Disputed Questions on the Mystery of the Trinity*. Translated by Zachary Hayes. Franciscan Institute, 2000.

——. *Itinerarium Mentis In Deum*. Edited by Zachary Hayes and Philotheus Boehner. Rev. and exp. ed. Vol. 2. Franciscan Institute, 2002.

Bos, Johanna W. H. "Oh, When the Saints: A Consideration of the Meaning of Psalm 50." *Journal for the Study of the Old Testament* 7, no. 24 (1982): 65–77. https://doi.org/10.1177/030908928200702404.

Boyce, James Petigru. *Abstract of Systematic Theology*. Founders, 2006.

Boyd, Gregory A. *God of the Possible: A Biblical Introduction to the Open View of God*. Baker Books, 2000.

Bradshaw, David. *Aristotle East and West: Metaphysics and the Division of Christendom*. Cambridge: Cambridge University Press, 2007.

———. "Introduction." In *Natural Theology in the Eastern Orthodox Tradition*, edited by David Bradshaw and Richard Swinburne. IOTA, 2021.

———. "The Philosophical Theology of St Cyril's *Against Julian*." *Phronema* 29, no. 2 (2014): 21–40.

Brakel, Wilhelmus à. *The Christian's Reasonable Service*. Edited by Joel R. Beeke. Translated by Bartel Elshout. Reformation Heritage, 1992.

Bray, Gerald Lewis. *The Attributes of God: An Introduction*. Short Studies in Systematic Theology. Crossway, 2021.

Brine, John. *A Vindication of Some Truths of Natural and Revealed Religion*. London, 1846.

Brock, Cory C. *Orthodox yet Modern: Herman Bavinck's Use of Friedrich Schleiermacher*. Lexham, 2020.

Brock, Cory C., and Nathaniel Gray Sutanto. "Herman Bavinck's Reformed Eclecticism: On Catholicity, Consciousness and Theological Epistemology." *Scottish Journal of Theology* 70, no. 3 (2017): 310–32. https://doi.org/10.1017/S003693061700031X.

———. *Neo-Calvinism: A Theological Introduction*. Lexham, 2023.

Brower, Jeffrey E. "Aquinas on the Problem of Universals." *Philosophy and Phenomenological Research* 92, no. 3 (2016): 715–35. https://doi.org/10.1111/phpr.12176.

———. *Aquinas's Ontology of the Material World: Change, Hylomorphism, and Material Objects*. Oxford University Press, 2014.

———. "Making Sense of Divine Simplicity." *Faith and Philosophy* 25, no. 1 (2008): 3–30. https://doi.org/10.5840/faithphil20082511.

Brueggemann, Walter. *The Message of the Psalms: A Theological Commentary*. Augsburg, 1984.

Brunner, Emil. *The Christian Doctrine of God*. Translated by Olive Wyon. Westminster, 1949.

Burton, Simon J. G. *Ramism and the Reformation of Method: The Franciscan Legacy in Early Modernity*. Oxford Studies in Historical Theology. Oxford University Press, 2024.

Calvin, John. *Commentaries on the Epistle of Paul the Apostle to the Romans*. Translated by John Owen. Christian Classics Ethereal Library, n.d.

———. *Commentaries on the Four Last Books of Moses Arranged in the Form of a Harmony*. Translated by Charles William Bingham. Baker Book House, 1981.

———. *Commentary on the Book of Psalms*. Translated by James Anderson. Baker Book House, 1979.

———. *Institutes of the Christian Religion*. Edited by John T. McNeill. Translated by Ford Lewis Battles. Westminster John Knox, 2006.

Cameron, Ross P. "Intrinsic and Extrinsic Properties." In *The Routledge Companion to Metaphysics*, edited by Robin Le Poidevin, Peter Simons, Andrew McGonigal, and Ross P. Cameron. Routledge, 2009.

Carson, D. A. *The Difficult Doctrine of the Love of God*. Crossway, 2000.

Carter, Craig A. *Contemplating God with the Great Tradition: Recovering Trinitarian Classical Theism*. Baker Academic, 2021.

Case, Brendan. *The Accountable Animal: Justice, Justification, and Judgment*. Bloomsbury Academic, 2021.

Castelo, Daniel. "Qualified Impassibility." In *Divine Impassibility: Four Views of God's Emotions and Suffering*, edited by Robert J. Matz and A. Chadwick Thornhill. InterVarsity Press, 2019.

Cessario, Romanus. *A Short History of Thomism*. Catholic University of America Press, 2005.

Charnock, Stephen. *The Existence and Attributes of God*. Edited by Mark Jones. Crossway, 2022.

Chemnitz, Martin. *Examination of the Council of Trent*. Vol. 1. Concordia, 1978.

Chrysostom, John. "An Exhortation to Theodore After His Fall." In *St. Chrysostom: On the Priesthood; Ascetic Treaties; Select Homilies and Letters; Homilies on the Statutes*, edited by Philip Schaff and translated by W. R. W. Stephens, Nicene and Post-Nicene Fathers, 1st ser., vol. 9. Parker & Company, 1899.

———. *On the Incomprehensible Nature of God*. Translated by Paul W. Harkins. Catholic University of America Press, 1984.

Coakley, Sarah. *God, Sexuality and the Self: An Essay "On the Trinity."* Cambridge University Press, 2013.

———. "What Does Chalcedon Solve and What Does It Not? Some Reflections on the Status and Meaning of the Chalcedonian 'Definition.' " In *The Incarnation: An Interdisciplinary Symposium on the Incarnation of the*

Son of God, edited by Stephen T. Davis, Daniel Kendall, and Gerald O'Collins. Oxford University Press, 2002.

Craig, William Lane. *God Over All: Divine Aseity and the Challenge of Platonism*. Oxford University Press, 2016.

———. *Time and Eternity: Exploring God's Relationship to Time*. Crossway, 2001.

Craigie, Peter C. *Psalms 1–50*. Word, 1983.

Crisp, Oliver D. *Analyzing Doctrine: Toward a Systematic Theology*. Waco: Baylor University Press, 2019.

———. "A Parsimonious Model of Divine Simplicity." *Modern Theology* 35, no. 3 (2019): 558–73. https://doi.org/10.1111/moth.12520.

———. *The Word Enfleshed: Exploring the Person and Work of Christ*. Baker Academic, 2016.

Crisp, Oliver D., Gavin D'Costa, Mervyn Davies, and Peter Hampson. "Theology in Search of a Handmaiden: Reason and Philosophy." In *Theology and Philosophy: Faith and Reason*, edited by Oliver D. Crisp, Gavin D'Costa, Mervyn Davies, and Peter Hampson. T&T Clark, 2012.

Cross, Richard. "An Accidental Reformation?" *The Hanover Review* 3, no. 1 (2024): 5–13.

———. *Christology and Metaphysics in the Seventeenth Century*. Oxford University Press, 2022.

———. *Duns Scotus*. Oxford University Press, 1999.

———. *Duns Scotus on God*. Ashgate, 2005.

———. "On the Interpretation of Church Councils." *TheoLogica: An International Journal for Philosophy of Religion and Philosophical Theology* 4, no. 2 (2020): 203–9. https://doi.org/10.14428/thl.v4i2.60613.

———. *The Medieval Christian Philosophers: An Introduction*. I. B. Tauris, 2014.

Cyril of Alexandria. "First Letter to Succensus." In *The Cambridge Edition of Early Christian Writings*, edited by Mark DelCogliano, translated by Matthew R. Crawford, 731–39. Cambridge University Press, 2022. https://doi.org/10.1017/9781107449640.052.

———. *Letters 51–110*. Translated by John I. McEnerney. The Catholic University of America Press, 1987.

——. *On the Unity of Christ.* Translated by John Anthony McGuckin. St. Vladimir's Seminary Press, 2000.

——. "Second Letter to Nestorius." In *The Cambridge Edition of Early Christian Writings*, edited by Mark DelCogliano, translated by Matthew R. Crawford, 564–69. Cambridge University Press, 2022. https://doi.org/10.1017/9781107449640.041.

——. "Second Letter to Succensus." In *The Cambridge Edition of Early Christian Writings*, edited by Mark DelCogliano, translated by Matthew R. Crawford, 740–46. Cambridge University Press, 2022. https://doi.org/10.1017/9781107449640.053.

——. "Third Letter to Nestorius." In *The Cambridge Edition of Early Christian Writings*, edited by Mark DelCogliano, translated by Matthew R. Crawford, 623–36. Cambridge University Press, 2022. https://doi.org/10.1017/9781107449640.046.

Dagg, John L. *Manual of Theology*. Southern Baptist Publication Society, 1859.

Dainton, Barry. *Time and Space*. McGill-Queen's University Press, 2001.

Daley, Brian E. *God Visible: Patristic Christology Reconsidered*. Oxford University Press, 2018.

Davidson, Robert. *The Vitality of Worship: A Commentary on the Book of Psalms*. Eerdmans, 1998.

Davis, Leo Donald. *The First Seven Ecumenical Councils (325–787): Their History and Theology*. Liturgical Press, 1990.

Davis, Stephen T. *Logic and the Nature of God*. Eerdmans, 1983.

Davison, Andrew. *Participation in God: A Study in Christian Doctrine and Metaphysics*. Cambridge University Press, 2019.

DelCogliano, Mark. "The Emergence of the Pro-Nicene Alliance." In *The Cambridge Companion to the Council of Nicaea*, edited by Young Richard Kim. Cambridge University Press, 2021.

Deng, Natalja. *God and Time*. Cambridge University Press, 2018. https://doi.org/10.1017/9781108653176.

Dieter, Theodor. "Luther as Late Medieval Theologian: His Positive and Negative Use of Nominalism and Realism." In *The Oxford Handbook of Martin Luther's Theology*, edited by Robert Kolb. Oxford University Press, 2014. https://doi.org/10.1093/oxfordhb/9780199604708.013.002.

Dixon, Thomas. *From Passions to Emotions: The Creation of a Secular Psychological Category*. Cambridge University Press, 2006.

———. *The History of Emotions: A Very Short Introduction*. Oxford University Press, 2023.

Dolezal, James E. *All That Is in God: Evangelical Theology and the Challenge of Classical Christian Theism*. Reformation Heritage, 2017.

———. *God Without Parts: Divine Simplicity and the Metaphysics of God's Absoluteness*. Pickwick, 2011.

———. "Review of Basil of Caesarea, Gregory of Nyssa, and the Transformation of Divine Simplicity." *Westminster Theological Journal* 73 (2011): 384–87.

———. "Strong Impassibility." In *Divine Impassibility: Four Views of God's Emotions and Suffering*, edited by Robert J. Matz and A. Chadwick Thornhill. InterVarsity Press, 2019.

Dorner, Isaak August. *Divine Immutability: A Critical Reconsideration*. Translated by Robert R. Williams and Claude Welch. Fortress, 1994.

Duby, Steven J. *Divine Simplicity: A Dogmatic Account*. T&T Clark, 2016.

———. "Divine Simplicity, Divine Freedom, and the Contingency of Creation: Dogmatic Responses to Some Analytic Questions." *Journal of Reformed Theology* 6, no. 2 (2012): 115–42. https://doi.org/10.1163/15697312-12341234.

———. *God in Himself: Scripture, Metaphysics, and the Task of Christian Theology*. IVP Academic, 2019.

———. *Jesus and the God of Classical Theism: Biblical Christology in Light of the Doctrine of God*. Baker Academic, 2022.

Dulles, Avery. *The Resilient Church: The Necessity and Limits of Adaptation*. Doubleday, 1977.

Dunn, James D. G. *Romans 9–16*. Word, 1998.

Duns Scotus, John. "Ordinatio." Translated by Peter L. P. Simpson, n.d. https://www.aristotelophile.com/Books/Translations/Ordinatio%20I.pdf.

———. *Philosophical Writings: A Selection*. Translated by Allan B. Wolter. Hackett, 1987.

———. *Selected Writings on Ethics*. Translated by Thomas Williams. Oxford University Press, 2017.

Durand, Emmanuel. *Divine Speech in Human Words: Thomistic Engagements with Scripture*. Edited by Matthew K. Minerd. Catholic University of America Press, 2022.

Edwards, Jonathan. "Dissertation I: Concerning the End for Which God Created the World." In *Ethical Writings,* vol 8. of *Works of Jonathan Edwards Online*, edited by Paul Ramsey. Yale University Press, 2008.

———. "Dissertation II: The Nature of True Virtue." In *Ethical Writings*, in vol. 8 of *Works of Jonathan Edwards Online*, edited by Paul Ramsey. Yale University Press, 2008.

Effingham, Nikk. *Introduction to Ontology*. Polity, 2013.

———. "The Wave Theory of Time: A Comparison to Competing Tensed Theories." *Journal of the American Philosophical Association* 9, no. 1 (2023): 172–92. https://doi.org/10.1017/apa.2021.49.

Emery, Gilles. "The Immutability of the God of Love and the Problem of Language Concerning the 'Suffering of God.' " In *Divine Impassibility and the Mystery of Human Suffering*, edited by James F. Keating and Thomas Joseph White, translated by Thomas Joseph White. Eerdmans, 2009.

———. *The Trinity: An Introduction to Catholic Doctrine on the Triune God*. Translated by Matthew Levering. Catholic University of America Press, 2011.

Fairbairn, Donald. "Interpreting Conciliar Christology: An Overview in the Service of Analytic Theology." *Journal of Analytic Theology* 10 (2022): 363–81. https://doi.org/10.12978/jat.2022-10.050013031403.

Feinberg, John S. *No One Like Him: The Doctrine of God*. Crossway, 2001.

Feser, Edward. *Five Proofs of the Existence of God*. Ignatius, 2017.

———. *Scholastic Metaphysics: A Contemporary Introduction*. Editiones Scholasticae 39. Scholasticae, 2014.

Floate, Cody. "Hosea, Figuration, and Impassibility: A Passioned Prophet and the Yahweh Without Passions." *Journal of Classical Theology* 1 (2022): 107–22.

Ford, David F. "Introduction." In *The Modern Theologians: An Introduction to Christian Theology since 1918*, edited by David F. Ford and Rachel Muers. 3rd ed. Blackwell, 2005.

Fox, Rory. *Time and Eternity in Mid-Thirteenth Century Thought*. Oxford University Press, 2006.

Frame, John M. *The Doctrine of God*. P&R, 2002.

———. *Systematic Theology: An Introduction to Christian Belief*. P&R, 2013.

Freddoso, Alfred J. "Human Nature, Potency and the Incarnation." *Faith and Philosophy* 3, no. 1 (1986): 27–53. https://doi.org/10.5840/faithphil1986312.

Friedman, Russell L. *Medieval Trinitarian Thought from Aquinas to Ockham*. Cambridge University Press, 2013.

Garrigou-Lagrange, Réginald. *God, His Existence and His Nature: A Thomistic Solution of Certain Agnostic Antinomies*. Translated by Bede Rose. B. Herder, 1936.

Gavrilyuk, Paul L. "God's Impassible Suffering in the Flesh: The Promise of Paradoxical Christology." In *Divine Impassibility and the Mystery of Human Suffering*, edited by James F. Keating and Thomas Joseph White. Eerdmans, 2009.

———. *The Suffering of the Impassible God: The Dialectics of Patristic Thought*. Oxford University Press, 2004.

Geach, Peter. *God and the Soul*. St. Augustine's, 2001.

Gerhard, Johann. *On the Nature of God and on the Most Holy Mystery of the Trinity*. Edited by Benjamin T. G. Mayes. Translated by Richard J. Dinda. Concordia, 2007.

Gerson, Lloyd P. *From Plato to Platonism*. Ithaca, NY: Cornell University Press, 2017.

Gill, John. *A Body of Doctrinal Divinity*. George Keith, 1769.

———. *What Is Theology?* Edited by Christopher Ellis Osterbrock. H&E, 2022.

Goldingay, John. *Isaiah*. New International Biblical Commentary. Hendrickson, 2001.

Gorman, Michael. *Aquinas on the Metaphysics of the Hypostatic Union*. Cambridge University Press, 2017.

———. *A Contemporary Introduction to Thomistic Metaphysics*. The Catholic University of America Press, 2024.

———. "The Essential and The Accidental." *Ratio* 18, no. 3 (2005): 276–89.

Gregory of Nazianzus. *On God and Christ: The Five Theological Orations and Two Letters to Cledonius*. Translated by Frederick Williams and Lionel R. Wickham. St. Vladimir's Seminary Press, 2002.

Grogan, Geoffrey. *Psalms*. Eerdmans, 2008.

Guarino, Thomas G. *Vincent of Lérins and the Development of Christian Doctrine*. Baker Academic, 2013.

Hall, Francis J. *The Being and Attributes of God*. Longmans, Green, 1909.

Hall, Robert. *God's Approbation, the Study of Faithful Ministers*. J. W. Piercy, 1771.

Hart, David Bentley. "Impassibility as Transcendence: On the Infinite Innocence of God." In *Divine Impassibility and the Mystery of Human Suffering*, edited by James F. Keating and Thomas Joseph White. Eerdmans, 2009.

——. *The Experience of God: Being, Consciousness, Bliss*. Yale University Press, 2013.

——. "No Shadow of Turning: On Divine Impassibility." *Pro Ecclesia* 11, no. 2 (2002): 184–206.

Hasker, William. "The Absence of a Timeless God." In *God and Time*, edited by Gregory E. Ganssle and David M. Woodruff. Oxford University Press, 2001. https://doi.org/10.1093/acprof:oso/9780195129656.001.0001.

——. *God, Time, and Knowledge*. Cornell University Press, 1998.

——. *Metaphysics and the Tri-Personal God*. Oxford University Press, 2017.

Helm, Paul. "Divine Timeless Eternity." In *God and Time: Four Views*, edited by Gregory E. Ganssle. InterVarsity Press, 2001.

——. *Eternal God: A Study of God without Time*. 2nd ed. Oxford University Press, 2010.

——. *John Calvin's Ideas*. Oxford University Press, 2004.

Henninger, Mark Gerald. *Relations: Medieval Theories, 1250–1325*. Oxford University Press, 1989.

Henry of Ghent. *Henry of Ghent's Summa: The Questions on God's Unity and Simplicity (Articles 25–30)*. Translated by Roland J. Teske. Dallas Medieval Texts and Translations 6. Peeters, 2006.

Herdt, Jennifer A. *Putting on Virtue: The Legacy of the Splendid Vices*. University of Chicago Press, 2012.

Hoenen, Maarten J. F. M. "Via Antiqua and Via Moderna in the Fifteenth Century: Doctrinal, Institutional, and Church Political Factors in the Wegestreit." In *The Medieval Heritage in Early*

Modern Metaphysics and Moral Theory, 1400–1700, edited by Lauge O. Nielsen and Russell L. Friedman. Kluwer Academic, 2003.

Holmes, Stephen R. "The Attributes of God." In *The Oxford Handbook of Systematic Theology*, edited by Kathryn Tanner, John Webster, and Iain Torrance. Oxford University Press, 2007. https://doi.org/10.1093/oxfordhb/9780199245765.003.0004.

Horton, Michael. "Knowing God: Calvin's Understanding of Revelation." In *John Calvin and Evangelical Theology: Legacy and Prospect*, edited by Sung Wook Chung. Westminster John Knox, 2009.

Hugh of Saint Victor. *On the Sacraments of the Christian Faith (De Sacramentis)*. Translated by Roy Deferraro. Ex Fontibus, 2016.

Hunter, Justus H. "Postmodernity and Univocity." Syndicate Network. https://syndicate.network/symposia/theology/postmodernity-and-univocity/. Accessed April 20, 2023.

Ingham, Mary B., and Mechthild Dreyer. *The Philosophical Vision of John Duns Scotus: An Introduction*. Catholic University of America Press, 2004.

Inman, Ross D. *Christian Philosophy as a Way of Life: An Invitation to Wonder*. Baker Academic, 2023.

———. *Substance and the Fundamentality of the Familiar: A Neo-Aristotelian Mereology*. Routledge, 2018.

———. *What Is Reality? An Introduction to Metaphysics*. IVP Academic, 2024.

Ip, Pui Him. *Origen and the Emergence of Divine Simplicity before Nicaea*. University of Notre Dame Press, 2022.

Irenaeus. *Against Heresies*. Edited by Alexander Roberts and James Donaldson. Ex Fontibus, 2010.

Jamieson, R. B., and Tyler Wittman. *Biblical Reasoning: Christological and Trinitarian Rules for Exegesis*. Baker Academic, 2022.

Jenson, Robert W. *Systematic Theology*. 2 vols. Oxford University Press, 1997.

John of Damascus. *On the Orthodox Faith*. Translated by Norman Russell. St. Vladimir's Seminary Press, 2022.

Johnson, Jeffrey D. *The Failure of Natural Theology: A Critical Appraisal of the Philosophical Theology of Thomas Aquinas*. Free Grace, 2021.

Johnson, Terry L. *The Identity and Attributes of God*. Banner of Truth Trust, 2019.

Junius, Franciscus. *A Treatise on True Theology*. Translated by David C. Noe. Reformation Heritage, 2014.

Kärkkäinen, Pekka. "Nominalism and the Via Moderna." Oxford University Press, 2017. https://doi.org/10.1093/acref/9780190461843.013.266.

Keating, James F., and Thomas Joseph White. "Introduction: Divine Impassibility in Contemporary Theology." In *Divine Impassibility and the Mystery of Human Suffering*, edited by James F. Keating and Thomas Joseph White. Eerdmans, 2009.

Kenny, Anthony. *The God of the Philosophers*. Clarendon, 2001.

Kibbe, Michael H. "Present and Accommodated For: Calvin's God on Mount Sinai." *Journal of Theological Interpretation* 7, no. 1 (2013): 115–31.

King, Peter. "Emotions in Medieval Thought." In *The Oxford Handbook of Philosophy of Emotion*, edited by Peter Goldie. Oxford University Press, 2009. https://doi.org/10.1093/oxfordhb/9780199235018.003.0008.

———. "Scotus on Metaphysics." In *The Cambridge Companion to Duns Scotus*, edited by Thomas Williams. Cambridge University Press, 2006.

Kooi, Cornelis van der, and Gijsbert van den Brink. *Christian Dogmatics: An Introduction*. Translated by Reinder Bruinsma and James D. Bratt. Eerdmans, 2017.

Koons, Robert C. "Does the God of Classical Theism Exist?" In *Classical Theism: New Essays on the Metaphysics of God*, edited by Robert C. Koons and Jonathan Fuqua. Routledge, 2022.

Koons, Robert C., and Timothy H. Pickavance. *Metaphysics: The Fundamentals*. Wiley Blackwell, 2015.

Le Poidevin, Robin. *And Was Made Man: Mind, Metaphysics, and Incarnation*. Oxford University Press, 2023.

———. *Travels in Four Dimensions: The Enigmas of Space and Time*. Oxford University Press, 2003.

Leftow, Brian. "Boethius on Eternity." *History of Philosophy Quarterly* 7, no. 2 (1990): 123–42.

———. *God and Necessity*. Oxford University Press, 2015.

———. "Immutability." In *The Stanford Encyclopedia of Philosophy*, edited by Edward N. Zalta, Winter 2016. https://plato.stanford.edu/archives/win2016/entries/immutability/.

———. *Time and Eternity*. Cornell University Press, 1991.

Leigh, Edward. *A Systeme or Body of Divinity*. William Lee, 1654.

Leithart, Peter J. *Creator: A Theological Interpretation of Genesis 1*. IVP Academic, 2023.

Leo the Great. *Sermons*. Translated by Jane Patricia Freeland and Agnes Josephine Conway. The Catholic University of America Press, 1995.

Leo of Rome. "The Second Tome (Letter to Emperor Leo)." In *The Cambridge Edition of Early Christian Writings*, edited and translated by Mark DelCogliano, 117–28. Cambridge University Press, 2022. https://doi.org/10.1017/9781009057103.005.

Levering, Matthew. *Scripture and Metaphysics: Aquinas and the Renewal of Trinitarian Theology*. Challenges in Contemporary Theology. Blackwell, 2004.

Levy, Ian Christopher. *Holy Scripture and the Quest for Authority at the End of the Middle Ages*. University of Notre Dame Press, 2012.

Lewis, C. S. *The Lion, the Witch and the Wardrobe*. HarperCollins, 2005.

Lewis, David. "Extrinsic Properties." *Philosophical Studies* 44, no. 2 (1983): 197–200.

Lewis, Delmas. "Eternity, Time and Timelessness." *Faith and Philosophy* 5, no. 1 (1988): 72–86.

Lilla, Salvatore Romano Clemente. *Clement of Alexandria: A Study in Christian Platonism and Gnosticism*. Oxford University Press, 1971.

Lister, Rob. *God Is Impassible and Impassioned: Toward a Theology of Divine Emotion*. Crossway, 2013.

Litton, E. A. *Introduction to Dogmatic Theology*. Elliot Stock, 1882.

Lombard, Peter. *The Sentences*. Translated by Giulio Silano. Pontifical Institute of Mediaeval Studies, 2007.

Louth, Andrew. *The Origins of the Christian Mystical Tradition from Plato to Denys*. Clarendon, 1981.

Loux, Michael J., and Thomas M. Crisp. *Metaphysics: A Contemporary Introduction*. 4th ed. Routledge, 2017.

Luther, Martin. *Lectures on Genesis*. Edited by Jaroslav Pelikan and Daniel E. Poellot. Luther's Works 2. Concordia, 1960.

Mander, William. "Pantheism." In *The Stanford Encyclopedia of Philosophy*, edited by Edward N. Zalta. Metaphysics Research Lab, Stanford University, 2022. https://plato.stanford.edu/archives/spr2022/entries/pantheism/.

Mann, William E. "Divine Sovereignty and Aseity." In *The Oxford Handbook of Philosophy of Religion*, edited by William J. Wainwright, 35–58. Oxford University Press, 2009. https://doi.org/10.1093/oxfordhb/9780195331356.003.0003.

———. "Simplicity and Properties: A Reply to Morris." *Religious Studies* 22, no 3–4 (1986): 343–53.

Marmodoro, Anna, and Erasmus Mayr. *Metaphysics: An Introduction to Contemporary Debates and Their History*. Oxford University Press, 2019.

Marshall, Bruce D. *Trinity and Truth*. Cambridge University Press, 2002.

Martens, Peter W. *Origen and Scripture: The Contours of the Exegetical Life*. Oxford University Press, 2014.

Martyr, Justin. *The First and Second Apologies*. Translated by Leslie W. Barnard. Paulist Press, 1997.

Mastricht, Petrus van. *Theoretical-Practical Theology*. Edited by Joel R. Beeke. Translated by Todd M. Rester. Reformation Heritage, 2018.

Mathewes, Charles T. *Evil and the Augustinian Tradition*. Cambridge University Press, 2001.

Mawson, T. J. *The Divine Attributes*. Cambridge University Press, 2019.

McCall, Thomas H. *Analytic Christology and the Theological Interpretation of the New Testament*. Oxford Studies in Analytic Theology. Oxford University Press, 2021.

———. "Trinity Doctrine, Plain and Simple." In *Advancing Trinitarian Theology: Explorations in Constructive Dogmatics*, edited by Oliver Crisp and Fred Sanders. Zondervan, 2014.

McDaniel, Kris. "Extended Simples and Qualitative Heterogeneity." *The Philosophical Quarterly* 59, no. 235 (2009): 325–31. https://doi.org/10.1111/j.1467-9213.2008.589.x.

McGrath, Alister E. *A Scientific Theology*. Eerdmans, 2003.

McShea, Daniel W. "Evolutionary Trends and Goal Directedness." *Synthese* 201, no. 5 (2023): 178. https://doi.org/10.1007/s11229-023-04164-9.

Milbank, John. *Theology and Social Theory: Beyond Secular Reason*. 2nd ed. Blackwell, 2006.

Miller, Alexander. "Realism." In *The Stanford Encyclopedia of Philosophy*, edited by Edward N. Zalta, Winter 2021. Metaphysics Research Lab, Stanford University, 2021. https://plato.stanford.edu/archives/win2021/entries/realism/.

Moltmann, Jürgen. *The Crucified God*. SCM, 2015.

More, Henry. *Divine Dialogues, Containing Sundry Disquisitions & Instructions Concerning the Attributes and Providence of God*. James Elesher, 1668.

Morris, Thomas V. *Our Idea of God: An Introduction to Philosophical Theology*. InterVarsity Press, 1991.

Motyer, J. A. *The Prophecy of Isaiah: An Introduction & Commentary*. Downers Grove: InterVarsity Press, 1993.

Muller, Richard A. *After Calvin: Studies in the Development of a Theological Tradition*. Oxford University Press, 2003.

———. *Dictionary of Latin and Greek Theological Terms: Drawn Principally from Protestant Scholastic Theology*. 2nd ed. Baker Academic, 2017.

———. *Divine Will and Human Choice: Freedom, Contingency, and Necessity in Early Modern Reformed Thought*. Baker Academic, 2017.

———. *Post-Reformation Reformed Dogmatics: The Rise and Development of Reformed Orthodoxy, ca. 1520 to ca. 1725*. 2nd ed. 4 vols. Baker Academic, 2003.

———. "Reformation, Orthodoxy, 'Christian Aristotelianism,' and the Eclecticism of Early Modern Philosophy." *Nederlands Archief Voor Kerkgeschiedenis* 81, no. 3 (2001): 306–25.

———. *Understanding the Divine in Early Modern Reformed Theology*. Grand Rapids, MI: Reformation Heritage Books, 2024.

Mullins, R. T. "Classical Theism." In *T&T Clark Handbook of Analytic Theology*, edited by James Arcadi and James T. Turner. T&T Clark, 2021.

———. "Classical Theism, Christology, and the Two Sons Worry." In *Impeccability and Temptation: Understanding Christ's Divine and Human Will*, edited by Johannes Grössl and Klaus von Stosch. Routledge Studies in Analytic and Systematic Theology. Routledge, 2021.

———. "Closeness with God: A Problem for Divine Impassibility." *Journal of Analytic Theology* 10 (2022): 233–45. https://doi.org/10.12978/jat.2022-10.17-51-65122018.

———. "The Difficulty with Demarcating Panentheism." *Sophia* 55, no. 3 (2016): 325–46. https://doi.org/10.1007/s11841-015-0497-6.

———. *The End of the Timeless God*. Oxford University Press, 2016.

———. *God and Emotion*. Cambridge University Press, 2020. https://doi.org/10.1017/9781108688918.

———. "Omnisubjectivity and the Problem of Creepy Divine Emotions." *Religious Studies* 58, no. 1 (2022): 162–79. https://doi.org/10.1017/S0034412520000220.

———. "Simply Impossible: A Case against Divine Simplicity." *Journal of Reformed Theology* 7, no. 2 (2013): 181–203. https://doi.org/10.1163/15697312-12341294.

———. "Why Can't the Impassible God Suffer? Analytic Reflections on Divine Blessedness." *TheoLogica: An International Journal for Philosophy of Religion and Philosophical Theology* 2, no. 1 (2018): 3–22. https://doi.org/10.14428/thl.v0i0.1313.

Murray, John. *The Epistle to the Romans*. Eerdmans, 1968.

Nagasawa, Yujin. *Maximal God: A New Defence of Perfect Being Theism*. Oxford University Press, 2017.

Newman, John Henry. *An Essay on the Development of Christian Doctrine*. Word on Fire, 2017.

———. *On Consulting the Faithful in Matters of Doctrine*. Edited by John Coulson. Rowman & Littlefield, 2006.

Oberman, Heiko A. "Via Antiqua and Via Moderna: Late Medieval Prolegomena to Early Reformation Thought." *Journal of the History of Ideas* 48, no. 1 (1987): 23–40.

O'Connor, Timothy. "The Unity of the Divine Nature: Four Theories." In *Classical Theism: New Essays on the Metaphysics of God*, edited by Robert C. Koons and Jonathan Fuqua. Routledge, 2022.

Oliphint, K. Scott. *God with Us: Divine Condescension and the Attributes of God*. Crossway, 2012.

Oord, Thomas Jay. *The Death of Omnipotence and Birth of Amipotence*. SacraSage, 2023.

——. *Open and Relational Theology: An Introduction to Life-Changing Ideas*. SacraSage, 2021.

Origen. *Origen: Contra Celsum*. Translated by Henry Chadwick. Cambridge University Press, 1980. https://doi.org/10.1017/CBO9780511555213.

——. *Origen: On First Principles*. Translated by John Behr. Oxford University Press, 2019.

Ortlund, Gavin. *Theological Retrieval for Evangelicals: Why We Need Our Past to Have a Future*. Crossway, 2019.

Otten, Willemien. "Christian Platonism: Some Comments on Its Past and the Need for Its Future." *The London Lyceum Ledger* (blog), August 3, 2022. https://thelondonlyceum.com/christian-platonism-some-comments-on-its-past-and-the-need-for-its-future/.

Owen, John. *The Holy Spirit—The Helper*. Edited by Andrew S. Ballitch. The Complete Works of John Owen 7. Crossway, 2023.

——. *Vindiciae Evangelicae; or, The Mystery of the Gospel Vindicated and Socinianism Examined*. Edited by William H. Goold. The Works of John Owen 12. Banner of Truth Trust, 1966.

Padgett, Alan G. "Eternity as Relative Timelessness." In *God and Time: Four Views*, edited by Gregory E. Ganssle. InterVarsity Press, 2001.

Panaccio, Claude. *Mental Language: From Plato to William of Ockham*. Translated by Joshua P. Hochschild and Meredith K. Ziebart. Fordham University Press, 2017.

Pasnau, Robert. *Metaphysical Themes: 1274–1671*. Clarendon, 2011.

Paul, Sarah K. *Philosophy of Action: A Contemporary Introduction*. Routledge, 2021.

Pawl, Tim. "Conciliar Christology and the Consistency of Divine Immutability with a Mutable, Incarnate God." *Nova et Vetera* 16, no. 3 (2018): 913–37.

——. "Conciliar Trinitarianism, Divine Identity Claims, and Subordination." *TheoLogica: An International Journal for Philosophy of Religion and Philosophical Theology* 4, no. 2 (2020): 102–28. https://doi.org/10.14428/thl.v4i2.23593.

——. "Divine Immutability." In *Internet Encyclopedia of Philosophy*, n.d. https://iep.utm.edu/divine-immutability/.

——. "The Incarnation of a Simple God." In *Classical Theism: New Essays on the Metaphysics of God*, edited by Robert C. Koons and Jonathan Fuqua, 303–17. Routledge, 2022. https://doi.org/10.4324/9781003202172-19.

——. *In Defense of Conciliar Christology: A Philosophical Essay*. Oxford University Press, 2016.

——. "Review of *God without Parts: Divine Simplicity and the Metaphysics of God's Absoluteness*, by James E. Dolezal." *Faith and Philosophy* 30, no. 4 (2013): 480–86. https://doi.org/10.5840/faithphil201330445.

Peckham, John C. *Divine Attributes: Knowing the Covenantal God of Scripture*. Baker Academic, 2021.

——. "Qualified Passibility." In *Divine Impassibility: Four Views of God's Emotions and Suffering*, edited by Robert J. Matz and A. Chadwick Thornhill. InterVarsity Press, 2019.

Pedersen, Daniel J., and Christopher Lilley. "Divine Simplicity, God's Freedom, and the Supposed Problem of Modal Collapse." *Journal of Reformed Theology* 16 (2022): 127–47. https://doi.org/10.1163/15697312-bja10028.

Penner, Sydney. "Suárez on the Reduction of Categorical Relations." *Philosophers' Imprint* 13, no. 2 (2013): 1–24.

Perkins, William. *A Reformed Catholic*. Edited by Shawn Wright and Andrew S. Ballitch. Vol. 7. Reformation Heritage, 2014.

Pike, Nelson. *God and Timelessness*. Wipf & Stock, 2002.

Pinnock, Clark H. "Open Theism: An Answer to My Critics." *Dialog: A Journal of Theology* 44, no. 3 (2005): 237–45. https://doi.org/10.1111/j.0012-2033.2005.00263.x.

Plantinga, Alvin. *Does God Have a Nature?* Marquette University Press, 1980.

——. *The Nature of Necessity*. Clarendon, 2010.

——. "Reason and Belief in God." In *Faith and Rationality: Reason and Belief in God*, edited by Alvin Plantinga and Nicholas Wolterstorff. Notre Dame: University of Notre Dame Press, 1983.

Plato. "The Republic." In *Great Dialogues of Plato: Complete Text of The Republic, The Apology, Crito, Phaedo, Ion, Meno, Symposium*. Translated by W. H. D. Rouse. Signet, 2008.

——. "Symposium." In *Great Dialogues of Plato: Complete Text of The Republic, The Apology, Crito, Phaedo, Ion, Meno, Symposium*. Translated by W. H. D. Rouse. Signet, 2008.

Pomplun, Trent. "John Duns Scotus in the History of Medieval Philosophy from the Sixteenth Century to Étienne Gilson (†1978)." *Bulletin de Philosophie Médiévale* 58 (2016): 355–445.

Price, Richard, and Michael Gaddis, trans. *The Acts of the Council of Chalcedon*. Vol. 1. Liverpool University Press, 2007.

Pruss, Alexander, and Joshua Rasmussen. "Time without Creation?" *Faith and Philosophy* 31, no. 4 (2014): 401–11. https://doi.org/10.5840/faithphil201412819.

Radde-Gallwitz, Andrew. "Gregory of Nyssa and Divine Simplicity: A Conceptualist Reading." *Modern Theology* 35, no. 3 (2019): 452–66. https://doi.org/10.1111/moth.12504.

Radner, Ephraim. *Time and the Word: Figural Reading of the Christian Scriptures*. Eerdmans, 2021.

Ratzinger, Joseph. *God's Word: Scripture–Tradition–Office*. Edited by Peter Hünermann and Thomas Söding. Translated by Henry Taylor. Ignatius, 2020.

Renberg, Adam R. "Is Eusebius of Caesarea a 'Nicene'? A Contribution to the Notion of Conciliar Theology." *International Journal of Systematic Theology* 25, no. 2 (2023): 290–311. https://doi.org/10.1111/ijst.12583

Renihan, James. *To the Judicious and Impartial Reader: A Contextual-Historical Exposition of the Second London Baptist Confession of Faith*. Founders, 2022.

Renihan, Samuel. *Deity & Decree*. Independently published, 2020.

———. *God without Passions: A Primer*. Reformed Baptist Academic, 2015.

Reymond, Robert L. "Calvin's Doctrine of Holy Scripture." In *A Theological Guide to Calvin's Institutes*, edited by David W. Hall and Peter A. Lillback. P&R, 2008.

Rhoda, Alan R. "Generic Open Theism and Some Varieties Thereof." *Religious Studies* 44, no. 2 (2008): 225–34. https://doi.org/10.1017/S0034412508009438.

———. "The Philosophical Case for Open Theism." *Philosophia* 35, no. 3–4 (2007): 301–11. https://doi.org/10.1007/s11406-007-9078-4.

Richard of St. Victor. "On the Trinity." In *Trinity and Creation*, edited by Boyd Taylor Coolman and Dale M. Coulter, translated by Christopher P. Evans. New City, 2011.

Richards, Jay Wesley. *The Untamed God: A Philosophical Exploration of Divine Perfection, Immutability, and Simplicity*. InterVarsity Press, 2003.

Ridgeley, Thomas. *A Body of Divinity*. Robert Carter & Brothers, 1855.

Rogers, Katherin A. "Anselmian Eternalism: The Presence of a Timeless God." *Faith and Philosophy* 24, no. 1 (2007): 3–27. https://doi.org/10.5840/faithphil200724134.

———. *Perfect Being Theology*. Edinburgh: Edinburgh University Press, 2000.

Ryland, John C. *Contemplations on the Beauties of Creation and on All the Principal Truths and Blessings of the Glorious Gospel; with the Sins and Graces of Professing Christians*. Thomas Dicey, 1779.

Sanders, John. "An Introduction to Open Theism." *Reformed Review* 60, no. 2 (2007): 34–50.

Scheeben, Matthias Joseph. *Handbook of Catholic Dogmatics*. Translated by Michael J. Miller. Emmaus Academic, 2019.

Schreiner, Thomas R. *1, 2 Peter, Jude*. Broadman & Holman, 2003.

Scrutton, Anastasia Philippa. *Thinking Through Feeling: God, Emotion, and Passibility*. Bloomsbury, 2013.

Shafer-Landau, Russ. *The Fundamentals of Ethics*. 5th ed. Oxford University Press, 2020.

Shalkowski, Scott A. "Theoretical Virtues and Theological Construction." *International Journal for Philosophy of Religion* 41 (1997): 71–89.

Shedd, William G. T. *Dogmatic Theology*. 3rd ed. P&R, 2003.

Sheridan, Mark. *Language for God in Patristic Tradition: Wrestling with Biblical Anthropomorphism*. IVP Academic, 2015.

Simons, Peter. "Extended Simples: A Third Way Between Atoms and Gunk." *The Monist* 87, no. 3 (2004): 371–84.

Simpson, William M. R. "From Quantum Physics to Classical Metaphysics." In *Neo-Aristotelian Metaphysics and the Theology of Nature*, edited by William M. R. Simpson, Robert C. Koons, and James Orr. Routledge, 2021.

Smith, Brandon D. *Taught by God: Ancient Hermeneutics for the Modern Church*. B&H Academic, 2024.

Solomon, Robert C. *The Passions: Emotions and the Meaning of Life*. Hackett, 1993.

Sonderegger, Katherine. *Systematic Theology*. Vol. 1. Fortress, 2015.

Soskice, Janet Martin. *Naming God: Addressing the Divine in Philosophy, Theology and Scripture*. Cambridge University Press, 2023.

Spencer, Mark K. "The Flexibility of Divine Simplicity: Aquinas, Scotus, Palamas." *International Philosophical Quarterly* 57, no. 2 (2017): 123–39. https://doi.org/10.5840/ipq201731682.

Spinoza, Benedictus de. *The Essential Spinoza: Ethics and Related Writings*. Edited by Michael L. Morgan. Translated by Samuel Shirley. Hackett, 2006.

Stanglin, Keith D. *The Letter and Spirit of Biblical Interpretation: From the Early Church to Modern Practice*. Baker Academic, 2018.

Steele, Jeff, and Thomas Williams. "Complexity without Composition: Duns Scotus on Divine Simplicity." *American Catholic Philosophical Quarterly* 93, no. 4 (2019): 611–31. https://doi.org/10.5840/acpq2019920185.

Steffaniak, Jordan L. "3 Terms about the Trinity You Should Know & How We Got Them." Word by Word, April 2023. https://www.logos.com/grow/hall-three-trinitarian-words/.

———. "Bound by the Word of God: John Calvin's Religious Epistemology." *Puritan Reformed Journal* 10, no. 2 (2018): 120–36.

———. "Everything in Nature Speaks of God: Understanding Sola Scriptura Aright." *Modern Reformation* 31, no. 3 (2022).

———. "The God of All Creation: A Critique of Evangelical Biblicism and Recovery of Perfect Being Theology." *Journal of Reformed Theology* 14, no. 4 (2020): 358–80. https://doi.org/10.1163/15697312-bja10008.

———. "Natural Theology and the Uneasy Conscience of Modern 'Calvinism.'" The London Lyceum, July 10, 2022. https://www.thelondonlyceum.com/natural-theology-and-the-uneasy-conscience-of-modern-calvinism/.

———. "Retrieving Reformed Philosophy of Mind: Herman Bavinck's Eclectic Harmonism as Gateway to Neo-Aristotelianism." *Evangelical Quarterly* 94 (2023): 1–25. https://doi.org/10.1163/27725472-09401006.

———. "Which Plato? Whose Platonism? Summarizing the Christian Platonism Symposium." The London Lyceum, September 2, 2022. https://www.thelondonlyceum.com/which-plato-whose-platonism-summarizing-the-christian-platonism-symposium/.

Stevenson, James, and W. H. C. Frend, eds. *Creeds, Councils, and Controversies: Documents Illustrating the History of the Church, AD 337–461*. 3rd ed. Baker Academic, 2012.

Stump, Eleonore. *The God of the Bible and the God of the Philosophers*. Marquette University Press, 2016.

Stump, Eleonore, and Norman Kretzmann. "Absolute Simplicity." *Faith and Philosophy* 2, no. 4 (1985): 353–82. https://doi.org/10.5840/faithphil19852449.

———. "Eternity." *The Journal of Philosophy* 78, no. 8 (1981): 429–58.

Suárez, Francisco. *Metaphysical Disputation I: On the Nature of First Philosophy or Metaphysics*. Translated by Shane Duarte. The Catholic University of America Press, 2021.

———. *On the Various Kinds of Distinctions*. Translated by Cyril Vollert. Marquette University Press, 2007.

Sweeney, Douglas A. *The Substance of Our Faith: Foundations for the History of Christian Doctrine*. Baker Academic, 2023.

Swinburne, Richard. *The Coherence of Theism*. 2nd ed. Oxford University Press, 2016.

Sytsma, David. "The Logic of the Heart: Analyzing the Affections in Early Reformed Orthodoxy." In *Church and School in Early Modern Protestantism*, edited by Jordan Ballor, David Sytsma, and Jason Zuidema, 471–88. Brill, 2013. https://doi.org/10.1163/9789004258297_035.

Taylor, Dan. *Fundamentals of Religion in Faith and Practice*. Leeds, 1775.

The Theological Interpretation of Scripture Roundtable. YouTube. The London Lyceum, 2023. https://www.youtube.com/watch?v=LWOC-LB2x-U&t=1614s.

Timpe, Kevin. "Introduction to Neo-Classical Theism." In *Models of God and Alternative Ultimate Realities*, edited by Jeanine Diller and Asa Kasher. Springer, 2013.

Turretin, Francis. *Institutes of Elenctic Theology*. Edited by James T. Dennison. Translated by George Musgrave Giger. P&R, 1994.

van Inwagen, Peter. *Material Beings*. Cornell University Press, 1995.

———. *Metaphysics*. 4th ed. Westview, 2015.

VanGemeren, Willem A. "Psalms." In *The Expositor's Bible Commentary: Psalms, Proverbs, Ecclesiastes, Song of Songs*. Zondervan, 1991.

Vincent of Lérins. "The Commonitory." In Sulpitius Severus, Vincent of Lerins, John Cassian, edited by Philip Schaff and Henry Wace, translated by C. A. Heurtley, Nicene and Post-Nicene Fathers, 1st ser., vol. 11. Eerdmans, 1978.

Viney, Donald. "Process Theism." In *The Stanford Encyclopedia of Philosophy*, edited by Edward N. Zalta. Metaphysics Research Lab, Stanford University, 2022. https://plato.stanford.edu/archives/sum2022/entries/process-theism/.

Voetius, Gisbertus. "God's Single, Absolutely Simple Essence." Translated by R. M. Hurd. *The Confessional Presbyterian* 15 (2019): 9–39.

Walden, Garrett M. "Revisiting John Gill's Doctrine of Eternal Justification." *International Journal of Systematic Theology* 26, no. 2 (2024): 176–96. https://doi.org/10.1111/ijst.12668.

Ward, Thomas M. "Duns Scotus, Classical Theist: A Vindication." *The Hanover Review* 3, no. 1 (2024): 14–25.

——. *Ordered by Love: An Introduction to John Duns Scotus*. Angelico, 2022.

Ware, Bruce A. "An Evangelical Reexamination of the Doctrine of the Immutability of God." PhD diss., Fuller Theological Seminary, 1984.

——. *God's Greater Glory: The Exalted God of Scripture and the Christian Faith*. Crossway, 2004.

Webster, John. *The Domain of the Word: Scripture and Theological Reason*. Bloomsbury, 2012.

——. *God Without Measure: Working Papers in Christian Theology*. T&T Clark, 2016.

——. *Holiness*. Eerdmans, 2003.

——. "Theologies of Retrieval." In *The Oxford Handbook of Systematic Theology*, edited by Kathryn Tanner, John Webster, and Iain Torrance. Oxford University Press, 2007. https://doi.org/10.1093/oxfordhb/9780199245765.003.0033.

Weinandy, Thomas G. *Does God Change? The Word's Becoming in the Incarnation*. St. Bede's, 1985.

——. *Does God Suffer?* University of Notre Dame Press, 2000.

White, Thomas Joseph. *The Incarnate Lord: A Thomistic Study in Christology*. Catholic University of America Press, 2017.

Whitney, Barry L. "Process Theism: Does a Persuasive God Coerce?" *The Southern Journal of Philosophy* 17, no. 1 (1979): 133–43.

Wierenga, Edward R. *The Nature of God: An Inquiry into Divine Attributes*. Cornell University Press, 1989.

Wilcoxen, Matthew A. *Divine Humility: God's Morally Perfect Being*. Baylor University Press, 2019.

Williams, Scott M. *The Trinity*. Cambridge University Press, 2025. https://doi.org/10.1017/9781009293105.Williams, Thomas. "Introduction to Classical Theism." In *Models of God and Alternative Ultimate Realities*, edited by Jeanine Diller and Asa Kasher. Springer, 2013.

Wippel, John F. *Metaphysical Themes in Thomas Aquinas II*. Rev. ed. Catholic University of America Press, 2007.

Wittman, Tyler. *God and Creation in the Theology of Thomas Aquinas and Karl Barth*. Cambridge University Press, 2019.

Wolterstorff, Nicholas. *Lament for a Son*. Eerdmans, 1987.

——. "Unqualified Divine Temporality." In *God and Time: Four Views*, edited by Gregory E. Ganssle. InterVarsity Press, 2001.

Wood, William. *Analytic Theology and the Academic Study of Religion*. Oxford Studies in Analytic Theology. Oxford University Press, 2021.

Young, Frances M. *Scripture, the Genesis of Doctrine*. Eerdmans, 2023.

Zachhuber, Johannes. *The Rise of Christian Theology and the End of Ancient Metaphysics: Patristic Philosophy from the Cappadocian Fathers to John of Damascus*. Oxford University Press, 2022.

Zagzebski, Linda Trinkaus. *Omnisubjectivity: An Essay on God and Subjectivity*. Oxford University Press, 2023. https://doi.org/10.1093/oso/9780197682098.003.0002.

Zahl, Simeon. "Tradition and Its 'Use': The Ethics of Theological Retrieval." *Scottish Journal of Theology* 71, no. 3 (2018): 308–23. https://doi.org/10.1017/S0036930618000340.

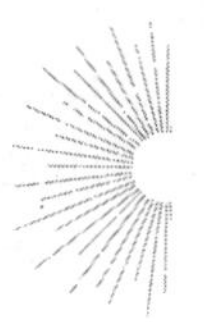

SUBJECT INDEX

SCRIPTURE INDEX

Old Testament

New Testament